T0313713

A PHILOSOPHER'S ECONOMIST

Portrait of David Hume attributed to William Millar reproduced
with kind permission by owner. Photo © Tom Nolan.

A
Philosopher's
Economist

Hume & the
Rise of Capitalism

Margaret Schabas *and*
Carl Wennerlind

The University of Chicago Press | Chicago and London

The University of Chicago Press, Chicago 60637
The University of Chicago Press, Ltd., London
© 2020 by The University of Chicago

For more information, contact the
University of Chicago Press, 1427 E. 60th St., Chicago, IL 60637.

Published 2020
Printed in the United States of America

30 29 28 27 26 25 24 23 22 21   2 3 4 5 6

ISBN-13: 978-0-226-59744-7 (cloth)
ISBN-13: 978-0-226-69125-1 (e-book)
DOI: https://doi.org/10.7208/chicago/9780226691251.001.0001

Library of Congress Cataloging-in-Publication Data

Names: Schabas, Margaret, 1954– author. | Wennerlind, Carl, author.
Title: A philosopher's economist : Hume and the rise of capitalism /
Margaret Schabas and Carl Wennerlind.
Description: Chicago : University of Chicago Press, 2020. |
Includes bibliographical references and index.
Identifiers: LCCN 2019037860 | ISBN 9780226597447 (cloth) |
ISBN 9780226691251 (ebook)
Subjects: LCSH: Hume, David, 1711-1776. | Economists—Biography. |
Capitalism—History.
Classification: LCC B1497 .S33 2020 | DDC 192—dc23
LC record available at https://lccn.loc.gov/2019037860

♾ This paper meets the requirements of ANSI/NISO Z39.48–1992
(Permanence of Paper).

The difference of fortune makes
less difference in happiness
than is vulgarly imagined.

DAVID HUME,
*An Enquiry concerning the
Principles of Morals*, 57

CONTENTS

ABBREVIATIONS
& MODIFICATIONS

For the primary sources by David Hume and Adam Smith, listed here in chronological order of original date, we have adopted the practice enshrined by other scholars, notably the series of the *Cambridge Companions*. We provide the page number and, if relevant, volume number as well, to the modern edition, using the following system of abbreviations. The bulk of our citations are to Hume's fifty essays, and we list them here without exception to provide a sense of Hume's breadth of interest. We use "E-" followed by an abbreviation for each specific essay. We provide the date the essay was first published but with the title as it appears in the modern volume published in 1987. For details on the date of publication for each essay or renaming, see that volume's introduction by its editor, Eugene F. Miller. We have created shorthand titles for some essays that are not on the lists of the *Cambridge Companions*. We have also adopted abbreviations for the Hume correspondence. The remaining primary sources by Hume and Smith that we cite but are not abbreviated are listed in the bibliography.

We quote Hume often and have retained the stylistic conventions of his day, with two exceptions. We alter his practice of using uppercase letters for proper names. By the 1760s, this convention had waned, and "PARIS," for example, had become "Paris" in his printed works. We have also removed italics when quoting Hume if and when he italicized the entire passage, a common convention at the time. We retain italics within quotations if there are single words used by Hume or if we wish to emphasize some wording, and then we make a note of that decision.

David Hume

HL   *The Letters of David Hume* [1727–65; 1766–76]. 2 vols. Edited by J. Y. T. Greig. Oxford: Oxford University Press, 1932.

MEM   *Early Memoranda* [unknown]. Unpublished and undated notes, compiled by Ernest Campbell Mossner, 1948. "Hume's Early Memoranda, 1729–40: The Complete Text." *Journal of the History of Ideas* 9 (4): 492–518.

NHL   *New Letters of David Hume* [1737–76]. Edited by Raymond Klibansky and Ernest C. Mossner. Oxford: Oxford University Press, 1954.

T   *A Treatise of Human Nature* [1739–40]. Edited by David Fate Norton and Mary J. Norton. Oxford: Oxford University Press, 2000. [Also referred to as *Treatise*.]

E   *Essays Moral, Political, and Literary* [1741–77]. Edited by Eugene F. Miller. Rev. ed. Indianapolis: Liberty Classics, 1987. [Also referred to as *Essays*.] Individual essays, listed alphabetically, are referred to as follows:

E-Av   "Of Avarice" (1741)
E-BG   "Whether the British Government Inclines More to Absolute Monarchy, or to a Republic" (1741)
E-BP   "Of the Balance of Power" (1752)
E-BT   "Of the Balance of Trade" (1752)
E-CL   "Of Civil Liberty" (1741)
E-Co   "Of Commerce" (1752)
E-CP   "Of the Coalition of Parties" (1758)
E-CR   "A Character of Sir Robert Walpole" (1742)
E-DM   "Of the Dignity or Meanness of Human Nature" (1741)
E-DT   "Of the Delicacy of Taste and Passion" (1741)
E-El   "Of Eloquence" (1742)
E-Ep   "The Epicurean" (1742)
E-EW   "Of Essay-Writing" (1742)
E-FP   "Of the First Principles of Government" (1741)
E-IM   "Of Impudence and Modesty" (1741)
E-In   "Of Interest" (1752)
E-IP   "Of the Independency of Parliament" (1741)
E-IPC   "Idea of a Perfect Commonwealth" (1752)
E-IS   "Of the Immortality of the Soul" (1777)
E-JT   "Of the Jealousy of Trade" (1758)

E-LM   "Of Love and Marriage" (1741)

E-LP   "Of the Liberty of the Press" (1741)

E-Mo   "Of Money" (1752)

E-MOL "My Own Life" (1777)

E-MP   "Of Moral Prejudices" (1742)

E-MSL "Of the Middle Station of Life" (1742)

E-NC   "Of National Characters" (1748)

E-OC   "Of the Original Contract" (1748)

E-OG   "Of the Origin of Government" (1777)

E-PA   "Of the Populousness of Ancient Nations" (1752)

E-PC   "Of Public Credit" (1752)

E-PD   "Of Polygamy and Divorces" (1742)

E-PG   "Of Parties in General" (1741)

E-PGB   "Of the Parties of Great Britain" (1741)

E-Pl   "The Platonist" (1742)

E-PO   "Of Passive Obedience" (1748)

E-PR "That Politics May Be Reduced to a Science" (1741)

E-PS   "Of the Protestant Succession" (1752)

E-RA   "Of Refinement in the Arts" (1752)

E-RC   "Of Some Remarkable Customs" (1752)

E-RP   "Of the Rise and Progress of the Arts and Sciences" (1742)

E-Sc   "The Sceptic" (1742)

E-SE   "Of Superstition and Enthusiasm" (1741)

E-SH   "Of the Study of History" (1741)

E-SR   "Of Simplicity and Refinement in Writing" (1742)

E-ST   "Of the Standard of Taste" (1757)

E-St   "The Stoic" (1742)

E-Su   "Of Suicide" (1777)

E-Ta   "Of Taxes" (1752)

E-Tr   "Of Tragedy" (1757)

EHU   *An Enquiry concerning Human Understanding* [1748; first published as *Philosophical Essays concerning Human Understanding*]. Edited by Tom L. Beauchamp. Oxford: Oxford University Press 2000. [Also referred to as first *Enquiry*.]

EPM   *An Enquiry concerning the Principles of Morals* [1751]. Edited by Tom L. Beauchamp. Oxford: Oxford University Press 1998. [Also referred to as second *Enquiry*.]

HE   *The History of England, from the Invasion of Julius Caesar to the Revolution in 1688* [1754–62]. 6 vols. Indianapolis: Liberty Classics, 1983. [Also referred to as *History of England*.]

DP   *Dissertation on the Passions* [1757]. Edited by Tom L. Beauchamp. Oxford: Oxford University Press, 2007. [Published with NHR.]

NHR   *Natural History of Religion* [1757]. Edited by Tom L. Beauchamp. Oxford: Oxford University Press, 2007. [Published with DP.]

DNR   *Dialogues concerning Natural Religion* [1779]. Edited by J. C. A. Gaskin. Oxford: Oxford University Press, 1993. [Published as *David Hume: Principal Writings on Religion*.]

Adam Smith

TMS   *The Theory of Moral Sentiments* [1759]. Edited by D. D. Raphael and A. L. Macfie. Oxford: Oxford University Press, 1976.

WN   *An Inquiry into the Nature and Causes of the Wealth of Nations* [1776]. 2 vols. Edited by R. H. Campbell, A. S. Skinner, and W. B. Todd. Oxford: Oxford University Press, 1976. [Also referred to as *Wealth of Nations*.]

LJ   *Lectures on Jurisprudence* [1762–63, 1766]. Edited by R. L. Meek, D. D. Raphael, and P. G. Stein. Oxford: Oxford University Press, 1978. [These are extant lecture notes of two of Adam Smith's students.]

PREFACE

Unlike his monumental *Treatise of Human Nature* (1739–40) that failed to gain recognition during his lifetime, David Hume's book on economics, *Political Discourses* (1752), was immensely successful. Over the next twenty-five years it underwent ten English editions and about a dozen translations, and over the next two centuries it continued to be read and valued by prominent economists. Nevertheless, there is as yet no monograph in English devoted to a comprehensive study of Hume's economics, let alone one that connects this body of thought to his philosophical tenets. This book fills that gap. One explanation for this scholarly lacuna is that Hume was a formidable philosopher. To understand his economics demands a full comprehension of his epistemology, metaphysics, political philosophy, and ethics—in short, a labor of a lifetime. Another reason is that to make sense of Hume's economics requires a multidisciplinary approach, one that develops a scholarly sensibility that transcends the boundaries that currently segregate economics from history or philosophy. Economics in Hume's day was not ahistorical, aethical, or apolitical. Quite the contrary: it was a discourse that embraced each and every one of these dimensions, as this book makes clear.

The three canonical thinkers on capitalism as a system writ large—Adam Smith, Karl Marx, and John Maynard Keynes—garner the lion's share of scholarly attention among historians of economics. Each man has had dozens of books and hundreds of articles written on his respective contributions to economics. Each one was also a philosopher, but none could compare with Hume in terms of philosophical breadth or depth. It is Hume's philosophical richness that makes his economics distinctive, his capacity to understand human motives and actions in both ethical and economic terms, to reflect on the human condition with an eye toward people's struggles with material scarcity, unmet desires, and a limited capacity to forge a full and meaningful life. Hume's economics adopts utilitarian goals in the sense that he saw people's efforts to produce, exchange, and consume as serving the greater end of happiness, but he also noted that few people sufficiently value the nonpecuniary goods of life, such as friendship or equanimity. Hume offered insight into the extent to which people's pursuit of wealth can at times conflict with their moral aims, while nevertheless celebrating the potential for their convergence, particularly for those among the middle class.

There is a sense in which Hume, more than Smith or Keynes, is an enthusiast for capitalism. Smith and Keynes each deprecated the human passion for money, particularly its tendency to render human beings into irrational creatures mired in petty forms of envy. Hume too recognized the core ingredient of avarice but nonetheless underscored its ennobling features, the sense in which the pursuit of profit could be channeled into prudential actions and, above all, promote the virtue of industriousness. The main obstacles to progress, for Hume, were war and the heinous practices of enslavement and colonization that accompanied national aggrandizement. In 1746, he participated, albeit as a noncombatant, in an aborted invasion of Lorient, headquarters for the French East India Company. In 1748, he was part of a diplomatic mission to Vienna to end the War of the Austrian Succession, traveling through enemy lines and the war-torn fields of Flanders. His economics was permeated by the realization that the costs of British military protection were increasing not just in nominal but also in real terms and that this expenditure would render the nation bankrupt. In that respect, his analysis of capitalism kept in the foreground the fact that peaceful relations are the exception and not the rule.

Hume was ever attentive to the political setting of economic activity, to the sense in which specific modes of government—autocratic, monarchical, or republican—could yield different economic outcomes, enhance standards of living, or induce more freedom. Hume believed that the stability, freedoms, and prosperity of Georgian Britain, particularly in comparison with the seventeenth century beset with civil war, regicide, and famine, were crowning achievements that deserved safeguarding. In that respect, he offered much policy advice, with detailed recommendations on trade as well as fiscal and monetary policy, as the instruments that might guide us to a more just and peaceful society.

Above all, Hume reflected on the essential mechanisms and defining properties of capitalism and its propensity for global expansion. He explicitly attended to the economic features of distant lands (as far away as China, Persia, or Africa) as well as the regions with which he was more familiar (Europe and North America). His primary focus was on modern Britain, France, and the Netherlands, but he also made frequent references to the economic practices of ancient Greece and Rome and offered economic explanations for their respective decline. In fleeting moments, he also speculated about the future; his economic principles, for example, posited concrete outcomes such as the tendency of the profit rate to fall or the public debt to rise in the long term.

Our book not only offers a detailed study of Hume's economics but also goes further and argues that economics was a unifying theme that runs throughout his written work and life as a cosmopolitan man of letters. Hume believed, passionately, that his capitalist world was at the vanguard of human flourishing, that commerce and the prosperity it engendered served to promote a more polite, civil, and secular society. He also believed that international and unrestricted trade was one of the best means to reduce war and conflict. We seek to understand Hume's arguments and his mission, without succumbing to their appeal. Certainly, given the human carnage of the past couple of centuries, it would be unimaginable by any measure to endorse Hume's conviction that the spread of capitalism would foster a more peaceful world. It is of great value, however, to understand the vision that Hume bequeathed, if only to gain insights into the paths not taken.

INTRODUCTION

On the first of April 1776, just months before his death, David Hume wrote to Adam Smith, "Euge! Belle! Dear Mr. Smith: I am much pleas'd with your Performance. . . . [The *Wealth of Nations* is] a Work of much Expectation, . . . [and] I trembled for its Appearance" (HL, 2:311).[1] As Smith's close friend and interlocutor for more than twenty-five years, Hume could take great pride in helping to shape what would prove to be the most seminal single book in the history of economics. Hume, however, was an important contributor to economics in his own right, as this book will establish. While he is still often relegated to the class of thinkers before economics became a well-recognized discipline, this book will bring to the foreground the wisdom, breadth, and depth of Hume's economic thought, his vision for the future of humanity, and the sense in which economic ideas permeated much of his philosophical writings.

Hume was a keen observer and analyst of the economic landscape of his day and forged much of his economic theory with distinct policies in mind. His enthusiasm for the commercial system we now call *capitalism* was arguably greater than that of any other eighteenth-century philosopher, including Smith. Hume laid down a maxim whereby the happiness of the people in the aggregate is directly linked to the degree of economic prosperity. As commerce and trade spread across Europe in the seventeenth and eighteenth centuries, the quality of life, he believed, had improved in virtually every respect. Nations such as the Netherlands and Britain had become more tolerant and peaceful in both the private and public spheres. The arts and sciences, manufacturing, and skilled husbandry were cultivated with unprecedented intensity and merit. Moreover, modern commerce, by spreading probity and industriousness, induced more civility and refined manners, which in turn fostered sociability and greater freedoms of association and expression. This was particularly true of Britain since the Glorious Revolution of 1688, where "so many millions," Hume declared, live "in a manner so free, so rational, and so suitable to the dignity of human nature" (E-PS, 508).

Hume's Enlightenment ideals spread well beyond the United Kingdom. As one of the most admired British philosophers in the decades leading up to the American and French Revolutions, Hume became a prominent voice for progressive ethical and political ideals. His writings on unrestricted trade (E-JT), freedom of the press (E-LP), and gender equality (E-PD, E-MP, E-LM) clashed with an age still encumbered by monopolistic privileges, censorship, and primogeniture. He in no way dismissed the illiberal practices of the day, the press-gangs, or, much worse, the slave trade, but his focus was primarily on the urban dwellers of Western Europe, whom he believed were at the vanguard of more cultivated modes of living, partly because they could easily meet to exchange ideas and sample novel products. Hume readily conjoined the progressive march of science and civility with innovations in manufacturing: "We cannot reasonably expect, that a piece of woollen cloth will be wrought to perfection in a nation, which is ignorant of astronomy, or where ethics are neglected" (E-RA, 270–71).

During the *siècle des lumières* in which Hume came of age, scientific associations were formed across Europe, from Dublin to Saint Petersburg, Lisbon to Uppsala. They served as important forums for the learned to exchange ideas and accolades, particularly in an age when universities were still beholden to the church. Their members were united by a reverence for the achievements of the seventeenth-century natural philosophers, Galileo and Newton above all, and their objectives were both utilitarian and theoretical. Papers on fertilizers or fortification were presented alongside estimates of the lunar orbit or the size of the earth. This spirit of inquiry perfectly suited a mind such as that of Hume, who served as joint secretary of the Philosophical Society of Edinburgh from 1751–63, and cofounded the Select Society in 1754. But Hume did not contribute directly to the natural sciences. It was his writings on the moral sciences, including his economics, that brought him, by the 1760s, "the applause of the whole world," not only in his native Scotland but also in Paris, the center of Enlightenment philosophy.[2] As Lord Elibank (Patrick Murray) wrote in a letter to Hume in 1763, "no author ever yet attained to that degree of reputation in his own lifetime that you are now in possession of at Paris."[3]

Hume left his mark on each of the four pillars of philosophy: epistemology, metaphysics, ethics, and political thought. His influence is greater in the first two than the second two, and considerably greater in ethics than in political thought. In each of these four fields, Hume issued a distinct set of beliefs and tenets that have spawned thousands of pages of commentary. A roving curiosity also led him to write extensively on virtually every other field in philosophy, including the philosophy of religion, aesthetics, probability theory, and the philosophy of sex and gender. The breadth of his thought was one of his greatest strengths, and his philosophical tenets continue to spread like the roots and branches of a majestic tree.

Among eighteenth-century philosophers, Adam Smith, Thomas Reid, and Immanuel Kant were Hume's most attentive readers. Among the nineteenth-century empiricists, John Stuart Mill, Auguste Comte, and Herbert Spencer each drew inspiration from Hume, as did the early twentieth century's logician Bertrand Russell and physicist Albert Einstein. Hume served as the patron saint for the logical positivists of the Vienna Circle and inspired the analytic philosophy that dominated much of Anglo-American philosophy for the rest of the twentieth century. Karl Popper, John Rawls, and Bernard Williams, for example, were each admirers of Hume. Since the 1960s, Hume has achieved such high standing that it is now common for philosophers to employ the adjective *Humean* in discourses on moral agency, personal identity, or the problem of induction.[4] If one narrows the sphere to philosophers who wrote in the English language, then Hume's standing in the canon is nonpareil.[5]

Yet for all the attention that Hume's work has garnered, his contributions to economics are still underappreciated. In contrast to his youthful tome, *A Treatise of Human Nature* (1739–40) that was never reprinted in his lifetime, or his two short philosophical texts, *An Enquiry concerning Human Understanding* (1748) and *An Enquiry concerning the Principles of Morals* (1751), Hume's *Political Discourses* (1752), by his own admission, was the only work "that was successful on the first publication. It was well received abroad and at home" (E-MOL, xxxvi). It consists of twelve essays, eight of which specifically focus on economic topics: commerce, consumption, money, the interest rate, trade, taxes, public credit, and demography. Among the remaining four essays that are directed more explicitly to political science, there are nonetheless some economic propositions worth extracting.

The publication success of the *Political Discourses* bears out Hume's estimation. It was initially published as a book in Edinburgh in January 1752 and sold so rapidly that a second edition, again as an octavo-sized bound book, was issued later that same year. By 1754, it had been translated twice into French, and by 1767 there were altogether nineteen printings, seven in English and a dozen translations in diverse European languages. The English editions after 1752 blended the *Political Discourses* with many of Hume's earlier essays of the 1740s and were released under the title *Essays and Treatises on Several Subjects*. Hume wrote additional essays on politics and economics right up until his death in 1776, and he spent considerable time and energy revising and regrouping his essays, issuing them as two- or four-volume sets with the title *Essays and Treatises on Several Subjects*.[6] From 1752 to 1777, there were a total of eleven editions of the essays in English that were first issued as the *Political Discourses*. The print run for each edition was normally one thousand copies.

On the Continent, Hume's *Political Discourses* endured as a book for decades; the myth that Hume did not write a book on economics, in contrast to Mill or Smith, is simply false. The dozen translations, particularly three in French — the language of the learned world — meant that Hume's single book on economics was widely known for the entire second half of the eighteenth century (HL, 2:343–46). It was displayed, for example, at the annual Frankfurt book fair. Each of the initial French translations, of 1754, were reprinted, in 1755, 1761, and 1767, respectively, and released in a number of cities: Paris, Amsterdam, Dresden, and Lyon.[7] James Steuart, who lived in France for decades, observed in his major work, *An Inquiry into the Principles of Political Oeconomy* (1767), that Hume's *Political Discourses* has "done much honour to that gentleman, and drawn the approbation of the learned world so much, that there is hardly a nation in Europe which has not the pleasure of reading them in their own language."[8]

The most influential translation of Hume was by Jean-Bernard Le Blanc; it was likened to "the latest novel" and "snapped up as fast as the most agreeably frivolous book."[9] In a letter to Hume on October 1, 1754, Le Blanc noted that "all those who are part of the [French] government have talked about your work as one of the best that was ever made on these matters."[10] A prominent French philosophe, François Véron de Forbonnais, issued a treatise in 1755 that favorably engaged Hume's analysis of public credit, and this work remained a focal point among French statesmen for several decades thereafter, not least because Forbonnais was a leading opponent of the physiocrats. As Loïc Charles has observed, "the delayed reception of Smith's political economy in Europe contrasts sharply with the quickness with which David Hume's *Political Discourses* penetrated the European public after its publication in 1752."[11]

Hume also gave copies of his *Political Discourses* to some of the leading statesmen in Scotland, several of whom he had befriended in his youth, either in Scotland or while living in London in his midtwenties, notably James Oswald, Lord Kames (Henry Home), and the third Duke of Argyll (Archibald Campbell), who because of his position of power became known as the "King of Scotland." Hume's endorsement of the policy for protecting the infant industry of Scottish linen in his analysis of trade could be viewed as a direct tribute to Argyll, who championed its expansion (E-BT 324).[12] As one prominent Edinburgh writer, John Home (no relation) observed, the "*Essays* are at once popular and philosophical, and contain a rare and happy union of profound Science and fine writing."[13]

For much of the second half of the eighteenth century, then, Hume's economic writings were in wide circulation and read by members of the learned academies and polite society as well as by those active in business, trade, or government. When François Quesnay, the founder in 1757 of an influential group of economists known as the *physiocrats*, decided to take up the study of economics, he first read Hume's *Political Discourses*. Hume was an inspiration to the American founding fathers as well, in particular Benjamin Franklin, whom he befriended, and Alexander Hamilton, who crafted many of the rules and regulations of the financial institutions of the new republic. Hume formed a close association with several leading economists of the 1760s and 1770s—Anne-Robert-Jacques Turgot, Steuart, and Smith. Insofar as modern economists still draw on the core principles inscribed in *The Wealth of Nations* (1776), Hume's legacy is profound and far-reaching. Moreover, several prominent economists of the twentieth century, notably Keynes and Friedrich Hayek, helped to disseminate Hume's ideas. As we will see, important strands of Humean thought pervade the discourse of economics to this day.

Although Hume was best known for his monetary theory, Hume's greater contribution stems from the philosophical acumen he used to enrich his economic analysis writ large. He fused his insights on moral and political philosophy, epistemology, and metaphysics with his "science of man" and his economics more specifically. In that respect, Hume was the progenitor of subsequent worldly philosophers, notably Smith, Mill, and Karl Marx, all of whom read Hume attentively.[14] Hume, however, is regarded as a more significant contributor to philosophy than any one of these three, but as a less significant economist. We wish to revisit this judgment and demonstrate that Hume was engaged in thinking and writing about economics for his entire adult life and that his contributions are extensive and significant. His imprint on economics becomes all the more relevant given recent interests in the normative and political dimensions of the subject—for example, the contributions of Elinor Ostrom or Daron Acemoglu. Whereas economics for much of the twentieth century had lost sight of its ethical and behavioral foundations, these seminal questions have been restored to the foreground of the discipline, as economists draw out the full implications of Rawls's theory of distributive justice or the psychological findings of Amos Tversky and Daniel Kahneman.[15]

The Unifying Thread of Economics

In treating any major philosopher, there is always the problem of authorial integrity and consistency. For the most part, Hume scholars have advanced the view that there is a unified project emanating from his *Treatise*. Barry Stroud, for example, emphasizes the theme of naturalism and Annette Baier the theme of moral sentimentalism.[16] Don Garrett positions Hume's mental machinery at the center of his philosophical project, while Paul Russell highlights the theme of irreligion.[17] More recently, James Harris argues that Hume's post-*Treatise* writings served diverse ends and thus cannot be subsumed under a single program.[18] Harris characterizes Hume as a man of letters who chose to tackle different problems at different times in his long and varied life. Certainly Hume's political diatribes, *A Letter from a Gentleman* (1745), *The Petition of the Grave and Venerable Bellman* (1751), and *Sister Peg* (1761) belie simple classification.[19] Add to this Hume's six-volume *History of England* (1754–62), his *Natural History of Religion* (1757), and his *Dialogues concerning Natural Religion* (1779), and it becomes clear that Hume had his hands on multiple strings; he played a harp, not a violin.

Our book seeks to restore the sense in which Hume's life and writings form an integral whole centered on economics, broadly construed, as a unifying thread. It may not be the only thread—we leave that for others to argue—but insofar as no other scholar has yet imposed this particular connective tissue on the body of Hume's thought, we will put forward a strong case. Hume, we argue, sought to understand economics both for its own sake and insofar as it enables us to understand and advance moral refinement, peace, and prosperity. To a large extent, he was a historical materialist; economic conditions shape fundamentally the political or cultural features of an age. Specific mores and manners, religious practices, or intellectual pursuits reflect the economic institutions of a given era. Yet Hume was not a reductionist; he also believed that political or cultural features acted symbiotically with economic conditions and spoke readily of an emergent "spirit of the age" (E-RA, 271). Hume's efforts to understand the rise of capitalism foreshadow arguments offered, more famously, by both Marx and Max Weber. Hume not only interprets the rise of representative government as the effect of the rise of commerce but also gestures to the significance of Protestant culture for fostering a more enterprising and liberal milieu.[20]

There are numerous economic insights to be found throughout Hume's correspondence and in virtually all of his published works. Economics was not a passing fancy for the two or three years during which he composed the *Political Discourses*. Hume's philosophical inquiry from the start was directed first and foremost to the study of human nature, and his objectives were to promote well-being and political stability, both of which, he argued, depended critically on a sound understanding of economics. His analysis of the passions positions pride in one's possessions as a fundamental human disposition, and his analysis of justice puts the spotlight on the institution of property. Both of these investigations segue readily into the study of economics. More generally, his enlightenment project extolls the unintended benefits of modern commerce, notably the spread of science and the arts, as well as more refined ethical norms.

Economic analysis also infuses Hume's historical narratives. For him, the gradual diminution of tyranny and the forward march toward greater liberty and representative government moved in step with the spread of commerce and trade. England's transition toward more democratic governance, albeit with the bloodshed of the civil war and the Glorious Revolution, was primarily the result of its burgeoning wealth, in both the agrarian and manufacturing sectors. Hume's political theory garnered originality largely because he attended to the underlying economic institutions that govern the production and distribution of wealth.[21] Hume drew many fine-grained distinctions between the degrees of representative government and the consequences for economic development emphasizing the importance of the rise of the middle class to power since the Reformation. Britain, he believed, had achieved a balanced "mixture of monarchy, aristocracy, and democracy" and was more tolerant of religious dissenters (E-NC, 207). Merchants and manufacturers were at the vanguard of secular culture, and in that respect economics was seminal to Hume's project to lift the yoke of superstition and idolatry. Hume's efforts to extend his "science of man" to virtually all facets of life were for the most part refracted through the lens of economic activity.

Hume's primary objectives were utilitarian. For him, it was a universal truth that "the great end of all human industry, is the attainment of happiness" (E-St, 148). Hume also recognized, however, that widespread happiness was not readily achieved, either by Sunday sermons or by facile attempts at self-enlightenment. As Hume observed, "all men, it is allowed, are equally desirous of happiness; but few are successful in the pursuit" (EPM, 51). Rather, the path forward depended critically on the civilities and liberties engendered by modern trade and commerce that in turn bolstered representative government. Britain, Hume believed, had already established itself as a paragon in this respect. Understanding the underlying mechanisms of the economic order, and the way they dovetailed with one another, was of far greater importance for utilitarian outcomes than the belief that an understanding of moral philosophy in and of itself would breed virtuous practices.

In what respects did Hume's own life accord with our characterization of him as an economist? Although born and raised in the Scottish lowlands, Hume willingly immersed himself in the hustle and bustle of commercial life in England. In 1734, at the age of twenty-three, he worked as a clerk for a Bristol sugar merchant with the aspiration of becoming a merchant himself (HL, 1:18). For about six years, at various intervals throughout his adult life, Hume lived in London, which, as the largest metropolis in Europe, was a beehive of trade, commerce, and manufacturing. In 1746, while initially serving as secretary to General James St. Clair, Hume kept the accounts of the ship's purchases and remittances.[22] In 1748, he joined St. Clair, who had been recently promoted to general, as his personal companion on a diplomatic mission to Vienna, and the yearlong trip exposed him to the diverse economic conditions across Western Europe. In his fifties, after securing his reputation with the *Political Discourses* and *A History of England*, Hume was invited to serve, for almost three years, in the British embassy in Paris, where he oversaw the reinstatement of British sterling in Québec (HL, 2:404–6). Like John Locke and Isaac Newton before him, Hume was drawn into the vortex of currency reform. And in 1767, despite protestations that he would rather retire to his home in Edinburgh, Hume elected to serve for two years in London as undersecretary of state for the Northern Department and, for the second of those years, this role included the ministry for Scottish affairs. As with the Parisian posting, this position required regular attention to trade agreements and financial settlements.

These stints in Bristol and on the Continent as a young man, and in government service in Paris and London in his fifties, which served as bookends for his life of letters, were in fact integral to his lifelong identity as an economist and not, as many commentators have supposed, tangential or idiosyncratic. In the initial editions of his *Political Discourses*, Hume recorded that he had been intrigued with the French term "circulation . . . ever since I was a school-boy" and could not, at least for many years, resolve to his satisfaction how wealth was created by the transactions of exchequer-notes or East India bonds (E-PC, 636–37). For Hume, it was labor that created wealth, particularly labor that had become more skilled and directed intensively for each working day. But insofar as he withdrew his appeal to his youthful puzzlement in the 1770 edition, this might be taken as a sign that he had also come to recognize more fully the importance of sophisticated capital markets.

Hume's habit of collecting economic data may have commenced around 1730. He recorded 320 distinct observations, of which at least 200 pertain to economics, in an unpublished list that has come to be known as the *Early Memoranda*, written sometime between 1729 and the early 1740s.[23] To give a sense of the range and detail of his data, Hume makes note of the import of wine per annum into Britain (20,000 tons), the number of bankruptcies per annum in Amsterdam (300), and the volume of Scottish linen exports before 1707 (1.8 million ells) (MEM, 506, 508, 509). Other observations attend, inter alia, to economic phenomena in France, Spain, Italy, Russia, Sweden, Ireland, Mexico, Antigua, Virginia, and Newfoundland. Hume records duties on sugar, taxes in ancient Athens and contemporary France, and one salient datum that would sound an alarm bell for him and his contemporaries: an annual interest payment of 45 million pounds on the British public debt (MEM, 507).

Hume was a veritable sponge for economic data, both ancient and modern. But he also undertook estimations and tested hypotheses with his empirical data and sought to establish stable indicators of economic prosperity such as population size, the money supply, or the interest rate. His essays and letters include scores of specific economic data from the far reaches of the world. To give three examples from his correspondence, in July 1769, Hume had a lengthy exchange with Abbé Morellet on the percentage rate of the debasement of the currency (HL, 2:203–5); from June to October 1772, he had several exchanges with Adam Smith about recent bank failures and undertook concrete estimates of their specific financial losses (HL, 2:262–67); and in October 1775 in a letter to William Strahan, Hume offered an estimation of the profit on the trade with the American colonies (HL, 2:299–302). If one read these and many other letters without knowing they were by Hume, one would have no idea that they were penned by one of the greatest philosophers in the English language.

Nor should one diminish the significance of Hume's close friendship with Smith that commenced by 1750 and lasted until Hume's death in 1776. Each served as an important sounding board for the other. It is even possible that Smith shaped some of the ideas in the *Political Discourses*; the fact that Smith was the first to deliver a public lecture on Hume's theory of commerce two weeks after the book appeared in print suggests a prior familiarity with the manuscript. During the 1760s, Hume made concerted efforts to read drafts of Smith's great tome and was delighted, as we saw with the opening quotation of this chapter, to finally hold and read Smith's *Wealth of Nations* (1776). Hume also voiced criticisms in his letter to Smith, including a penetrating one that Smith was at fault to include rent in the formation of a price, an indication that Hume was still pondering fundamental questions in economic theory in the last year of his life (HL, 2:311–12).[24]

Hume's sustained interests in economics are evident in his many texts. His first work, *A Treatise of Human Nature*, makes clear that his primary objective is to devise a "science of man" that has practical and not just theoretical applications. Hume's analysis of human nature describes in detail how we experience and process the external world and how we link our internal motives with manifest actions so as to achieve ethical judgments, establish and obey legal systems, and promote practical wisdom. Book 1 of the *Treatise* establishes the limits of our knowledge as grounded in our mental and perceptual faculties, and it emphasizes the fact that our knowledge of the physical world is inextricably beholden to our knowledge of human nature and the social world. To establish natural laws requires an attention to moral laws, particularly the laws of the mind. Book 2 of the *Treatise* attends to human agency and the manner in which our passions, accompanied by reason, forge uniform behavior analogous to the uniformity of the physical world. The first two books set the stage for Book 3 on moral and political philosophy, where Hume anchors his inquiry to the long-standing *verité* passed down from the Greeks: to wit, that individual happiness could only be sustained by the pursuit of virtue. Hume advances an evolutionary and cultural account of the virtues and foregrounds the institutions of property, markets, and money as the best means to develop and safeguard moral improvement. Commercial institutions are sustained by explicit and implicit rules and conventions that uphold contractual obligations that in turn feed upon trust and honesty. As several scholars have argued, there is much to glean about Hume's economic thought from a close reading of the *Treatise*.[25]

Economic considerations persisted, if not intensified, in Hume's post-*Treatise* writings, including many of his early *Essays* dating from 1741, such as "That Politics May Be Reduced to a Science" (E-PR), "Of Civil Liberty" (E-CL), and "Of Avarice" (E-Av). A year later, he added more essays that offer important insights on economics, notably "Of the Middle Station of Life" (E-MSL), "Of the Rise and Progress of the Arts and Sciences" (E-RP), and his so-called happiness quartet, a set of four essays on ancient moral philosophy (E-Ep, E-St, E-Pl, E-Sc). In 1748, Hume composed "Of National Characters" (E-NC) and "Of the Protestant Succession" (E-PS), both of which reflect on economic development. The *Political Discourses* can rightfully be taken as Hume's most concentrated contribution to economics, but it is important to bear in mind that he added a new essay, "Of the Jealousy of

Trade" (E-JT), in 1758 and continued to revise many of his essays, substantially in some instances, over the rest of his life.

Hume decided to reissue his *Treatise* as three separate works, corresponding to each of the three Books. The first one, his *Enquiry concerning Human Understanding* (1748), based on Book 1, delves more deeply into the question of free will and determinism that is central to the understanding of economic agency. Hume also uses economic examples to illustrate key philosophical tenets and speaks at one point of the "empty and transitory nature of riches" (EHU, 35). Moreover, he shows a stronger inclination than in the *Treatise* to legitimate our ascriptions of causal connections, a significant if not necessary step if one is to develop a science of economics.[26] But it was the second one, the *Enquiry concerning the Principles of Morals* (1751), based on Book 3 of the *Treatise* and written at the same time as the *Political Discourses*, that we argue can be read as an important contribution to economic discourse. We therefore disagree with Duncan Forbes, who maintains that Hume's "striking economic orientation" in the *Treatise* was softened in the second *Enquiry*.[27] Quite the contrary, we read the latter work as a vade mecum to instruct the prospering merchants and bankers of Hume's day to enhance their moral standing. Hume underscores the virtues of honesty and trustworthiness and argues that the world of commerce pivots on the cultivation of good character and reputation as an honorable person.[28]

Book 2 of the *Treatise* became Hume's *Dissertation on the Passions*, devised before 1752 but initially published as part of the *Four Dissertations* in 1757. Hume positions "reason" with our "calm desire of riches and a fortune" and thus gives birth to a set of profound insights into economic agency (DP, 24).[29] Hume asserts that "in the production and conduct of the passions, there is a certain regular mechanism, which is susceptible of as accurate a disquisition, as the laws of motion, optics, hydrostatics, or any part of natural philosophy" (DP, 29). As Albert Hirschman argued forcefully, the "taming of the passions" by an appeal to the more overriding pursuit of self-interest was an essential step for the justification of commercial capitalism.[30] Hume went further by redefining reason as a passion, albeit a calm and indirect one, and thus highlighting the predictability of human action. In sum, Hume's reissuing of the *Treatise* as the two *Enquiries* and the *Dissertation on the Passions* are replete with important philosophical material that pertain directly to his science of economics.

This judgment extends to Hume's writings on religious beliefs and practices, as they promote the secular culture of a thriving commercial world. His *Treatise* and several essays cast aspersions on the practice of transubstantiation and on the belief in the afterlife. Hume's essay "Of Suicide" (E-Su) develops a strong allegiance to materialism, a position he also develops in his essay "Of the Immortality of the Soul" (E-IS).[31] Hume's *Natural History of Religion* argues that religious beliefs came into existence to placate human fears of the unknown, fears that would abate in the age of reason. Hume's *Dialogues concerning Natural Religion* emphasizes the vast imperfections of our world and undercuts to the core the long-standing belief in a providential order. Hume's critical stance toward religion had a strong subversive thrust and played a central role in his mission to bring about greater freedoms and enlightenment.[32]

How does this position on religion pertain to his economic thought? Commerce, like science, is often at loggerheads with religious beliefs and practices in that the latter tend to suppress individual ingenuity. The Bible contains several reprimands against the pursuit of wealth and, above all, the practice of usury. It taught piety and obedience in opposition to cultivating an independent state of mind. As Voltaire recognized, "where there is not liberty of conscience, there is seldom liberty of trade, the same tyranny encroaching upon the commerce as upon Religion."[33] Hume echoed this insight in arguing that "liberty of thinking, and of expressing our thoughts, is always fatal to priestly power" (E-PGB, 65–66). Hume deemed the Roman Catholic Church to be "less tolerating" than the Protestant Church and to be a greater perpetrator of superstition and idolatry that had thwarted freedom of thought and rationality (E-PS, 510). "Superstition," Hume maintained, "renders men tame and submissive" and turns the priest into a "tyrant and disturber of human society, by his endless contentions, persecutions, and religious wars." Moreover, superstition "is an enemy to civil liberty," as witnessed in the "dismal convulsions" to which all of Europe had been subjected by the church in Rome (E-SE, 78).

Hume emphasized the importance of practical knowledge in the development of manufacturing, commerce, and trade that he believed, rightly or wrongly, stemmed from a state with greater religious tolerance. Hume believed that the Reformation, by overcoming the corrupt practices of the Vatican and by promoting greater individual freedom, had fostered an enterprising ethos and hence the spread of commerce. As proof of the fact that religious tolerance and commercial advancement move in tandem, Hume observed that "the three greatest trading towns now in Europe, are London, Amsterdam, and Hamburgh; all free cities, and protestant cities; that is, enjoying a double liberty" (E-CL, 92). Britain, Hume argued, was the most tolerant nation in Europe; it had put to rest the previous "mutual rancor" between Catholics and Protestants and allowed minorities such as the Quakers to "become very free reasoners" (E-PS, 508; E-SE, 78). In Ireland, by contrast, Hume argued, because the Protestants and Catholics have no "common intercourse" and engage in "severe revenges," one finds "disorder, poverty, and depopulation" (E-PA, 640). Like Voltaire, Hume celebrated the mingling of persons of different faiths and saw it as a potent and progressive force. He honored the Jewish moneylenders of medieval England and the Huguenot immigrants who brought their artisanal skills to England in the late 1680s. Hume has much to say about the links between economic development, good government, and religious toleration and, whether soundly or not, believed that the advent of Protestantism served these ends.

Finally, there is substantial material on economic practices and policies woven throughout Hume's six-volume *History of England*. While scholars have long viewed this work as Hume having retired from philosophy, he had not forsaken economics. His *History* records numerous decrees by the English Crown over the centuries to fix prices and wages, impose taxes or tariffs, and reconstitute the currency. He also weighs in on the various measures to finance wars and colonial expansion, and he treats the expansion and maturation of the agrarian and manufacturing sectors as the primary reason for England's current prowess. Hume astutely locates the initial impulse toward commercial development in the sixteenth century, under the Tudor reign. Moreover, he discerns the many and diverse ways in which trade, public finance, and political stability were interwoven. It is not difficult to read Hume's account of England's empowerment over the course of seven centuries as an important contribution to economic history.[34]

An inquiry into the ideal economic conditions to promote political stability and peace more strongly connects Hume's entire corpus of writings, from his *Treatise* on through to his *History of England* and posthumous *Dialogues*, than anything drawn specifically from his epistemology or metaphysics. We do not make this claim lightly. Hume feared that the hard-earned liberties of his day would disintegrate and that poor governance, stemming from ignorance of economics, might lead to rapid decline and instability. The plight of Spain was a constant reminder of the folly of restricting the flow of money and failing to promote capital investment. Hume also discerned that the system for collecting taxes in France was its Achilles' heel. If France were to reform its system and emulate the more efficient one in Britain, "the difference between that absolute government and our free one, would not appear so considerable as at present" (E-CL, 95; see also HL, 1:136). As Hume noted at the start of Book 3 of the *Treatise*, entitled "Of Morals," the reason the study of ethics is so critical is because we rightfully believe "the peace of society to be at stake in every decision concerning it" (T, 293). And his analysis of ethics moves readily to questions of justice and property, the observance of commercial contracts, and obedience to the law more generally. For Britain and the world to find the path to peace, stability, and human well-being, a firm understanding of commerce and trade was required. Book 3 of Hume's *Treatise*, together with his *Political Discourses* and *The History of England*, demonstrate that economic and political institutions emerge and evolve without human design or foresight. Although his ethics, epistemology, and metaphysics have been given far more weight and attention in the scholarly literature than have his economic and political thought, it is the latter that govern and infuse the former.

As several scholars have recognized, Hume was one of the first to identify the specific factors that promote economic growth.[35] John Locke, in his *Two Treatises of Government* (1689), had observed that the agrarian yield of cultivated land in Devonshire was ten times more than uncultivated English soil, and one hundred times more than the forests in America. But his argument was directed primarily at the virtue of industriousness rather than intended as a full-blown account of the production and distribution of wealth or the importance of capital accumulation and trade. Hume, as we will show, also highlighted the virtue of industriousness but provided a more coherent account of the interdependent components of economic growth, with specific attention to the role of capital accumulation, enterprising merchants, sophisticated bankers, and the inventors of new products. Hume's account also had little in common with Locke's puritanism.[36] Hume believed that human labor, suitably specialized and channeled wisely, was the key to the creation of wealth, but it was a labor drawn to new desires and proclivities. The consequent import of novel luxuries would foster a culture of imitation, inventiveness, and improvement, Hume argued. Hume emphasized the dramatic transformation of British manufacturing since the Tudor period and maintained that it stemmed almost entirely from the emulation and subsequent improvement of foreign crafts (E-JT, 328). He recognized the inversion of the "natural progress of opulence," to use Smith's term—namely, that the expansion of farming in the regions surrounding a town follows its prosperity as first a trading port and then a manufacturing hub, and not the other way around (WN, 1:376–80).

Hume's avidity for commerce and manufacturing was more pronounced than Adam Smith's, but it was not unqualified. As the merchant class garnered more political power, their strong inclinations to expand overseas and fund imperial efforts resulted in excessive taxation and public indebtedness. These in turn had the potential to destabilize the domestic polity, and Hume worried that in the centuries ahead, republican states or constitutional monarchies would degenerate into autocratic rule. Hume also expressed some disdain for the avaricious and insatiable desire for luxuries that might detract from higher-order pursuits such as knowledge, friendship, health, or inner equanimity (EPM, 82). A life of excessive luxury, he remarked, might become "destitute of humanity or benevolence" (E-RA, 269). Like Mandeville, Hume acknowledged some of the dehumanizing and hypocritical effects of commerce that feigned civility in the pursuit of profit. Both thinkers were nonetheless drawn to modern urban life, in contrast to Jean-Jacques Rousseau, who romanticized about a more rustic lifestyle of a bygone era. Hume believed that his current age was the superior one, if only because basic necessities such as bread were cheaper in real terms.

Economic growth brought in its wake moral refinement, Hume contended. A pervasive work ethic meant that, to a man of business, "indolence will seem a punishment" (E-Sc, 171). If "men are kept in perpetual occupation," as in the new commercial era, they not only cultivate many virtues, such as diligence and perseverance, but also find that "the mind acquires new vigour; [and] enlarges its powers and faculties . . . in honest industry" (E-RA, 270). At the close of his second *Enquiry*, Hume reminded his readers that "honesty is the best policy," and that even to "cheat with moderation and secrecy" makes one vulnerable to additional temptations that inevitably hasten a fall from grace (EPM, 82). Far better, he averred, to retain a clean conscience and one's integrity than to risk losing a reputation for a few additional trinkets. It is in this respect that trust and a "spirit of industry" took hold and thus polished and softened manners that in turn enhanced sociability, Hume believed. Urban centers became preferable to country life. People "flock into cities; love to receive and communicate knowledge; to show their wit or their breeding. . . . Both sexes meet in an easy and sociable manner; and the tempers of men, as well as their behavior, refine apace" (E-RA, 271). Hume did not fear that such urbanity would render men effeminate or reduce the martial spirit of liberal nations. Rather, education would invigorate modern citizens to be courageous and willing to fight for their liberty (E-RA, 274–75). Hume, incidentally, wrote several essays that addressed the status of women, and he questioned the practice of premarital chastity and restrictions for divorce (E-PD). His ethical predilections were radical for the period, favoring libertine over puritan mores and treating the modern secular ways of living in the mercantile towns of Western Europe as beacons for the future.

Hume's aspirations for a more enlightened and liberal world ran strong and deep but were tempered by his attention to the fragile forces at play. There were, in short, many critical institutions of a contractual or political nature that required vigilant scrutiny, both of their internal operations and of their alignment with one another. His account of the balance of trade is mirrored by his analysis of the balance of state power. Hume thought in terms of costs and benefits and tended to weigh a question at the margin rather than in absolute terms. If one includes his private letters, then all told, Hume wrote hundreds of pages to explain why certain kinds of taxes, trade policies, types of monetary issue, and types of political rule were more effective than others. In some instances, he wrote with a categorical voice, that some propositions are virtually indubitable. But for the most part, his economic propositions were qualified rather than dogmatic, with full recognition of the difficulties of settling definitively any specific core principles on the production and distribution of wealth.

Plan and Purpose

This is the first comprehensive study, in the English language, of Hume's economics. The closest alternative on offer is the lengthy introduction, by Eugene Rotwein, to an edited collection of Hume's economic writings. It was written in 1955, reissued in 1970, and reprinted with a new introduction and in paperback in 2007, a testament to its enduring value. There are four books in other languages that directly address Hume's economics, the most recent one, in 1995, by Tatsuya Sakamoto in Japanese.[37] Three more recent books in English feature Hume's economics but with different objectives than our own. John Robertson demonstrates strong analogues between the economic Enlightenment in Scotland and in Naples; Willie Henderson traces the ancient and early modern sources on which Hume drafted his economic thought; and Jia Wei extracts the theme of commercial development in Hume's *History of England*.[38] None of these studies, however, provides a detailed analysis of Hume's economic theory and policies nor conjoins them to his epistemology and ethics. It is our belief that to make sense of Hume's economics, one has to comprehend his entire life's work, not only his writings on philosophy, politics, and history but also his writings on science and religion and, albeit more tangentially, his analyses of aesthetics, gender, and race. This is an inherently interdisciplinary project that cannot be done simply by attending to the economic essays in isolation.

In undertaking this study of Hume's economics, we are fully cognizant that there is no consensus on the name for the discipline extant in his day. Nonetheless, the science that came to be called economics was a well-formed discourse in the first half of the eighteenth century, well before Hume. Money and trade were identified as central topics of inquiry; some leading examples were the tracts by John Law (1705), Isaac Gervaise (1720), Joshua Gee (1729), Jacob Vanderlint (1734), and Ferdinando Galiani (1751). Hume used several labels for the study of economic phenomena. The title of his main contribution to the field, *Political Discourses*, not to mention an earlier essay of 1741, "That Politics May Be Reduced to a Science," indicate that the "science of politics" served Hume as an umbrella term for economic inquiry. Hume also groups the science of politics with the natural sciences, primarily because it can posit general truths or laws. In his first *Enquiry* he demarcates two kinds of sciences: those based on "particular facts" such as history, geography, or astronomy, and those that treat "general facts," notably "politics, natural philosophy, physics, [or] chemistry" (EHU, 122).

Hume's first essay in the *Political Discourses* is entitled "Of Commerce," and he refers as well to the "science of commerce." This seems to have been the most pervasive label for economics at the time. It was used, for example, by Samuel Ricard, *Traité général du commerce* (1700), and entrenched by the titles of two leading texts of the 1730s, by Jean-François Melon (1734) and Charles de Ferrère Du Tot (1738), respectively. Coincident with Hume, we find "commerce" as the main designation in the works of Forbonnais, *Éléments du commerce* (1754), Josiah Tucker, *The Elements of Commerce and the Theory of Taxes* (1755), and Richard Cantillon, *Essai sur la nature du commerce en général* (1755). Later prominent texts that upheld "commerce" as the operative term are by Étienne Bonnot abbé de Condillac, *Le commerce et le gouvernement* (1776) and Henry Vaughan, *New and Old Principles of Trade Compared; or a Treatise on the Principles of Commerce between Nations*, (1788). The term "political œconomy" was not commonly in use until after Hume's *Political Discourses*, for example, in the titles of works by Jean-Jacques Rousseau (1755) and James Steuart (1767). *Political economy*, spelled without the diphthong, only took hold in the early nineteenth century, and the current term, *economics*, was not cemented until 1890 with Alfred Marshall's *Principles of Economics*.

In keeping with practices in the history of science that take the history of physics or biology back to the ancient Greeks, we will use the term *economics* throughout this book, and we mean by it a study of a specific domain of phenomena, particularly money, trade, and commerce. Hume cited Xenophon's work on "*œconomy*" and referred to Cato as "a great *œconomist*," but both references are in the spirit of the ancient sense of managing the *oikos*, or household (E-PA, 392–94; MEM, 515). Furthermore, Hume used the term *œconomy* about a dozen times, but he tended to denote either the act of budgeting or an orderly system, such as the "œconomy of nature."[39] The one major exception to this pattern can be found in the opening section of the first *Enquiry*. Having acknowledged recent achievements in the natural sciences, Hume submitted that "there is no reason to despair of equal success in our enquiries concerning the mental powers and *œconomy*" (EHU, 11; our emphasis). This is the closest he comes to an explicit recognition of a science of economics using the term with which we are now familiar. It is important to note that Hume expressed the desire to treat his inquiry on the *œconomy* as comparable to the natural sciences and that he links it with his investigation into mental powers, since he also devoted much pen and paper to the "laws of the mind." We will replace Hume's references to the science of politics or commerce by economics, except when we believe doing so would distort his intentions—for example, when he is squarely engaged in the field practiced at present as political theory.

As a science, economics posits some initial assumptions about the uniformity of human behavior, the sense in which we as a species forge beliefs about the world and act on them, presumably in the pursuit of material betterment or a happier life, broadly construed. Neoclassical economics famously settled on a few simple generalizations—for example, that agents maximize utility or firms maximize profits. In its heyday, the post–World War II decades, neoclassical economists kept a fair distance from any detailed assertions about human psychology. More recently, economists have rekindled an interest in psychology, and the field of behavioral economics has grown by leaps and bounds. Appeals to power relations and strategizing have also reentered the discourse, particularly under the guise of game theory. Many of these predilections, we will see, are already to be found in Hume's economics, insofar as it discerns the central importance of human agency composed of a complex set of motives and deliberations, and it attends to people's propensities for self-deception or lack of prudence.[40] Hume is also cognizant of the imbalance of power, the formation of contracts with asymmetric information, and the manner by which coordinated activities might emerge without design. In sum, many of the efforts by mainstream economists since the late twentieth century to reclaim a more nuanced account of human behavior are to a large extent retrieving insights that were evident to Hume.

There is, perhaps, a tendency among some scholars to attribute too much rigor to Hume's account of human agency, to see him as a progenitor, for example, of formal modeling, game theory, or rational choice theory.[41] It is easy to be seduced by Hume's brilliance and agility with abstract analysis, and these ascriptions of formal methods to Hume are of much value. Nevertheless, we prefer to treat Hume in the context of eighteenth-century economics and philosophy and, for the most part, not impose contemporary analytical tools on his work. Moreover, we do not wish to convey the impression that Hume got everything right or that everything he wrote was original. What we find most valuable in Hume is his account of human nature, his measured skepticism, and his efforts to connect his philosophical principles to the global trajectory of human advancement over the centuries. We appreciate Hume's historical sweep; his average interval of temporal analysis is about three hundred years, and the short-run period is about twenty-five years. He thus offers a dynamic account that is absent in much of contemporary economic discourse, where the long-term is five years and the past hardly exists except as a source of empirical support for the models.[42]

Hume not only made extensive references to economic practices in ancient Greece and Rome, as well as to the medieval period, but he also projected centuries into the future. He conjectured, for example, that the Netherlands would continue to hold a dominant place in global shipping and brokering, even though it had reached its saturation point domestically. Britain, because it had built its wealth on the export of wool and, more recently, silk and linen, would secure its economic prowess with textile production and finished goods. Hume also believed that economic dominance was never permanent and that the global center would migrate from nation to nation. He discerned, as would Smith, that America, because of its rapid growth in population, would become the economic hegemony in the not-too-distant future, but that if China were to open itself up to global trade, in conjunction with a lower cost for shipping, it might be the next one to gain dominance (E-RP, 122). Finally, in part because financial wealth was overtaking landed wealth and because it was more portable, Hume believed that representative governments were vulnerable and, in the remote future, likely to resort back to autocratic rule. Hume thus appealed to many of the forces that govern long-term economic development, those that are robust and those that are vulnerable to decay, and he embellished these with his penetrating grasp of human nature. In sum, Hume's economics is about the potential of human flourishing, past, present, and future.

This book is divided into seven chapters. We first trace the remarkable path that brought Hume into contact with many of the leading savants and statesmen of his day. From a young age, Hume cultivated knowledge of the new commercial world, whether in Bristol, London, and Edinburgh or on his visits to the Continent. We will also assess the extent to which Hume learned and kept abreast of the growth of scientific knowledge, both the natural and the moral sciences, as part of the context in which he forged his economic theory. Our account is not meant to be a comprehensive biography but rather to persuade our readers that Hume was an active and inquisitive economist for the better part of his adult life.

After sketching Hume's life qua economist, we then unpack his arguments for elevating the science of economics. Doing so demands a preliminary sketch of Hume's empiricist project and his epistemology more generally. We argue that, for Hume, economics was superior to the physical sciences in certain respects; it was able to use our intuitions about human nature to detect erroneous views more adequately than ascriptions regarding the microphysical world, and it tended to engage shorter inferential chains that were therefore less susceptible to error. Furthermore, the phenomena emanated from robust uniformities of human agency that, Hume believed, are as stable and constant as the laws that governed natural phenomena. We canvass some of the methods Hume used in devising his economic theory, such as thought experiments or analogical modes of explanation, and show that Hume was an avid collector of economic data on prices, taxes, and capital markets and devised various methods, such as estimation techniques or weighted averages, to measure the leading indicators of his economic landscape. Hume also had a predilection to detect the degrees of variance of a particular phenomenon and appreciated the tendency of mean-reverting patterns. As markets expanded, there were forces that induced price uniformities and manifest what we would now call the law of one price.

We then turn to Hume's rich narrative of the entangled web of wealth and justice. The emergence of capitalism in the sixteenth and seventeenth centuries constituted a profound transformation of the practices and institutions pertaining to the markets for land, labor, and capital. These markets were sustained by contractual obligations nestled within the all-pervasive rule of law that protected property rights. Hume famously delimits the pursuit of justice to the laws that govern property and thus narrows the gaze to economic conditions. His analysis of justice also underscores the sense in which the social utility of upholding promises fosters a path of economic betterment independently of legal enforcement. As commercial relations take hold, we police ourselves to obey and respect the property of others. But Hume also provides arguments that motivate the need for political authority, notwithstanding the ubiquitous tendency of politicians for knavery. He develops these conflicting predilections both theoretically, in the *Treatise*, the second *Enquiry*, and in his *Essays*, and empirically, in his colorful account of English history.

Modern commerce, Hume believed, has modified and will continue to modify human behavior and induce more polite and convivial interactions. Montesquieu had famously promoted the doctrine of *doux commerce*, which states that commerce polishes mores and subdues human conflict, both domestically and internationally.[43] Hume, we argue, expanded and deepened the many respects in which commercial societies become more virtuous. Instead of sparking an increase in greed and degenerate gluttony, as critics argued, Hume maintained that active participation in commercial society promotes interactions that are conducive to fostering refined moral sentiments. Modern citizens not only enjoy greater material wealth but also benefit by living in a well-functioning society. The human species is, at best, at the halfway point of its development, Hume thought, and, given the complex interplay of all of the political and economic forces of his age, people ought to expect significant changes in the future (E-PA, 378).[44] As Hume observed of the recent rise of commerce and trade in his day, "such mighty revolutions have happened in human affairs, and so many events have arisen contrary to the expectation of the ancients, that they are sufficient to beget the suspicion of still further changes" (E-CL, 89).

Hume's most celebrated contributions are in monetary theory. One important proposition that builds on the quantity theory of money is Hume's specie-flow mechanism that renders money neutral on a global scale. But Hume also, under certain local conditions, grants money the potential to stimulate economic production and exchange. The two propositions appear to contradict each other, but we show that this inconsistency evaporates under scrutiny. The first mechanism is broached as a thought experiment to isolate a propensity that is never fully actualized—money is in fact not neutral—while the second claim describes a process that had in fact transpired in Britain and elsewhere and thus meant that an influx of money due to a trade surplus could yield a greater domestic product. As a result, Hume advocated both the unrestricted import and export of specie and the domestic circulation of privately issued paper banknotes.

One of Hume's most brilliant arguments is that the interest rate, at root, is not a monetary phenomenon. Rather, the interest rate indicates the maturation of capital accumulation and the degree of competition in financial markets. Prosperous countries have low interest rates and, while these may be correlated with abundant money supplies, the latter is not a direct cause. National efforts to stockpile gold and silver were therefore futile, insofar as the forces governing international trade and hence the global flow of specie exceeded the control of any single nation. Hume also used his monetary theory to reflect on banking and financial institutions at large. As his correspondence attests, Hume changed his views on a host of economic topics specific to money, banking, and public finance. He had an active mind that matured as the years unfolded; nevertheless, his tone in his *Political Discourses* is confident throughout, even when he offers qualifications or indulges in hyperbole, most likely because he sought to influence those in power.

Hume singled out Niccolò Machiavelli for his genius but "profound silence" on the subject of trade (E-CL, 88); in his *Early Memoranda* he remarked on how strange this silence was "considering that Florence rose only by Trade" (MEM, 508). It was only in the seventeenth century, Hume believed, that commerce and trade began to appear in political thought, particularly in England and the Netherlands. As Hume underscored, "the great opulence, grandeur, and military achievements of the two maritime powers" was a key motivation for placing economic analysis front and center (E-CL, 89). His argument for the gains from trade draws heavily on the principle of absolute advantage—that each nation has distinctive resources and skills that make it preferable for specialized exports—but he also gestured toward the principle of comparative advantage—that a nation might better produce the good which is most cost-effective and import the other goods even if they could both be produced more cheaply domestically. Hume mapped out a long trajectory of global diversification and of the adoption of increasingly sophisticated manufacturing techniques in the richer regions of the world. These improvements would also, on average, lower real prices while at the same time raise wages. Goods that were once luxuries, such as paper, would become conveniences and perhaps even necessities. Trade meant that each nation had a greater quantity and more diverse basket of goods to enjoy. As people's patterns of consumption evolved and became more interdependent, the need to conquer other nations would be eclipsed by the efficient practice of trade.

But this Humean vision of widespread peace and international trade lay in the future. Throughout Hume's own life, Britain was mostly at war with France, albeit offshore, with the notable exception of the brief and ill-planned skirmish in Brittany in which Hume partook in 1746, as a last-minute alternative to a planned attack on Québec. To fund this and other military campaigns, Parliament raised and imposed new kinds of taxes and resorted to a number of other remunerative schemes, such as lotteries, annuities, and government bonds. Hume was worried about the long-term consequences of excessive public borrowing. He feared a lack of restraint in the extension of public credit meant that the government would become bankrupt. His fears, however, proved to be unfounded. Even with the prolonged Napoleonic wars, the British state was not, as Hume predicted, rendered bankrupt. Because Hume wrote before industrialization, he underestimated the dramatic economic growth that was still to come.

We will close by first sketching Hume's imprint on Adam Smith and then evaluating Hume's legacy up to the present. The young Smith of the 1740s was a careful student of Hume's epistemology and ethics, and his first book, *The Theory of Moral Sentiments* (1759), was directly indebted to Hume. It built on Hume's insights on sympathy and the human propensity to admire wealth and power, as well as many of his utilitarian predilections. By contrast, the received view submits that Smith's *Wealth of Nations* (1776) dissented from many of the core tenets of Hume's economics. We challenge this interpretation and argue that there was in fact considerable overlap in their economic thought, particularly on the subjects of trade and development. Hume was carefully studied by many of the leading economists of the twentieth century; Milton Friedman and Paul Samuelson single Hume out for his insightfulness. Many present-day economists, including Robert Lucas, Amartya Sen, and Paul Krugman, praise Hume. One of the most striking features of Hume is his versatility: economists of both libertarian and liberal stripes look to him for ideas and inspiration. We will show that Hume's broad appeal across the political spectrum stems from his probing philosophical analysis of economic phenomena.

Hume was a consummate stylist in an age when prose, rather than poetry, was much esteemed among men and women of letters. As we have seen, he wrote several short political diatribes that cultivated a pronounced satirical tone and he had an irrepressible flair for irony. For all his efforts to write succinctly, there is an irreverent side to Hume. At the close of Book 1 of his *Treatise*, he instructed his reader to put aside any skeptical musings or inclinations for solipsism that tend to induce "melancholy and delirium" and instead have dinner with friends and play backgammon (T, 175). Are we to believe that after more than one hundred pages of painstaking analysis into the core questions of epistemology and metaphysics, Hume's philosophical inquiry is but a diversion? The more plausible way to view this disclaimer is that Hume wished to prompt his readers to refresh themselves and struggle anew with the same set of ideas.

To grasp the core elements of Hume's philosophical work demands that we try hard to extract his more recondite meanings, a challenge that pertains to understanding any primary text in the philosophical canon but is belied by Hume's efforts at plain prose. As Hume warned his readers at the start of the *Treatise*, "if truth be at all within the reach of human capacity, 'tis certain it must lie very deep and abstruse; and to hope we shall arrive at it without pains, . . . must certainly be esteem'd sufficiently vain and presumptuous" (T, 3). With that warning in mind, we nevertheless try to pull away some of the covers and capture a succinct account of the philosopher the French called *le bon David*. Our aim is to canvass Hume's economics in conjunction with his writings on philosophy and history and to foreground the position that economics serves as a unifying thread in Hume's oeuvre. We will also adjudicate the sense in which Hume understood the human trajectory, while entirely secular and without any boost from a providential order, to be nonetheless potentially progressive. Michel Foucault may have argued, in *The Order of Things* (1966), that the "science of man" has not yet begun because we cannot transcend our self-reflexivity, but if there is one philosopher who made some preliminary inroads and was able to step out of his time and mentalité, it was David Hume.[45]

CHAPTER 1

"A Rising Reputation"

Hume's Lifelong Pursuit of Economics

As the second-born son of a Scottish laird, David Hume entered the world as David Home in 1711 with neither wealth nor title. On coming of age, Hume received an annual stipend of fifty pounds, a meager sum that forced him to practice considerable austerity. His first effort to augment his annuity was to work as a clerk for a Bristol merchant, during which time he changed his name from Home to Hume. While living in London in his late twenties and for part of his thirties, Hume considered himself "a good Oeconomist," meaning that he lived within his means; he also acquired a reputation for dining at his friends' homes but avoided the custom of tipping the servants (NHL, 26). Notwithstanding this youthful disposition, in later years as his income rose, Hume became known for his generosity and hospitality.[1] By his fifties, he could boast an annual income of a thousand pounds, earned primarily from the sale of his books. At age fifty-two, Hume bought a large flat in one of the more fashionable districts of Edinburgh and, in 1770, built a small house near Princes Street where he spent the last six years of his life.

Many poor gentlemen in Hume's position would enter the law or become a clergyman or soldier, and most would marry and have children. Hume did none of these. As a young man, Hume was accused of fathering a child out of wedlock; he had already departed for England when his name was cleared in court. There were later infatuations, but the young Hume lacked the means to marry in accordance with his station and remained a bachelor his entire life. Hume's family assumed that he would enter the law, the profession of his father, Joseph Home (1681–1713), and maternal grandfather, Sir David Falconer (c. 1640–1685), who had served as President of the College of Justice. But by 1729, Hume had abandoned that pursuit, later describing his four years of study of the law as "nauseous" (HL, 1:13). The church was not an option for Hume; while observant in his youth, he confessed later in life that "I am not a Christian" (HL, 1:470). Hume did, however, wear a British uniform while serving as secretary and judge advocate under General James St. Clair (1746–48), but he did not train as a soldier nor engage in combat.

Rather than take up the sword, Hume derived his income from his pen, as clerk, tutor, secretary, librarian, statesman, and, above all, "Scholar & Philosopher" (HL, 1:13). As Hume observed at the start of his autobiography, "almost all my life has been spent in literary pursuits and occupations" (E-MOL, xxxi). Nevertheless, Hume never held an academic position. His candidacies for a professorship at both the University of Edinburgh (1745) and the University of Glasgow (1752) were each denied, purportedly for his irreligious writings. He also struggled to make a name as a scholar. Although his first and now best-known work, *A Treatise of Human Nature* (1739–40) did not gain the recognition he had expected, his first two volumes of *Essays, Moral and Political* (1741–42) proved more successful. He was given the princely sum of 150 pounds for each print run, but five years later, with nothing new to show, he was forced back to dependency on his elder brother, John Home of Ninewells. In a heartfelt letter to his mentor Lord Kames, at age thirty-six, Hume worried about "continuing a poor Philosopher for ever," noting that it was too late for him to enter the law (NHL, 24–26).

Hume's decision to remain a poor philosopher bore fruit in the years 1747 to 1751, while residing at Ninewells, the family estate.[2] In just three years, Hume wrote his two *Enquiries* (1748 and 1751), *A Dialogue* (1751), and substantial parts of the *Four Dissertations* (1757)—namely, *A Dissertation on the Passions*, based on Book 2 of the *Treatise*, and *The Natural History of Religion*. Less well known is the fact that he completed, in 1750, a work entitled *A Dissertation on Geometry and Natural Philosophy* that was intended as one of the *Four Dissertations* but was never published and subsequently lost.[3] By 1751, Hume had also drafted the *Dialogues concerning Natural Religion* that was published posthumously in 1779. Most important for our study here, he completed the highly acclaimed work on economics, the *Political Discourses* (1752). Hume's only remaining major work after these three intensive and productive years was not in philosophy but did the most to lift him out of his financial straits. *The History of England* (1754 62) took about five years to gain a following; however, by 1760 he could boast that "the copy-money given me by the booksellers, much exceeded any thing formerly known in England" (E-MOL, xxxviii). It is estimated that Hume earned at least 3,200 pounds from the sales of his *History* and became one of the first Britons to live comfortably as the author of nonfiction.[4]

Hume did not live entirely on book royalties. Several appointments provided modest incomes, the first in 1745 as a tutor and companion to the Marquess of Annadale, one of the wealthiest aristocrats in England and the second, in 1746 and 1748, in the service of General St. Clair. In each case, Hume disputed a breach of contract on the terms of employment, and he subsequently wrote dozens of letters to secure full payment from the marquess and the promised half pension from the British army. From 1752 to 1757, Hume was keeper of the Advocate's Library in Edinburgh, receiving a meager stipend but gaining access to an invaluable collection for his research on English history (E-MOL, xxxvi). In 1763, Hume returned to salaried work for the British government, first as secretary and then, in 1765, as acting ambassador at the embassy in Paris. Two years later, in 1767, he moved to London to serve as undersecretary of state for the Northern Department until 1769. Hume had already attained financial independence; presumably he took these posts in part for the challenge. They also came with ample pensions and, for the first time in his life, Hume could declare himself a wealthy man.

In 1776, Hume composed a short autobiographical essay "My Own Life," that mutes his relatively turbulent path through life. Hume experienced numerous accusations of impropriety, dismissals, or rejections from suitable posts, a near excommunication from the Church of Scotland, protracted efforts to secure payments or recognitions due, and subsequent vilifications from several people he had befriended, most famously Jean-Jacques Rousseau. Hume observed in an early essay that wisdom is necessarily in short supply (E-DM, 83). Evidently, in his case what wisdom he acquired, along with his "rising reputation," was hard earned (E-MOL, xxxvi). In contrast to the prudent and steady path taken by his closest friend, Adam Smith, Hume did not always navigate life's shoals adroitly.

Ernest Mossner depicts Hume's life as beset with many disappointments and intrigues, both personal and professional.[5] Hume comes across as his own worst enemy, too forthright and too trusting of others who could not always see that his objective was not to offend but to enlighten. More recently, James A. Harris's *Hume: An Intellectual Biography* (2015) offers an account of Hume's life that downplays the sensationalist details that preoccupied Mossner. Harris portrays Hume's life as segmented, broken into distinct chapters rather than unified by a single mission. Hume is depicted as a brilliant man of letters who contributed to philosophy but also to many other subjects, including economics. Mossner registers that Hume's *Political Discourses* "established him at the summit of British economists," but it is Harris who provides the substance for this accolade.[6]

Hume corresponded with many of the leading philosophers of his day, including Francis Hutcheson, Voltaire, Montesquieu, Rousseau, Edmund Burke, and Thomas Reid. He befriended many prominent savants, Jean d'Alembert, Denis Diderot, Comte de Buffon, and Benjamin Franklin, as well as the historians Catharine Macaulay, Edward Gibbon, and James Boswell. He was on close terms with the Scottish stadial theorists Lord Kames, Adam Ferguson, and John Millar. He also exchanged ideas with leading contributors to economics, such as Lord Elibank, Robert Wallace, Abbé Morellet, Anne-Robert-Jacques Turgot, James Steuart, Isaac de Pinto, and, last but not least, Adam Smith.

During Hume's life he became known as "the Socrates of Edinburgh" and his native town as "the Athens of the North."[7] One contemporary, William Smellie, boasted that if one were to stand at the "Cross of Edinburgh," at a suitable time in the day, some fifty men of genius and learning would pass in the span of a few minutes.[8] Roger Emerson estimates, with considerable attention to the historical record, that there were about seven hundred Enlightened Scots in 1760.[9] England might have had ten times that number and France twenty, but in total, the number of readers of philosophical works would not have exceeded thirty thousand across Europe. Hume's success as an author, selling approximately ten thousand copies of each of his mature works, his two *Enquiries*, his *Essays* (including the *Political Discourses*), and *The History of England*, is thus remarkable.

Only Edinburgh could rival Paris in terms of contributions to philosophy during the Enlightenment.[10] Hutcheson, Hume, Smith, and Reid brought Scottish philosophy to the attention of the learned world. Although Hutcheson lived in Glasgow, Reid in Aberdeen, and Smith only briefly in Edinburgh, it was Hume's city that became preeminent, mostly because as the seat of local governance, it drew the most educated elite at the time. According to Harris, the Edinburgh in which Hume retired was a very different, more secular and intellectually advanced place than the one he had lived in as a young man up through the 1750s.[11] By the 1760s, professors at the University of Edinburgh whom Hume counted as friends and equals included William Cullen, Hugh Blair, William Robertson, and Adam Ferguson. He befriended the artist Allan Ramsay, who painted Hume twice, and novelists and poets such as Tobias Smollett, John Home, James Macpherson, and William Wilkie. In Hume's opinion, these Scottish writers were the most eloquent in all of Europe.[12]

The Scottish Enlightenment had a strong association with the natural sciences. The Select Society of Edinburgh (1754–64) that Hume cofounded listed as its primary objective the promotion of scientific methods in agriculture, engineering, and medicine. This objective suggests that for much of

the 1750s, Hume willingly if not enthusiastically kept abreast of scientific research, particularly research that led to practical results, a proclivity evident
in his *Treatise*, *Early Memoranda*, and *Dialogues concerning Natural Religion*.
Hume may have been deemed an *amateur*, but an amateur in the full sense of
the word: a lover of knowledge including the natural sciences.[13] He formed
associations with Colin Maclaurin, John Pringle, Joseph Black, and James
Hutton, the most eminent contributors to Scottish mathematics and science
of the eighteenth century. From 1751 to 1763, Hume served as joint secretary to the Philosophical Society of Edinburgh. This society was formed in
1737 and was intended to facilitate the exchange of ideas between physicians
and naturalists. Over time, it grew to include intellectuals such as Hume who
were neither. At the meetings, members would present their research and
sometimes conduct experimental demonstrations. The initial publications
were exclusively on medical topics but, under the urgings of Maclaurin, expanded to include essays on general science. In 1754 and 1756, Hume co-
edited with Alexander Monro II, a leading physician, two volumes entitled
Essays and Observations, Physical and Literary. A third volume was published
in 1770 and includes a number of entries from the early 1760s that Hume
would have edited.[14]

By the 1760s, the University of Edinburgh could boast one of the most
prestigious medical schools in the Western world, primarily because of such
scientific luminaries as Cullen, Black, and three generations of Alexander
Monros.[15] A sign of its sustained eminence in science is the fact that the two
most prominent British scientists of the nineteenth century, Charles Darwin and James Clerk Maxwell, studied at Edinburgh. Black and Cullen were
Hume's personal physicians and attended Hume in his terminal months after
a diagnosis of intestinal cancer (HL, 2:449–50). In 1754, Black was the first
to isolate a new gas that he called "fixed air," now known as carbon dioxide.
In 1756, Cullen devised an important analysis of evaporation that prompted
Turgot to formulate the physical theory of state change, that all substances
with enough heat could expand from solid to liquid to gas. These break-
throughs discredited the Aristotelian doctrine of the elements and facilitated
the establishment of modern chemistry, grounded in the discoveries of oxy-
gen and hydrogen in the 1760s and 1770s.[16] Hume's close association with
some of the leading contributors to science of his day strongly suggests he
brought an informed understanding of science to bear in his plan to develop
and elevate the science of economics.

We will not rehearse Hume's personal life in much detail here. Our emphasis is rather on the various experiences and encounters that informed his economics, and moral and political thought more generally. Hume recognized

the value of "a cautious observation of human life" in making "any addition to our stock of knowledge" (T, 6; EHU, 12). Hume, we will show, was ever attentive to learning about agricultural and artisanal techniques, mercantile trade, and the rise of private and public finance, and he wove these topics into his economic thought. As Emma Rothschild has noted, Hume's *Political Discourses* "includes a mass of details of commercial existence."[17] Our case also emphasizes that Hume's firsthand experience with Scotland figured prominently in his economic thought. His close contact with the leading Scottish improvers, merchants, and bankers gave him considerable opportunity to reflect on the symbiotic relationship between economic and political betterment.

It is our ambition to highlight the sense in which economic ideas and policies pervaded Hume's entire adult life, in his publications and correspondence as well as his actions. Hume proclaims at the start of his first *Enquiry*, the *Enquiry concerning Human Understanding* (1748), that "a philosopher may live quite remote from business," but this does not undercut the potential of philosophy to "diffuse itself throughout the whole society" (EHU, 8). Quite literally, economics was Hume's applied philosophy, the ideal domain in which to develop his prolonged reflections of human nature. This is an underappreciated side to Hume, but one that seems obvious when one is reminded that his closest and most enduring friendship for more than twenty-five years was with Adam Smith and that one of the last books he read with care was Smith's newly issued *Wealth of Nations*.

Hume's Education and Travels Abroad

Hume was born in Edinburgh on April 26, 1711, and spent his childhood at Ninewells, a large estate in the southeast of Scotland. His father died when he was two years old. Hume was very close to his mother (1683–1745) and sister (1710–90), both named Katherine. Hume spoke glowingly of his mother, particularly her intelligence and devotion to "the rearing and educating of her children" (E-MOL, xxxii). She had come to live at Ninewells at the age of five when her widowed mother, Mary, married Hume's paternal grandfather, John Home. Hume's parents were thus stepsiblings, together for twenty years before their brief and purportedly happy marriage of five years. Ninewells remained Hume's official home until his older brother, John Home, married in 1751.

In 1721, at the age of ten, Hume and his brother went together to study for four years at the University of Edinburgh.[18] At the time, the University of Edinburgh was more like a preparatory college than a full-blown university.

It paved the way, more often than not, for students to pursue a degree in law or medicine at one of the Dutch universities. The strong imprint of Dutch thinking on Scottish savants meant that Hume would have absorbed the ideas of Hugo Grotius, Baruch Spinoza, and Pierre Bayle, who lived most of his life in exile in the Netherlands.[19] The core curriculum at Edinburgh included the study of Latin, Greek, history, literature, and philosophy, notably logic, metaphysics, and ethics. Hume studied mathematics for at least three years, including geometry, trigonometry, and algebra.[20] In his last year (1724–25), he studied natural science, for which we have extant the catalog of books required by the students, with Hume's signature among the list of subscribers. In addition to an extensive list of books in the natural sciences and mathematics, there were volumes on "Book-keeping, Trade and Manufacture," as part of his pursuit of "mixed mathematics."[21] Hume's *Early Memoranda* suggests a sustained interest in these subjects, including commerce and fortification.[22]

After four years in Edinburgh, Hume returned home to Ninewells, ostensibly to study the law, but actually to read philosophy and literature (E-MOL, xxxiii). Given Hume's close attachment to his mother, and hers for the memory of her own father, a leading barrister, not to mention the strained family resources, it would not have been easy for Hume to forgo the pursuit of law that had been chosen for him. He records that at age eighteen he had an important philosophical breakthrough. While we do not know the gist of these insights, we know that they prompted him to begin to work on his monumental *Treatise of Human Nature* that he would publish ten years later.

Hume still went up to Edinburgh from time to time, where he continued to study mathematics extramurally, with George Campbell, and the extant lecture notes indicate that he had studied calculus, or fluxions, as it was then known.[23] He also went to Berwick-upon-Tweed, the English port ten miles to the east that had a thriving book trade.[24] Hume was an avid collector and by 1740 — when he was not yet thirty years old — boasted that he had more than 400 volumes to his name. He bequeathed most of his library to his nephew, Baron David Hume, and the catalog that records the contents, some 1,300 volumes, informs us as to what Hume might have read and owned in his formative years.[25] The library contains surprisingly few core works in philosophy and leans more toward literature, the arts, history, and economics. There are dozens of books on economic topics, including texts by John Locke, Charles Davenant, John Law, Ferdinando Galiani, François Véron de Forbonnais, and Abbé Morellet, as well as pamphlets on the subjects of taxes, duties, public debt, and trade. Unfortunately, we cannot know for certain when Hume acquired these books, or whether some of them were purchased by his nephew.[26]

At age twenty-two, in February 1734, Hume left the comforts of his family for the first time and ventured out on his own for five years. His first destination was Bristol, via London, to try his hand in commerce.[27] Before leaving, Hume wrote a heartfelt letter to a learned physician in London, quite possibly John Arbuthnot or George Cheyne, seeking help for his persistent "melancholy."[28] He registered a decision to become a merchant in part to cure his "distemper" (HL, 1:18). This struggle with what today might be recognized as depression may be partly why Hume more than once in his later published works advised his readers not to remain brooding at their desks but to be active and engage the world (T, 175). In the opening pages of the first *Enquiry*, he contrasts the life of the philosopher with that of the businessman and suggests that a mixture of the two would yield "the most perfect character" (EHU, 6–7). The reasons stem from the fact that the latter pursuit forges an "easy style and manner" that counterbalances the tendencies toward "pensive melancholy" to which philosophers are susceptible; quite possibly, Hume was looking in a mirror.[29]

Bristol at the time was the second largest city in England and a thriving port for the sugar and slave trade. In his *Tour through the Whole Island of Great Britain* (1724–26), Daniel Defoe opines that Bristol might swell to twice the population were it not for its cramped housing stock and policy of "corporation-tyranny" that restricted trade to "subjects of their city sovereignty."[30] Hume worked as a clerk for Michael Miller, who imported Caribbean sugar with a business worth twenty thousand pounds.[31] Although Hume had expressed intentions of setting out into a business of his own, he stayed only four months. In that brief time, however, Hume would have reconciled many accounts and discharged bills of exchange, promissory notes, and banknotes. He made good friends with men in the mercantile trade, some of whom were also men of letters, and this may have prompted him to read the influential *Essay on the State of England in Relation to Its Trade, Its Poor, and Its Taxes* (1695) by John Cary, a Bristol merchant of some renown who had died in 1720.[32] Moreover, Hume might have learned something about the equity market that had made its way west from London. Prior to the construction of a Royal Exchange in 1741, merchants conducted their trade in the open air, known generically as the "Tolsey." Defoe describes this as a place of "great business, yet so straitened, so crowded, and so many ways inconvenient, that the merchants have been obliged to do less business there, than indeed the nature of their great trade requires."[33] Mandeville remarks on two traders from London's Change-Alley who might normally "act with not much greater civility than bulls," but on meeting by chance in Bristol "would be glad of one another's company."[34]

Hume was dismissed from his position in Bristol for correcting Miller's grammar.[35] It is only fitting that as a future man of letters, Hume exhibited an early tendency to precise prose if not pedantry. This came as a blessing, since Hume reminisced that he knew by then that his true calling was that of a philosopher and that he must suffice with his small annual stipend. Hume later observed that the average Englander spends half a shilling a day, "yet is he esteemed but poor" if expending half a crown (E-PA, 429). Hume's fifty pounds per year worked out to slightly more than 2.7 shillings per day, just marginally above the poverty line of half a crown, or 2.5 shillings.[36] He seemed well enough informed to know that living in London or Paris would prove too costly but chose, for whatever reasons, not to return home.[37]

Hume was drawn to France, where he lived for almost three years. He stayed briefly in Paris and then for about a year in Reims, where he enjoyed the company of the renowned savant and Cartesian Noël-Antoine Pluche, who had assembled an excellent library. Pluche is primarily known for his multivolume and immensely popular work, *Spectacle de la Nature* (1732–51) that included a study of commerce.[38] Reims owed much to the interventions of its native son, Jean-Baptiste Colbert, who had developed its woolen industry in the previous century and set in motion the transformation of France into a manufacturing nation.[39] Hume had planned to stay in Reims but found it to be too expensive, notwithstanding that he was welcomed into the homes of numerous burghers, whom he found to be "a polite Sociable People" (HL, 1:22). Hume observed, in a letter of 1734 to his Bristol friend James Birch, that although the well-heeled citizens earned no more than the equivalent of five hundred pounds, each family kept a coach. They also built their homes off the main avenues, so as to conceal their wealth. Already in his twenties, Hume was taking notice of the specific patterns of consumption among those in the middle rank.

La Flèche, where Hume settled in 1735, was home to a small Jesuit college, the most famous student of which was René Descartes a century before. Although Descartes had deemed his education a waste of time, the college ironically had become a center for Cartesian philosophy. Moreover, several of the priests at the college had served as missionaries abroad. Hume records the fact that he conversed with them, and because he dined at the college daily, he was probably privy to many stories regarding the cultures and religions of distant lands. This exposure may have partly informed his study of comparative religions in the *Natural History of Religion* as well as his efforts to extend his economic principles worldwide.[40] For example, Hume refers to China or India dozens of times in his written work and correspondence.

The college library had some forty thousand volumes, and Hume undoubtedly availed himself of its collection. The sources he cites in his *Treatise* include works by the leading Continental philosophers Descartes, Spinoza, Bayle, Blaise Pascal, and Gottfried Leibniz. Hume most likely also had access to the works of the well-known French economists whom he later cites — namely, Jean-François Melon, Charles de Ferrère Du Tot, and Joseph Pâris-Duverney. Some scholars speculate that Hume may also have come across the writings of a former associate of John Law, Richard Cantillon, whose *Essai sur la nature du commerce en général* (*Essay on the Nature of Commerce in General*), published posthumously in 1755, had allegedly circulated in manuscript in the mid-1730s.[41] Cantillon's *Essai* is among the list of books in the Baron Hume library of 1840, but whether or not it was bought or read by David Hume remains unknown.[42] Although Hume responded actively to the work of Josiah Tucker that appeared in 1755, there are no references to Cantillon, nor is there any clear evidence that Cantillon influenced Hume when he undertook various revisions of his economic writings. It is possible that Hume had read Cantillon in the 1730s, or after 1755 when the work was in print, but it is unlikely that we will ever know for certain.[43]

Hume found the cost of provisions in La Flèche one-third the price of a similar basket of goods in England.[44] He attributed the higher prices back home to the "greater Encrease of Money in England."[45] He thus had some command, even in his twenties, of the notion of the relative purchasing power of money and hence the key tenet of the quantity theory of money: that an increase in the money supply prompts a rise in the overall price level, or what we now term inflation. This understanding is also made clear in his *Early Memoranda*; he makes note that "what costs 3 pence at Paris is sold for half a crown in Mexico," where silver was abundant (MEM, 504). We will argue that Hume was not an unqualified exponent of the quantity theory, but suffice it to say here that he had some empirical exposure to the fact that price levels were regional and in part governed by the volume of trade and hence the supply of money in circulation.

During his three years in France, Hume completed the first two books of his *Treatise*. In 1737, he moved to London to shepherd them into print. After several setbacks, they were published at the end of 1738, with a 1739 date for the printing. Before he left France, Hume may have already drafted parts of the third book, on moral and political philosophy, published in 1740, but we know that he had not completed it until after the first two books were in print and that he contemplated adding two more books. The *Treatise* was published anonymously, as was customary at the time, but Hume's authorship came out into the open in 1745 when he was refused the chair in philosophy at the University of Edinburgh and composed *A Letter from a Gentlemen to His Friend in Edinburgh*, initially a private letter to John Coutts, Lord Provost of Edinburgh, that was subsequently published as a pamphlet. It takes up the charges of atheism and makes direct reference to the *Treatise*. Hume's book set him on a path that was in clear opposition to the established views on virtually every prominent question in philosophy and religion.

For a Scottish man of letters, Hume saw a great deal of Europe. After his sojourns in Bristol, France, and London, he traveled extensively with St. Clair. In 1746, they landed briefly in Lorient (or as Hume and his contemporaries called it, L'Orient) in Brittany as well as set anchor in Plymouth, Portsmouth, Cork, and London. In 1748, Hume served on a diplomatic mission with St. Clair that took him across the Continent. They sailed to the Netherlands and traveled to Vienna, where they succeeded in settling the diplomatic agreement that had prompted their mission, only to learn on the journey home, while in Turin, that the War of the Austrian Succession had come to an end with the Treaty of Aix-la-Chapelle (1748) and that their mission had been in vain.[46] But this also meant that they could travel home via France, spending time in Lyon and Paris.

There are some important events to note in the years that Hume spent with St. Clair. In addition to serving as his secretary, he was appointed judge advocate because of his knowledge of the law.[47] In the St. Clair papers, there are some documents in Hume's hand regarding his adjudication and sentencing of the deserters of the aborted attack on Lorient, a seemingly unwarranted loss of life since no significant battle had transpired and nothing was gained by the incursion. This was no doubt a source of anguish for Hume.[48] Young men were executed for what was unequivocally a futile expedition; no one had expected that such a small force, about three thousand soldiers, could capture the province of Brittany, let alone all of France. The ostensible reason for attacking was, ironically, to harm French trade—Lorient was headquarters for the French East India Company—since Hume would later famously argue for the flourishing of French trade (E-JT, 331). Hume undoubtedly performed his duties well, because he was asked a year later to accompany St. Clair, as his sole companion, on the diplomatic mission to Vienna. But it is also reasonable to suppose that Hume did not succeed in washing that figurative blood off his hands for several years to come. On more than one occasion, Hume decried the folly and barbarity of war.[49]

The St. Clair papers also indicate that Hume kept the accounts and budget for the expedition, which means that he had to record purchases and reconcile accounts; he was in effect a clerk, much as in his Bristol days. For most of the campaign of 1746, they were docked in Plymouth or Cork. As such, he was forced to pay close attention to economic conditions, including local price variations. His observation about relative prices between La Flèche and England in his twenties was just the start of a lifetime habit of noticing the economic features of his world. However much the philosopher, Hume paid close attention to economic data.

During his tour of the Continent with St. Clair, Hume kept a journal that provides us with a detailed account of the "Variety of Scenes" (HL, 1:125). At almost every town he visited, Hume comments on the diet, dress, and overall state of the inhabitants. They sailed to Rotterdam and spent several days in Breda, in March 1748, where they encountered a beleaguered French army just defeated in the battle at Bergen-op-Zoom. Of the five thousand French troops, one thousand were captured as prisoners and paraded through town. Hume describes them as "ragged Scarecrows" and attributes their mal-nourishment and the economic depravity of the region directly to the decline of trade and the oppressive taxes of the Flemish by the French (HL, 1:118). It was a sorry sight of what Hume had believed to be "the greatest Army [the French], that ever was assembled together in the World" (HL, 1:118). Hume estimated some 206,000 British men fought that same year in the War of the Austrian Succession, more than ever partook in a Roman war. The cost in economic terms alone was staggering and resulted in a significant spike in the public debt. "We have so much exceeded, not only our own natural strength, but even that of the greatest empires," Hume asserted. "This extravagance is the abuse complained of, as the source of all the dangers, to which we are at present exposed" (E-PC, 358–59).

After leaving Breda, they traveled on an iceboat on the frozen canals. East of Nijmegen, they rode in what Hume called a "Berline," a type of carriage that used an ingenious suspension system to provide greater comfort, and near Cologne, Hume marveled at "a very pretty Machine" known as a "fly-ing Bridge" to traverse the rapids of the Rhine (HL, 1:117–21). They mostly traveled overland, following along the banks of the main river routes, taking them to Cologne, Bonn, Koblenz, and Frankfurt, before sailing down the Danube to their point of destination, Vienna. En route, they encountered French troops once more attempting to reclaim the town of Dettingen, near Würtzburg, that had been lost to the British in 1743. Hume and St. Clair made a hasty escape, traveling "in great Security" because of reports that more French troops lay in their path (HL, 1:123). No doubt these adventures emboldened Hume into a more resilient man.

Hume found the Dutch and Italians worse off than the Germans, and he was impressed by the prosperity of the region along the Rhine and the Maine rivers. He found the palaces at Cologne and at Würzburg magnificent and comparable, he speculated, to Versailles. The region around Cologne was "very populous" and "the Inhabitants well cloth'd & well fed" (HL, 1:119). Hume was particularly struck with Frankfurt, which he noted was a Protestant town and which had in its vicinity the best cultivated farms that he had ever witnessed. More striking was that "every body, except the Farmers, live here in Towns: And these [the farmers] dwell all in Villages" (HL, 1:122). Hume would later argue that more Western Europeans lived in towns than in the countryside and that urban demand for nearby agrarian products was a critical link for economic development. The first pervasive poverty that Hume witnessed was in Bavaria, and he mused in a letter as to the reasons, pointing to recent wars, the adherence to Roman Catholicism, and the type of government (HL, 1:124–25). In his economic essays, Hume argues that the institutions of Catholicism and monarchy reinforce each other and tend to fuel war and conquest, and that all three of these factors hinder economic prosperity. His brief exposure to Bavaria evidently made a strong impression.

Hume found the Germans to be honest and industrious, two virtues he would make salient in his moral philosophy. Although he found Germany to be weak militarily, he remarked presciently that, if unified into a German nation, it "would be the greatest power that ever was in the world" (HL, 1:126).[50] He found the region heavily populated—the basis, perhaps, for his subsequent claim that Germany had twenty times more people than in the Roman era (E-PA, 453). In his essay "Of Money," Hume compares the diminished size of the army in Germany and its heightened level of "industry, people, and manufactures" over the past three centuries (E-Mo, 289). His point was that, while a region can be densely populated and economically thriving, it could also lack the capacity to collect taxes effectively and thus fail to fund a substantial standing army. Much of the specie in Europe, Hume believed, had drained to France, which also had by far the largest army in Europe (E-BP, 338).

Hume was less enthralled by what he observed in Austria. He found Vienna smaller than expected for an imperial capital and made note of the complete lack of Italian opera or French comedy that were both on offer in Cologne (HL, 1:129–30). While in Vienna, Hume met the empress Maria Theresa and found her more approachable than he had anticipated. She would not be the only royalty he and St. Clair would meet on this trip. On December 18, 1748, on the outskirts of Paris in Fontainebleau, they chanced upon Charles Edward Stuart, the Young Pretender, disgraced from the defeat at

Culloden and en route to his exile in Rome.⁵¹ Fifteen years later, Hume returned to Fontainebleau, where he met Madame de Pompadour. He then visited Versailles and had a brief audience with the French royal family, including Louis XV and his two sons, ages ten and eight, who would become Louis XVI and Louis XVIII (postrevolution), respectively. Hume described the encounters with royalty in both Vienna and France, particularly their mannerisms, as converging on the comical, a judgment Smith would echo (HL, 1:127; 1:408; 1:414; TMS, 54). Hume disliked autocratic power and observed that both the Austrian and French courts exhibited a "spirit of bigotry and persecution" (E-BP, 338).

Hume met one Viennese statesman who impressed him deeply: Count von Zinzendorf, who later became the controller of finance for the Austrian empire and who wrote about state banking. There is no extant correspondence, but at some point, Zinzendorf gave Hume an account of the influx of gold and silver into Spain, and Hume passed this booklet on to Smith to assist him in writing the *Wealth of Nations*.⁵² Hume's encounter with Zinzendorf may have been the source of Hume's later misapprehension about the relationship between money and wealth prevalent in Austria. In "Of Money" he wrote, "the Austrian dominions in the empire are in general well peopled and well cultivated, and are of great extent; but have not a proportionable weight in the balance of Europe; proceeding, as is commonly supposed, from the scarcity of money" (E-Mo, 289). But Hume insisted that the lack of specie was only the apparent and not the primary cause because the price level can always adjust downward (E-Mo, 289–90). The primary reason for the scarcity of money and hence the means to mount an effective army stemmed from "the manners and customs of the people," and Hume gestured to "experience" as a source of this proposition (E-Mo, 290).

After departing Vienna, Hume made note that the landscape of Styria, the region near Graz, was enchanting, but that he found the inhabitants "deform'd & monstrous in their appearance" (HL, 1:130). The Tyrolian Alps offered the converse; the landscape was more "barren" but the people "as remarkably beautiful as the Stirans are ugly. An air of humanity, & spirit & health & plenty is seen in every face" (HL, 1:131). In his *Early Memoranda*, Hume had posited the generalization that "people commonly live poorest in Countrys, which have the richest natural Soil" (MEM, 510). The contrast between the Styrian and the Tyrolian regions, witnessed firsthand several years later, served to instantiate this maxim. Crossing the Alps into Italy, Hume settled in Turin. He there received a copy of Montesquieu's *Spirit of the Laws* (1748), just released, a book that makes a strong case for geographical determinism. While Hume initially seemed drawn to some of Montesquieu's arguments, his more mature reflections on the subject mostly discredited the effects of physical causes, "air or climate," on the resulting national character (E-NC, 204). He argued that the natural conditions underdetermine the cultural and economic ones, and put much more weight on the mechanism of sympathy among those who share a language or form kinships and alliances.

Hume found Italy poorer than Austria and weighted down under exorbitant taxes (HL, 1:132). He would later remark that, notwithstanding the size of cities such as Milan or Turin, both of which he visited, Italy, "it is probable, has decayed" since Roman times (E-PA, 457). Although Hume did not go to the south, he decried the long-standing tax burden exacted by the Vatican, reaching back a thousand years. Nevertheless, the money, he claims, drained out of Rome even more effectively by "secret and insensible canals," and hence "the want of industry and commerce renders at present the papal dominions the poorest territory in all Italy" (E-BT, 326). He had noted earlier that Italy had only recently begun to import British manufactured goods (MEM, 505) and included Italy in his list of countries he hoped would no longer be subject to the ill-begotten sentiment of the "jealousy of trade" (E-JT, 331).

Hume's tour of the Continent also gave him a valuable sampling of forms of political rule: the Dutch republic, the German principalities, the Austrian empire, the Italian city-states, and the French absolutist kingdom. Seeing the contrasts between Lyon and Paris, analogous in certain respects to the contrasts between Bristol and London, may well have prompted additional insights on economic geography. As the second largest city in France, Lyon was not as thriving as Bristol. Hume made explicit note of the diminution of silk manufacturing in Lyon from eighteen thousand workers at its height down to four thousand looms by the year 1698 (MEM, 510). This reduction in the workforce was mostly due, Hume recognized, to the expulsion of the Huguenots after the Revocation of the Edict of Nantes in 1685. Hume would later make note of this mass migration. Many of those who were exiled went to London and worked in the silk-weaving industry: "Above half a million of the most useful and industrious subjects [Huguenots] deserted France; and exported, together with immense sums of money, those art and manufactures, which had chiefly tended to enrich that kingdom" (HE, 6:471).[53] Evidently, Hume's travels in 1748 exposed him to a wide array of cultural, political, and economic phenomena that clearly left their mark on his *Political Discourses*, written upon his return to Scotland in 1749 and completed by 1751.

Political and Economic Transformations

Hume's life coincided with a rapid expansion of the British Empire. The defeat of the Spanish Armada in 1588 may be taken as the moment imperial ascent commenced, but it was only in the eighteenth century that the British were firmly entrenched with colonies on five continents. As the great-grandson of Joseph Johnstone of Hilton, Hume was related to the wealthy and influential Johnstone family that sent its many sons overseas to India, Africa, and the Americas.[54] Through his familial ties, Hume would most surely have heard regular reports of the adventures of his many cousins. As a young man, Hume had considered a post in Massachusetts and yearned to "toss about the World, from one Pole to the other" (HL, 1:18). In 1746, Hume prepared to sail to Canada to secure it from the French, but the plan was aborted due to poor winds. Hume never crossed the Atlantic. During the 1760s, however, while serving the British Crown for five years, first in Paris and then in London, he would have participated in numerous discussions and read many documents pertaining to Britain's reach across the globe.

Scotland had once harbored imperial ambitions. In the wake of a grain famine in the 1690s, Scotland sought ways to avert another calamity. One effort was the Darien scheme, the establishment of an entrepôt called Caledonia on the Isthmus of Panama, close to where the current canal is now situated. But without sufficient naval protection, the Scots were undercut by the Spanish and forced to uproot. This setback provided additional impetus for them to sign a Treaty of Union, in 1707, with England and Wales, and hence give birth to the United Kingdom of Great Britain. Hume was born four years later and thus grew in step with the new regime, the largest region of unrestricted trade in Europe. Glasgow in particular prospered, driven by shipbuilding and trade with the Americas. By the 1760s, the ironworks at Carron near Stirling became the largest single factory in Europe, with about one thousand workers producing the armaments for British forts and naval ships. The union brought considerable economic gains but also political humiliation, demoralizing the Scots for failing to uphold national autonomy and forcing their elected Members of Parliament to reside in Westminster.

Hume would have been too young to understand the significance of the first Jacobite rebellion of 1715–16, but the uprising in 1719 may have prompted a keener awareness, since he would have been able to read broadsides and pamphlets by that point in time. The next Jacobite rebellion, 1745–46, tore at the heart of Scottish society. Sir James Steuart was one of many Jacobite sympathizers forced into exile in France, and Hume, in his correspondence, voiced much concern and affection for the older statesman. Hume would later remark, in a letter of September 1757, that "the most terrible *ism* of them all, [is] that of Jacobitism" (HL, 1:264).

Hume was residing in England in 1745 when the Highlanders captured Edinburgh. He nonetheless jumped into the fray, writing in defense of his close friend, Archibald Stewart, who, as provost of Edinburgh during the siege, was accused of a breach of duty.[55] Hume's pamphlet also established his own loyalty to the British Crown, an allegiance made even clearer the following year when he joined the British army and partook in the war against France, where many Jacobites lived in exile. Hume was surely marked by his Scottish roots, but his gaze was more toward England in the south than to Inverness in the north.[56] The fact that he would change the spelling of his name from *Home* to *Hume* in 1734 to aid and abet the citizens of Bristol, or that he would write a history of England and not, as he had initially preferred, of Britain, reinforces this line of interpretation.[57]

When the South Sea Bubble burst in 1720, Hume was nine years old and thus old enough to register that calamity; he may also have heard about the more dramatic collapse of the Mississippi Company (Compagnie des Indes) in France that same year, if only because John Law, a Scot, was held directly responsible. In his second *Enquiry*, the *Enquiry concerning the Principles of Morals* (1751), Hume made pejorative comments about the stockjobbers of Paris on the rue Quincampoix. Hume related the story of the traders for the Mississippi Company hiring a man with a humpback to use his back as a signing table during the frenzies leading up to the crash of 1720 (EPM, 29). In his *Political Discourses*, Hume expressed considerable skepticism of financial markets, noting that the only value of Change-Alley, the place for London brokers, was to increase the consumption of "coffee, and pen, ink, and paper" (E-PC, 637). Hume quipped in his essay on public credit that were those traders to be "for ever buried in the ocean," it would not make one whit of difference to the world (E-PC, 637).

Hume would not be the first or the last economist to criticize brokers and the rentier class more generally, but perhaps only John Maynard Keynes could rival his flair or wit. Ironically, in 1761, Hume borrowed and invested one thousand pounds in securities, under the guidance of his good friend Andrew Millar, with the aim of selling when peace was restored (HL, 1:356).[58] Hume subsequently found himself "exposed to the many jokes of his friends. His rebuttal was that he had bought real stock and was not a jobber."[59] We cannot be sure what he meant by this remark; he had held a small annuity since his youth, but this remark suggests that he had purchased publicly traded funds, either bonds or shares in a mercantile company, but without the intentions of speculating as a stockjobber might. In 1766, Hume lent money to a friend to invest in a Caribbean plantation, which suggests Hume was willing to risk his savings and, hypocritically, support the practice of slavery that he had condemned in print. In the next edition of his *Essays* (1768), Hume removed the remarks about the coffee consumption of Change-Alley, perhaps because he had come to see "the advantages that result from a circulation [of stocks]" (E-PC, 637). Hume kept a careful eye on his investments and mused about the best time to sell in order to capitalize on the height of the market. In March 1764, Hume remarked in a letter to William Strahan that the price of stocks was unusually low but he was pleased to see his own fund earn a 4 percent return (HL, 1:427).[60] This rate, however, was only slightly above the return on a bank deposit, thus verifying Hume's argument that the return on capital would, ceteris paribus, converge on the prevailing interest rate (E-In, 302–3).

Hume was fortunate to live in an age of relative domestic peace and prosperity, at least in comparison with the previous century. The succession of queens and kings was far more orderly than previous centuries, and much of the violence surrounding the enclosures was subsiding. The Toleration Act of 1689 had made possible the cohabitation of faiths, and religious persecution became far less frequent. As Hume observed, England welcomed nonconformity. "All sects of religion are to be found among [the English]. And the great liberty and independency, which every man enjoys, allows him to display the manners peculiar to him" (E-NC, 207). The burning of witches, not to mention plague or famine, no longer troubled Britons. Apart from the Jacobite rebellions, all of the combat during Hume's lifetime by the British Crown was offshore.

Nevertheless, Hume's world was profoundly marred by war, particularly with France. Hume was born during the reign of Queen Anne (1702–14) and lived to see the three Hanoverians, George I, II, and III, keep Britain on an ambitious—and from a modern standpoint, unwarranted—path of imperial expansion and empowerment. The War of the Spanish Succession (1701–13) was particularly brutal and transformative of the European map, setting the stage for subsequent wars. The War of the Austrian Succession (1740–48) and the Seven Years' War (1756–63), which was settled the same year Hume arrived in Paris as secretary at the British embassy, were each fought on an unprecedented scale. In 1773, conflicts with the American colonists grew into a full-blown war that was only settled in 1783. Britain's efforts at forging an empire also included confrontations in the Spanish colonies and the Indian subcontinent, as well as many prolonged assaults on and appropriations of ancestral lands of the indigenous peoples of the Americas and the South Pacific. The trade in African captives and the mass production of sugar and tobacco in the colonies required constant military coercion and violence. All of this activity was extremely costly, in terms of lives lost, ships sunk, and debts incurred. Hume recorded his antipathy toward slavery, war, and the ballooning national debt, fearing Britain might be brought to ruin.

Hume's death in 1776 coincided with the American Revolution, a rupture Hume had anticipated with mixed emotions. Like Smith, he did not view colonization in a favorable light, and he believed that the Americans had been excessively taxed. For these reasons, as well as other strategic considerations, Hume sincerely hoped that Britain would release its claim rather than go to war. He did not believe that the use of force, even an army of thirty thousand redcoats, could keep Americans subordinate to British rule. As Hume revealed in a letter of October 27, 1775, "I am an American in my principles, and wish we woud let them alone to govern or misgovern themselves as they think proper" (HL, 2:303).

Notwithstanding his approval of American independence, Hume was by and large conservative in temperament. He welcomed gradual and legal changes through parliamentary acts but opposed insurrections or revolutions. The London riots of 1768 protesting the imprisonment of John Wilkes only deepened Hume's aversion to mob turmoil and radical sentiments. Hume's father and grandfathers were Whigs, who supported the 1707 union and opposed the Jacobite cause. But Hume was not one to follow tradition. He was liberal in terms of individual proclivities, and more drawn to the new middle class than the landed aristocracy from which he sprung, yet he did not explicitly endorse either party, Whigs or Tories.[61] The primary reason is that Hume opposed party politics in principle because such allegiances were often orthogonal, he believed, to political stability and reasonable governance.[62] He sought the diminution of factionalism because beneficial policies in the moment tend to be diverted by party interests. In his account of an ideal commonwealth, Hume favored the republican system of governance but was in fact more drawn to the mixed form of constitutional monarchy as in Britain (E-IPC, 527–28; E-BG, 52). In either case, elections would be frequent to mitigate the groundswell of party sentiment and prompt the government to be accountable to the electorate. More than once, he asserted that his contemporary Britain had achieved the best form of government in recorded history because, as he had discerned at a young age, "the Legislature has not force enough to execute the Laws without the Goodwill of the People" (MEM, 506; E-PS, 508).

The Pull of Great Cities:
London, Paris, and Edinburgh

From time to time, Hume refers to himself as a "Briton," but it is fair to say that he never warmed to the English, certainly not in comparison with the joy he felt in his fifties while living in Paris, a city he considered making his permanent home.[63] Hume lived in or visited London many times. The first exposure was in 1734, en route to Bristol, and the first proper sojourn, in 1737–39, while guiding his *Treatise* into print. He returned a year later to oversee the publication of Book 3 of the *Treatise* and then in 1745–46 for about six months while officially serving as a tutor in nearby St. Albans. Hume considered settling in London at that point but lacked the financial means. However, his service to General St. Clair, from 1746–48, included several short stays in London. Hume returned to London for about a year in 1758–59, to oversee the publication of a new volume of his *History of England*. During his final residence in London in 1767–69, while working for the Northern Department, Hume suffered from widespread anti-Scottish sentiment that had been fomented by King George III, and he returned to Edinburgh as soon as his position came to an end. In April 1776, he visited London for the last time, very briefly for medical attention.

Hume lived in London for about six years in total, an experience that proved invaluable for exposure to commerce and culture. In a letter of 1754 to his friend John Clephane, Hume noted drawing on the wisdom of Pierre Bayle that "a man of letters ought always to live in a capital" (HL, 1:205). Many years later, on reading the *Wealth of Nations*, Hume remarked to Smith that "it is probably much improved by your last Abode in London" (HL, 2:311). This remark suggests that Hume comprehended how important it was to have personal experiences of life in the commercial metropolis of London. For comparative purposes, it was also important to observe surrounding regions. He remarked, for example, in a 1750 letter, "the manufactures of London, you know, are steel, lace, silk, books, coaches, watches, furniture, fashions. But the outlying provinces have the linen and woollen trades" (HL, 1:143–44). The regional pattern he observed would become more apparent with the Industrial Revolution a few decades later. While factories in the provincial towns would revolutionize the scale of production, Hume was strongly impressed by the scale and breadth of artisanal activities in London. He contrasted the large size of its many ateliers to that of ancient Rome, where one of the largest reported manufacturers employed but twenty cabinetmakers (E-PA, 429). Hume proclaimed of London that "by uniting extensive commerce and middling empire, [it] has, perhaps, arrived at a greatness, which no city will ever be able to exceed" (E-PA, 448).

Once known as a cramped and dirty city, London had become more spacious and spectacular in the Georgian era.[64] Wealthy citizens, in particular, participated in a vibrant and fashion-conscious culture. According to Daniel Defoe, a number of London shopkeepers spent more than five hundred pounds on displays and fixtures, including the innovation of bow windows—curved bay windows extending into the passageways to catch the eyes of passersby. The city bustled with peddlers and shopkeepers seeking to satisfy the desires and vanity of discerning consumers. Citizens displayed their finery at the Royal Exchange, the pleasure gardens, or the opera. Conspicuous consumption forged a new kind of sociability; to be seen in public became a new pastime.[65] Wearing finely woven cloth dyed with novel colors produced from exotic plants, the new cosmopolitan wife and husband might be painted sipping sweetened coffee or chocolate in a fine porcelain cup or smoking Chesapeake tobacco in a Dutch pipe. Their Georgian townhouse would be furnished with ornate rococo chairs and tables from France or Italy, with walls covered with chinoiserie wallpaper and windows draped by Indian chintz. Ornamental mirrors, landscape paintings, and family portraits completed the interior decor. Luxury items imported from the far reaches of the world were visible markers of bourgeois taste and refinement.[66]

Hume estimated that London acquired approximately five thousand additional inhabitants each year and might exceed one million (E-PA, 388, 428). It was certainly the commercial center of Britain. While networks of turnpikes and canals were rapidly developed in the 1750s and 1760s, in the 1730s and 1740s, the period that most informed Hume's economics, the River Thames served as the main inland artery. In an age when travel by land was slow and arduous, the Thames offered a natural highway, bringing corn from Oxfordshire and fish from Sussex to the metropolis of London. As Hume observed, "men naturally flock to capital cities, sea-ports, and navigable rivers. There we find more men, more industry, more commodities, and consequently more money" (E-BT, 314–15).

The new consumer culture was made possible by a massive expansion in global trade, much of which flowed through London. British export revenues doubled in the first half of the eighteenth century.[67] The Thames was teeming with ships and barges of various sizes coming and going, loading and unloading, buying and selling. Quays, wharfs, docks, jetties, and bridges were built at a rapid pace to facilitate the circulation of commodities. The London riverbank was abuzz with grain merchants, boatswains, porters, coopers, and customs officials. As trade expanded and the infrastructure improved, mercantile specialization promoted clustering by trade, such as tobacconists row in the West End. It would have been challenging for any visitor crossing the newly erected Westminster Bridge in 1750 not to marvel at the commercial frenzy playing out below.

London became the major site for wholesale markets and specialized traders in a wide array of commodities, including coal, cattle, and cloth. A series of parliamentary acts during the seventeenth and eighteenth centuries overhauled long-standing wholesale or retail regulations, such as transpired in Billingsgate fish market.[68] Such changes resulted in considerable competition, price reductions, and price convergences. Between 1700 and 1750, it is estimated that prices on a wide range of goods, particularly in London, declined in real terms by some 15 percent. This trend was most marked in the 1740s, when output rose by a higher percentage than in any previous decade of that century.[69] Hume was evidently attentive to these variations in prices, which factored into his efforts at theorizing the relationship between trade and prices: "Any man who travels over Europe at this day, may see, by the prices of commodities, that money . . . has brought itself nearly to a level; and that the difference between one kingdom and another is not greater in this respect, than it is often between different provinces of the same kingdom" (E-BT, 314). Just as he had made note of the much lower prices in La Flèche, Hume recognized new patterns of price convergence around London. "There is more difference between the prices of all provisions in Paris and Languedoc, than between those in London and Yorkshire," Hume observed (E-PC, 354–55).[70]

Although Hume witnessed and recognized the rise of the consumer society and the initial takeoff of what came to be known as the Industrial Revolution, he failed to grasp the extent to which the British economy was poised to grow over the final third of the eighteenth century, transforming into the "workshop of the world."[71] He understood that the future lay in the production of cloth, and he made specific note of the importance of wool, linen, and silk, but he had no inkling of the surge in cotton production that would occur by the 1780s, much of it facilitated by the steam engine. To be charitable, when Hume wrote his *Political Discourses* in 1749–51, he could not have anticipated the dramatic shifts ahead, however much he celebrated the manufacturing sector. This great transformation to an industrial nation was not fully apparent to Smith, at least when he issued his *Wealth of Nations* in 1776.[72] The expansion of canals and turnpikes, the dredging of harbors, and various inventions for mechanizing the spinning and weaving of cloth, not to mention important chemical discoveries for bleaching, dyeing, and smelting, transpired between 1752 and 1776, but the significant harnessing of steam power only came after the improvements by James Watt and Matthew Boulton in 1776—notably, the separate condenser and sun-and-planet gears. Both Hume and Smith analyzed a protoindustrial commercial world, one in which artisanal production tended to be carried out on a smaller scale, such as the ten men of Smith's paradigmatic workshop producing steel pins, using hand tools without additional sources of power. Hume's capitalist world did not yet resemble the coal-drenched and hardscrabble cityscapes of Sheffield or Manchester that were famously depicted by Charles Dickens and Elizabeth Gaskell in the nineteenth century.

In his role as public servant, Hume was directly engaged in a variety of reforms and policies. For example, while serving with the British embassy in Paris in 1763–66, he oversaw the restoration of metallic coins in Québec, where paper money had circulated for more than sixty years. In 1685, because of the harsh winter in Montreal, bullion could not arrive by ship for six months of the year, and the intendant issued thirty-nine thousand livres in the form of stamped playing cards. The paper bills were initially issued as a temporary measure, to be redeemed once specie arrived, but by 1705, the authorized playing cards were made legal tender. Due to persistent chronic shortages of specie, they were de facto irredeemable. After Québec fell to the British in 1759, the paper notes were declared illegal, but the transition to a metallic currency proved much more complicated than anticipated as many trade agreements, including with English merchants, were still represented by the Canadian notes. Hume drafted the formal agreement, dated September 25, 1765, noting the current discounting of the bills at the usurious rate of 35 percent and demanding full restitution for English merchants. Hume thus put to good use his knowledge of the law and of monetary theory.[73]

While in Paris, Hume befriended Isaac de Pinto, a wealthy Dutch financier originally of Portuguese Sephardic heritage. Pinto had written a critique of Hume's essay "Of Public Credit," and he appears to have influenced Hume's thinking on the topic.[74] Hume had written sympathetically about the Jewish moneylenders in York, who in 1189–90 were severely persecuted under King John. About five hundred of them were burned to death to annul outstanding debts. As Hume reflected, "the most barefaced acts of tyranny and oppression were practised against the Jews, who were entirely out of the protection of law, were extremely odious from the bigotry of the people, and were abandoned to the immeasurable rapacity of the king and his ministers" (HE, 1:483).[75] Hume wrote at least six letters to British officials urging them to provide Pinto with a pension for the services he had rendered in settling the Treaty of Paris in 1763.[76] Hume was unsuccessful at first but persevered and, while working for the Northern Department in London as undersecretary of state, secured Pinto an annual pension of five hundred pounds. There is reason to believe that Hume and Pinto continued as good friends throughout this period and that Hume helped shepherd an English translation of Pinto's book *Traité de la circulation et du crédit* (1771) into print as *An Essay on Circulation and Credit, in Four Parts; and a Letter on the Jealousy of Commerce* (1774).

For all his fascination with the metropolis of London and the culture of Paris, Hume lived most of his life, over fifty of his sixty-five years, in his native country. His adulthood was mostly spent in Edinburgh, but even as a child he spent winters there, living in the family pied-à-terre. He would have witnessed many features of the burgeoning Scottish economy—for example, the linen trade that was given a considerable boost by a series of Linen Acts passed in Scottish Parliament. Hume was well acquainted with the prominent founders of the British Linen Company and Royal Bank: Lord Kames, the third Duke of Argyll, and Charles Erskine. By the end of the century, almost one-third of the laboring class in Scotland was employed full-time or part-time in the linen trade.[77] He would also have learned about other facets of the economy from his many friends. General St. Clair, his close companion for some eighteen months, was a proprietor of coal mines in Fife. James Oswald, who from 1751 to 1759 served as commissioner of trade for Scotland, was an expert on Canada and naval politics. Hume discussed economics regularly with Oswald starting in the mid-1740s. Hume befriended Corbyn Morris, who wrote pamphlets on economic topics and served as commissioner of customs, and John Boyle, a shipping magnate who later administered the Office of Customs and Excises as the Earl of Glasgow (HL, 1:380; 1:44). Hume considered William Mure, who oversaw the commercial development of western Scotland and was appointed Baron of the Exchequer for Scotland in 1761, to be one of his closest friends (HL, 1:392; HL, 2:312). Among bankers, Hume knew or befriended Archibald Stewart of Allanbank; John Coutts, whose family bank in London provided Hume with a personal line of credit; and Adam Fairholm, who extended credit notes "honored from Riga to Naples."[78] These are just some of the men leading Scotland's economic expansion in Hume's day, and he undoubtedly learned a great deal from each one of them.

No window into economic development at the time could have been more evident to Hume than the improvements undertaken by John Home, his older brother, on the family estate. Hume was pleased to see his brother's yield and income rise over the course of their lifetime; he was deemed "one of the pioneers in introducing modern methods of farming into Scotland."[79] This was an era when it was commonplace for landowners to read about new techniques for breeding or fertilizers and to experiment with new crops such as turnips, new methods of storage, or improved fences or hedges.[80] They would also attend meetings in town to pool information or listen to special lectures. Both Cullen and Hutton conducted experiments on agricultural practices.[81] In his essay "Of Commerce," Hume observed that "the proprietors of land, as well as the farmers, study agriculture as a science" (E-Co, 261). As early as 1700, the yield per arable acre in Britain was twice that of France, making it sufficient for only one-third of the population to work the land.[82]

Hume's gaze was also directed toward the world of money and banking; he acknowledged the expansion of credit with the advent of bills of exchange and promissory notes in place of specie in Genoa, Dublin, and Amsterdam (E-PR, 24; E-Mo, 284). He also referenced the advent of banking in Sweden (MEM, 507). In his own country, Hume lived through a dramatic increase in banking; from 1744 to 1772, bank assets in Scotland increased tenfold, facilitated by the opening of thirteen provincial banks. Scottish bankers were also highly innovative; for example, they introduced paper notes for ten shillings and invented daily-interest lines of credit. Hume praised both expedients (E-BT, 319–20). Hume singled out a group of men, who "are half merchants, half stock-holders" (E-PC, 353). With the development of secondary and tertiary markets for capital assets, Hume estimated that roughly 60 percent of the money in circulation in Scotland was comprised of paper instruments, and close to 70 percent in England (E-BT, 317–20). Paper money, he underscored, was a permanent feature of a modern commercial state.

Toward the end of his life, in June 1772, Hume witnessed the collapse of the first large land bank in Scotland, the Ayr Bank, and reflected in a letter to Adam Smith on the vulnerability of such institutions (HL, 2:262–64).[83] He believed that the foolish actions of that bank, which exposed virtually every other bank to near closure as well, "will prove of advantage in the long run, as it will reduce people to more solid and less sanguine projects, and at the same time introduce frugality among merchants and manufacturers" (HL, 2:263). Hume's letters to Smith on this subject indicate not only that he was aware of the details of the plights of several Scottish banks but also that the tightening of credit might result in massive unemployment, shutting down the ironworks at Carron. This is a rare inkling that in 1772 Hume grasped the dramatic shift toward industrialization and its strong dependency on financial capitalism.

Hume's correspondence reflects a sustained interest in economic thought and activity long after the first publication of the *Political Discourses*. Not only did he continue to edit his essays, often quite significantly, and in 1758 insert a brand new essay, "Of The Jealousy of Trade," but he also wrote, also in 1758, an anonymous preface to a pamphlet on the corn trade that argued for unrestricted trade.[84] Hume continued to actively engage with the world of commerce and the realm of economic ideas after his retirement from public office. Even while debilitated by cancer, he debated the problem of the public debt with his friend and fellow companion, the author John Home, en route to Bath in April 1776.[85]

When the end finally came, Hume confronted death in a remarkably noble manner. One might even suspect that it was staged were it not for the fact that there were multiple witnesses, each one proclaiming a profound admiration for Hume's courage, stoic indifference, and equanimity. This is all the more surprising since a rumor had spread in 1772 that he was engaged to Anne (Nancy) Ord, daughter of the Lord Chief Baron of the Court of the Scottish Exchequer, even though she was half his age. He wrote her a very moving letter in June 1776, just two months before he died, promising to see her soon and to kiss her hand. He also left her ten guineas in his will, to buy her a ring in memory of their "friendship and attachment."[86] But the letter also made plain that he knew "what an egregious Folly it is for a Man of my Years to attach himself too strongly to one of Yours."[87]

Hume had acquired the nickname of "Saint David," first by Voltaire and then by his friend John Home. They each paid homage to his virtuous and generous character, notwithstanding his near excommunication from the Church of Scotland in 1756. Ord, circa 1770, had chalked "St. David's Street" in front of Hume's new house on St. Andrews Square in Edinburgh. The incident gained notoriety, and with time the street name was adopted even though Hume refused last rites from a priest and thus died a non-Christian. Hume was also recorded as having achieved inner peace; he wrote down that he had completed all of his life's missions and there remained nothing left for him to accomplish. He took steps to ensure that his unpublished manuscripts, including his essay questioning the immortality of the soul, would be printed posthumously. He clearly knew that his name would live on for many generations, but most likely he had no inkling of the magnitude of his philosophical reach some three centuries hence.

CHAPTER 2

"A Cautious Observation of Human Life"

Hume on the Science of Economics

Although Adam Smith, among others, addressed the scientific standing of economics during the Enlightenment, none of them can match David Hume's sophisticated set of arguments on the subject.[1] Insofar as Hume grappled extensively with fundamental problems of epistemology (and more specifically the means by which we forge and legitimate our mathematical principles and scientific theories), and kept a steady eye on the primary goal of forging the moral sciences, he also developed a detailed and cogent account of the scope and method of economics. He provided a rich array of insights on inferential tools and methods for establishing principles on a wide range of economic phenomena. In that respect, Hume served to initiate a line of inquiry now known as *economic methodology*, to which John Stuart Mill and Milton Friedman, most notably, contributed.

Hume's primary aim to forge and expand the science of economics was predicated on the belief that the moral sciences could achieve a comparable if not greater degree of certainty than the physical sciences. This conviction depended critically on his belief that there are tractable uniformities to human agency that produce observable patterns in the social realm. To demonstrate this belief, Hume employed a number of distinct methods to ascertain and measure features of the social world, particularly prices, the balance of trade, the supply of money, and the size of the population. He made use of analogical inferences, thought experiments, and a number of protostatistical methods to isolate and estimate these key indicators of economic prosperity as well as to establish salient functional relationships. The empirical record was central to Hume's economics and he drew extensively on data available at the time to confirm his theoretical analysis.

In his essay of 1741 entitled "That Politics May Be Reduced to a Science," Hume included banking, public credit, and trade, and hence treated politics as inclusive of economics. He also broached the possibility of securing laws in this domain, "general truths, which are invariable" and do not depend on personal dispositions (E-PR, 18). In his essay "Of Commerce," Hume asserted that his primary task was to find general principles of the kind beyond "what we can learn from every coffee-house conversation" (E-Co, 253). With his characteristic lack of humility, he asserted that, "the difference between a common man and a man of genius is chiefly seen in the shallowness or depth of the principles upon which they proceed" (E-Co, 254). Hume also remarked that, as a man of genius, he would unearth some principles that were abstruse and not readily discernible (E-Co, 254). As he observed in another essay, "of all sciences there is none, where first appearances are more deceitful than in politics" (E-PA, 400). Nevertheless, he maintained that the laws he seeks, once found, will have "consequences almost as general and certain . . . as any which the mathematical sciences afford us" (E-PR, 16).

Hume decreed that his science of economics ought to collect a large number of particulars and to seek out "the common circumstance in which they all agree" (E-Co, 254). This method might require extracting the "pure and unmixed" elements and putting aside "the other superfluous circumstances," or what we would call *statistical noise* (E-Co, 254). Astute moral philosophers, however, if they could transcend the "intricate and obscure" features of the situation, might "enlarge their view to those universal propositions, which comprehend under them an infinite number of individuals, and include a whole science in a single theorem" (E-Co, 254). Hume thus harbored high aspirations for the degree of abstraction and applicability of his science, the search for economic principles that are universal in scope.[2] Hume never found that single theorem, but he made a concerted effort to engage the entire sweep of human history across the globe, citing economic data from far and wide: China, India, the East Indies, Greenland, Jamaica, Mexico, and Turkey, not to mention about a dozen European countries. This effort to include evidence from across time and space—for Hume makes considerable use of the record in ancient Greece and Rome—suggests a strong predilection to render his science general. At the very least, Hume realized that, if he were to succeed in elevating economics to epistemic parity with the natural sciences, it must be universal in scope.

The science of commerce is defined by a distinct group of phenomena that pertain to the production and distribution of wealth. Hume's list first included "commerce, luxury, money, interest, etc.," but for the 1760 and subsequent editions, he omitted "luxury" and added "balance of trade" (E-Co 255;

631). The composition of the list itself is less meaningful than the fact that he conceives of his inquiry as encompassing a distinct set of phenomena. The titles of his essays, each named for one salient phenomenon, may be indebted to Montesquieu, who had approached the study of economics in a similar manner in his *Spirit of the Laws* (1748). James Steuart (1767) would continue the pattern, fleshing out Hume's etcetera with topics Hume also addressed— namely, "Population, Agriculture, . . . Industry, Coin, . . . Circulation, Banks, Exchange, Public Credit, and Taxes."[3] Smith, while subordinating everything to the study of "the wealth of nations," offers a comparable breadth of inquiry. It is worth noting the persistence of these core phenomena as defining the science of economics, and the dearth of genuinely novel phenomena adopted since Hume and Smith.[4]

By the eighteenth century, economics was a mature discourse and had spawned several distinct "disciplinary matrixes," notably the Salamanca school in Spain, the Colbertistes in France, and the political arithmeticians in England and Ireland.[5] The most renowned school in the eighteenth century, in terms of both allegiances and influence, is undoubtedly that of the physiocrats, who flourished from the late 1750s to the mid-1770s. Cameralism was also a widespread discourse in the German and Scandinavian regions of Europe and lasted for well over a century. There were schools of *economia civile* (civil economy) and *pubblica felicità* (public happiness) in the Italian principalities of Naples and Milan.[6] And in Scotland we find the "four-stages school" of economic development, forged by some of Hume's correspondents: Lord Kames, John Millar, and Adam Ferguson.

Many of the formal principles and methods that became de rigueur in twentieth-century economics—game theory, decision theory, and the binomial theorem—were formulated before Hume, by Blaise Pascal (1670), Daniel Bernoulli (1738), and Abraham de Moivre (1738), respectively.[7] Much of the differential and integral calculus that was adopted in economics by the end of the nineteenth century had been cemented by the mid-eighteenth century by, for example, Jean d'Alembert, whom Hume befriended. Thomas Bayes arrived at his famous theorem in the 1750s, and there is good evidence that Hume would have read its published version in 1764.[8] In economics, specifically, political arithmeticians such as Charles Davenant had devised demand schedules for corn, and William Petty had identified and estimated the four variables of the quantity theory of money, including its velocity. Quesnay constructed one of the first formal models, the *Tableau économique* (1758) that served to demonstrate the path by which an equilibrium might or might not be achieved with the annual product in a closed economy.[9]

Another feature of eighteenth-century economics was its spectacular growth, both written and institutional. Joseph Massie, a contemporary of Hume, published a number of prominent tracts in the 1750s and 1760s on economics, including a *Catalogue of Commercial Books* that spans almost two hundred years (1557–1763). Massie lists nearly 2,400 works and had in his possession about 1,500 of them. A recent study of Massie, by Julian Hoppit, found significant spikes in the number of publications corresponding to the South Sea Bubble (1720) and the Jacobite rebellion of 1745.[10] Christine Théré has estimated that in eighteenth-century France, there were more than 3,500 publications on various economic subjects, notably wealth, trade, money, and taxation.[11] We cannot simply add the figures, since Massie collected French works as well. Nevertheless, a modest estimate of eighteenth-century writings in English and French would bring the number to well over 4,000 publications. Needless to say, there were hundreds more in other languages that Hume did not read.

Hume thus had access to a flourishing print culture. London newspapers started to advertise shop prices in 1658. By the 1750s, there were more than a dozen newspapers, some issued daily. The *Gentleman's Magazine*, pamphlets, and broadsides also provided Hume with a vast array of price charts and descriptions of wares.[12] He made use of classic works on trade: Sir Josiah Child, *A New Discourse of Trade* (1665; mentioned in MEM, 508); Charles Davenant, *An Account of the Trade between Great-Britain, France, Holland, Spain, Portugal, Italy, Africa, Newfoundland, &c* (1715; also mentioned in MEM, 511); and Joshua Gee, *The Trade and Navigation of Great-Britain Considered* (1729; cited in E-BT, 310). He cited several works on economic geography, including Sir William Temple, *Account of the Netherlands* and *Observations upon the United Provinces of the Netherlands* (1673; in MEM, 507; E-Ta, 344), and Jonathan Swift, *Short View of the State of Ireland* (1727–28; in E-BT, 310). Hume probably read and benefited from the popular work by Daniel Defoe, his *Tour through the Whole Island of Great Britain* (1724–26), because it records innumerable details regarding manufacturing and farming practices. Hume's *Early Memoranda* lists specific data from the *Dictionnaire universel du commerce* (1723–30) by Jacques Savary des Brûlons, a text owned by Pluche, Hume's mentor in 1734 (MEM, 499, 510).[13] Soon after the publication of the *Political Discourses*, Hume may have read Malachy Postlethwayt's popular *Universal Dictionary of Trade and Commerce* (1751–55) that offered extensive economic observations as well as lengthy translations of sections of Savary's *Dictionnaire*.[14] Postlethwayt also published a book entitled *Great Britain's True System* (1757) in which he advocated that the study of economics be introduced at university.[15] This book serves as an indication that the field of economics had gained legitimacy by the 1750s, the same decade in which the *Encyclopédie* of Diderot and d'Alembert gave strong representation to the moral sciences, including economics. In sum, Hume's efforts to gather economic data and formulate economic theories rode the crest of an ascending wave.

One commonplace caveat was not to take numerical facts at face value. In *England's Treasure by Forraign Trade* (1664), Thomas Mun had warned his readers to question the data on customs and duties and to adjust up or down by a figure of 25 percent when calculating the volume of trade.[16] This recommendation did not stem from the influence of illicit activities, although those surely colored the estimates, but because of the accounting problems that included the freight and insurance costs, or items with no customs, such as fish. In short, Mun provided a detailed explanation as to why the adjustments are warranted. Hume echoed this admonition in his *Early Memoranda* and in his essay "Of the Balance of Trade," suggesting that the "custom-house books" and rates of exchange are "insufficient" sources for devising more general principles (MEM, 505; E-BT, 310). He claimed that every writer on trade "has always proved his theory, whatever it was, by facts and calculations, and by an enumeration of all the commodities sent to all foreign kingdoms" (E-BT, 310).

Hume, however, was not adversely disposed to use quantitative data in other contexts, whether in his analysis of interest rates, taxes, or birth or mortality rates.[17] As with his analysis of the belief in miracles, there are many systematic steps to follow in endorsing the testimony of others. Hume recognized that we must value these sources, especially historical records, but proceed cautiously: "A wise man, therefore, proportions his believe to the evidence" (EHU, 84). The point is to bring additional judgment, fed by theoretical acumen, to bear, as Hume does in adjusting the historical consensus on the money supply in the time of Henry VII. He reasoned that the recorded figure of 2,700,000 pounds was probably only three-fourths of the money that was in England at the time (E-BT, 321). The upward adjustment stems from Hume's insights into the specie-flow mechanism and the use of Bills of Exchange.

Whereas it is important for the development of the science of economics to lay down maxims and general principles, Hume almost always followed these by additional comments, situating, qualifying, and exemplifying. He criticized the French policy of outlawing the planting of new vineyards, or Britain's tax on silver plate intended to augment the specie reserves in the mint (E-BT, 315–18). Another is his proposal to reform the English parish-rates system, which supported the poor and destitute (E-PA, 457). Like the mathematics of the period, Hume's science of economics was "mixed"—that is, forged with the aspiration of discovering general laws but also with an eye to practical applications. In that respect, he paved the way toward Adam Smith's understanding of the science of "political œconomy" as a "branch of the science of a statesman or legislator" (WN, 1:428). There is a strong political tenor to their respective treatments of economics.

Philosophy of Mathematics and Science

The two hallmarks of good science for Hume were the presence of "quantity or number" and "experimental reasoning concerning matter of fact and existence" (EHU, 123). At the time, the word *experimental* was more a synonym for empirical pursuits writ large than a systematic or contrived investigation. Laboratories, apart from alchemical ones, were still not prevalent in the middle of the eighteenth century. New instruments, the electrostatic generator and the capacitor (Leyden jar), prompted more systematic experimentation during the first half of the eighteenth century, but the devices were more often used for parlor displays than to measure. As Lorraine Daston has observed, Francis Bacon "did not fix the fluid meanings of *observation*, *experimentum*, and *experiential*," and it was only gradually over the eighteenth century that these terms were made distinct.[18] During the 1730s and 1740s, when Hume forged his philosophical tenets, the word *experimental* was used capaciously to mean a general appeal to observation.

Initially, Hume drew a firm line between the empirical sciences and the formal sciences of mathematics and logic. While mathematics serves as the exemplar of scientific truth, it appeared to be without content. For Hume, mathematics was in essence about the relations drawn between ideas, such as the idea of five added to the idea of seven, and not about matters of fact. But all ideas have antecedent impressions, and Hume gestured to the possibility that numbers are themselves empirical in origin. Hume stated in a footnote in the first *Enquiry—An Enquiry concerning Human Understanding* (1748)— "that all the ideas of quantity, upon which mathematicians reason, are nothing but particular, and such as are suggested by the senses and imagination" (EHU, 118n). Numbers arose from observations of strongly resembling objects and then acquired abstract properties, for example, infinite divisibility.

Furthermore, the process of discovery in mathematics is empirical. Hume asserted that "there is no algebraist nor mathematician so expert in his science, as to place entire confidence in any truth immediately upon his discovery of it, or regard it as any thing, but a mere probability. Every time he runs over his proofs, his confidence encreases" (T, 121). Hume then pointed to the importance of consensus within the community of mathematicians, reaching the point such that a particular proposition has "universal assent" (T, 121). He thus underscored the empirical standing of mathematical knowledge in three respects: the source of mathematical objects, the process of discovery, and the path by which a new insight comes to be widely endorsed. Hume would be the first to submit that the mere agreement to the truth of a claim is not a reason to endorse it. Otherwise the ascription of religious miracles would be veridical. As a result, he reminded the reader that the universal "assurance is still nothing more than the addition of new probabilities . . . according to past experience and observation" (T, 121). There is no certainty for Hume; all knowledge is fallible and hence subject to revision.

There is a brief and sophisticated passage at the start of part 4 of Book 1 of Hume's *Treatise* that speaks authoritatively of merchant accounts. Hume's main point is to assert that certainty in knowledge, even in mathematics, is unattainable: "All knowledge resolves itself into probability" (T, 122). There is a process of discovery such that with each revisit to the proof of a proposition, the confidence in the truth increases, by degrees. Likewise, as other mathematicians assent to its validity, the confidence rises. An analogy to merchant accounting is then drawn: "In accompts of any length or importance, merchants seldom trust to the infallible certainty of numbers for their security; but by the artificial structure of the accompts, produce a probability beyond what is deriv'd from the skill and experience of the accomptant" (T, 121). The "artificial structure" is a reference to the innovation of double-entry accounting, almost surely practiced by Hume while clerking in Bristol.

Hume also drew an epistemic distinction between geometry and algebra. Because geometric objects have prior empirical sources, and because many propositions, such as the parallel postulate, require extrapolation to infinity, it is always important to assume that there is "no standard of a right line so precise as to assure us of the truth of this proposition" (T, 51). It is possible, Hume suggested, that the two right lines might have a "sensible inclination," even though the deviation from a right angle is "extremely small" (T, 51). Parallel lines might converge in this case. Geometry surpasses "the loose judgments of the senses and imagination" but cannot achieve the purported certainty that others, Plato or René Descartes in particular, have asserted in the past. Hume believed that the rigorous nature of geometrical inference is such that many demonstrations are valid, provided we keep the ideas of each geometric object "steady and precise" and never lose sight of their empirical origins (T, 52).

Unlike geometry, algebra (by which Hume meant, for the most part, arithmetic) achieves "a perfect exactness and certainty." Two plus five equals seven, and there can be no doubt about this formal relation. Simple arithmetic thus approximates Cartesian certainty, but one must not forget that the source of numbers is empirical. Hume imported this spectrum of fallibility in mathematics into his reflections on the natural and moral sciences. There too we find degrees of uncertainty in the core propositions.

In his essay of 1742, "The Rise and Progress of the Arts and Sciences," Hume remarked that the Cartesian system had begun to weaken. He also observed of the Newtonian theory that the most critical scrutiny had come "not from his own countrymen, but from foreigners; and if it can overcome the obstacles, which it meets with at present in all parts of Europe, it will probably go down triumphant" (E-RP, 121). Hume seemed drawn to Newton, but we know that he had also read the works of Descartes and Gottfried Leibniz, and this is what he meant by "obstacles." We argue here that if Hume became an adherent to Newtonian physics, it was not until the early or even late 1750s, after he had penned his two *Enquiries* and the *Political Discourses*. Most philosophers, including Hume, were still hesitant to endorse Newton's supposition of a gravitational force because it was occult and acted at a distance by some unknown medium. In his first *Enquiry*, Hume asserted in a footnote that Newton employed an "etherial active fluid" to serve as the seat of gravitational attraction but conceded that it was "a mere hypothesis, not to be insisted on, without more experiments" (EHU, 58n). Moreover, Hume rarely cited Newton. There is no mention of Newton in the main body of the *Treatise*, only in a footnote (T, 47n2). There is one implicit reference in the first *Enquiry* and the footnote just cited, but the first explicit acknowledgment of Newton in Hume's main text of a philosophical work is in the second *Enquiry*—*An Enquiry concerning the Principles of Morals* (1751)—and this was in reference to Newton's rule of reasoning rather than his scientific theories (EPM, 27).[19] Hume also paid tribute to Newton once in the *History of England* but in the same passage expressed considerable skepticism, observing that Newton has shown "the imperfections of the mechanical philosophy; and thereby restored her ultimate secrets to that obscurity, in which they ever did and ever will remain" (HE, 6:542).[20]

The commonplace assertion that Hume was a follower of Newton when he forged his moral sciences is thus overblown.[21] Hume did not view the physical sciences as having yet achieved the epistemic heights that we have unequivocally come to take for granted today. The triumph of the Newtonian theory came more toward the end of the 1750s. In the 1740s, when Hume composed his economic essays, there was still little consensus among natural philosophers on the major issues of the nature of matter and motion.[22] There was mounting empirical and analytical support for Newton, which Smith registered in his essay on the "History of Astronomy" and that we have reason to believe Hume had read in the early 1750s, but in the years when Hume wrote his main economic and philosophical works, he remained in doubt about the merits of Newtonian metaphysics. As he noted in his footnote in the *Treatise*, "nothing is more suitable to that philosophy [the Newtonian], than a modest scepticism to a certain degree, and a fair confession of ignorance" (T, 47n2).

The three grand systems in ascendance during Hume's youth—the Cartesian, Leibnizian, and Newtonian—differed over fundamental claims regarding the vacuum, the conservation of motion, the existence of forces, and the nature of the microphysical world. Hume dove right into these debates in Book 1 of his *Treatise*, famously casting doubt on the existence of a vacuum or our ability to know about underlying forces or powers. The early Hume appears to be more informed about Descartes than about Leibniz or Newton. In Book 2 of the *Treatise*, in a passage that has escaped scholarly attention thus far, he remarks that no one could value the branch of mathematics that attends to the conic sections (T, 287). But this was the critical branch of mathematics used by Newton to demonstrate that a central force would entail the known empirical laws of Johannes Kepler and Galileo, each of which committed a planet or projectile to a path that describes one of the conic sections: circle, parabola, or ellipse. If Hume had read Newton before 1739, it is clear that he did not understand the core argument or he would have spoken more favorably about the study of the conic sections.

In his *Abstract* to the *Treatise*, and in his first *Enquiry*, Hume defined the principle of inertia in geometric and kinematic terms that closely resemble the Cartesian formulations (T, 411–14; EHU, 58n). Hume also committed to one of Descartes's fallacious laws, whereby a smaller body sets in motion a larger body, and he makes no mention of acceleration, a critical feature for Newtonian mechanics (EHU, 28). The fact that Hume referred to several laws of mechanical action—Descartes had seven in total—is also at odds with Newton, who had only one such law.[23] There is reason to believe that Hume was still grappling with these competing systems when he issued his first *Enquiry* in 1748. Hume also referred to the famous vis viva controversy that was prevalent in the 1730s and 1740s that set battle lines between the two Continental systems (EHU, 60–61n). The Cartesians believed that something akin to our modern concept of momentum was conserved in collisions between bodies, while the Leibnizians believed that something resembling our modern concept of kinetic energy was conserved. In a sense, both sides were right, but insofar as they did not use the modern defining methods of vector analysis or stipulate other conditions (a closed system, for example), both sides were not quite right. The fact that conservation principles were at the foreground of these debates is important because they seeped readily into economic discourse.[24]

Hume appealed to this controversy over matter and force partly to promote the claim that we can never grasp the inner workings of physical nature, asserting that there is "no proof, that we are acquainted, in any instance, with the connecting principle between cause and effect, or can account ultimately for the production of one thing by another" (EHU, 61n). To know the nature of these causes, the specific powers or forces that give rise to the observed causal patterns, will forever elude our grasp, he believed. As Hume had previously confessed, "my intention never was to penetrate into the nature of bodies, or explain the secret causes of their operations" (T, 46). We are advised to "confine our speculations to the *appearances* of objects to our senses, without entering into disquisitions concerning their real nature and operations" (T, 46n). It suffices, for "the conduct of life" and for philosophical inquiry, to stay at the surface and rely on empirical patterns (T, 46). We can be confident that these patterns exist because of the manner by which we function as creatures.

Although Hume emphasized our limited engagement with the physical world, he nonetheless granted that there is some explanatory gain derived from the reduction of observable events to more fundamental states—to powers, forces, or microphysical particles—but whatever level of reduction we reach will at best scratch the surface of things. If the world is like an onion, and we experience the outer skin with our senses, our reason will never get much beyond the second or third layer because "nature has kept us at a great distance from all her secrets, and has afforded us only the knowledge of a few superficial qualities of objects; while she conceals from us those powers and principles, on which the influence of those objects entirely depends" (EHU, 29). Our knowledge of the physical world is highly limited and shrouded in mystery.

Hume's efforts to expose the limits of human understanding did not mean he devalued the importance of scientific and technical knowledge per se. Quite the contrary, he believed that there were legitimate means to establish practical knowledge about the world, both physical and moral, and to apply these means with results, particularly to advance commerce and industry. Hume believed that knowledge could grow and that this growth in turn served to foster consensus and forge a more civil society. In his moral philosophy, Hume argued that many key features of our social world are the product of tacit agreement and are more stable than meets the eye. Habits and customs, conventions, and more overarching institutions such as the judicial system are part of the features of the social realm that make it amenable to scientific inquiry.

To ascribe the term *science*, at least in the English language, is to denote the existence of a theoretical edifice centered on a set of laws, for which there is an ongoing effort to amass empirical support. Some of the laws are about theoretical entities, such as Newton's inverse-square law of gravitational attraction, and some are low-level empirical regularities, such as Kepler's first law of elliptical planetary orbits. This was Hume's understanding of science, and he was clearly of the view that such a set of laws could be discovered for political and economic phenomena, comparable to those in the natural sciences. But as Alex Rosenberg has pointed out, Hume was skeptical that exceptionless laws exist.[25] He was inclined to believe in the existence of uniformities in nature and the social realm, just not ironclad uniformities without exceptions. Hume would have been at home with the subsequent shift toward probabilistic laws, whether in thermodynamics, genetics or the genuinely stochastic laws of quantum mechanics.

Hume was also aware that scientific laws were always subject to revision and that it was wise to remain skeptical about the theoretical entities since so many had proved fallacious, whether epicycles as in Ptolemaic astronomy or Cartesian vortices. For the Newtonian theory, it proved useful to appeal to gravitational attraction or the specific properties of the material substratum and to see them as useful instruments for forging scientific theory without making a full commitment to their existence. Even were we to make some headway in understanding those mechanisms, however, that would just raise more questions. As Hume observed, "the ultimate springs and principles are totally shut up from human curiousity and enquiry. . . . The most perfect philosophy of the natural kind only staves off our ignorance a little longer" (EHU, 27–28).

By 1750, Hume was immersed in the philosophical community of Edinburgh, and he may have become more inclined to accept the superior standing of the Newtonian system. But the critical empirical finding that cemented the Newtonian system did not come until the return of Halley's comet in 1757. Smith espoused a similar position. In the early 1750s, he sent Hume a draft of his essay "The History of Astronomy" that voices skepticism regarding Newton, a skepticism that abated after 1757. This window of doubt vis-à-vis Newton, if one could put it that way, was thus critical in giving Hume the conviction that the moral sciences could fare just as well, if not better. Hume developed the view that we could know with greater conviction in the moral sciences when our reasoning is erroneous than in the natural sciences.

He expressed this view in his *Treatise* and underscored this belief in his first *Enquiry*. Although, as Hume remarked, there is pervasive "human blindness and weakness" in all philosophical inquiries, in the moral sciences one can at least "discover larger portions of our ignorance" than one can in the natural sciences (EHU, 28). Significantly for Hume, this grasp of what we cannot know and the belief that we could quantify our ignorance is positioned in a favorable light.

These beliefs motivated Hume to proclaim an epistemic superiority of the moral over the natural sciences. In his *Treatise*, he asserted that:

> We must certainly allow, that the cohesion of the parts of matter arises from natural and necessary principles, whatever difficulty we may find in explaining them: And for a like reason we must allow, that human society is founded on like principles; and *our reason in the latter case is better than even that in the former*; because we not only observe, that men *always* seek society, but can also explain the principles, on which this universal propensity is founded. (T, 258; first italicized phrase is our emphasis; Hume italicized *always*)

Whereas in the physical sciences, we must "confine our speculations to the *appearances* of objects," as Hume had said, with human actions we can also venture into the internal causes, presumably via the same process of introspection that Hume used to establish the mental laws of association. The moral sciences have this advantage of permitting us to grasp a layer of causation that is blocked for the most part in the natural sciences. The inferences we draw regarding human action feed on our own personal acquaintance and introspection with the mechanisms that connect motives with observed actions: "We mount up to the knowledge of men's inclinations and motives, from their actions, expressions, and even gestures; and again, descend to the interpretation of their actions from our knowledge of their motives and inclinations" (EHU, 65). As evidence in support of this set of inferences, Hume pointed to our understanding of predictable economic activities: that goods are produced, wages paid, and wares sold in the market to meet human demands (EHU, 68).

Hume bolstered this claim with several more arguments. First, there is as much or more uniformity among persons than is likely to hold true for the basic building blocks of the physical world. Our ever-present inclination to sympathize with those around us, and to behave in accordance with customs and habits, puts all the weight toward uniformities in the human realm.

Given that we have no knowledge of the powers and forces, or microscopic particles, that purportedly compose the universe, however, we must be skeptical as to their degree of uniformity. Indeed, it is plausible to believe that the fundamental entities of the physical world lack uniformity, and hence that the patterns we observe are merely provisional. As Hume's celebrated analysis of inductive inference demonstrates, the course of the universe could change at any moment. The sun might not rise tomorrow, or the bread we eat might not continue to sustain human lives. Because we cannot know the inner constituents of physical bodies, we must be open to the possibility that the patterns established up to the present might not persist in the future.

Second, Hume argued, human actions confirm on a daily basis that we are creatures of habit and custom. We understand the motives and actions of historical agents, such as the ancient Greeks or Romans, by transferring to them what we observe of the French or English (EHU, 64). But more important, Hume emphasized that the historical record provides a fund of data for the human sciences: "These records of wars, intrigues, factions, and revolutions, are so many collections of experiments, by which the politician or moral philosopher fixes the principles of his science; in the same manner as the physician or natural philosopher becomes acquainted with the nature of plants, minerals, and other external objects, by the experiments, which he forms concerning them" (EHU, 64). In sum, the degree of uniformity in human behavior is pronounced and has been stable for some two thousand years, or as far back as our records permit.

Third, Hume argued, because of what we know by introspection and quotidian observations, we are more likely to detect fallacious inferences in the moral sciences than in the physical sciences. We are more likely to know when an ascription of human behavior is false than to know that a proposition is false in the natural sciences: "Should a traveller, returning from a far country, bring us an account of men, wholly different from any, with whom we were ever acquainted; men who were entirely divested of avarice, ambition, or revenge; who knew no pleasure but friendship, generosity, and public spirit; we should immediately, from those circumstances, detect the falsehood, and prove him a liar, with the same certainty as if he had stuffed his narration with stories of centaurs and dragons" (EHU, 64–65). In Cartesian metaphysics, by contrast, "we are got into a fairy land, long ere we have reached the last steps of our theory" (EHU, 57). Hume mocks Descartes's ready ascription of vortices to every system in nature and its offshoot, Malebranche's doctrine of occasionalism that positioned God as the proximate cause of all physical change: "This fancied experience has no authority, when we thus apply it to subjects, that lie entirely out of the sphere of experience" (EHU, 57). It had been thoroughly discredited as a wrongheaded chapter in the history of science.

Adam Smith wrote in a similar vein. In part 7 of *The Theory of Moral Sentiments* (1759) that provides a history of ethics, Smith observed that the French had subscribed to the Cartesian system of vortices for nearly a century. In Smith's own time, he claimed that "it has been demonstrated, to the conviction of all mankind, that these pretended causes [Cartesian vortices] . . . not only do not actually exist, but are utterly impossible, and if they did exist, could produce no such effects as are ascribed to them" (TMS, 313). "But it is otherwise with systems of moral philosophy," Smith remarked, since an account of "the origin of our desires and affections, of our sentiments of approbation and disapprobation" could not "deceive us so grossly, nor depart so very far from all resemblance to the truth" (TMS, 314). The argument is motivated by drawing an analogy to the case of a traveler, one borrowed from Hume's first *Enquiry*. A person may describe a distant country and provide absurd fictions that he disguises as matters of fact, Smith allows, "but when a person pretends to inform us of what passes in our neighbourhood, and of the affairs of the very parish which we live in, though here too, if we are so careless as not to examine things with our own eyes, he may deceive us in many respects, yet the greatest falsehoods which he imposes upon us must bear some resemblance to the truth, and must even have a considerable mixture of truth in them" (TMS, 314). Natural philosophy is the distant country; moral philosophy our local parish. We may still be told falsehoods, but the account must "preserve some little regard to the truth, . . . [and contain] some foundation" (TMS, 314).

Let us here underscore this common ground between Hume and Smith: both deflate the epistemic standing of the natural sciences and in the same breath inflate the epistemic standing of the moral sciences precisely because there is an added resource to detect erroneous beliefs. In other words, we could be radically wrong in the physical sciences and be unaware of this fact. The subscription to a geocentric system for the planets upheld until the sixteenth century, or to Cartesian vortices for almost a century, proves that point. But in economics, we have an added resource that tells us when we have entered into absurd lines of thought, and we are thus able to circumscribe or expose our ignorance that much the better. We know, for example, that people do not always act rationally, and so we must recognize that as an ideal condition in economics rather than as descriptively true. One could challenge these claims as self-serving rhetoric. Hume demanded far too much of both introspection and instinct, neither of which was well understood. Nevertheless, he clearly believed that we might achieve more reliable and enduring knowledge in the moral sciences, and in economics more specifically, than in the natural sciences.

Uniformities in the Science of Human Nature

The moral sciences have in common the aim of understanding human nature, both its internal operations of the mind (reason, imagination, memory, and the passions) and its external manifestations (our individual and collective actions). The greater the degree of uniformity that could be ascribed to the internal operations, the greater the degree of uniformity will be observed in the external behavior that is their effect. Although Hume is a strong adherent of empiricism, he allows for internal sources of our mental impressions—namely, the passions—so in that respect, there are sources of our knowledge that do not come from without. Hume put a great deal of epistemic weight on the mechanisms of the mind: the role of memory, intuition, imagination, and analogical thinking. Finally, there is a clear role for reason, in deductive inferences and mathematical demonstrations as well as in the "distinction of reason" between resembling objects (T, 21–22).[26]

Since the seventeenth century, a familiar trope declared that all humans were alike when it came to the capacities of the mind. Descartes announced, at the start of his *Discourse on Method* (1637) that "the power of forming a good judgment and of distinguishing the true from the false, which is properly speaking what is called Good sense or Reason, is by nature equal in all men."[27] Many subsequent philosophers, including Leibniz, Baruch Spinoza, John Locke, and Denis Diderot, articulated a similar *verité*. Hume also joined this chorus. His essay "Of the Original Contract" asks us to "consider how nearly equal all men are in their bodily force, and even in their mental powers and faculties, till cultivated by education" (E-OC, 467–68). In his essay "Of Public Credit," Hume remarks that "people in this country [Britain] are so good reasoners upon whatever regards their interests, that such a practice [debasement or an arbitrary tax] will deceive nobody" (E-PC, 638). Smith echoed this sentiment with his famous example comparing the philosopher to the street porter; what differentiated persons, for the most part, could be attributed to education. At birth and even in early childhood, Smith avers, our capacity for common sense and reason are much the same (WN, 1:30).

For Hume, the probability was high that our minds are in harmony with the patterns the world has to offer. This harmony could have come about either by natural processes or by divine arrangement. It is clear that Hume favored the secular account. In fact, Hume suggested in more than one place that the human species is on an evolutionary trajectory and that there is a natural process of birth and death for species that mirrors that of individual organisms (E-PA, 377). This suggestion owes something to Hellenic philosophy that also considered the world as an organism that evolved over time. In his essay "Of the Immortality of the Soul," Hume, drawing inspiration from the Stoics, maintained that there is some basic substance, a "kind of paste or clay . . . [and that nature] modifies it into a variety of forms and existences; dissolves after a time each modification; and from its substance erects a new form" (E-IS, 591). Hence, "every being, however seemingly firm, is in continual flux and change" (E-IS, 597).

There is no divine plan to explain the organic realm of plants and animals, a point Hume put forth in several of his essays and most forcefully in his posthumous *Dialogues concerning Natural Religion*. He there unleashed the idea that our actual world is highly imperfect and, as a result, we are also only partially adapted to our surroundings. Hume also adopted the Stoic view that we humans are but a small speck of dust; our life is of no more value than that of an oyster (E-Su, 583). Hume's evolutionary stance does not posit mechanisms by which to account for the evolution of life forms, only the not fully developed intuition that it is a distinct possibility. But given the considerable weight he places on the process of adaptation of our species as a whole to our surroundings, he was inclined to believe that there is an exclusively secular explanation as to why the contents of our minds are consonant with the physical world.

This explanation only makes sense because of a belief in the uniformity of nature and hence the existence of laws. Hume never offered a satisfactory argument for this belief. It was the reigning view at the time, since most philosophers of his day took science to be the study of God's first bible and to be in essence an effort to record the laws of nature that God had issued from the beginning of time. But Hume had no truck with that position. He seemed, much as we might today, to adopt an inductive justification. For him, laws would not be possible if there were not sufficiently robust patterns in nature, or at least the nature we access with our human cognitive and perceptual faculties, and insofar as we do find these patterns, there is reason to believe that they exist. As Hume averred, "a wise man . . . regards his past experience as a full *proof* of the future existence of that event" (EHU, 84). For Hume, this served to strengthen his conviction in the uniformity of human minds—however idiosyncratic the path by which each of us walks through our respective life—and this bedrock of uniformity provided the spawning ground for scientific generalizations, economics included.

Much ink has been spilled on Hume's account of free will and necessity, but only a few scholars have extended this scrutiny to his efforts to forge the science of commerce.[28] Hume recognized that the moral sciences are only possible if there is uniformity in human agency—that is, that the same motives give rise to the same actions: "No union can be more constant and certain, than that of some actions with some motives and characters" (T, 260). Hume provided examples drawn from economics: "A prince, who imposes a tax upon his subjects, expects their compliance. . . . A merchant looks for fidelity and skill in his factor or super-cargo" (T, 260). But it is a complicated matter to parse the degree of uniformity since it is readily evident that people have different characters and that the same person acts differently at different stages of his or her life, or even in the course of one day. Capricious actions are possible, Hume admitted. A steadfast friend might succumb to an unexpected frenzy, much as an earthquake could arise without warning and topple one's home. Nonetheless, we see these as unlikely events and operate and function in the world on the supposition that the behavioral patterns obtain; we use the same inferences and appeals to uniformity as we do with physical events. Furthermore, the nexus that joins motives and actions is, Hume submits, of the same kind of necessity as that in the physical world. There is, Hume insisted, but one kind of necessity.

Let us slow down a bit. Hume was adamant that everything appears to have a cause; nothing happens by chance, and there is no supernatural intervention. Whatever we cannot explain is due to our ignorance. Any exceptions to a pattern could be explained. The necessity by which human intentions are bound to actions, however, is the same necessity that we ascribe to the motion of physical objects, planets or projectiles, light or water (DP, 29). This is particularly the case in the commercial realm. As Hume observed, a man takes his goods to market expecting to find buyers, and the buyers come expecting to find purveyors of desirable goods, and they both expect customary prices unless there are extreme circumstances such as war or famine that might raise prices, but that too could be readily explained (EHU, 68). We think it significant that the place Hume turned to in the social world to illustrate his nexus of motives and actions was the marketplace: this supports our claim that economic thought figures prominently in his philosophical works and that the market more specifically offers the paradigmatic case of uniform behavior.

According to Hume—at least post-*Treatise* Hume—reason itself is a passion: "Reason . . . is nothing but a general and a calm passion, which takes a comprehensive and distant view of its object, and actuates the will, without exciting any sensible emotion. A man, we say, is diligent in his profession from reason; that is, from a calm desire of riches and a fortune" (DP, 24).

If reason is the dominant passion that motivates action in the commercial realm, it appears to be less myopic than other passions. Nevertheless, there is much in this claim that is left unclear. How does a passion gain a view of the future, and how does Hume know that reason can actuate the will, particularly when there is no "sensible emotion"? In the *Treatise*, he took the opposite position: that reason, insofar as it can never motivate actions, is always distinct from the passions. Hume more consistently cast aspersions on the existence of the will as an illusory ascription to an invisible entity. Although we believe that our bodily movements are commanded by our will, the actual means by which this process transpires escapes the "most diligent enquiry" (EHU, 52). True, our capacity for self-command is highly variable. Different persons have different amounts, and even for the same person, Hume thought that our self-command is stronger in the morning than in the evening, better when we have an empty stomach than when we are sated, and better if we are in good health than sickly (EHU, 55). This variation, however, is comprehensible at the surface without the added metaphysical step to the will as the cause.

Hume conceded that we may never grasp the nature of the nexus that links motives with actions, and thus we must rest content with the empirical record that points to so many instances of uniform links between motives and actions. History offers a rich trove of examples of human engagement, Hume contended: "A man acquainted with history may, in some respect, be said to have lived from the beginning of the world, and to have been making continual additions to his stock of knowledge in every century" (E-SH, 567). But Hume attributes to the study of history far more than a mere chronology:

> What would become of *history*, had we not a dependence on the veracity of the historian, according to the experience, which we have had of mankind? How could *politics* be a science, if laws and forms of government had not a uniform influence upon society? Where would be the foundation of morals, if particular characters had no certain or determinate power to produce particular sentiments?" (EHU, 68)

Every general proposition in the science of humankind clearly stems from this inference—namely, that people's beliefs or sentiments are the proximate causes that determine the ensuing and observable actions. In forging a science of economics, the key is to find that degree of similitude to past experiences. While conditions are never identical, there are sufficient degrees of similarity for merchants to infer patterns between motives and actions, and this finding is manifest in the stability of market phenomena. As we will see, Hume's conviction in the law of one price is due to persistent efforts of modern citizens to seek out more remunerative work or more profitable lines of industry (HL, 2:94).

An appeal to the manifest sociability of our species also supports Hume's argument for the uniformity to human behavior. The belief in the "constant character" of human nature dominates our every action; we would not be able to function otherwise. Hume believed that the patterns are deeply entrenched. For example, "a manufacturer reckons upon the labour of his servants, for the execution of any work, as much as upon the tools" (EHU, 68). The wage contract is built upon a complex array of obligations and mutual interests that forge a predictable world. Furthermore, when something does happen out of the ordinary, it has a reason, and we seek out that reason. For example, a man of good nature happens to be peevish, but there is an explanation, argued Hume: he has not eaten or has a toothache (EHU, 67). Hume thus conveyed the view that even extraordinary actions could be subsumed under more overarching patterns.

Hume thus allowed for interruptions or exceptions to the uniform flow of nature, both physical and human. There are hailstorms on a summer evening, or a seemingly healthy person might suddenly die for no apparent reason. Hume thus allowed for two kinds of disturbing factors that take people down from perfect uniformity. There is the normal array of deviating factors (weather or health), and there are the very rare ones that are entirely unexpected (an earthquake or a bout of frenzy). But neither of these, he believed, robs people of the conviction that laws govern all events and that the only thing that people lack in the case of the exceptions is a complete understanding of the relevant causes and factors. Indeed, he argued, the exceptions are the gateway to discovering new laws (EHU, 67).

Necessity in human agency, for Hume, is identical to the necessity of the nonhuman realm. People's expectations of patterns in the moral realm may be no better than their expectations of the daily flux of atmospheric pressure. But that people govern themselves, and form society and government based on these patterns, for Hume at least, there is no doubt. Furthermore, people have always known this to be the case and do not need the proofs of a philosopher: "The mutual dependence of men is so great, in all societies, that scarce any human action is entirely complete in itself, or is performed without some reference to the actions of others, which are requisite to make it answer fully the intention of the agent" (EHU, 68). All human actions depend on ascribing to others a high degree of uniformity, of linking motives to actions, or people would never have formed societies and thus acted cooperatively in the first place. Hume's metaphysical analysis of human agency in the *Treatise* and the first *Enquiry* are of direct application to his science of economics.

Individuals and Groups

Hume's strong appeal to human sociability led him to foreground the action of groups such that he resisted the reduction down to individuals.[29] Hume was drawn toward methodological holism in the sense that he recognized that much knowledge could be gleaned at the level of the group or the whole nation.[30] He also believed in emergent properties; there are attributes to a particular group that may not be found among the individual parts. Hume pointed to the destructive tendency of a rioting mob (E-PGB, 66n1), the falling rate of profit due to the rivalry between merchants (E-In, 302), or the fact that the British "people are animated with such a national spirit" (E-BP, 338).

Because Hume believed in a descriptive version of the law of large numbers, he was inclined to attend to the actions of groups rather than individuals. In an essay of 1742, Hume emphasized the following proposition: "What depends upon a few persons is, in a great measure, to be ascribed to chance, or secret and unknown causes: What arises from a great number, may often be accounted for by determinate and known causes" (E-RP, 112). He recognized that each case would be particular with respect to the specific circumstances and that it takes "sagacity" to distinguish a random event from a genuine pattern. As justification, he appealed to the analogy of throwing a six-sided die. If the die is unevenly weighted, the bias will only manifest itself with a "great number" of tosses. The analogy is then drawn to nonartificial cases, such that if there is a prevalent cause of a certain "inclination or passion," it will only be manifest with "the multitude," since some individuals "may escape the contagion" (E-RP, 112).

To eliminate the outliers, Hume appealed to our inviolable passions: "Those principles or causes, which are fitted to operate on a multitude, are always of a grosser and more stubborn nature, less subject to accidents, and less influenced by whim and private fancy, than those which operate on a few" (E-RP, 112). The moral philosopher thus strives to sift out the accidental features of a given individual and foreground the central and common propensities at work. To achieve a full understanding of the causes at work, one has to appeal to properties of the group and not the individual, precisely because the group as a whole acts in a "more stubborn" manner. The reason for this stubbornness derives from the contagious process by which sympathy diffuses.[31] According to Hume, people in close proximity are inclined to "be seized by the common affection, and be governed by it [sympathy] in all their actions"

(E-RP, 112). It is for this reason there are manifest national characters: "The human mind is of a very imitative nature; nor is it possible for any set of men to converse often together, without acquiring a similitude of manners" (E-NC, 202). A common language serves to reinforce national traits. Hume frequently referred to the actions that bind us into groups as analogous to a contagion, whether of "popular opinion" or political faction (E-RP, 120). We are more like sheep than we realize.

Hume's discourse is replete with appeals to "the multitude" that are equivalent to mean-reverting tendencies, as in the case of throwing a weighted die to detect its bias (E-RP, 112). Individual actors are outliers and can be eliminated once one attends to the salient properties of a group: "The distinct orders of men, nobles and people, soldiers and merchants, have all a distinct interest" (E-PG, 60). As Hume described them, merchants are enterprising and industrious; landowners are prodigal; peasants are indolent; politicians are knaves, and so forth. Hume drew numerous contrasts between social groupings, by rank, profession, sex, or nationality. For example, "a soldier and a priest are different characters, in all nations, and all ages; and this difference is founded on circumstances, whose operation is eternal and unalterable" (E-NC, 198). Even within the priesthood Hume found subgroupings that, again, have less to do with geographical factors and more to do with institutional arrangements brought on by social channels: "The Jesuits, in all Roman-catholic countries, are also observed to have a character peculiar to themselves" (E-NC, 205). Hume's essay "Of National Characters" abounds with propositions that ascribe properties to social groupings that are bound by a common language, rank, or religion.

Little to nothing was gained, analytically, by reducing a given group down to the level of individuals, precisely because one would lose sight of the group attribute. Note, too, that Hume explicitly and frequently used forms of the verb *to reduce* in his critical appeal to reach general maxims. He was aware that all social phenomena have outliers or noise but that there is de facto a reversion to the mean. Hence, the path to scientific principles or laws consists in reducing the variance. One of his most tantalizing assertions, in the first *Enquiry*, compares the degree of variance in the natural and social realms. His claim is that we ascribe a greater number of uniformities in the human realm because "from observing the variety of conduct of different men, we are enabled to form a greater variety of maxims, which still suppose a degree of uniformity and regularity" (EHU, 65). In other words, there are laws that govern specific types of natural phenomena (planets or pendulums), and laws that govern human phenomena (money or trade), but it so happens that we see a greater variety of such "maxims" among humans. This finding could imply that there is a greater degree of uniformity among the fundamental entities of the natural realm, but not necessarily. Alternatively, the greater number of regularities in the human realm might be viewed as providing added justification for the metainduction that establishes the uniformity of human nature. As will become clear in our analysis of Hume's methodology, he was clearly apprised of a nonrigorous understanding of the concepts that motivate the reversion to the mean, degrees of variance, and the importance of distinguishing reductionist from nonreductionist thinking.

Methodology

A long-standing answer to the question "What is science?" proceeds by appealing to the methods rather than the content of science. Science is distinct from other types of knowledge, the arts or practical skills, because it develops theories using distinct methods of inference, modes of explanation, experimentation, measurement, and the construction of theories. If economics is to count as a science, it behooves it to adopt the same types of inferential tools and methods as the natural sciences. Hume, we will see, contributed to this mission. Although his economics is strongly literary, he enlisted a wide array of methods and techniques to estimate and measure various key phenomena, and he developed his economic theory using a number of modes of reasoning that could be found in the natural sciences at the time.

Inferential Tools

In Hume's texts, there are numerous rules of reasoning or maxims regarding inferential tools. Some are systematically presented, even enumerated, and others are mentioned in passing. Although induction is ubiquitous, it rests on an appeal to habit and custom, and thus it draws on other mental processes—namely, memory, analogy, and what Hume calls "the distinction of reason" (T, 20–22). In his first *Enquiry*, Hume listed four rules for adjudicating the testimony of others, particularly reports of miracles from ancient times (EHU, 88–91). In his second *Enquiry*, Hume referred to Newton's rule for ascribing uniform causes to similar types of phenomena (EPM, 27). In his essays specifically on economic topics, Hume also spelled out certain maxims and offered several systematic rules to guide him in his theoretical endeavors. Our focus will be on both his implicit and explicit appeals to inferential tools in his economic analysis, but in many cases these tools hold more generally for both the moral and natural sciences.

According to Hume, the rules of scientific inference are in and of themselves "certain and infallible," but upon their application, it is easy to "fall into error" (T, 121). Recollect the analogy to the accounts of merchants, who know that the final computation might be false; much depends on "the skill and experience of the accomptant" (T, 121). The critical criterion to bear in mind is the number of inferences in a given demonstration. Insofar as there are on average more inferences in the mathematical sciences, Hume asserted, there is more reason to assume that error will creep in. This higher risk of falling into error is compensated, however, by the fact that mathematical concepts are more "clear and determinate" (EHU, 49). In the moral sciences, while the "ideas are apt, without extreme care, to fall into obscurity and confusion, the inferences are always much shorter" (EHU, 49). Hume saw this as a virtue: "The intermediate steps [in the moral sciences], which lead to the conclusion, [are] much fewer than in the sciences which treat of quantity and number" (EHU, 49). It is critical, therefore, to find precise concepts in the moral sciences. Hume believed that the outcome of such reasoning might compare favorably to geometry. "In reality, there is scarcely a proposition in Euclid so simple, as not to consist of more parts, than are to be found in any moral reasoning which runs not into chimera and conceit" (EHU, 49).

Because Hume was an empiricist, the relevant place to start in building up a body of knowledge is to ascertain particular facts, or what he called "phenomena," and the more unusual they are, the better. There is no logic of discovery for Hume. These unusual phenomena that prove fecund are "often discovered by chance, and cannot always be found, when requisite, even by the most diligent and prudent enquiry" (EHU, 50). The chance discovery of a meteor on earth is a good example. But Hume also pointed to an unanticipated political event—namely, the creation of English factions, the Whigs and the Tories. Hume deemed the emergence of political factions one of "the most extraordinary and unaccountable *phænomenon*, that has yet appeared in human affairs" (E-PG, 60). A systematic reading of Hume makes plain that he was ever alert to such oddities, since they will prove to be the entry point for new knowledge.

Hume was strongly inclined to forge general theories: "We must endeavour to render all our principles as universal as possible, by tracing up our experiments to the utmost, and explaining all effects from the simplest and fewest causes" (T, 5). Thus, one rule of thumb is to seek the simplest and fewest causes that are also the most prevalent. For any given phenomenon, there are competing explanations. In his analysis of justice, for example, Hume observed, "no questions in philosophy are more difficult, than when a number of causes present themselves for the same phænomenon, to determine which is the principal and predominant. There seldom is any very precise argument to fix our choice, and men must be contented to be guided by a kind of taste or fancy, arising from analogy, and a comparison of similar instances" (T, 323n71). Hume thus recognized the role of *heuristics*, less precise guiding principles that boil down to "taste or fancy" and the appeal to analogies.

For Hume, nothing is due to chance. He was strongly committed to a belief in *determinism*, that every event has a cause, if not multiple causes. If we do not know what caused a particular phenomenon, then our ignorance is like that of the peasant who does not understand why the pocket watch stopped working (EHU, 66). Hume never resolved whether he believed causes are veridical, only that we are drawn to seek out causes precisely because uniformities abound in the human sphere. In other words, the constant conjunction of events drives us to a belief in necessity, a belief that enters into "*every* deliberation of our lives, and in *every* step of our conduct and behaviour" (EHU, 71; emphasis added). Hume illustrated this belief with the institution of the market. It is the product of cooperation and association among persons, fed by conventions that establish "a reasonable price" and the utility of money. There are sellers and buyers of many kinds of goods, necessities and conveniences, perhaps luxuries as well. All traders, he claimed, "firmly believe, that men, as well as all the elements, are to continue, in their operations, the same, that they have ever found them" (EHU, 68).

Another example on offer in the first *Enquiry* has remained folk wisdom in economic discourse to this day. "A man who at noon leaves his purse full of gold on the pavement at Charing Cross, may as well expect that it will fly away like a feather, as that he will find it untouched an hour after" (EHU, 69–70). Hume made this assertion as if it were obvious to his reader; when economic gain is clear-cut, someone will seize the opportunity.[32] Hume went on to assert, without any evidential support whatsoever, "above one half of human reasonings contain inferences of a similar nature, attended with more or less degrees of certainty, proportioned to our experience of the usual conduct of mankind in such particular situations" (EHU, 70). Hume noted that there are degrees of certainty that govern human inferences and that there are specific contexts, money and markets, where the behavior tends to be uniform; the probability for a pattern to be obeyed is greater than one-half. Hume did not assert that this pattern happens without exception; nor, however, did he provide reasons why the pattern falls short of complete uniformity. But the critical point is that the majority, over half, of our inferences derive from appeals to uniform behavior and are thus predictable to some degree.

How did Hume apply these insights, inscribed in his first *Enquiry* text, to his economic analysis, particularly the *Political Discourses* composed shortly thereafter? One theme we advance here is that Hume was all the more committed to causal efficacy in the science of commerce. It is in these essays that he became the "New Hume," more so than in his first *Enquiry*.[33] We will see that there are numerous causal ascriptions, such as the increase in prices due to the influx of specie (gold and silver money) or the increase in population due to higher wages. More significantly, Hume distinguished the correlation of two variables from the genuine cause. The interest rate is correlated with the profit rate and the supply and demand for loanable funds, but its motion is governed by different factors—namely, the customs and habits of the lenders and borrowers and their efforts to accumulate capital. When prudent merchants and bankers become widespread, the interest rate will decline, tugged down by the same factors that lower the rate of profit: increased competition and the increased concentration of capital.

How can we tell correlation from causation, especially when the two rates move in step with each other? To some extent this judgment draws on "taste and fancy." For example, night is correlated with the appearance of stars, but we do not declare that night causes the stars. In the same essay, "Of Interest," where Hume distinguished concomitant effects from a cause, he laid down a maxim: "an effect always holds proportion with its cause" (E-In, 296). The example he gave is the fourfold increase in prices since 1492 but the fact that the interest rate has "not fallen much above half" (E-In, 296). He concluded that "it is in vain, therefore, to look for the cause of the fall or rise of interest in the greater or less quantity of gold and silver" (E-In, 297). A low interest rate is not caused by an increase in money but rather by the spread of ever-increasing industry and commerce, which may bring with it more specie, but not necessarily. It is the competition between merchants, as well as the concentration of capital holdings, that bring about lower profits, or so Hume argued. Interest rates will fall as commerce matures. Interest rates are correlated with profit rates and, as merchants accumulate capital sums, they are content to receive a lower rate of return. It is also the case, Hume recognized, that banks hold large quantities of specie and thus can pool risk and lower the interest rate. The more developed the financial sector, the lower the interest rate. It is lower in Amsterdam than in London, and lower in London than in Paris. Thus we see Hume's maxim at work: "If we consider the whole connection of causes and effects, interest is the barometer of the state, and its lowness is a sign almost infallible of the flourishing condition of a people" (E-In, 303). Hume made plain, in his economic essays, that he sought to distinguish causes from correlations and that he believed he had the methods to achieve this end.

Evidential Support and Estimations

Knowledge, Hume recognized, relies on the testimony of others; hence we need to employ various precautionary measures in taking any report as a fact of the matter. Hume believed that a single rumor of a marriage spreads like wildfire in a province even if the two persons have met but twice (EHU, 89). Speculations are thus contagious, especially in cases where people are disposed to believe in a given proposition, as in the case of a religious miracle. Hume famously discredited our belief in miracles. First, there were no contemporary miracles in his day; all such reports stemmed from past witnesses who could not be questioned, most of whom were preliterate. Moreover, no reported miracle, in his view, had been attested by a "sufficient number of men, of such unquestioned good-sense, education, and learning" (EHU, 88). Hume issued four maxims when confronted with testimonial evidence, and the critical ones that pertain also to testimony in general can be summarized as follows.[34] Is the testimony by reporters who have a reliable character of "undoubted integrity" such that we ought to believe them? Are they impartial? We must keep in mind that the pleasure gained from learning about reports of extraordinary events or creatures tends to cloud our judgment. Reason tells us that "what we have found to be most usual is always most probable" (EHU, 88). Insofar as every testimonial falls short of certainty, it is important to weigh reports to the contrary, much as a judge in a courtroom facing contradictory witnesses would do. When "two kinds of experience are contrary, we have nothing to do but subtract the one from the other, and embrace an opinion, . . . with that assurance which arises from the remainder" (EHU, 97). For Hume, this rule yields an "entire annihilation" to the account of a purported miracle, since all the evidence is on the opposing side: "No testimony for any kind of miracle has ever amounted to a probability, much less to a proof" (EHU, 96–97).

The last rule is the most interesting. If the probability that a law of nature holds true is, say, 0.8, and the probability that the report of a miracle holds true (given the preceding rules) is 0.2, then subtracting one from the other means that we assign 0.6 to the remainder and that of course weighs in favor of the law. Now the law holds true and the probability of the miracle that violates it drops to zero. Hume allows for the reverse situation, although he believes it would be hard to imagine a law of nature where the probability was lower than that of the testimonial report of a miracle. As for pitting reports of miracles in one religion to that of another religion, because the probabilities are equal (or so he assumes), Hume reaches the conclusion that "we may establish it as a maxim, that no human testimony can have such force as to prove a miracle" (EHU, 97).

Hume distinguished between reports of miracles that serve as the foundation for a system of religion, and miraculous reports that appear to contradict the laws of nature as such. He presented as an example two hypothetical reports of events in January 1600, during the reign of Elizabeth I. One is a report that for eight days there was total darkness over the entire earth, but that this was observed by everyone in "all languages" and was still affirmed down through the centuries (EHU, 97). He considered this information sufficient to accept that this report is true and that we must seek causes for such an unusual event.[35] But a different report, that some physicians and members of court attested that the queen had died on January 1, 1600, and then come back to life shortly after, should be very much doubted. There is good reason to suppose that she had reasons to simulate the death and to collude with those close by. As Hume remarked, "I should rather believe the most extraordinary events to arise from their concurrence, than admit of so signal a violation of the laws of nature" (EHU, 98).

The source of a specific knowledge claim is thus important. Hume presumed that enduring truths are recondite and thus only found after prolonged probing. But he also believed that the results, if attained properly, will be of considerable value. In the "science of man," the observations must be taken "as they appear in the common course of the world, by men's behavior in company, in affairs, and in their pleasures. Where experiments of this kind are judiciously collected and compar'd, we may hope to establish on them a science, which will not be inferior in certainty, and will be much superior in utility to any other of human comprehension" (T, 6). Hume was thus keen to elevate the epistemic standing of the moral sciences, and this objective, to a considerable extent, framed his entire set of writings.

Insofar as a philosopher seeks to find patterns and analogies, the key is to find evidence that has multiple and reliable reporters. This was the case of the week in 1600 of no sunshine, as opposed to the resurrection of Elizabeth I. Hume had at his disposal a considerable amount of data about economic conditions, qualitative and quantitative, contemporary and historical. Some facts he quoted directly from a reliable published source (such as Cicero or William Petty), or from his friends in high office (such as James Oswald), while others he estimated using a variety of inferential tools. He also tried to explain more fully some of the more peculiar phenomena and most certainly questioned the observations of others that he found unreliable. Hume had quite a number of figures about the money supply in various countries, the size of the public debt, the number of banks and availability of credit, and the fluctuations in the value of the currency. He also had access to charts with price data for corn, both in Britain and in France. He had some estimates of average interest rates and wages in various regions of the globe. He knew a fair amount about national differences for the collection and issuance of taxes, and since most of this tax money went to support the military, he had some knowledge about relative sizes and costs for provisioning armies and navies. And he was familiar with figures for customs, duties, and tariffs and remarked on variations in them from country to country, century to century. In fact, numerical assertions are found in each and every one of Hume's essays on economics and throughout his correspondence.

Here are some examples of Hume's attention to quantitative phenomena:

"There are near three million [pound]s a year at the disposal of the crown. . . . An enormous sum, and what may fairly be computed to be more than a thirtieth part of the whole income and labour of the kingdom." (E-BG, 49)

"It was found, upon the recoinage made after the union, that there was near a million of specie in [Scotland]: . . . the current specie will not now amount to a third of that sum." (E-BT, 320)

"I have heard it has been computed, that all the creditors of the public [i.e., holders of government bonds constituting the public debt in Britain], natives and foreigners, amount to only 17,000 [persons]." (E-PC, 364n19)

"It is computed, that every ninth child born at Paris, is sent to the hospital . . . to turn over the care of him upon others." (E-PA, 400)

Hume also drew from his extensive reading of Greek and Roman sources; over one-half of the entries in the *Early Memoranda* register facts about the ancient economy—for example, higher interest rate in Rome than in Greece (MEM, 506).[36] Some of Hume's figures are precise and some, he notes, are averages.

To illustrate the degree of sophistication of Hume's calculations, let us look at a lengthy footnote in his essay "Of Money" in which Hume attempted to estimate the cost of mounting the Roman legion using Tacitus, circa 100 AD, as his main source (E-Mo, 282–83n). The Roman emperors, he claimed, normally had twenty-five legions in pay and assigned five thousand men to each legion. Ordinary soldiers were paid a denarius each day. Hume noted that there also were auxiliaries and that their numbers and pay were less certain. But he also observed that the number of officers was considerably lower than in 1750 and that a centurion would only receive double the pay of a common Roman soldier. Tacitus also reported that each soldier had to pay for his own provisions, clothing, arms, tents, and baggage.

Hume then estimated, based on the standard of living he discerned in the accounts by Tacitus, that the pay for a soldier would be "somewhat less than eight-pence" in his own time (E-Mo, 282n). Hume did not reveal how he arrived at this figure, but he noted that the average wage for a London unskilled worker was twelve pence per day (and could range up to twenty pence in times of prosperity). And he observed that in ancient times clothing for men and women was very drab, white or gray flannel that "became dirty" from overuse (E-PA 416). He contrasted this with the dress of his time, when it would be normal to have some embroidery, ruffles, and buttons (HE, 6:143). Hume may not have had more to go by, but the point is that he was making some effort to use a rudimentary notion of purchasing power parity to estimate the modern equivalent of a Roman denarius.[37] Putting aside the pay for officers and auxiliaries, "the pay of the [125,000] private men could not exceed 1,600,000 pounds [per annum]" (E-Mo, 283n).

It is not entirely clear how Hume arrived at that last figure. He would have had to decide how many days in the year each legionnaire was paid. Assuming they were paid for 360 days each year that would come to a total bill slightly below the figure he provides—namely, 12 pounds per annum, or 1,500,000 pounds in total. The additional 100,000 pounds is left unjustified, but Hume makes it clear that his figure of 1,600,000 is a ceiling: "To consider only the legionaries, the pay of the private men could not exceed 1,600,000 pounds" (E-Mo, 283). Were he to add the pay of officers, at 24 pounds per year, that would mean there would have been slightly more than 4,000 officers, or 160 per legion, which comes to 96,000 pounds per year or, rounded up, the additional 100,000. Hume expressed considerable doubt that the total bill for officers would have cost that much, which may be a reason why he kept to the figure of 1,600,000 as a ceiling. From his good friend James Oswald, Hume learned that the cost of the British navy was 2.5 million pounds, which meant that the navy alone cost 900,000 pounds more than the Roman legions. Hume thus established that the cost of military protection in the eighteenth century had risen considerably, by more than 50 percent: "The English fleet, during the late war [1740–48], required as much money to support it as all the Roman legions, which kept the whole world in subjection, during the time of the emperors" (E-Mo, 282). Hume also noted that the wages of British soldiers were twice those of the French army, mostly because as a wealthy nation, it must resort to hiring mercenaries (E-Mo, 282).

Another estimate Hume undertook was price indexing. He was by no means the first. In 1517, Nicholas Copernicus wrote a short text that addressed the shifts in the purchasing power of the Prussian currency due to its devaluation: "Money can lose its value also through excessive abundance, if so much silver is coined as to heighten people's desire for silver bullion."[38] By the late seventeenth century, efforts to stabilize the currency prompted numerous estimates of price fluctuations for a nation. The price of corn was usually taken as the benchmark, even though it would vary from region to region and from year to year depending on the quality of the harvest. The problem was compounded by efforts of authorities to fix the price of bread and to undertake the debasement or devaluation of the currency itself. To arrive at a long-term and customary price for corn was thus no mean feat; outliers had to be trimmed, certain markets used as representative for the nation, and knowledge of the metallic content and regulations of the mint brought into the analysis. If one could normalize for both the price of corn and the value of the prevailing currency, then it was possible to get some sense as to whether the price of corn had risen or fallen in real terms over a period of time.

Hume estimated the cost of corn in France, using figures from 1683 and 1750. He argued that the price of corn had declined by almost 40 percent and was thus considerably cheaper in real terms in 1750. Hume relied on figures from Charles de Ferrère Du Tot's *Réflexions politiques sur les finances et le commerce* (1738) but also expressed skepticism as to their reliability: "I must confess, that the facts which he [Du Tot] advances on other occasions, are often so suspicious, as to make his authority less in this matter" (E-Mo, 287n).[39] But the anchor points that seem more reliable are that the nominal price of corn was the same in 1683 as in 1750. Hume's argument relied on figures from the French mint and knowledge of frequent debasements by the French crown. The same amount of silver used for the coins such as the mark was thirty livres in 1683 and diluted to fifty livres in 1750. If one adds to this the fact that there had been a "great addition of gold and silver . . . into that kingdom since the former period," then there is all the more reason to expect inflation and a rise in the nominal price of corn (E-Mo, 287). The fact that the price had remained the same, however, could only mean that purchasing power had increased and economic growth transpired. The price of corn had fallen in real terms and people were better fed. The peasants had become "rich and independent" (E-RA, 277). Hume noted as well that the increase in money by a factor of three-sevenths had augmented prices by at best one-seventh. The additional money was used to service the economic growth over the sixty-seven years between 1683 and 1750.

As for the metallic value of the French coins, Hume's data were fairly accurate.[40] He also pointed to the widespread inflation in early eighteenth-century France that was promulgated by John Law. The primary sources that Hume cited were those by Du Tot, Jean-François Melon, and "Paris De Verney," and their primary method of calculation took the silver price of corn as an index (E-Mo, 288n).[41] Moreover, as we have seen, Hume recognized the regional variations in French and English prices, noting the gravitational tug of the metropolis (E-PC, 354–55). He had ready access to current charts of regional corn prices in the *Gentleman's Magazine* that made clear a pattern whereby the London price tended to fall somewhere in the middle and might be taken as the average price because the market was the largest.[42] This is a good example of Hume's appeal to both the convergence to the mean and a preliminary understanding of variance.

Hume was also apprised of the quantitative law of demand and noted it in several passages; for example: "Every thing is dearer, where the gold and silver are supposed equal; and that because fewer commodities come to market" (E-Mo, 293). In a letter to Smith, Hume observed "that the Price is determined altogether by the Quantity and the Demand" (HL, 2:311). This is a clearer statement of the same analysis found in his essay "Of Money," where he stated that "it is only the overplus [supply], compared to the demand, that determines the value" (E-Mo, 290). The Hume library contains a copy of Charles Davenant's *An Essay upon the Probable Methods of making a People gainers in the Balance of Trade* (1699), which includes time series data on corn compiled by Gregory King. Hume referred to Davenant in his *Early Memoranda*, so it is likely that he had purchased this book before 1740 and that he had absorbed the importance of its contents. The chart shows an inverse function of price as a quantity bought that reduces by one-tenth in each period. The price rises by three-tenths above the common rate with a reduction of one-tenth, and by the time the grain supply is reduced by 50 percent, the price has risen to 4.5 tenths above the common rate—that is, by nearly 45 percent. This came to be known as the King-Davenant law of demand. Davenant argued that no legal action, except perhaps in a tyrannical regime, could mitigate this "law" since "in the natural course of trade, each commodity will find its price."[43] In addition to Davenant, Hume might also have availed himself of William Fleetwood's well-known *Chronicon Preciosum; or an Account of English Money, the Price of Corn and Other Commodities for the Last 600 Years* (1707). The silver price of corn remained the primary benchmark for annual price indexing for Adam Smith (WN, 1:53–54). Hume was thus steeped in an established discourse that undertook a number of strategies to ascertain the distinction between nominal and real prices, singling out the price of corn as the best index.

Abductive Reasoning and Thought Experiments

Another mode of estimation that Hume employed resembles the type of argument found in William Harvey's treatise on the circulation of the blood, *De Motu Cordis* (1628), which we have reason to believe Hume knew.[44] Harvey's breakthrough was a significant milestone of the previous century and has long been assumed to be of critical importance in prompting Quesnay to highlight circulation in his *Tableau économique*.[45] Harvey's work had imposed a mechanical sensibility on the human body that reached its apogee in 1747 with Julien Offray de La Mettrie's *L'homme-machine* (*Man a Machine*), widely known for its scandalous assertions of thoroughgoing materialism. Hume was in Paris at the end of 1748 and would have found La Mettrie's denial of free will very appealing, coinciding with his own first *Enquiry* where this is argued. The strict mechanical treatment of the human body was reproduced in the first volume of Comte de Buffon's *Histoire Naturelle* (1749) that also caused much controversy in learned circles. It is very likely that Hume read Buffon's book at the time it was published.[46]

Harvey set out to refute the belief, passed down from Aristotle and Galen, that our daily food is turned into blood that is then absorbed into the body. He could not know with precision how much blood is expelled from the left ventricle with each heartbeat, but he argued quite brilliantly that, given the size of the ventricle, it could contain at best between 1.5 and 3 ounces of blood (he found 2 ounces in a human corpse). For each contraction, he supposed that one-eighth to one-fourth of that amount is expelled per beat. In a half hour, the heart beats between one thousand and four thousand times. Suppose we assume that half an ounce is expelled with one thousand beats; it follows that we would need 500 ounces of blood in half an hour. But no amount of food could produce this much blood, nor even approximate the amount. The same blood must therefore circulate. Moreover, Harvey demonstrated, using ligatures, that the blood flows in one direction, from the arteries to the veins and back through the heart from right to left. Harvey recast the heart as a powerful pump, and the valves in the veins were essential for ensuring at each impulse that the blood could ascend up from our toes and reach our extremities. Harvey, however, lacked one critical part of the process. He did not have a good microscope and could thus not observe the capillaries that join the arterial to the venal systems. Until Marcello Malpighi observed the capillaries, in 1661, the theory of the circulation of the blood was still hypothetical. Yet it was adopted and promulgated by Descartes in his *Discourse on Method* (1637) as well as by many others before Malpighi's observations. This is because, once one grants the magnitude of the quantitative discrepancies, there is only one plausible explanation.

Hume used much the same type of argument, an inference to the best explanation, when establishing that there had been growth in the European economy over the previous few centuries. His argument employs crude estimates but rests on establishing the quantitative gap that he submitted existed between the at least sevenfold increase in specie since 1492 versus the at-best fourfold increase in prices. If nominal prices had risen by an identical amount to the influx of specie, then real prices would not have changed. But because, from 1492 to 1750, nominal prices had not risen by more than a factor of four, the only explanation is that there are more goods and services in the market that are serviced by the additional specie. This is a remarkable demonstration that there had been significant economic growth in Western Europe over that period of time. If one rounds up to an eightfold increase in specie and down to a fourfold increase in prices, the output, according to Hume's reasoning, could potentially have doubled. As he emphasized, "it is the proportion between the circulating money, and the commodities in the market, which determines the prices" (E-Mo, 291).

Hume could not always give exact measurements; he lacked the tools to forge a reliable price index or to make more than a rough estimate of the growth of the money supply. His dates and spatial ascriptions are also vague. But the sizable gap between the estimated specie to arrive in Europe and the estimated increase in the price level overall cries out for explanation. Hume estimated that, circa 1500, the annual influx of specie was about six million (of an unspecified currency). Allowing for one-third to leak to the East Indies, he estimated that in ten years, the rate of influx would be sufficient to double the reserve of money from before the New World was discovered (E-Mo, 292). Implicit in this estimate is the claim that four million are injected per year for ten years, or that the premodern money supply was forty million, and that sum had doubled from 1492 to 1502. Insofar as much of the specie entered through Spain and Portugal, where prices were subsequently depressed, this makes the point even more obvious. Hume also knew that prices in southern France were one-tenth that of northern Spain circa 1550 and hence, most of the silver and gold was transported, illegally, over the Pyrenees until no more arbitrage opportunities could be extracted (E-BT, 312). This illicit movement so drained the Iberian peninsula of its specie that prices sank to the point that, as Hume observed, Spain had "decayed from what it was three centuries ago" (E-PA, 455).[47]

Much as Harvey lacked the critical link of the capillaries, Hume lacked the means to observe the full chain by which the money diffuses or manifests itself in higher prices and economic growth. But he offered a scenario nonetheless that was predicated on the assumption that people would spend rather than hoard the new specie that came to Britain from Spain. In his essay "Of Money," he gives an account that is best understood literally, as a process Hume took to be veridical. An inflow of silver money from Cádiz (a port in Spain) enters Britain and stimulates economic activity before raising prices, but the inflation transpires in a sequential and dispersed manner over time rather than *tout court*. In this respect, Hume followed out the causal paths by which money prompts growth and a disproportionate increase in the price level. We will return to this account, but suffice it to say here that Hume adopted a very useful type of argument, most probably from Harvey.

Hume announced at the start of his essay "Of Commerce" that he sought general principles with universal applicability. The question lurking in the background is the degree of abstraction he was willing to adopt, and the answer appears to lie in his use of thought experiments. According to Gerald Massey, "perhaps no other philosopher has conducted his thought experiments with the degree of care and sophistication that Hume bestowed on his."[48] In his essays on economics, Hume used several examples of *thought experiments*—although the term did not exist as such—in his analyses of money, the interest rate, and taxation.[49] Thought experiments commence with a jarring counterfactual to a hypothetical world. But for the most part, the rest of the experiment engages features familiar to our own world before reaching a conclusion that articulates the core principle.[50] Thought experiments thus dredge up some deeper intuition and help to rearrange the components in the laboratory of the mind, without in fact introducing any new empirical content.

Hume's predilection for thought experiments might also explain why he was adversely disposed toward models. Although the term was not in use in economics at the time, we might define a *model* as a set of propositions, each of which is false but which together form a coherent structure that serves to explain the patterns offered by a set of phenomena. The model has deep structural analogies to our actual world. Unlike a thought experiment, which need only be performed once to reach the desired demonstration, a model (at least a good model) is used in multiple ways, and later variants might extract different propositions.[51] There are only a few examples of genuine models in eighteenth-century economic discourse. According to Hont, three are found in Melon's *Essai politique sur le commerce* (1734), a work that was translated into English in 1738 and circulated widely.[52] For example, Melon posited different hypothetical islands, each one producing a single good, and then followed out the possible implications once trade commenced. Hume had read Melon with care and voiced strong criticisms of the analysis (E-Co, 256n; E-Mo, 288n).[53]

Hume was even more scathing about the abstractions undertaken in Quesnay's celebrated *Tableau économique*. He could not accept the stylized division of the French population into 50 percent farmers, 25 percent landowners, and 25 percent artisans. His criticism of Quesnay's model was motivated by the claim that these figures did not conform to the actual distributions in France at the time, or even in the recent past. Hume believed that there were more people working in the artisanal sector and more living in towns (E-Co, 256n). He seemed unable to grasp that models by their very nature must abstract from the empirical record and use stylized assumptions. The ratios chosen by Quesnay were designed to enable mathematical closure. If the only net surplus is in the agrarian sector, but it is assumed that there is full reproduction, such that for every seed sown in the spring, two are reaped in the autumn, then the zigzag circular flow of grain and artisanal goods yields an annual cycle of production that is self-sustaining. Quesnay had in effect devised a model with an income multiplier effect that achieved equilibrium not just for one period but indefinitely. He was also able to introduce new variations, either with capital depreciation or a deviation toward luxury consumption. Hume was not impressed. In a letter to Morellet, Hume declared with operatic language that the physiocrats are, of all the economists, "the most chimerical and most arrogant that now exist," and he urged Morellet to "crush them, and pound them, and reduce them to dust and ashes!" (HL, 2:205).

It is worth underscoring that Hume was troubled by the degree of abstraction undertaken in model building. He showed no compunction about engaging the counterfactual reasoning of a thought experiment or many other forms of conjectural or hypothetical reasoning. But he did not accept the degree of stylization of the extant models of his day. In models, strictly speaking, every proposition is false because it invokes ideal conditions or removes some properties altogether. A thought experiment, conversely, does the work of conceptual dredging, by keeping everything else in place except the strong counterfactual, which in turn isolates an underlying propensity. Hume used thought experiments in the spirit of empiricism. The entry point to the experiment is fictitious, and that means that the conclusion reached must, strictly speaking, be false as well, but the tendency that is unearthed may well hold in our actual world. Again, an analogical leap is needed to make this claim, but Hume seemed comfortable with this type of demonstration.

Probability

Hume wrote explicitly about the concept of probability in his *Treatise* and first *Enquiry* and makes many probabilistic ascriptions in his economic essays. He may have first learned about the fundamental principles from reading Pascal,

Locke, and Christiaan Huygens, each of whom applied probabilistic concepts to moral judgments. We know that Hume had read Pascal's *Pensées (Thoughts)* before writing the *Treatise* and that, in his first *Enquiry* Hume refers to Pascal and the Port-Royal logicians more generally (T, I12n; EHU, 95n). Hume also knew about the work of Locke and Huygens, and it is possible that he had read Abraham De Moivre's *Doctrine of Chances* (1718), a seminal text in the field, because De Moivre had moved to England in 1688 and his ideas had become popular.[54]

John Arbuthnot, a leading physician in London, had compiled birth records, for eighty-two years, from a central London hospital and established that more boys were born than girls. Needless to say, the ratio of male to female births varied each year, but Arbuthnot took as his null hypothesis an equal ratio of male to females and showed that the probability this held true, given his extensive set of data, was vanishingly small.[55] He thus demonstrated that there was an excess of male to female births, an asymmetry that has since become an established fact—indeed, one also found in a wide range of non-human species.

It is highly likely that Hume knew about Arbuthnot's study of 1710, for several reasons. He had purchased a copy of Arbuthnot's *Essay on the Usefulness of Mathematical Learning* (1723) and cited another work by Arbuthnot, on ancient coins, in his *Political Discourses* (E-BT, 323). In a "Fragment on Evil" that Hume purportedly sent to his Bristol friend John Peach in his youth, Hume noted that the matter of more male than female births had been determined with certainty.[56] Hume started to make note of population data in his *Early Memoranda*, such as 95 million in the Roman Empire or 8 million in England (MEM, 508–9). Hume's essay on demography depends critically on understanding the factors that govern high or low rates of birth, and he noted that among slaves, there was a preference for male workers over females (E-PA, 388). The unequal sex ratio was widely cited and modified for much of the eighteenth century, in the respective work of Nicholas Bernoulli, William Derham, and Johann Peter Süssmilch, among others, and used by natural theologians to establish a providential order.[57]

Arbuthnot's study resonates with Hume's own predilection for obtaining large samples rather than generalizing from a few observations and using a similar mode of reasoning. Hume took as a null hypothesis that the ancient population was larger than in his own Europe and then set out, using a variety of sources of methods of computations, to show that the probability this was true was virtually zero. Hume appealed to the low birth rate among ancient slaves, the low standard of living in ancient Rome, the lack of trade and commerce, the many conflicting and exaggerated accounts of populations—to motivate his conclusion that the European population of 1750 exceeded that of ancient Rome, a hunch he had broached in his *Early Memoranda* (MEM, 514). Much of Hume's argument rests on weighing likelihoods and questioning received views. His reasoning is not always sound, but one cannot help but admire the zeal with which he took up his cause and the informal grasp of probabilistic modes of thinking, including a nascent version of the test enshrined in statistics as the Neyman-Pearson lemma.

Hume wrote at length about the theory of probability and is celebrated for discerning that there are two distinct types, or "species," of probability (T, 86–104; EHU, 45–80).[58] The first is the concept of *equiprobability*—namely, that a coin would be assumed to exhibit an equal number of heads and tails when tossed many times. This type of probability is confined to games of chance as in the use of dice and gives rise to the concept of *likelihood*, as Hume defined the term. Hume asserted, however, that humans do not perceive equiprobable events, even if they exist: "In proportion as any man's course of life is governed by accident, we always find, that he increases in superstition; as may particularly be observed of gamesters and sailors, who, though, of all mankind, the least capable of serious reflection, abound most in frivolous and superstitious apprehensions" (DNR, 41). Adam Smith issued a remark that also suggests people misrepresent the genuine distribution of events and might in fact be risk seeking: "The chance of gain is by every man more or less over-valued, and the chance of loss is by most men under-valued" (WN, 1:125). The ascription or actualization of equiprobability, while a key concept of the mathematical theory of probability, may not be found in common everyday practices.

The second species of probability is grounded in observable patterns and appeals to variances, often drawn from everyday life. As Hume asserted, "it is more probable, in almost every country of Europe, that there will be frost sometime in January, than that the weather will continue open throughout the whole month; though this probability varies according to the different climates, and approaches to a certainty in the more northern kingdoms" (EHU, 47). Another case looks to medicine. Because the "human body is a mighty complicated machine," governed by "many secret powers," there are cases where a prescribed medicine cures and cases where it fails; for example, rhubarb, a good cure for constipation, does not always purge the body (EHU, 47). Nevertheless, the fact that we discern an irregularity in some cases does not mean that the body is any less law-governed. As Hume pointed out, "the irregular events, which outwardly discover themselves, can be no proof, that the laws of nature are not observed with the greatest regularity in its internal operations and government" (EHU, 67). Hume reaffirmed that whereas the laws in mechanics admit of no exceptions, in meteorology or medicine, we must be content with the assignment of degrees of probability.

Hume also emphasized the effects of collecting additional evidence and that doing so might alter the ascribed frequency of a given pattern. Scholars have suggested that Hume might have apprised himself of the insights of Thomas Bayes, whose seminal theorem was broached circa 1755 and published posthumously in 1764 by one of Hume's main adversaries, Richard Price. We know that Price used Bayesian analysis in his *Four Dissertations* (1767), that it included a lengthy critique of Hume on miracles, and that Price had sent Hume a copy. Hume's letter thanking Price suggests that he read the work with care and might therefore have absorbed the gist of the method and incorporated it into his own posthumous *Dialogues* (NHL, 234).[59] All of this transpired after Hume had written his *Political Discourses*, and although he was still reissuing and revising his essays, there is no evidence of a firm imprint on his core economic thinking. Suffice it to say that Hume sought to apply probabilistic measures in the case of an ongoing accumulation of evidential support, but without the formal rigor of Bayes or Price. In short, his thinking is resonant of Bayesianism. In general, Hume was part of a zeitgeist that embraced probabilistic modes of thinking, stemming from the Continental mathematicians, Pascal, Huygens, Pierre de Fermat, and Jacob Bernoulli.[60] Hume's estimations, mean-reverting analyses, and general remarks about degrees of probabilities, served to capture the quantitative face of the economic landscape of his day.

In conclusion, we have seen the extent and depth to which Hume believed the moral sciences have the potential to ascend to, if not surpass, the epistemic heights of the natural sciences. Hume was a strong advocate of the moral sciences, above all economics, and held out much optimism for theoretical analysis and empirical confirmation. He believed that human behavior was sufficiently uniform to warrant robust generalizations, such as the ones he identified in the theory of money and trade, and he believed that some of these laws in politics and commerce were universal, that they held across time and place. Above all, Hume grasped that empirical claims required caution and care. One had to sift through the evidence, assess the accuracy of testimony, and attend to the degrees of resemblance between each case. Probabilistic inferences and quantitative measures, if carefully ascertained, were thus of critical importance. Hume's insights into methodology and application of these findings are a critical part of his overarching plan to forge a science of economics.

CHAPTER 3

"A More Virtuous Age"

Hume on Property and Commerce

David Hume believed that commercial nations tend to be "both the happiest and most virtuous" (E-RA, 269). This belief challenged the tide of ancient and medieval thought that had by and large cast commerce in a negative light. No one, including Hume, disputed the fact that commerce feeds on and fuels avaricious tendencies, but the traditional arguments against mercantile activities ran more deeply. Aristotle pointed to the story of Midas, who starved before a heap of gold; the unfettered pursuit of wealth would distort means and ends, and thus lead citizens away from achieving virtue and wisdom. It was permissible for artisans and merchants to set prices to cover their costs and a reasonable profit in order to maintain their place in the polity, but it would be unethical to exceed these limits. In the thirteenth century, Thomas Aquinas went further and maintained that merchants, by their incessant pursuit of gain, violated the golden rule: to buy low and sell high necessarily involves deception. Usury was also deemed unethical; idle funds should be lent to those who were in need, with no expectations of interest payments. Aquinas recognized some exceptions, but the legal recognition of lending with interest, for the most part, only came about in the late sixteenth century.

As capitalism took hold in early modern Europe, the scholarly analysis of commerce and trade also became more favorable.[1] Although he was not the first to do so, Bernard Mandeville, in his *Fable of the Bees* (1714), famously demonstrated that the pursuit of wealth and power has the potential to generate modern prosperity.[2] It was the pursuit of "private vices," he argued, that enabled "public virtues." By emphasizing the beneficial consequences of luxury consumption, in direct defiance of both religious doctrine and sumptuary laws, Mandeville significantly recast the debate. Bishop Butler and Francis

Hutcheson, most notably, considered Mandeville's intervention to be scandalous, and each one issued harsh rebukes.[3] Montesquieu's *Spirit of the Laws*, however, served to quell the dispute by advancing the notion of *doux commerce*. As he observed, "it is an almost general rule that everywhere there are gentle mores, there is commerce and that everywhere there is commerce, there are gentle mores."[4] Market interactions induce civility and thus temper the passions.

Hume built on these ideas, taking from Mandeville a clear understanding of how self-interested action could result in unintended benefits, from Hutcheson a secular approach to ethics, and from Montesquieu the idea that commerce promotes respect for others. Hume accepted that "avarice, or the desire of gain, is an universal passion, which operates at all times, in all places, and upon all persons" (E-RP, 113) and went on to argue that the love of gain, however, ensures that the wealthy merchant does not succumb to extravagant pleasures but instead remains enterprising and industrious, building personal wealth while at the same time engendering widespread prosperity. Furthermore, Hume argued, commerce fosters a number of virtuous traits, such as prudence, industry, and ingenuity, all of which tend to bolster social stability and good governance.

While Hume did not explicitly appeal to a providential order or to an "invisible hand," he secured the links between our built-in dispositions—selfishness and greed included—to foster utilitarian outcomes. Property, markets, and money are the key institutions that set these beneficial paths in motion, insofar as they offer powerful incentives for individuals to channel their self-interest in ways that promote their own ends as well as the common good.[5] Yet, to be sure, these institutions could not guarantee favorable outcomes. Much like the mechanical operations of a pocket watch, there are several intricate and interconnected moving parts that coordinate with one another. Each one of these parts is prone to breaking down and thus preventing the watch from functioning. If the vicious tendencies become too excessive, if too many citizens fail to honor their contracts or respect property rights or indulge in the excessive consumption of luxuries, then the fragile threads that join individual and collective actions might unravel and thus hinder the path to progress. Hume, as we will see, offered a number of penetrating and subtle insights regarding human proclivities to form and honor contracts, to establish rules and protocols, and to forge and sustain a set of enduring institutions. The end result, ceteris paribus, is to promote a just society with greater freedoms and human flourishing.

Reason and Moral Sentiments

In Book 3 of the *Treatise of Human Nature*, Hume developed a detailed analysis of the institutional foundations of a modern commercial society. It has been described as "one of the most complex, original, and successful parts of the *Treatise*."[6] Hume questioned whether people by nature have a sufficient capacity for sociability to predispose them to form convivial and prosperous communities. He argued, in opposition to Thomas Hobbes, that humans are not only capable of living collectively in peace but also to do so without formal contracts. In his 1748 essay "Of the Original Contract," Hume mocked both Hobbes and John Locke for supposing there were such inscriptions: "in vain, are we asked in what records this charter of our liberties is registered. It was not written on parchment, nor yet on leaves or barks of trees. It preceded the use of writing and all the other civilized arts of life" (E-OC, 468). Although Hume maintained that ancient polities were more likely to have been born in violence and usurpation, he nonetheless put much weight on the bond of love within the family and the disposition toward sociability that it encourages. The historical record, he claimed, demonstrates that there were innumerable small groups living in prolonged periods of peace. The challenge, Hume remarked, is to preserve this capacity for cooperation as societies expand and as trade brings strangers into contact with one other. For such cooperation to be possible, it was imperative to secure the means to channel human passions and interests toward peaceful and productive ends and not allow selfish tendencies to undercut the good of the community.

As with many philosophers at the time, Hume thus sought the best means to bridle our passions for power or pleasure in a manner that would "promote the interests of our species, and bestow happiness on human society" (EPM, 12). Religious sanctions had proven only partly effective toward that end. Hume considered the possibility that reason or moral sentiments could provide the necessary restraints, but he did not believe that either one was sufficiently powerful to rely on singly or jointly. He reflected on the ideas advanced by Anthony Ashley Cooper, the third Earl of Shaftesbury (1711) and by Hutcheson (1725)—to wit, that people are born with a moral sense that inspires a natural affection toward others and that this moral sense operates in a manner analogous to our aesthetic sense; we feel virtue and vice the same way that we feel beauty and deformity. Hume agreed with them that this innate moral sensibility is strong enough to inspire a natural affection within the family, but not necessarily between strangers.

Sympathy provided the solution. Essentially a physiological response found in all human beings across time and place; sympathy enables people to cultivate fellow-feeling and to share in the feelings of others, even strangers.[7] Our capacity to conjure up, in our mind's eye, the pains or pleasures of another is critical to the means by which we refine our conduct over time. As Hume observed, "no quality of human nature is more remarkable, both in itself and in its consequences, than that propensity we have to sympathize with others, and to receive by communication their inclinations and sentiments" (T, 206). Once our sentiments are polished by "tender sympathy" and "softer affections," as well as by education and experience, we are able to develop a more complete and sophisticated repertoire of social virtues. Praiseworthy virtues, such as "beneficence and humanity, friendship and gratitude, natural affection and public spirit," make social life more civil and pleasing (EPM, 8–9). However, for these virtues to become salient requires the formation of a set of social institutions—in essence, rules for implicit action that coordinate human needs and reduce potential frictions.

Channeling our passions, rather than our reason, is the key to forming a stable and peaceful society. Giving full recognition to our desires for power and wealth is paramount. Contrary to thinkers in the natural law or civic republican traditions, Hume did not believe in the existence of a transcendental moral universe that we access through reason. While we can reflect in the abstract on the principles that would form the ideal commonwealth, reason alone is not powerful enough to ensure that people will act in ways that make such a society possible. When deciding on a course of action, people gather information and use reason to judge its worth, but reason alone is unable to propel people to act. It is our passions and desires that inspire actions, while "reason is, and ought only to be the slave of the passions, and can never pretend to any other office than to serve and obey them" (T, 266). Reason is ever present but subordinate to the true motor-engine of human action.

A specific action could be judged ethical either by the intentions that motivated the action or by the consequences that ensue. Hume weighed in on both ends but tended to put more weight on intentions than consequences, much as the law issues a harsher sentence for murder than manslaughter (EPM, 86). Nevertheless, Hume offered some examples wherein good intentions and misplaced benevolence might prove detrimental to public utility, or what he calls the "happiness of mankind" (EPM, 12). Gifts and donations, for example, while normally viewed as signs of generosity, often yield negative unintended consequences in that they tend to erode the spirit of industry. Giving alms to the poor is often regarded as an estimable act, but "when we observe the encouragement thence arising to idleness and debauchery, we regard that species of charity rather as a weakness than a virtue" (EPM, 11). Princely largesse, while a sign of beneficence, brings more harm than good:

"When it occurs, . . . the homely bread of the honest and industrious is often thereby converted into delicious cates for the idle and the prodigal, [and] we soon retract our heedless praise" (EPM, 11).

Hume also pointed to actions that at first appear to be detrimental to society, but when their effects are taken into account, they come to be seen as beneficial. A good example is luxury consumption, a long-standing "bugbear of Christian and republican political morality."[8] Condemning luxury consumption seems to be "little less than a contradiction in terms, to talk of a vice, which is in general beneficial to society" (E-RA, 280). Because most luxury goods have the capacity to prompt an "encrease of industry, civility, and arts," however, they shift from "pernicious and blameable" to "laudable and innocent" (EPM, 11–12). Hume thus tailored his judgments to different contexts; an action might have merit because of good intentions or good consequences, or both. The primary consideration is whether the action promotes public utility. For Hume, a robust and prospering society is built upon core institutions that in turn revolve around our self-interest. Reason assists people in making decisions, and moral sentiments gradually polish people's dispositions toward their fellow citizens, but the main force that keeps society intact is the individual pursuit of one's interests, which provides the fundamental impetus behind the formation of property, markets, and money. These institutions, in turn, channel our self-interest in ways that strengthen our proclivities for industry, commerce, and the arts and sciences, and therefore promote both economic growth and the further refinement of our social virtues.

Property

For Hume, the institution of property constituted the most essential condition for a prosperous and stable society. Only when people enjoy secure rights over land and possessions are they able to engage peacefully with other people and collaborate in the construction of complex societies. Property became increasingly important with the spread of trade and commerce. While certain forms of exchanges could take place in what Hume called "barbaric" societies, for a society to prosper and grow, "the ideas of property become necessary in all civil society" (EPM, 16). Property was such a constitutive part of society that, for Hume, it was synonymous with justice.

The need for property, Hume insisted, is virtually universal. To prove his point, he considered hypothetical scenarios to the contrary, where property is purportedly redundant or not possible. He examined a case of extreme abundance such that there are sufficient goods to satisfy, without effort, people's most "voracious appetite" or "luxurious imagination wish or desire" (EPM, 13). No labor, tillage, or navigation would be necessary to obtain unlimited amounts of conveniences and superfluities, thus removing the most common source of societal discord. Here, justice would be "totally useless," a mere "idle ceremonial." This scenario led Hume to ask, "Why call this object *mine*, when upon, the seizing of it by another, I need but stretch out my hand to possess myself of what is equally valuable?" (EPM, 13). A similar effect would follow, Hume continued, if we supposed that people miraculously became self-sufficient in both basic necessities and superfluities: if man's "natural beauty . . . surpasses all acquired ornaments: The perpetual clemency of the seasons renders useless all cloaths or covering: The raw herbage affords him the most delicious fare; the clear fountain, the richest beverage. . . . Music, poetry, and contemplation form his sole business: Conversation, mirth, and friendship his sole amusement" (EPM, 13).

A system of property would also prove redundant if people transcended their selfish tendencies and became entirely benevolent. Hume hypothesized that if "the mind is so enlarged, and so replete with friendship and generosity, that every man has the utmost tenderness for every man, and feels no more concern for his own interest than for that of his fellows: It seems evident, that the use of justice would, in this case, be suspended by such extensive benevolence." He added, "Why raise land-marks between my neighbour's field and mine, when my heart has made no division between our interests; but shares all his joys and sorrows with the same force and vivacity as if originally my own?" (EPM, 14). Conversely, in the case of extreme deprivation such as a severe famine or a siege, it might prove impossible to uphold property rights. In such circumstances, there would be no rule of law: "No rule of justice known: No distinction of property regarded: Power was the only measure of right; and a perpetual war of all against all was the result of men's untamed selfishness and barbarity" (EPM, 17).

Humans have yet to enjoy a utopia and are rarely in a situation of such extreme scarcity or deprivation that they suspend the rule of law. Because most societies recorded in history have fallen somewhere in the middle between these two extremes, Hume observed, the institution of property has taken hold and proved effective (EPM, 16). The perpetual condition we have faced is one of scarcity: we have "numberless wants and necessities" and only "slender means" whereby to meet them (T, 311). While philosophers for generations had lamented humankind's voracious appetite for pleasure and material enjoyment, Hume belonged to a new generation of Epicurean-inspired thinkers who posited an inexhaustible appetite for pleasure as a congenital condition of human nature.[9] In this respect, Hume contended, animals have an advantage in that they enjoy a finely calibrated balance between their wants and means. The lion, for example, possesses the proper temper, agility, and force to readily satisfy his voracious appetite, whereas the sheep need fewer advantages because "their appetites are moderate." Humans, on the other hand, lack the "natural abilities" to meet their countless desires (T, 312).

Hume submitted that the remedy for this shortfall is the formation of societies. By living and, more important, working and trading together, Hume asserted, man's "infirmities are compensated; and tho' in that situation his wants multiply every moment upon him, yet his abilities are still more augmented, and leave him in every respect more satisfy'd and happy, than 'tis possible for him, in his savage and solitary condition, ever to become" (T, 312). For Hume, one person working alone is not strong enough to accomplish critical tasks, such as building homes or cultivating the land. But when people join together in societies, they derive benefits from the "conjunction of forces" and the "partition of employments" (T, 312). Hume thus recognized the value of the division of labor and specialization by trade. Cooperative and specialized labor constitutes the most productive way to challenge the condition of scarcity.[10]

Property rights constitute the sine qua non of thriving society. Hume argued that people come to appreciate, through trial and error, that by respecting the property of others, they feel more secure in their own. This respect for property in the form of external goods thus "arises gradually, and acquires force by a slow progression, and by our repeated experience of the inconveniences of transgressing it" (T, 315). Eventually, we internalize these outcomes and cooperate tacitly and instantaneously, as when "two men, who pull the oars of a boat, do it by an agreement or convention, tho' they have never given promises to each other" (T, 315).

In Hume's account, property rights are upheld more by individual regulation than by legal enforcement. People in stable communities recognize that their "passion [of avidity] is much better satisfy'd by its restraint, than by its liberty, and that by preserving society, we make much greater advances in the acquiring possessions, than by running into the solitary and forlorn condition, which must follow upon violence and an universal licence" (T, 316). As the respect for property becomes universal and "every single act is perform'd in expectation that others are to perform the like," social interactions become more predictable and transparent (T, 320). As virtually all people join the community and thus subscribe to these conventions, a general sense of trust emerges, which is crucial to peaceful relations. The stability of possessions sustains the peace and hence the "first rudiments of justice must every day be improv'd, as the society enlarges" (T, 316). This kind of trust does not rely on people's expectations of each other's benevolence or honesty. Instead, it revolves primarily around the belief that people will fulfill their obligations (repay their loans, for example), since doing so serves their long-term interests in the accumulation of wealth.[11] Promises are "human inventions, founded on the necessities and interests of society," and a single breach bears "the penalty of never being trusted again" (T, 334–35). Crucially, the practice of keeping one's promises becomes habit-forming.

Hume had a profound appreciation for the many types of tacit conventions that bring people together. He points to various instances of mutual cooperation, such as passing one another on the right side of the road in accordance to the rules of the wagon-way, or two neighbors who "agree to drain a meadow, which they possess in common; because 'tis easy for them to know . . . that the immediate consequence of his failing in his part, is, the abandoning the whole project" (T, 345).[12] The respect for property stems from the same disposition, "by a convention enter'd into by all the members of the society to bestow stability on the possession of those external goods, and leave every one in the peaceable enjoyment of what he may acquire by his fortune and industry. By this means, every one knows what he may safely possess; and the passions are restrain'd in their partial and contradictory motions" (T, 314).

Justice, for Hume, at least in the *Treatise* and the first *Enquiry* (*An Enquiry concerning Human Nature*), did not stem from a sense of fairness or reciprocity.[13] Rather, Hume sought to highlight the basic condition of security to ensure that social and, above all, economic interactions were sustained, whether among those living in urban squalor or in the splendor of a country estate. Several scholars have expressed perplexity with Hume for limiting his theory of justice to the legal ascription of property rights.[14] As this book shows, however, Hume's theory of justice, when read in the context of his economics, can be understood as part of his pronounced enthusiasm for the advent and spread of trade and commerce and the moral benefits of economic growth. In short, as we will show more carefully in chapter 4, Hume put much stock in the potential of commerce to engender more refinement, prudence, and liberty. He also believed that the concomitant urbanization would induce more civility, friendship, and humanity. Above all, the modern economy would foster a wide array of social virtues, notably honesty, politeness, and beneficence. All of this depended critically on upholding the system of property rights and hence the rule of law. It was these beneficial outcomes, the effects of the law, that gave it warrant, not a more primitive appeal to fairness or equality.

While the formation of property rights required a slight redirection of people's self-interest, a more complicated process, involving sympathy, was required for the respect of property rights to solidify into a virtue. Once people could, more or less, take it for granted that property will be respected, violations of property rights take on a different moral connotation (T, 320). Witnessing a theft no longer conjures up anxieties about the collapse of the social order. Instead, we isolate our focus on the experience of the dispossessed individual. Our sympathy for the victim draws us to his or her suffering, and the violation of property rights thus becomes anchored more deeply in our moral sentiments. Contrastingly, when a person observes someone respecting the property of others, an awareness of its favorable effects creates a pleasurable feeling. It is this pleasure that grounds our sense of respecting property as a virtue.[15] Moreover, it is critical to note that, for Hume, we anchor this cultivated sense of an "extensive sympathy" in public order and justice (T, 374).[16] Hume thus asserted, *"self-interest* is the original motive to the *establishment* of justice: But a *sympathy* with *public* interest is the source of the *moral* approbation, which attends that virtue" (T, 320–21). In this respect, Hume went beyond both Samuel Pufendorf and Mandeville, who argued, respectively, that societies arise as the solution to the penury of solitude. Hume put much weight on our capacity to inculcate moral sentiments that appeal to the public utility of our actions and thereby reinforce the criteria for justice.[17]

The moral sentiments gradually elevate the observance of justice into a virtue that no longer requires constant motivation. This process occurs without any external involvement, either by the government or by preachers. There are, however, certain actions that governments could take to further strengthen the sense that justice is a virtue. For example, statesmen could endeavor to instill a greater appreciation for justice in the population by warning people about the damages that follow from widespread violations. Hume believed that it is in the interest of the government to do so, as it improves the stability of society and thus renders the population more easily governable.

In addition to the efforts undertaken by the government, Hume also encouraged the use of education to bolster respect for justice. If parents would teach their children from an early age to obey social conventions and strive for honor, Hume argued, they would also foster a culture in which justice is recognized as virtuous (T, 321). Hume promoted the study of history as a way to provide moral instruction. He was of the opinion that the reading of history was beneficial, "as it amuses the fancy, as it improves the understanding, and as it strengthens virtue" (E-SH, 565).[18] Finally, the need to safeguard one's reputation feeds into the institution of property.[19] Apart from our avidity and pleasure-seeking pursuits, which Hume viewed as the strongest forces operating on the human mind, there is little that matters more to civilized people than their reputation. "For this reason," Hume noted, "every one, who has any regard to his character, or who intends to live on good terms with mankind, must fix an inviolable law to himself, never, by any temptation, to be induc'd to violate those principles, which are essential to a man of probity and honour" (T, 321).

To briefly recapitulate the analysis thus far, Hume argued not only that justice is coextensive with property rights but also that these rights provide the foundation for commercial society and hence serve to bring about the economic, political, and moral improvements that he much valued. Hume also explained why the practice of justice is better seen as an "artificial virtue," albeit the most natural of the set of artificial virtues. In using this phrase, Hume drew attention to the modern concept of justice as grounded in a human artifice. "Mankind is an inventive species," he declared, "and where an invention is obvious and absolutely necessary, it may as properly be said to be natural as any thing that proceeds immediately from original principles, without the intervention of thought or reflection." In this respect, "no virtue is more natural than justice" (T, 311).

Markets and Money

Property, for Hume, constituted a necessary institution for the forging of a stable and expanding society, but it is not sufficient. Two additional conventions—markets and money—are also required for human beings to enjoy the full benefits of society. To make productive use of society's resources and to distribute wealth in a manner that enables the satisfaction of people's heterogeneous wants, a regular mechanism of exchange is required. As Hume observed, "the invention of the law of nature, concerning the *stability* of possession, has already render'd men tolerable to each other; that of the *transference* of property and possession by consent has begun to render them mutually advantageous" (T, 334). One person might have plentiful wheat, a second person equipment useful to baking, and a third person fuel suitable to heating an oven, but no single person has access to the right mix of property necessary to produce bread. To rectify this situation, every owner of property must have the right "to bestow [the property] on some other person" (T, 330). The formation of markets is not simply motivated by local wants and needs; rather, it ripples out across the globe. "Different parts of the earth," Hume explained, "produce different commodities; and not only so, but different men both are by nature fitted for different employments, and attain to greater perfection in any one, when they confine themselves to it alone. All this requires a mutual exchange and commerce" (T, 330). In a rare gesture to a deity, Hume claimed that it would be wrong to "deprive neighbouring nations of that free communication and exchange which the Author of the world has intended, by giving them soils, climates, and geniuses, so different from each other" (E-BT, 324).

Hume noted that most contractual agreements depend on the future delivery of goods and therefore require trust and confidence that promises will be kept, particularly in the exchange of services. Hume illustrated this concept with the case of two farmers facing a decision whether to cooperate with each other. One farmer declares, "your corn is ripe to-day; mine will be so to-morrow. 'Tis profitable for us both, that I shou'd labour with you to-day, and that you shou'd aid me to-morrow" (T, 334). But because there is insufficient assurance of reciprocity, they do not form such an implicit contract, leading the first farmer to conclude, "both of us lose our harvests for want of mutual confidence and security" (T, 334). Hume submitted, however, that such unfortunate outcomes had long been buried in the past. Even if people did not harbor feelings of benevolence toward their neighbors, the recognition of mutual gain led them to exchange services delivered sequentially rather than simultaneously.

Similar to the motivations for respecting property, the solution to the lack of surety in commercial contracts involves a redirection of individual self-interest and the recognition that each person is better served in the long run by respecting contracts. Hume argued, "hence I learn to do a service to another, without bearing him any real kindness; because I foresee, that he will return my service, in expectation of another of the same kind, and in order to maintain the same correspondence of good offices with me or with others" (T, 334–35). If a society fails to develop these interdependencies, then "the mutual commerce of good offices [is] in a manner lost among mankind, and every one reduc'd to his own skill and industry for his well-being and subsistence" (T, 334). In short, if trust in contracts fails, industry and commerce would suffer: "The freedom and extent of human commerce depend entirely on a fidelity with regard to promises" (T, 349).

Hume's analysis of property and markets provides the conceptual foundation for the most important representation of contractual obligations: money. Hume insisted that money is intrinsically semiotic; it represents, like language, the value of goods or services, and it is in many respects the crystallization of pledges and promises between traders.[20] Coins, like words, are fungible and circulate. Foreign coins, like foreign words, can be converted into the native medium of exchange. Hume went further and conjectured that in the distant past, money and natural languages arose in tandem: to give "us a confidence of the future regularity of their [our fellow human beings'] conduct, . . . are languages gradually establish'd by human conventions without any promise. In like manner do gold and silver become the common measures of exchange, and are esteem'd sufficient payment for what is of a hundred times their value" (T, 315). He provided no empirical sources to confirm this claim, but it is a tantalizing hypothesis that serves to bolster his belief that money is the product of tacit and collective agreements, drawing on innumerable conventions. His analysis of the origins of language also resonates with these insights into money, in particular, the respective imperfect capturing of its representation of meaning or value.

In his epistemology, Hume cast much doubt as to whether human language genuinely refers to features of the external world. He showed that insofar as people process impressions, copy them into ideas, and employ linguistic utterances to represent these ideas, they must also use their memory to compare any given idea at present in terms of its resemblance with past impressions and ideas. It is not that people are incapable of doing so, or that they mostly err, but rather that the resemblance is never perfect; there are only particulars in the world, and words demand an appeal to an abstract type. In that sense, people ascribe words inductively, and therein lies the source of the fallibility. Words are always clothed in this ambiguity and never fully map onto the world. Money is like this as well. It is always, whether one realizes it or not, embedded in a virtually infinite chain of transactions that also appeal to some degree of resemblance of the value of two things. But as Aristotle had recognized, the ascription of a price, an exchange value, masks the inescapable impossibility of equating two commodities.[21] Prices, like words, dupe people into believing that they can ascribe more resemblance than actually exists.

In addition to explaining the inadequacy of money, Hume also queried the possibility of a symbol serving as surety of promises in commercial agreements.[22] The exchange of a good or service in return for an object that might lack any intrinsic value, what Hume called a "symbolical" exchange, constituted a truly "remarkable event," a profound achievement of the human mind (T, 331). By using a "certain form of words," Hume emphasized, they convey to others that, notwithstanding our own self-interest, they will honor their promises and agreements (T, 335). These words provide a standardized way to express that whoever uses them is committed to honoring his or her promises and accepting the negative consequences of failing to do so. We thereby bind ourselves to the performance of our promises. As such, another convention emerges, Hume observed, one "which create[s] a new motive, when experience has taught us, that human affairs wou'd be conducted much more for mutual advantage, were there certain *symbols* or *signs* instituted, by which we might give each other security of our conduct in any particular incident" (T, 335). People learn the benefits of honoring their word and upholding the trust people place in them. "After these signs are instituted," Hume cautioned, "whoever uses them is immediately bound by his interest to execute his engagements, and must never expect to be trusted any more, if he refuse to perform what he promis'd" (T, 335).

Money is, for Hume, one of these signs. It symbolizes an indefinite chain of promises, past and future, and fosters surety in the minds of traders. As more and more people participate in the convention, the promises embodied in the symbol become all the more cemented and generalized—money thus acquires "chiefly a ficticious value" (E-In, 297). All people now "have a sense of interest in the faithful fulfilling of engagements, and express that sense to other members of society" (T, 335). Again, similar to the motivations for property rights, when people grasp the full sense in which the public utility is served by using money and upholding commercial contracts, Hume asserted, their new "sentiment of morals concurs with interest, and becomes a new obligation upon mankind" (T, 335).

Hume submitted that the transference of property is at bottom conducted by words. Every time a commodity or service is exchanged in the marketplace, and money is used to symbolize a temporary store of value, a new promise and concomitant obligation arises. The money used for trading could thus be thought of as incorporating this additional linguistic property. Hume pointed out that market exchange is analogous to the metamorphosis that Roman Catholics invoke with the ritual of transubstantiation (T, 331). Although absolution requires only "a certain form of words, along with a certain intention, [it] changes entirely the nature of an external object, and even of a human creature" (T, 336). The heart of the analogy stems from the fact that the priest must fully intend the outcome. Were he to fail in carrying out the ritual fully, or were his intentions inattentive at the time, the absolution of the soul of the parishioner would not be achieved (T, 337). But there is no means to know this, Hume contended, because people's minds are distracted by the symbolic representations and rituals at work: "*Roman Catholics* represent the inconceivable mysteries of the *Christian* religion, and render them more present to the mind, by a taper, or habit, or grimace, which is suppos'd to resemble them." Hume continued, "So lawyers and moralists have run into like inventions for the same reason, and have endeavour'd by those means to satisfy themselves concerning the transference of property by consent" (T, 331). Like the sacrament, in the case of market exchange, whether of money or possessions, there is an implicit set of pledges and beliefs that are never fully acknowledged or known.

There is an isomorphism, Hume suggested, between a coin and the Eucharistic wafer. In the *Natural History of Religion*, he related a story of a priest who had inadvertently given the communicant a piece of money that had accidentally fallen into the wafers only to be told that God "is so hard and tough there is no swallowing him" (NHR, 67).[23] But for Hume, this is where the visible similarities end. Whereas the obligation to uphold commercial promises becomes a widespread practice because of the manifest public benefits, "those other monstrous doctrines are mere priestly inventions, and have no public interest in view" (T, 337). The promises of the afterlife are never perceived, hence their delivery remains in doubt. In his posthumously published essay "Of the Immortality of the Soul," Hume argued that on strict empirical grounds, we have no knowledge of the soul or the afterlife. In the commercial world, by contrast, the benefits of market exchanges are visible and finite. Money, like religion, has a fictitious component, but at least the benefits of market exchanges are verifiable.

The analogy to transubstantiation served Hume well in his efforts to articulate the dimensions of monetary abstraction; he looked beyond the material composition of money and extracted its more essential property of a pledge. For many commentators in the early modern period, there was still a sharp distinction between money as a substance and credit as a figment of the imagination. Credit was seen as spirit-like, as something ephemeral that could disappear as readily as it was created. In 1698, Charles Davenant, for example, remarked that "of all Beings that have Existence only in the Minds of Men, nothing is more fantastical and nice than Credit: 'tis never to be forc'd; it hangs upon Opinion; it depends upon our Passions of Hope and Fear."[24] A few years later, during the financial crisis of 1710–11, Daniel Defoe described credit as like the wind: "We hear the *sound* thereof, but hardly know *whence it comes*, or *whither it goes*."[25] Credit, for Defoe, was inherently elusive. It is, he submitted, "*like the Soul* in the Body, it acts all Substance, yet is it self Immaterial; it gives Motion, yet it self cannot be said to Exist; it creates *Forms*, yet has it self *no Form*; it is neither Quantity or Quality; it has no *Whereness*, or *Whenness*, *Scite*, or *Habit*."[26] Defoe noted that credit rests upon the fulfillment of contractual obligations, but he failed to take these insights further, as Hume did, and recognize that money is identical to credit in this respect. Money is about a set of relations and conventions between humans, and in that respect, it is about beliefs and not about material objects. As Hume submitted, "money is not riches, as it is a metal endow'd with certain qualities of solidity, weight and fusibility; but only as it has a relation to the pleasures and conveniences of life" (T, 203).

In the second *Enquiry* (*An Enquiry concerning the Principles of Morals*), Hume illustrated the fact that credit forms a continuum, listing several different forms in terms of their increasing degrees of liquidity: mortgages, bonds, promissory notes, and bills of exchange (EPM, 22). In his *Political Discourses*, he referenced another set of credit arrangements. He described a system of bank credit pioneered in Edinburgh. Loans were issued to merchants on the collateral of their idle inventories and immovable assets. By extending lines of credit to creditworthy merchants, banks monetized idle capital. This practice increased the quantity of money in circulation, particularly in the wholesale sectors where contractual obligations with suppliers were settled at irregular temporal intervals. In addition, Glasgow banks had begun to issue paper notes as low as ten shillings (half a pound), which were widely used in place of silver coins to cover "all payments for goods, manufactures, tradesmen's labour of all kinds." Such notes "passed as money in all payments throughout the country" (E-BT, 320). These paper notes increased the circulation of money and greased the wheels of trade.

Hume was also well aware of the uses of paper money in the American colonies. The shortage of specie (silver and gold) forced certain regions to adopt paper notes as money. Benjamin Franklin promoted the system of banking in Pennsylvania, which used land as collateral for the issuance of paper money.[27] Up to one-half of the value of the land could be manifest as credit money, provided the planter paid back 10 percent of the loan per year to the issuing office. Hume was also aware that there were cases of non-redeemable money, as was introduced in Montreal in 1685.[28] As Hume observed, for almost a century "this paper currency passed in all payments, by convention" (HL, 2:204). Paper money, he opined, had become a permanent feature of modern commercial societies.

The various credit currencies in circulation in the eighteenth-century world were interconnected with the rest of the financial system. Because it had become relatively easy to move wealth from one asset to another, Hume observed, "no merchant thinks it necessary to keep by him any considerable cash" (E-PC, 353). Rather, with any residual cash, merchants could purchase bonds or stocks and thus earn a rate of return on their idle capital. Even public securities, which had "with us become a kind of money," could be liquidated in as little as "a quarter of an hour" (E-PC, 353). This liquidity held true for both government bonds and shares in large public companies, such as the East India Company. "In short," Hume concluded, "our national debts furnish merchants with a species of money, that is continually multiplying in their hands, and produces sure gain, besides the profits of their commerce" (E-PC, 353).

By abstracting the essence of money from its material composition, Hume advanced the understanding that all forms of money are part of a wide spectrum of credit arrangements. That is, both notes and coins are at their core a type of contract—a credit contract, to be more exact. These arrangements result from a long chain of implicit promises and obligations, each transaction affirming the "fictitious value" of money (E-In, 297). For the symbols representing these contracts to change hands, both participants, buyers and sellers, must agree that the particular object of transfer is in fact redeemable for future purchases. When money circulates smoothly through society, there is a clear sense of the collective recognition grounded in experience: "The sense of interest has become common to all our fellows, and gives us a confidence of the future regularity of their conduct" (T, 315).

Hume thus thought of a coin as a fiduciary symbol mediating commercial contracts, rather than as a counter with the same intrinsic value as the commodity for which it was exchanged. Money is thus not "one of the subjects of commerce; but only the instrument which men have agreed upon to facilitate the exchange of one commodity for another" (E-Mo, 281).[29] As such, his thinking shares important commonalities with that of George Berkeley, who suggested that money is nothing but "Tickets or Tokens."[30] For Hume, the material, color, or design of the monetary symbol was inconsequential: nonmetals such as "sheep, oxen, [and] fish, [have been] employed as measures of exchange, or as money" (HL, 2:204). He noted that Lycurgus, king of Sparta, used iron lumps (E-Mo, 318). The key is that the symbol is incorruptible and universal. "Nothing should be as exempt from variation as that which is the common measure of everything," Hume wrote, echoing Montesquieu's earlier observation that "trade itself is very uncertain, and it is a great ill to add a new uncertainty to the one founded on the nature of the thing."[31] If mints and banks act with the utmost integrity, then merchants can rely on the monetary system without doubt or fear of sudden losses. Moreover, although the system of denomination is purely conventional, Hume grasped that some modes of representation are better than others. Arabic numerals are a better system than the Roman, which Hume described as "rather inconvenient" (E-Mo, 285). Analogously, coins that are too small or banknotes that are in large denominations tend to be ineffective. He also thought Lycurgus would have been wiser to have issued paper credit, given the shortfall of silver and gold, than to resort to iron (E-Mo, 318).

Hume emphasized the social utility of commercial activities: "Who sees not, for instance, that whatever is produced or improved by a man's art or industry ought, for ever, to be secured to him, in order to give encouragement to such *useful* habits and accomplishments?" (EPM, 21). Moreover, who sees not that "property ought also to descend to children and relations, for the same *useful* purpose?" (EPM, 21). But above all, he focused on the benefits of property transfers by consent: "Who sees not, . . . that it [property] may be alienated by consent, in order to beget that commerce and intercourse, which is so *beneficial* to human society? And that all contracts and promises ought carefully to be fulfilled, in order to secure mutual trust and confidence, by which the general *interest* of mankind is so much promoted?" (EPM, 21). Public utility provides the rationale behind these institutions, without which a thriving commercial society would be impossible.

Government

Although the institutions that foster commercial practices are upheld by members of the community through their everyday interactions, there is nonetheless, Hume argued, a critical need for the government to secure these systems. He was far from a libertarian; capitalism, for Hume, could not exist without government. Hume located the need for government in our human shortcomings. The human tendency to discount the future, to fall short of self-knowledge, or to succumb to weakness of the will means that we need to establish protective measures. To put it another way, were we able to transcend these frailties, there would be no need for government. As Hume observed:

> Had every man sufficient *sagacity* to perceive, at all times, the strong interest, which binds him to the observance of justice and equity, and *strength of mind* sufficient to persevere in a steady adherence to a general and a distant interest, in opposition to the allurements of present plea-sure and advantage; there had never, in that case, been any such thing as a government or political society. (EPM, 28)

Active participation in commercial society promotes these proclivities, and the government offers further reinforcement and safeguarding. Civil laws are necessary to correct for human frailty: "As all men are, in some degree, sub-ject to the same weakness [of discounting the future], it necessarily happens, that the violations of equity must become very frequent in society, and the commerce of men, by that means, be render'd very dangerous and uncertain" (T, 343).

Several of Hume's texts address the pervasive problem of property vio-lations. In his essay "Of the Origins of Government," he explained that al-though people recognize the "necessity of peace and order for the mainte-nance of society," some people nevertheless commit injustices because of the allure of present gains (E-OG, 38). For Hume, "this great weakness is incur-able in human nature" (E-OG, 38). As a result, we must establish a government "to point out the decrees of equity, to punish transgressors, to correct fraud and violence, and to oblige men, however reluctant, to consult their own real and permanent interests" (E-OG, 38). He concluded that protecting property is the primary responsibility of the government. People should therefore, Hume insisted, "look upon all the vast apparatus of our government, as having ultimately no other object or purpose but the distribution of justice," by which he meant property rights (E-OG, 37).

Due to their long histories and complex political genealogies, most existing property systems were marked by ambiguity and inconsistency. Laws distinguishing ownership were subject to countless "statues, customs, precedents, analogies, and a hundred other circumstances" (EPM, 23). With a nod, perhaps, to his youthful study of the law, Hume voiced considerable skepticism about the possibility of reaching full closure in any given legal settlements. The sheer volume of legal judgments spoke to this persistent problem, "a hundred volumes of laws, and a thousand volumes of commentators, have not been found sufficient" to settle disputes definitively, he contended (EPM, 25). Nevertheless, as Hume stated unequivocally in the *Treatise*, "property, and right, and obligation, admit not of degrees." At any given moment, he declared, an "object must either be in the possession of one person or another" (T, 340). However, because of the many contingent factors from one nation to the next, legal systems vary. Hume illustrated this point with an analogy to the animal kingdom; whereas "all birds of the same species in every age and country, build their nests alike, . . . [humans] in different times and places, frame their houses differently: Here we perceive the influence of reason and custom" (EPM, 26). The responsibility of any specific government is thus not to impose, in a procrustean spirit, one uniform template but to tailor its laws to the needs of the nation. It is more critical, however, to recognize that the rule of law be upheld, whatever its specific denotations. As long as ownership of possessions remains stable and inviolable, problems of interpretation in the commercial sphere would abate.

Hume offered four specific criteria to guide the deliberations of the magistrate in disputes over ownership. First, in most cases, objects belong to the person who enjoyed first possession, or *occupation*. And second, in cases where this principle is impossible to establish firmly, whoever has been in possession of the object for the longest time should have the right of property, or *prescription* (T, 323–26). If someone creates or produces an item, it belongs to that person, not on the basis of having mixed his or her labor with physical nature, as Locke would have it, but rather because he or she was the first person to establish a relation with the object (T, 324n72). Third, to address circumstances in which an object comes into the world anew, but no free person was responsible for its creation, Hume posited the principle of *accession*, whereby we are "connected in an intimate manner with objects that are already our property, and at the same time are inferior to them" (T, 327). Examples of such circumstances include the fruits that grow in our garden, the offspring of our livestock, and "the work of our slaves," all of which become property because they originate from our primary property (T, 327). Fourth, Hume considered what should happen to an item when its owner dies, the principle of *succession*. The rule here should be that the item becomes the property of the person whom the deceased cared for the most. The main consideration is not the emotional bond per se, but rather the broader public utility, because it is "the general interest of mankind, which requires, that men's possessions shou'd pass to those, who are dearest to them, in order to render them more industrious and frugal" (T, 329).

It should be noted here that Hume did not limit the role of the government to the legal protection of property. He also insisted that the government was responsible for providing what we would today call *public goods*, for which the classic example is a lighthouse. "'Tis very difficult, and indeed impossible, that a thousand persons shou'd agree" to undertake a project that requires a complicated design or a challenging execution (T, 345). Hume gestured briefly to the potential for *free riders*, to use a modern term: "Each seeks a pretext to free himself of the trouble and expence, and wou'd lay the whole burden on others" (T, 345). This meant, Hume noted, that a modern government must oversee the provision of many public services for transportation and defense, making sure that "bridges are built; harbours open'd; ramparts rais'd; canals form'd; fleets equip'd; and armies disciplin'd" (T, 345). Governments thus solve the collective action problem; they undertake projects that are time-consuming, "distant and remote" (T, 345).

In order for the government to protect property and provide public goods, it was not necessary for the government to be composed of "Great Men." Hume did not subscribe to the civic republican tradition, which held that the choice of political leaders was fundamental to the morality and stability of society, and that only men of exceptional caliber and integrity should be allowed to serve.[32] For this tradition, rulers must have the right pedigree and must have exhibited bravery on the battlefield, skill and dexterity in public affairs, wise management of their estates, and eloquence in speech and letters. For Hume, it was far more important that civil servants cultivate the skills to protect the core institutions of commercial society. Hume suggested that members of the middle station are better equipped to serve in government than the aristocracy, as they are more likely to protect the laws and conventions of commercial society, in part because their recently elevated social standing had come as the result of success in commerce (E-RA, 277–78). Hume thus granted governments, either directly or indirectly, the potential to shape the workings of commercial society.

Governance and Commercial Development in Hume's *History of England*

Hume offered a colorful narrative of economic development in his *History of England*, tracing the roots of the modern commercial world back to Tudor England.[33] Much of his historical analysis was designed for pedagogical purposes, to illustrate successes and failures of past governments in order to instruct the legislators of his own day. His emphasis was on the prolonged and somewhat painful path by which modern commerce took hold. He records that King Henry VIII instituted a number of polices conducive to commerce, such as establishing "a more regular police" and "stricter administration of justice" (HE, 3:329). However, these policies were only partially successful, in part because the "principles of commerce are much more complicated, and require long experience and deep reflection to be well understood in any state" (HE, 3:74). Because of a lack of economic literacy, the Crown passed a number of laws and statutes that resulted in widespread dislocation, and, as a result, "trade and industry were rather hurt than promoted" (HE, 3:77). Hume was well aware of the violence and hardship accompanying the transition to capitalism, with vast numbers of people struggling to make a living, some of whom resorted to crime or vagrancy. He reported an estimate that approximately "72,000 criminals were executed during this reign for theft and robbery, which would amount nearly to 2000 a-year" (HE, 3:329). However brutal, Hume believed that these laws were necessary to ground and foster the right institutions and protocols. They would eventually produce a higher standard of living across the board and provide more regular and more skilled employment. The harsh measures were a necessary condition because they contributed "to the encrease of industry and of the arts, which have given maintenance, and, what is almost of equal importance, occupation, to the lower classes" (HE, 3:329).

By the early seventeenth century, trade became "an affair of state" (E-CL, 88). As Hume observed, the British Crown began to pass laws in support of commerce and manufacturing:

> During no preceding period of English history, was there a more sensible encrease, than during the reign of this monarch [James I], of all the advantages which distinguish a flourishing people. Not only the

peace which he maintained, was favourable to industry and commerce: His turn of mind inclined him to promote the peaceful arts: And trade being as yet in its infancy, all additions to it must have been the more evident to every eye, which was not blinded by melancholy prejudices. (HE, 5:142)

The subsequent regime engendered considerably more economic expansion. Hume described how "the commerce and industry of England encreased extremely during the peaceable period of Charles's reign" (HE, 6:148). This momentum was interrupted by civil war, but after the interregnum of Oliver Cromwell until the Glorious Revolution of 1688, the surge in economic development was without precedent. As Hume noted, "the commerce and riches of England did never, during any period, encrease so fast as from the restoration to the revolution" (HE, 6:537). He thus depicted an upward trajectory of economic betterment for much of the seventeenth century.

As Hume recognized, the new legislation promoted mercantile and manufacturing interests, which in turn accelerated the dissolution of the traditional agrarian order. Many people opposed the changes, sparking frequent and bloody confrontations between rioters and the king's armies.[34] While Hume acknowledged the suffering that followed in the wake of the Enclosure Acts, he nonetheless strongly supported them and the harsh measures necessary for their execution. He described the disruptive conditions that prevailed after the pasturage of livestock had become more profitable than traditional "unskilful" English farming: "Whole estates were laid waste by inclosures: The tenants regarded as a useless burden, were expelled [from] their habitations: Even the cottagers, deprived of the commons, on which they formerly fed their cattle, were reduced to misery" (HE, 3:369). Nevertheless, he dismissed Thomas More's appeal to "sheep eating men," as mere hyperbole; how ridiculous, Hume retorted, that "a sheep had become in England a more ravenous animal than a lion or wolf, and devoured whole villages, cities, and provinces" (HE, 3:370). If anything, the Crown was too clement in its efforts to protect the evicted commoners, Hume contended. He blamed the English peasantry for their poor work habits and lack of initiative. With hindsight, Hume argued, it was clear that they benefited from the enclosures by being forced to become more industrious and frugal (HE, 3:79). As he opined, it was "difficult for the people to shake off their former habits of indolence; and nothing but necessity could compel them to such an exertion of their faculties" (HE, 3:370). True to character, Hume highlighted the importance of establishing what to him constituted good habits and customs as the key to human betterment.

Hume blamed "*religious* fanatics" for mounting resistance to the enclosures. In 1649, a militia organized by the landed aristocracy had put down an uprising by the Diggers, led by William Everard and Gerrard Winstanley.[35] In tearing down the enclosures and cultivating the wastelands, they sought to restore the earth as a common treasury for all to share. Although their rebellion was quickly quelled, their subversive vision for a more egalitarian society lingered on and, in Hume's eyes, continued to pose a threat to the new property regime. To him, the Diggers were fanatics who quixotically believe that "dominion is founded on grace, and that saints alone inherit the earth" (EPM, 20). He reported with pleasure that "the civil magistrate very justly puts these sublime theorists on the same footing with common robbers, and teaches them by the severest discipline, that a rule, which, in speculation, may seem the most advantageous to society, may yet be found, in practice, totally pernicious and destructive" (EPM, 20). Hume was slightly kinder in his assessment of the Levellers, whom he referred to as "a kind of *political* fanatics" (EPM, 20).[36] He conceded that their principles in the abstract, "in speculation," are not obviously disadvantageous. In his essay "Of Superstition and Enthusiasm," Hume added that their cause was one of emancipation and civil liberty and thus, in principle, for the common good. Their methods, however, were problematic. Hume expressed optimism that once their initial "thunder and tempest" had abated, they would "become more gentle and moderate" (E-SE, 76–77).

Commoners displaced by the enclosures were particularly exposed to the vicissitudes of market forces. Not only did they lose access to their firewood or the means to graze their livestock, but they also had to purchase their food and were thus subject to price fluctuations in times of dearth. If the Crown interfered and imposed price ceilings on bread or regulated the export of corn, suffering tended to intensify, Hume asserted (HE, 3:327). If the markets were left unregulated, Hume believed, the higher price for bread would force the poor to become more frugal and prudent and, above all, to work more diligently. Hume believed the supply of labor was fairly elastic, both in terms of working additional days or weeks and in terms of the intensity of the labor per day. For example, he made note of the many saint's days in Medieval Europe that, in his mind, enabled excessive leisure time (MEM, 510). Faced with the proper incentives, farmers and weavers would work with much greater alacrity and attentiveness.[37]

In his essay "Of Taxes," Hume asserted that in "years of scarcity, if it be not extreme, . . . the poor labour more, and really live better, than in years of great plenty, when they indulge themselves in idleness and riot" (E-Ta, 635).[38] To him, regulating wages and prices to protect the poor only served to sustain their proclivity for idleness.[39] In support of his argument, Hume referenced the statues undertaken by Henry VIII to fix prices on poultry, cheese, butter, and beef. While these measures were intended to "remedy the evil . . . [of a] decay of commerce, and industry," they in fact did nothing but exacerbate the food shortages (HE, 3:330). This outcome led Hume to conclude, "it is evident, that these matters [the setting of wages and prices] ought always to be left free, and be entrusted to the common course of business and commerce" (HE, 3:78). It should be noted here, however, that even though Hume supported the exacting logic of the marketplace, he did not subscribe to the doctrine of the "utility of poverty." Nor did he endorse the view that would become widespread with Arthur Young, who proclaimed that "everyone but an idiot knows that the lower classes must be kept poor, or they will never be industrious."[40] Hume maintained that high wages combined with low prices served as the best means to promote industriousness, since ordinary laborers could then enjoy many conveniences, as well as some luxuries.

In addition to safeguarding market forces, Hume also underscored the importance of the government protecting the sanctity of commercial contracts, including both credit and coins. In particular, like many of his contemporaries, he was concerned about the widespread practices of forging banknotes and counterfeiting coins. Illicit tampering with money dangerously threatens the fiduciary basis of contracts and infuses a contagious doubt in the minds of commercial subjects. John Locke had earlier been forced to contend with the consequences of excessive clipping, hammering, and counterfeiting of coins that occurred after the Glorious Revolution. He deemed it a greater threat to England's national safety than the military might of Louis XIV.[41]

In 1696, inspired by the writings of Locke, the British Parliament instructed Isaac Newton, then warden of the mint, to undertake a massive recoinage of the silver currency. He was also made responsible for the pursuit of counterfeiters, a task Newton zealously carried out, delivering the perpetrators to the hangman.[42] Although Hume did not comment directly on Newton's measures for enforcement, he expressed admiration for efforts to punish counterfeiters during the reign of Henry I. Hume described approvingly how "false coining, which was then a very common crime, and by which the money had been extremely debased, was severely punished by Henry" (HE, 1:277). He further remarked that these anticounterfeiting laws were well received by the public and seemed to have yielded favorable results: "Near fifty criminals of this kind were at one time hanged or mutilated; and though these punishments seem to have been exercised in a manner somewhat arbitrary, they were grateful to the people" (HE, 1:277–78). This account speaks to Hume's belief that the money supply, as the fiduciary basis of society, must be safeguarded, if need be, through the execution of the people who jeopardized it. It was part of his broader appeal to the sense in which justice and property were in essence synonymous.

Hume paid careful attention to the ethical dimensions of commerce, striking a careful balance between self-interest and benevolence, wealth and virtue, liberty and authority. He articulated a social theory that foregrounds the critical importance of contractual obligations and thus the institutions of property, markets, and money. These conventions incentivize people to engage in industry and commerce, to pursue knowledge, and, in turn, to strengthen the virtuous pursuits that enhance life's pleasures. His historical account demonstrated the sense in which these conventions took time to become anchored, that as commerce took hold and spread, social norms evolved in step. Commercial societies, he believed, were on a trajectory that served to achieve the proper mix of prudence and trust, discipline and order, industry and pleasure, all in the name of individual and collective happiness. As shown, Hume was for the most part unfailingly optimistic about the potential of commerce to promote a wide array of improvements for humanity writ large. Yet, it should not be forgotten that he was well aware that the institutions of capitalism could break down; he was not opposed to the use of capital punishment to protect them.

CHAPTER 4

"That Indissoluble Chain of Industry, Knowledge, and Humanity"

Hume on Economic and Moral Improvement

The protagonists of commercial societies, the burgeoning middle class, David Hume argued, not only served as the engine of material affluence but also contributed to the formation of a more enlightened and humane world. Merchants and manufacturers solidified the institutions of money and markets, as well as the social norms of probity and trust. Superstition and ignorance had given way, at least among the mercantile classes, to more refined tastes and an increased interest in the arts and sciences. There were still reasons to be concerned that corrupt politicians, the rebellious poor, or bellicose neighbors might interfere with the continued development of commerce and thus impede future progress, but on the whole, Hume affirmed, the modern era had taken a turn for the better. Certainly in Georgian Britain, the quality of life had improved significantly and, he believed, there were many indications that it would continue to do so for many generations to come.

Commercial prosperity built on the cultivation of ingenuity, enterprise, and perseverance. The results were novel types of manufacturing, improved agricultural methods, and expanding markets, all of which brought people into closer proximity and thus tended to induce more civility and gentler manners. It was not wealth per se that served as the catalyst for moral refinement. Nor did education, moral suasion, or religious piety provide the critical impetus. As Bernard Mandeville had wryly observed earlier in the century, "Envy and Emulation have kept more Men in Bounds, . . . than all the Sermons that have been preach'd since the time of the Apostles."[1] Instead, it was the quotidian experience of commercial life, Hume argued, that engendered a more virtuous age. An active life of commerce and industry served as an elixir that polished the moral sentiments of the bourgeoisie. The experience of working diligently, negotiating and transacting with strangers, or developing novel skills in finance or manufacturing mitigated their passions and tended to make them more *"sociable, good-natured,* [and] *humane"* than the rest of the population (EPM, 8).

Some ancient societies had achieved a modicum of refinement among the elites, Hume conceded, but added that these societies tended to be held back by a general culture of "sloth, ignorance, and barbarism" (E-RA, 328).[2] Only commercial societies, Hume argued, have the capacity to simultaneously promote *both* wealth and virtue across a broad spectrum of the social strata. Hume succinctly captured this with his famous catena:

> Thus *industry, knowledge*, and *humanity*, are linked together by an indissoluble chain, and are found, from experience as well as reason, to be peculiar to the more polished, and, what are commonly denominated, the more luxurious ages. (E-RA, 271)

While not inevitable or guaranteed, Hume was strongly optimistic that his version of *doux commerce* would launch society on a progressive path. The group most responsible for building this path was drawn from the ranks of the rapidly expanding middle classes. Composed of merchants, bankers, traders, and manufacturers, the commercial vanguard forged a cosmopolitan society in which the pursuit of profits and sophisticated pleasures developed in tandem with a humane life and the pursuit of knowledge. As Britain turned into "a nation of shopkeepers," to use Adam Smith's apt phrase, it also became a more refined and gentler place to live (WN, 2:613). Urban consumers, particularly those in the middle ranks, enjoyed a wide array of conveniences and luxuries, which in turn transformed their modes of self-expression and habits of engagement. Moreover, as the political power of the mercantile classes grew in tandem with their wealth, they successfully transformed the government into a steward of the new commercial order. From their position of power they recognized the benefits of representative government—an elected parliament or council—and thus fostered a more liberal society. Hume celebrated the increased personal and public freedom in commercial societies of his time and asserted that the nouveau riche formed "the best and firmest basis of public liberty" (E-RA, 277).

In Hume's view, members of the rising middle class were more likely to find their way on the road to virtue. They lived with honesty and moderation and cultivated "humanity, generosity, [and] beneficence" (EPM, 80). Notwithstanding the temptations of "profit or pecuniary advantage," they grasped the greater value of achieving an "inward peace of mind, [and a] consciousness of integrity" (EPM, 82). They were neither beleaguered like the peasants by a "meanness of spirit," nor harbored "hopes of tyrannizing over others, like the barons" (E-RA, 277–78). Hume proclaimed that those in "the Middle Station, as it is most happy in many Respects, so particularly in this, that a Man, plac'd in it, can, with the greatest Leisure, consider his own Happiness, and reap a new Enjoyment, from comparing his Situation with that of Persons above or below him" (E-MSL, 546).

The middle classes cohered as a group as a result of their day-to-day practices, their overarching interest in gain, and, above all, the faculty of sympathy. "The human mind," Hume suggested, "is of a very imitative nature." It is impossible, he continued, "for any set of men to converse often together, without acquiring a similitude of manners, and communicating to each other their vices as well as virtues. The propensity to company and society is strong in all rational creatures; and the same disposition, which gives us this propensity, makes us enter deeply into each other's sentiments, and causes like passions and inclinations to run, as it were, by contagion, through the whole club or knot of companions" (E-NC, 202). Because class barriers were still significant, the "greats," the "middle ranks," and the "lower orders" each developed their own respective ethical norms. Hume noted that it was well known that the aristocracy had long indulged in more libertine mores. Ethical norms, however, evolve; just as chastity and piety dominated the medieval period, so more sociable virtues characterized Hume's time (EPM, 119–23). For Hume, it was those of the middle ranks who formed the core of a happy and prosperous society. Indeed, the progressive dynamic of commercial societies that brought people together meant that the ethical norms of the separate ranks would converge over time to those of the middle rank.

Hume traced the roots of modernity back to the Tudor era, when commerce began to alter the patterns of consumption among the nobility. The aristocrats adopted "a more civilized species of emulation, and endeavoured to excel in the splendour and elegance of their equipage, houses, and tables" (HE, 3:76). Their newfound extravagance stimulated trade while at the same time releasing their subordinates to pursue a variety of enterprising careers. The former vassals, "no longer maintained in vicious idleness by their superiors, were obliged to learn some calling or industry, and became useful both to themselves and others." This was, without doubt in Hume's mind, a favorable development. As anyone would agree, he argued, "an industrious tradesman is both a better man and a better citizen than one of those idle retainers" (HE, 3:76). In Hume's view, the birth of a commercial society also had salutary effects on the poor, who could now find employment with greater ease. Able to provide for their families, the poor no longer had to resort to theft and robbery, at least not to the same extent as before. By the latter part of the reign of Elizabeth I, the number of criminals executed had dropped dramatically, from two thousand per year under Henry VIII to only four hundred annually under Elizabeth—a figure that led Hume to declare that "if these facts be just, there has been a great improvement in morals since the reign of Henry VIII" (HE, 3:329). As mentioned in chapter 3, although Hume recognized that the enclosures caused widespread suffering, he did not blame the new property regime for generating the desperation and destitution that propelled certain people to rob and steal.

Starting in the Tudor era, commercial men acquired considerable amounts of liquid wealth that empowered them as a group. The landed aristocracy became increasingly beholden to the merchants who supplied them with their coveted goods and loaned them the money that enabled these expenditures. As a result, Hume noted, the titled classes "retained only that moderate influence, which customers have over tradesmen, . . . which can never be dangerous to civil government" (HE, 4:384). Their diminished "riches" and "influence" prompted the landed aristocracy to try to augment their agrarian yield by introducing new types of crop rotation, seeds, fertilizers, and livestock. Many of these measures required the consolidation of landholdings, prompting wave after wave of enclosures.[3] The landlords sought "to turn their lands to the best account with regard to profit, and either inclosing their fields, or joining many small farms into a few large ones, dismissed those useless hands, which formerly were always at their call in every attempt to subvert the government, or oppose a neighbouring baron" (HE, 4:384). These developments made England a net exporter of wool and corn by the seventeenth century, and the aristocrats became more aware of the pursuit of profits as they invested more capital into the land. Primogeniture also forced many second sons, such as Hume, to enter commerce. In each of these respects, the upper and middle classes tended to converge.

Over the course of the sixteenth century, Hume observed, as "the cities encreased; the middle rank of men began to be rich and powerful" (HE, 4:384). Towns and cities began to attract newcomers—merchants capitalizing on new opportunities and commoners looking for new ways of making a living. Hume underscored the significance of urbanization in England as a major solvent of traditional mores. However, along with new forms of sociability, new conflicts and frictions also arouse, sometimes prompting hostilities toward outsiders. Under Henry VIII, Hume reported, "all foreign artificers were prohibited from having above two foreigners in their house," and a tax on foreigners was enacted (HE, 3:328). Hume opposed these measures since he believed that cultural diversity tends to stimulate economic growth, as evidenced by the immigration of the French Huguenots into England after 1685. He wished that more could have been done to increase the immigration of "foreign merchants and artizans . . . [since this] might have excited the emulation of the natives, and have improved their skill" (HE, 3:328). The arrival of novel wares and foreign methods, Hume argued, tends to prompt domestic industry and thus economic development.

Hume's Edinburgh exemplified the new mercantile spirit and novel forms of sociability. Its rich intellectual life spawned clubs that welcomed burghers as well as aristocrats. One of the first, the Rankenian Club, founded a few years after Hume's birth, sought to promote "freedom of thought, boldness of disquisition, liberality of sentiment, accuracy of reasoning, correctness of taste, and attention to composition."[4] Hume was an active member and coeditor of the *Proceedings* of the Philosophical Society of Edinburgh, also known as the Society for the Improving Arts and Sciences. Hume also belonged to the Poker Club and was a founding member of the Select Society. Here he rubbed shoulders with some of Edinburgh's exemplary citizens, bankers, and merchants, such as John Coutts and Adam Fairholm; manufacturers and agricultural improvers, such as William Johnstone and George Dempster; politicians, such as Archibald Campbell, the third Duke of Argyll, and Corbyn Morris; and fellow philosopher-economists, including Lord Elibank, Adam Ferguson, William Robertson, and Adam Smith.[5] Some of them were gentlemen, like Hume, but others belonged to the middle ranks. Hume's high regard for the latter group was undoubtedly reinforced by the many friendships formed in these Edinburgh clubs.[6] Their civility and intellectual sophistication made palpable the positive effects of commercial society.

Those in the middle ranks were not only the protagonists of Hume's historical narrative but also the primary audience. Hume believed that those in the middle class constituted "the most numerous Rank of Men, that can be suppos'd susceptible of Philosophy" (E-MSL, 546). Indeed, Hume opined that all "discourses of Morality ought principally to be address'd to them," because "the great" are too busy indulging in "pleasure" and the poor are too preoccupied with providing for "the Necessities of Life" (E-MSL, 546). Moreover, Hume found the middle class to be more knowledgeable of the subtleties of human nature than many philosophers were, because the hustle and bustle of their daily work demanded a constant engagement with the full swathe of humanity. In his first *Enquiry*, the 1748 *Enquiry concerning Human Understanding*, he asserted that it is the "mixed kind of life" of "business and occupation" that enlarges the "bounds of human understanding," and not the "pensive melancholy" of the philosopher (EHU, 7).

Hume's second *Enquiry*, the 1751 *Enquiry concerning the Principles of*

Morals, could be read as a vade mecum for those participating in commerce, providing insights and the means to cultivate a reputation for honor and honesty.[7] Moral judgments, Hume argued, while initially based on observed actions, necessarily require an assessment of the motives and hence the forged character of an individual comprehended over time. Philosophers tend to be brooding and solitary and thus slide easily into the set of "monkish virtues" that Hume most deplored. The "most perfect character," by contrast, would engage with the world and cultivate commercial ties. Such a person would retain "an equal ability and taste for books, company, and business; preserving in conversation that discernment and delicacy which arise from polite letters; and in business, that probity and accuracy which are the natural result of a just philosophy" (EHU, 7). Hume thus sought to bridge the separate realms of philosophical and commercial life. On the one hand, he asked, "what Possibility is there of finding Topics of Conversation fit for the Entertainment of rational Creatures, without having Recourse sometimes to History, Poetry, Politics, and the more obvious Principles, at least, of Philosophy?" (E-EW, 534). And, on the other hand, if philosophers do not pay attention to what is happening in the actual world and instead stay "shut up in Colleges and Cells, . . . secluded from the World and good Company," philosophy would cease to be relevant to the modern citizenry (E-EW, 534). Previous generations of philosophers, Hume averred, failed in this regard. What came to pass among them as belles lettres was "totally barbarous, being cultivated by Men without any Taste of Life or Manners, and without that Liberty and Facility of Thought and Expression, which can only be acquir'd by Conversation" (E-EW, 534). Hume believed that there would always be a demand for books, but not necessarily the authors to feed the supply (E-RA, 113).

Hume was intent on offering the middle ranks a genuinely worldly philosophy. By serving as "an Ambassador from the Dominions of Learning to those of Conversation," he declared that it would be his "constant Duty to promote a good Correspondence betwixt these two States, which have so great a Dependence on each other" (E-EW, 535). He continued with this analogy of trade between intellects and merchants to proclaim: "I shall give Intelligence to the Learned of whatever passes in Company, and shall endeavour to import into Company whatever Commodities I find in my native Country proper for their Use and Entertainment" (E-EW, 535). Hume thus appealed to a vernacular of economics to make sense of the production and distribution of knowledge. In this "Balance of Trade," he added, "we need not be jealous. . . . The Materials of this Commerce must chiefly be furnish'd by Conversation and common Life: The manufacturing of them alone belongs to Learning" (E-EW, 535).

Hume assigned women a central role in mediating between the worlds of the learned and those in business (E-EW, 536). Women were not only better judges of literature, he suggested, but also more often responsible for staging and curating spaces for polite conversation. Hume befriended a number of such women. In 1758, for example, he became acquainted with Mrs. Anderson, a Scot who owned and managed the British Coffee-House near Charing Cross in London.[8] It served as the meeting place for displaced Scots of an artistic or political bent, much like the Parisian salons Hume would frequent in the mid-1760s. Here, women, Hume declared, had become the "Sovereigns of the *learned* World" (E-EW, 536).[9] Hume acquired a reputation as a favorite with elite *Parisiennes*, including a lengthy attachment and enduring affection for the Comtesse de Bouffleurs. He also took a particular interest in women of letters, most notably the historian Catharine Macaulay and the novelist Marie-Jeanne Laboras de Mézières Riccoboni (HL, 2:82; 1:426–27).

As urban populations increased and commercial mores became more deeply entrenched, the rapport between the sexes also refined, as men and women cultivated the habit of "conversing together" (E-RA, 271).[10] Hume added that "when the tempers of men are softened as well as their knowledge improved, this humanity appears still more conspicuous, and is the chief characteristic which distinguishes a civilized age from times of barbarity and ignorance" (E-RA, 274). In several of his essays, Hume favored greater equality between men and women, and he promoted the "feminine" virtues of trust and tenderness that commence with maternal love.[11] To Hume, feminization of the modern life was emblematic of a kinder and more benevolent world. Hume offered a detailed account of the progression of manners and customs centered on the widespread adoption and intensification of industry, commerce, and the refinement of the arts and sciences. In Hume's view, more benevolent and gentle mores had spread across the whole of society but were particularly manifest among those in the middle station, who promoted a new set of virtues—"industry, discretion, frugality, secrecy, order, perseverance, forethought, [and] judgment"—and helped bury the more austere virtues of "self-denial, humility, silence, [and] solitude" (EPM, 78, 73).

Industry

Hume defined *industry* as the systematic, methodical, and ingenious application of human labor. The spread of the virtue of *industriousness* was particularly important in the shaping of customs and habits, turning individuals into attentive and enterprising agents. Hume was not the only early modern philosopher to pay homage to the virtues stemming from industry; John Locke, for example, decreed that God had intended for people to clear and cultivate the land and therefore "gave it [the land] to the use of the Industrious and Rational, (and *Labour* was to be *his Title* to it;) not to the Fancy or Covetousness of the Quarrelsom and Contentious."[12] As Locke maintained, "virtue and industry . . . [are] as constant companions on the one side as vice and idleness are on the other."[13] Locke and Hume helped redeem labor from its prior status as befitting only those in the lower ranks. They also dismissed the utopian call for a prelapsarian world of abundant leisure.[14] For Hume, homo faber was the happiest and most virtuous of men: "There is no craving or demand of the human mind more constant and insatiable than that for exercise and employment; and this desire [to labor] seems the foundation of most of our passions and pursuits" (E-In, 300).

Labor, for Hume, was also a source of *happiness*, which he defined as consisting of three major components: "action, pleasure, and indolence" (E-RA, 269). He posited that while the relative weights of these three components differ for each person, no one could achieve sustained happiness without all three. Action and pleasure, Hume insisted, are more important and should take up the greater share of one's day. But they are not mutually exclusive, since when commerce flourishes, "men are kept in perpetual occupation, and enjoy, as their reward, the occupation itself, as well as those pleasures which are the fruit of their labour" (E-RA, 270). Activity and industry are thus intrinsically pleasurable, especially for the commercial avant-garde. Hume noted that "if the employment you give him [a man in business] be lucrative, especially if the profit be attached to every particular exertion of industry, he has gain so often in his eye, that he acquires, by degrees, a passion for it, and knows no such pleasure as that of seeing the daily encrease of his fortune" (E-In, 301).

The third component, indolence, offers a necessary respite from the intensity of work or gratification, Hume asserted, since no one can "support an uninterrupted course of business or pleasure. That quick march of the spirits, which takes a man from himself, and chiefly gives satisfaction, does in the end exhaust the mind, and requires some intervals of repose, which, though agreeable for a moment, yet, if prolonged, beget a languor and lethargy, that destroys all enjoyment" (E-RA, 270). If indolence becomes too prevalent, however, as it had among the aristocracy, Hume believed, it might turn one to ruin: "Deprive a man of all business and serious occupation, he runs restless from one amusement to another; and the weight and oppression, which he feels from idleness, is so great, that he forgets the ruin which must follow him from his immoderate expences" (E-In, 300–301). Hume thus positions industry in a strongly favorable light and links pleasure as much to the activity itself as to the enjoyment of its fruits.

Hume insisted that by working diligently in one's profession, one would not only find happiness but also inadvertently cultivate various virtues and thus contribute to the refinement of society. Because work occupies the majority of one's waking hours, it offers the means to discipline and dignify one's life. Rather than move in a rudderless manner from one frivolous or destructive activity to another, the pursuit of a profession dictates that one follows a daily routine, commits oneself to a sustained process, and focuses one's energies on a specific purpose. Hume thus encouraged his readers: "By art and attention alone thou canst acquire that ability, which will raise thee to thy proper station in the universe" (E-St, 147). Such an effort would reach far beyond providing for one's household, Hume contended: when one conscientiously pursues a career in manufacturing or commerce, industriousness becomes a "powerful means of reforming the mind, and implanting in it good dispositions and inclinations" (E-Sc, 170–71).

A proper work ethic thus ensures that the "mind acquires new vigour; enlarges its powers and faculties; and by an assiduity in honest industry, both satisfies its natural appetites, and prevents the growth of unnatural ones, which commonly spring up, when nourished by ease and idleness" (E-RA, 270). Once good habits are formed, they become self-reinforcing, Hume posited: "A man, who continues in a course of sobriety and temperance, will hate riot and disorder: If he engage in business or study, indolence will seem a punishment to him" (E-Sc, 171). Because industriousness is habit-forming, it seeps into daily practices and routines, strengthening one's character, and shoring up the path to virtue.

Hume reiterated this message most emphatically in his *Dialogues concerning Natural Religion*. His proxy, Philo, states that "almost all the moral as well as natural evils of human life, arise from idleness; and were our species, by the original constitution of their frame, exempt from this vice or infirmity, the perfect cultivation of land, the improvement of arts and manufactures, the exact execution of every office and duty, [would] immediately follow" (DNR, 110–11). He asserted that "in order to cure most of the ills of human life, . . . I am contented to take an increase in one single power or faculty of his soul. Let him be endowed with a greater propensity to industry and labour; a more vigorous spring and activity of mind; a more constant bent to business and application" (DNR, 110). Humans do not require superhuman fortitude, such as the "force of an ox," "the wings of the eagle," or the "sagacity of an angel," to bring about a more virtuous and happier world (DNR, 110). The practical bent of Hume's vision entails that more attentive commerce and industry would suffice to elevate humankind.

In his analyses of causal inference and the passions, Hume emphasized the similarities between humans and other animals. In the appeal to industry, however, he highlighted the differences. Whereas nature provides animals with their food, humans must cultivate skills and labor so as to turn the "rude and unfinished" materials of nature into the means to survival (E-St, 147). Even as they seek to perfect their "bodily powers and faculties," humans must ensure that their minds are challenged by their efforts to labor, Hume entreated: "Wouldest thou *meanly* neglect thy mind, and from a preposterous sloth, leave it still rude and uncultivated, as it came from the hands of nature?" (E-St, 147). As we depart from a primitive and rude state and ascend up the ladder of civilization, we will find our intelligence directed at a multitude of ends, but always with utilitarian outcomes, Hume pointed out: "The great end of all human industry, is the attainment of happiness. For this were arts invented, sciences cultivated, laws ordained, and societies modelled" (E-St, 148).

In Hume's view, industry thus promotes virtuous ends for everyone, but especially for those in the professional middle ranks. Their stock of morals was constantly augmented as they dedicated their lives to the pursuit of industry. The labor of the poor, by contrast, constituted nothing but drudgery and toil: "Poverty and hard labour debase the minds of the common people, and render them unfit for any science and ingenious profession" (E-NC, 198).[15] Because a person's character is in large part determined by his or her everyday activities, Hume continued, the "same principle of moral causes fixes the character of different professions, and alters even that disposition, which the particular members receive from the hand of nature." Hume declared, for example, that a "*soldier* and a *priest* are different characters, in all nations, and all ages" (E-NC, 198). Although soldiers acquire many admirable traits, because "they use more the labour of the body than that of the mind, they are commonly thoughtless and ignorant" (E-NC, 199). Priests by definition are cerebral, but beyond that, Hume had little good to say about them as a group (E-SE, 75–76). The point is rather that each profession tends to demand certain virtues to the exclusion of others.

Although the employment among the lower orders was unsatisfying, they nevertheless had good reasons to dedicate themselves to a lifetime of diligence, Hume believed. For example, the "constant *bent* of mind" and the "repeated *habit*" that hard work brings introduced them to proper discipline and order (E-Sc, 171). Industriousness on the part of the lower sorts was also critical to the nation's economic growth, which would eventually bring about higher wages and cheaper commodities. Hume disliked the taxation system of parish rates that provided for those in extreme poverty or destitution. He believed that the only way forward was to inculcate a habit of industry, which he hoped in the future would lead to improvements in the standard of living across society. In a letter to Anne-Robert-Jacques Turgot of September 1766, Hume remarked that the commercial classes in France or England had, in the process of becoming "very opulent," unwittingly provided "labour to the poorer sort" (HL, 2:94). Thus, Hume contended, it was possible for peasants to "become rich and independent" and for the ordinary street porter to relish a meal of "bacon and brandy" (E-RA, 276–77). The situation in England also made evident to Hume that the widespread vagrancy and violence associated with the enclosures would fade away if enough people were kept in regular employment and if wages remained relatively high.

In sum, whether one belonged to the lower, middle, or upper classes, a life of concentrated work was the catalyst for developing the individual virtues prevalent in commercial societies, Hume asserted. The recognition that "industry render[s] the cultivating of our mind, the moderating of our passions, the enlightenment of our reason" should convince all people to cure themselves of their "lethargic indolence" and dedicate themselves wholeheartedly to the pursuit of industry. While some personal initiatives may be challenging, the reorientation of one's life to industry "is not difficult: You need but taste the sweets of honest labour" (E-St, 149–50).

Commerce

A thriving commerce, Hume argued, was essential if material and moral improvements were to proceed apace. While nascent markets could be found in virtually every known society, the rise of capitalism in early modern Europe prompted a radical intensification in market transactions.[16] The key factors of production—land, labor, and capital—were now incorporated into an interconnected and increasingly sophisticated system of markets.[17] Land tenure reforms depleted access to the commons and traditional rights to the produce of ancestral lands. The majority of the people became wage earners, in both the agrarian and manufacturing sectors, and often took up seasonal work in either sector, wherever work could be found. Shops and outdoor stalls replaced the traditional seasonal and weekly fairs; ordinary workers purchased their food from the butcher, baker, or brewer, to use Smith's apt characterization. Newcomers to London purchased manuals to instruct them on the protocols of shopping, to learn the rituals of cultivating a rapport with one's purveyors and the art of price negotiations over time.[18]

Merchants contributed to the overall welfare of society by detecting and servicing unmet needs. For example, in the case of a city with "fifty workmen in silk and linen, and a thousand customers; . . . these two ranks of men, so necessary to each other, can never rightly meet, till one man erects a shop, to which all the workmen and all the customers repair" (E-In, 300). Hume also considered a province with dairy cattle and another with abundant corn. The merchant who "discovers" this demand and supplies both regions with what the other has to offer is deemed "a common benefactor" (E-In, 300). The gains from trade were undeniable.

As population grows and the merchant expands his trade, Hume continued, his operation becomes more sophisticated and specialized; he constantly "divides, subdivides, compounds, and mixes to a greater variety" (E-In, 300). Hume here was paying tribute to the rise of the middleman and wholesale markets.[19] The cattle market, for example, was already specialized at each node in the product chain: breeders, graziers, drovers, stockers, and butchers at the wholesale and retail levels. Because middlemen made a living, often a prosperous one, there was widespread suspicion that they profited from the long-reviled practices of forestalling, regrating, and engrossing and therefore forced consumers to pay higher prices.[20] Hume insisted that the opposite was the case: economies of scale and capital investments de facto lowered the final price, as various efficiencies were introduced. Hume contrasted the production of wine in Burgundy, where the capital stock cost little more than twenty shillings and the peasants remained trapped in poverty, with the capital-intensive production of beef in rural England. He described how the "grasiers are most at their ease of all those who cultivate the land. The reason is [that] . . . men must have profits proportionable to their expence and hazard" and thus must be "carefully managed, and by a method which gives not the full profit but in a course of several years" (E-Co, 266–67). Profits received for fattening cattle constituted just returns on capital investments that require foresight and risk taking. Moreover, as commerce developed and rivalries between merchants intensified, profits would fall, thus reducing prices even further.

The term *merchant* was often reserved for someone engaged in overseas trade, but Hume used the term capaciously, as anyone whose livelihood engaged market trade. As he observed in a letter to Turgot, "besides Merchants, properly speaking, I comprehend in this Class all Shop-Keepers and Master-Tradesmen of every Species" (HL, 2:94). Hume was well aware that to succeed in their endeavors, merchants had to possess an impressive array of skills to carry out the many aspects of their business: establish partnerships and corporations, seek out and negotiate with creditors and insurers, engage factors and workers to produce and acquire goods, outfit ships, hire crews, manage inventories, transport goods across the world, arrange for foreign buyers, negotiate sales, keep accounts, and utilize bills of exchange and foreign currencies.[21]

Thomas Mun, a prominent trader for the East India Company and a central voice in the debate on the commercial crisis of the 1620s, had recorded a long list of skills and expertise requisite for the successful merchant in his *England's Treasure by Forraign Trade* (1664). His book was widely read in the eighteenth century; Smith lectured on Mun to his students in Glasgow, for example, and references him in the *Wealth of Nations* (WN, 1:431). Although we do not know for certain whether Hume read Mun, the likelihood is high. First on Mun's list of merchant expertise were penmanship, arithmetic, and accounting. A merchant also had to know about measures and weights as well as the purities and specific grades of precious metals used in currencies around the globe. Each country and every port had specific customs, tolls, taxes, shipping rates, and insurance costs. Merchants might need to repair their ship and certainly provision it abroad, possibly hiring additional hands. They would need to know about foreign merchandise and keep track of suitable prices; they would need to attend to financial markets to settle their bills of exchange. It would help to speak other languages, understand the customs and laws of foreign regions, and perhaps serve as temporary ambassadors as a means to create advantages for their native country. Finally, Mun proposed that a merchant, to excel, ought to have studied Latin in his youth, presumably to present himself as a learned man, well-versed in the philosophical discourse of the day.

Mun did not see merchants as simple money-grubbers. Rather, he depicted them as honorable men and professionals with an impressive array of skills that enabled them to navigate a complex world full of risk and uncertainty. Mun wrote, "The Merchant in his Qualities, which in truth are such and so many, that I find no other Profession which leadeth into more worldly Knowledge."[22] In consistently promoting the diffusion of such "worldly knowledge," the merchants contributed to a new culture in which literacy and numeracy, as well as more specialized knowledge, would be valued and revered.

Joseph Addison, writing in the *Spectator* in 1711, the year of Hume's birth, underscored the extent to which merchants facilitate ties between distant regions and thereby transcend differences in national sentiments and religious beliefs.[23] The diverse array of nature's bounty around the globe motivated the need for trade and hence a mutual dependency on one another. International trade, Addison believed, would therefore reduce animosity and warfare and, as a result, there could not be any "more useful Members in a Commonwealth than Merchants."[24] Addison's cosmopolitanism prompted him to depict merchants as ambassadors of the trading world; "they negotiate Affairs, conclude Treaties, and maintain a good Correspondence between those wealthy Societies of Men that are divided from one another by Seas and Oceans."[25] This multicultural world was daily on display in the Royal Exchange of London. As Addison remarks after several visits:

> I have often been pleased to hear Disputes adjusted between an Inhabitant of *Japan* and an Alderman of *London*, or to see a Subject of the *Great Mogul* entering into a League with one of the *Czar of Muscovy*. I am infinitely delighted in mixing with these several Ministers of Commerce, as they are distinguished by their different Walks and different Languages: Sometimes I am justled among a Body of *Armenians*: Sometimes I am lost in a Crowd of *Jews*; and sometimes make one in a Groupe of *Dutch-men*. I am a *Dane*, *Swede*, or *French-man* at different times, or rather fancy my self . . . a Citizen of the World.[26]

Recall that Voltaire had similarly depicted the London stock market; not only was it a place of remarkable diversity and tolerance, but it also thrived on the fluidity of languages and a diverse array of religious denominations.

Another prominent writer of the early eighteenth century who praised merchants was Daniel Defoe. In his *Complete English Tradesman* (1726), Defoe outlines a list of mercantile skills similar to those enumerated by Mun but adds directives regarding the personal conduct of the successful merchant. Never underestimate, Defoe entreated, the importance of plain language, honest dealings, and mutual respect. While it might appear to be in the immediate interest of a merchant to undermine the reputation of a competitor, he should always keep in mind that his own reputation is as fickle and precarious. The tradesman ought therefore "in some degree to have the same care of his neighbour's [credit and reputation]." Given that a tradesman's reputation is "the life of his trade," a merchant who defames his rival and slanders his good name is tantamount to "a murderer in trade."[27] To make his point about the dangers of rumor and innuendo more forcefully, Defoe employed the imagery of a woman, Lady Credit. He exploited the double meaning of the term *commerce*—as sexual intercourse and trade—and advocated that a "tradesman's credit and a virgin's virtue ought to be equally sacred from the tongues of men."[28] Defoe's emphasis on propriety, honesty, and reputation suggests that notwithstanding the inherent competition among merchants, the community as a whole had come to forge a semblance of civility and respect for one another.

Hume also advanced the trope of the honorable merchant, building on Mun, Addison, and Defoe. He emphasized that it is the merchant who keeps the world together and sustains our lives in an age of urbanization. Of the merchant, Hume wrote in a pamphlet on the corn trade, "his Purpose, no doubt, is to acquire Profit: But how can he acquire it? By buying Corn where it is cheap, and selling where it is dear. Now can any thing be more useful than to make thus an equal Distribution of that Commodity, so essential to Life, and thereby enabling one Part of the Community to assist another."[29] By moving goods from one place to another, the merchant provides for everyone indiscriminately and ignites industry throughout the land. At the start of his second *Enquiry*, Hume described and praised the "humane, beneficent man, . . . [from whom] the hungry receive food, the naked cloathing, the ignorant and slothful skill and industry" (EPM, 9). Hume then concluded this passage by giving a name to such a man. It is the merchant, or manufacturer, whom he likens to a "minister of providence. . . . Can any thing stronger be said in praise of a profession, such as merchandize or manufacture, than to observe the advantages which it procures to society?" (EPM, 10). This paean echoes his sentiment, expressed in the *Political Discourses*, that the merchant is "one of the most useful races of men" (E-In, 300).

The sense in which a merchant might serve as a "minister of providence" segues readily to the spread of happiness. As much as Hume valued philosophical reflection, he put as much weight on actions or industry. According to Hume, pleasures result from three types of goods: "the internal satisfaction of our mind, the external advantages of our body, and the enjoyment of such possessions as we have acquir'd by our industry and good fortune" (T, 313). While Hume held the internal satisfaction of the mind in higher regard than the consumption of "worthless toys and gewgaws" (EPM, 82), the consumption of trivial goods nevertheless motivated people to develop a stronger work ethic, he believed. In contrast to most countries in Europe, where esteem for aristocratic birth and rank predominated, England had become a place "where riches are the chief idol" (EPM, 57), which in turn meant that English "arts, manufactures, commerce, [and] agriculture flourish," and a more republican type of government had taken hold (EPM, 57–58).

Although all forms of trade were advantageous, Hume argued that foreign trade is particularly beneficial as it brings different regions of the world together, exposing citizens to a greater array of consumer goods, for which they cultivate new tastes and desires. Foreign trade "rouses men from their indolence; and presenting the gayer and more opulent part of the nation with objects of luxury, which they never before dreamed of, raises in them a desire of a more splendid way of life than what their ancestors enjoyed" (E-Co, 264).

This new, more differentiated and sophisticated material culture played an indispensable role in galvanizing economic development: "Thus men become acquainted with the *pleasures* of luxury and the *profits* of commerce; and their *delicacy* and *industry*, being once awakened, carry them on to farther improvements, in every branch of domestic as well as foreign trade" (E-Co, 264). The cultivation of commerce induces more domestic production that also serves hitherto unmet demand: "Commerce increases industry, by conveying it readily from one member of the state to another, and allowing none of it to perish or become useless" (E-In, 301). The desires for new commodities are in principle insatiable, and "many [now have] the opportunity of receiving enjoyments, with which they would otherwise have been unacquainted" (E-Co, 256). Once awakened, this desire also unleashes a political force; those in trade and manufacturing become the center of power. "As the ambition of the sovereign must entrench on the luxury of individuals; so the luxury of individuals must diminish the force, and check the ambition of the sovereign" (E-Co, 257).

Hume had very little patience for philosophers such as François de Fénelon or Claude-Adrien Helvétius, who each condemned the consumption of luxuries as a source of moral and political decline.[30] Fénelon had argued in 1699 that luxury, a product of inequality, promotes corruption and prioritizes cities over the countryside, eventually leading to rural depopulation and a general moral decay.[31] Helvétius, with the fall of the Roman Empire in mind, argued that, "the epocha of the greatest luxury of a nation is generally the epocha preceding its fall and debasement."[32] Hume's position on luxury was more consonant with the views of Jean-François Melon, Voltaire, and Montesquieu, who had each, independently, argued that there was nothing inherently wrong with pleasure derived from consumption and who had thus emphasized the contingent standing of a luxury good.[33] Hume agreed that what counts as a vicious or virtuous indulgence cannot be fixed and depends on time and place (E-RA, 268).[34] For example, in the medieval period, a "dish of peas" for noblemen at Christmas cost the peasants their much-needed bread, but such vegetables had become affordable fare by the eighteenth century (E-RA, 279).

For Hume, the enjoyment of luxuries was a source of pleasure. Men value goods because they give pleasure, such as the "champagne and ortolans" at the baron's banquet (E-RA, 276). "To imagine," he wrote, "that the gratifying of any sense, or the indulging of any delicacy in meat, drink, or apparel, is of itself a vice, can never enter into a [reasonable] head" (E-RA, 268). Indeed, by his late thirties, the avuncular and overweight Hume was renowned for taking great delight in his consumption of oysters, mutton, and good claret.[35] Notwithstanding his own proclivities, however, Hume believed that the modern and refined patterns of consumption brought in their wake a sense of proportion and restraint. Excessive consumption of food or drink is "destructive," he asserted, as can be seen, for example, in Hume's condemnation of the vulgar eating habits of the Tartars who feasted on dead horses, or in his praise for the prevailing abhorrence for drunkenness as the most "odious" of vices (E-RA, 271–72). By contrast, the "refinements of cookery" in the European courts meant that gluttony was no longer countenanced (E-RA, 272). Luxuries must not impede other pursuits, such as acts of charity, friendship, or the cultivation of the mind. As Hume observed, "to be entirely occupied with the luxury of the table, for instance, without any relish for the pleasures of ambition, study, or conversation, is a mark of stupidity, and is incompatible with any vigour of temper or genius" (E-RA, 269). Such judgments, however, would be best left to individuals, Hume believed: it was better to dismantle sumptuary laws, permit the full importation of goods, and let each person forge his or her own pursuits or indulgences.

The benefits of luxury consumption, Hume argued, outweigh the disadvantages not only because they spark industry and trade but because they also instill esteem. As Mandeville had observed of London society, everyone dresses to a higher station. When it comes to clothing, "we all look above our selves, and, as fast as we can, strive to imitate those, that some way or other are superior to us."[36] To Hume, people's natural inclination is to sympathize with the rich and spurn the poor, and the sympathy one garners is enhanced the more one appears to be of high rank. Hume remarked that "when a poor man appears, the disagreeable images of want, penury, hard labour, dirty furniture, coarse or ragged cloaths, nauseous meat and distasteful liquor, immediately strike our fancy" (EPM, 57). Conversely, Hume noted, "when we approach a man who is, as we say, at his ease, we are presented with the pleasing ideas of plenty, satisfaction, cleanliness, warmth; a cheerful house, elegant furniture, ready service, and whatever is desirable in meat, drink, or apparel" (EPM, 57). These goods offer pleasure, but even more, they serve to fill the imagination with the sense by which one's otherwise imperfect life might be completed. We are thus doubly motivated to better our condition.

In agreement with Smith, Hume argued that wealth is sought by the middle and upper classes primarily because it engenders admiration and that this capacity to "beget esteem" in others is the "very nature or essence" of riches (EPM, 56).[37] As for the "vain man," he secures "the best that is any where to be found. His houses, equipage, furniture, cloaths, horses, hounds, excel all others. . . . His wine, if you'll believe him, has a finer flavour than any other; . . . [even] his fruits ripen earlier and to greater perfection" (T, 202).

Each facet of his estate, even its "expert servants" or clean air, constitutes "a new subject of pride and vanity" (T, 202). Furthermore, because money, whether paper notes or coins, can command these goods and services, its acquisition also becomes a source of pride (T, 203). In general, Hume argued, the pleasures that such acquisitions generate—namely, their "utility, beauty, or novelty"—is always accompanied by the passion of pride (T, 203).

In spite of Hume's enthusiastic support of luxury, he nevertheless voiced a note of caution about the unfettered pursuit of wealth. Wealth undoubtedly keeps the world together and serves as the anchor for people's obedience to the laws of the land, particularly the protection of property rights, and hence the system of justice. It also prompts people to build cities and roads and harbors and to engage in trade. But a wise person comes to see that wealth is not the trait that most deserves respect. He or she discerns that "the difference of fortune makes less difference in happiness than is vulgarly imagined; such a one does not measure out degrees of esteem according to the rent-rolls of his acquaintance" (EPM, 57). Riches may be a convenient way to establish rank, but for a wise person, "his internal sentiments are more regulated by the personal characters of men, than by the accidental and capricious favours of fortune" (EPM, 57). It is easy to supply the necessities for life, but to secure nonpecuniary goods such as friendship, good health, or equanimity is a far more satisfying outcome (EPM, 82). The paradox is that because wisdom is in short supply and acquired only after much "experience and philosophy," the knowledge that wisdom is of far greater worth can only be attained and appreciated if one has achieved a certain degree of wisdom (EPM, 57).

Although few people become wise enough to transcend vanity or greed, Hume believed that the world in which he lived had found its path forward insofar as most people would come to march in step with the middle rank. Merchants and manufacturers would be unlikely to overconsume precisely because the habits of industriousness and the acquisition of wealth rein in such tendencies. The desire to stockpile one's wealth induces frugal patterns of consumption and prudent investments, and hence the merchant becomes all the wealthier. He comes to dread the plight of bankruptcy and holds back in his expenditures. His frugality could become excessive and transform him into a miser. The pursuit of money for its own sake, unfettered greed, is more destructive of one's equanimity than lust or power. As Hume noted, "none of the most furious excesses of love and ambition are in any respect to be compared to the extremes of avarice" (E-Av, 571). But, if kept in moderation, and Hume believed the activities of those in the middle rank tended to be this way, the tempered pursuit of wealth achieves a perfect balance between the calmer passions and the enjoyment of luxuries. The alternative, Hume pointed out, would be "worthless prodigals," who waste "their fortune in wild debauches, thrusting themselves into every plentiful table, and every party of pleasure" (EPM, 50).

The Arts and Sciences

Although industry and commerce provide the foundation for economic growth and moral refinement, it is also imperative, Hume maintained, to cultivate the arts and sciences. To Hume, the *arts* included almost anything produced by artisans or artists and further encompassed anything with a design, such as a garden, building, or fountain. Hume listed tables and chairs, saddles and plows as "arts," in addition to "the finer arts" of "sculpture, painting, music, as well as poetry" (E-CL, 90). He emphasized that both types are the result of considerable skill and learning and are appreciated because of their aesthetic properties that accompany refined tastes. There can be as much pride in one's beautiful scritoire or garden as in the comprehension of a fine poem (T, 183). In his aesthetics, Hume stressed the importance of expert and informed judgment, conceding that "few are qualified to give judgment on any work of art" (E-ST, 241). Hume was good friends with a number of leading artists and writers and notably championed the great musicologist and critic of his time, his friend Charles Burney.[38]

The term *arts* thus included an appeal to knowledge as well as practice. It is telling that Hume normally referred to "the arts and sciences" as a single phrase. He wished to convey their overlap as much as their distinct identities. Hume, for example, looked favorably on the mechanical arts or the sense in which the science of anatomy might assist the painter. The term *sciences* in the early modern period denoted any specific field of knowledge, theoretical or applied. Hume's specific list includes history, chronology, geography, and politics as well as the traditional branches of natural philosophy—namely, astronomy, physics, and chemistry (EHU, 122).

The application of scientific and practical knowledge by farmers, artisans, and manufacturers had intensified during the seventeenth century and had become an integral feature of society by the time Hume wrote the *Political Discourses*.[39] Galileo had famously turned the spyglass into a telescope, but he also assisted in or inspired the construction of the first microscopes, thermometers, and barometers. By the mid-seventeenth century, enterprising savants might apprentice with established artisans, attend meetings of scientific societies such as the Royal Society or the Académie des Sciences, or join up with the groups of improvers organized by, for example, Samuel Hartlib or Théophraste Renaudot. These associations enabled them to absorb new methods for more systematic observation and measurement and to employ the many new instruments. Early modern science is replete with inventions and improvements of optical instruments, clocks, explosives, lamps, paper, glass, dyes, metals, and pottery. A cursory glance at the illustrations in the *Encyclopédie* of Diderot and d'Alembert indicates many sophisticated tools and machines used in shipbuilding, mining, minting, masonry, iron foundries, and textile manufacturing.[40] Large-scale production in factories was still, for the most part, a few decades away when Hume put pen to paper, but the rapid spread of artisanal ateliers characterized his age and paved the way to the industrial era that transformed Britain into the workshop of the world.[41]

Novel techniques in agriculture, manufacturing, and mining precipitated a broader transformation in eighteenth-century culture.[42] Efforts to standardize measurements became widespread, facilitating commerce as much as scientific inquiry.[43] Hume recognized the symbiotic development of multiple strands of knowledge: "The same age, which produces great philosophers and politicians, renowned generals and poets, usually abounds with skilful weavers, and ship-carpenters" (E-RA, 270). Hume continued:

> The spirit of the age affects all the arts; and the minds of men, being once roused from their lethargy, and put into a fermentation, turn themselves on all sides, and carry improvements into every art and science. Profound ignorance is totally banished, and men enjoy the privilege of rational creatures, to think as well as to act, to cultivate the pleasures of the mind as well as those of the body. (E-RA, 271)

Hume thus underscored the sense in which the new culture of inquiry and ingenuity penetrated every sphere of human knowledge, both practical and scientific.

Although the "spirit of the age" inspired many people to take up new improvements, there was still, for Hume, no logic of discovery. A breakthrough in science or manufacturing was to a large extent a random event, he thought, much as genius crops up unexpectedly at disparate times and places. It is much easier to provide an account of the rise and progress of commerce in any nation, than to account for the discoveries that in turn enhance human knowledge. Hume contended: "Avarice, or the desire of gain, is an universal passion, which operates at all times, in all places, and upon all persons: But curiosity, or the love of knowledge, has a very limited influence" on the relatively small group of people who are involved in breaking new ground in the arts and sciences (E-RP, 113). "What depends upon a few persons," Hume had argued, "is, in a great measure, to be ascribed to chance, or secret and unknown causes: What arises from a great number, may often be accounted for by determinate and known causes" (E-RP, 112). Hume concluded, "Chance, therefore, or secret and unknown causes, must have a great influence on the rise and progress of all the refined arts" (E-RP, 114).

Hume nevertheless recognized that there were certain circumstances that tended to promote advancements in knowledge. Without the security that well-defined property rights engender, few people would invest their time and energy into the development of new knowledge. As Hume succinctly declared, "from law arises security: From security curiosity: And from curiosity knowledge" (E-RP, 118). Friendly relations between nations, mediated by trade and diplomacy, also contribute to the formation and expansion of an inquisitive culture. International commerce was particularly important to the improvement of the mechanical arts. Although a nation may initially be content with importing goods from abroad, enterprising artisans and manufacturers will soon try to produce the commodities themselves. "Imitation soon diffuses all those arts," Hume noted, "while domestic manufactures emulate the foreign in their improvements, and work up every home commodity to the utmost perfection of which it is susceptible" (E-Co, 264). English manufacturing over the previous two hundred years owed much to the adoption of foreign inventions and improvements, particularly in textiles and ceramics. Hume thus concluded that "every improvement, which we have since made, has arisen from our imitation of foreigners; and we ought so far to esteem it happy, that they had previously made advances in arts and ingenuity" (E-JT, 328). Commercial nations, by virtue of foreign trade, are thus more likely to embody the kind of spirit that yields gradual, if not accelerating, improvements in knowledge, Hume believed.

While it is self-evident that advancements in the arts and sciences promote economic growth, Hume also noted that such advancements polish people's moral sentiments. For this purpose, he made a distinction between two personality types: people who exhibit a *"delicacy* of *passion"* and people who are characterized by their *"delicacy* of *taste."* People in the first category are extremely sensitive to fortune and accident, Hume explained, experiencing "lively joy upon every prosperous event, as well as a piercing grief, when they meet with misfortunes and adversity" (E-DT, 3–4). In Hume's view, such people are easygoing and pleasant, but also superficial, lacking deep and measured criteria for decision-making. Whatever moves their passions procures them happiness. They are easy to befriend, but since their friendships are not based on substance, these are quick to dissolve. Hume described how "favours and good offices easily engage their friendship; while the smallest injury provokes their resentment. Any honour or mark of distinction elevates them above measure; but they are as sensibly touched with contempt" (E-DT, 4). They are capable of strong emotional highs and lows, yet on average they tend to live rather unhappy lives because "great pleasures are much less frequent than great pains" (E-DT, 4). Additionally, because they are moved so strongly by their passions, they are likely to act without prudence and discretion, which frequently leads them to the type of conduct that has "irretrievable" consequences (E-DT, 4).

On the surface, people with a delicacy of passion did not readily appear dissimilar from those who exhibit a delicacy of taste, Hume found. Their respective dispositions produced the same "sensibility to beauty and deformity of every kind, as that does to prosperity and adversity, obligations and injuries" (E-DT, 4). They tended to be equally moved by a sublime poem and a beautiful painting, as well as deriving the same level of satisfaction from a polite conversation. "In short," Hume suggested, "delicacy of taste has the same effect as delicacy of passion: It enlarges the sphere both of our happiness and misery, and makes us sensible to pains as well as pleasures, which escape the rest of mankind" (E-DT, 5).

Yet, despite certain superficial commonalities, Hume concluded that it is far superior to be guided by a delicacy of taste. Indeed, he asserted, "delicacy of taste is as much to be desired and cultivated as delicacy of passion is to be lamented, and to be remedied, if possible" (E-DT, 5). The drawback of being at the mercy of the passions was that one maintains very little control over the accidents, good or bad, that spark or trigger reactions. Those enthralled by the passions are subject to the vagaries of fortune or luck, which cannot provide a solid foundation for sustained happiness. But when good taste is used to guide decisions, the likelihood of sustained happiness is much improved. Since every "wise man" seeks to "place his happiness on such objects chiefly as depend upon himself," one is better off developing a sense of taste. After all, Hume noted, we are "pretty much masters [of] what books we shall read, what diversions we shall partake of, and what company we shall keep" (E-DT 5). Hume held in high regard such experiences as conversation, reading, and socializing, because they produce an "internal satisfaction of our mind" (T, 313).

The command of one's passions and the cultivation of a more refined standard of taste require the simultaneous development of what Hume called a "delicacy of sentiment" (E-DT, 5). Once a person develops this delicacy of sentiment, Hume asserted, "he is more happy by what pleases his taste, than by what gratifies his appetites, and receives more enjoyment from a poem or a piece of reasoning than the most expensive luxury can afford" (E-DT, 5). In this process of refinement, people gradually change their preferences and begin to appreciate aesthetic pleasures, thus reducing their preoccupation with material goods. But how does this delicacy of taste develop? How is it possible to acquire the requisite temper and disposition to maintain good taste?

The answer Hume offered is that the "higher and more refined" tastes can best be cultivated by an active pursuit of the arts (E-DT, 6). The liberal arts, in particular, provide the best training of the mind because they strengthen people's judgment of character and genius and guide people in their quest to "form juster notions of life" (E-DT, 6). Hume explained that a serious study of the liberal arts "improves our sensibility for all the tender and agreeable passions; at the same time that it renders the mind incapable of the rougher and more boisterous emotions" (E-DT, 6). "Many things," Hume posited, "which please or afflict others, will appear to us too frivolous to engage our attention: And we shall lose by degrees that sensibility and delicacy of passion, which is so incommodious" (E-DT, 6). By indulging in the "finer arts," such as music or literature, people cultivate their calmer and more polished passions and internalize a standard for good taste. Hume continued:

> Nothing is so improving to the temper as the study of the beauties, either of poetry, eloquence, music, or painting. They give a certain elegance of sentiment to which the rest of mankind are strangers. The emotions which they excite are soft and tender. They draw off the mind from the hurry of business and interest; cherish reflection; dispose to tranquillity; and produce an agreeable melancholy, which, of all dispositions of the mind, is the best suited to love and friendship. (E-DT, 6–7)

With poetic flourish, Hume included a line from his favorite poet, Ovid: "A faithful study of the liberal arts humanizes character and permits it not to be cruel" (E-DT, 6n4).

Hume thus concluded that the chief benefit of studying philosophy, history, and literature "arises in an indirect manner, and proceeds more from its secret, insensible influence, than from its immediate application" (E-Sc, 170). This benefit is not unlike the benefits of industry as described by Hume. Recall that it is not the fruit of industry, but rather the work itself, that promotes moral refinement. No specific set of books will provide the remedy to a person who lacks proper virtue and honor, but through a dedicated study of philosophy and the liberal arts, the likelihood that a person might acquire the requisite disposition increases. To Hume, "it is certain, that a serious attention to the sciences and liberal arts softens and humanizes the temper, and cherishes those fine emotions, in which true virtue and honour consists." He also pointed out that "it rarely, very rarely happens, that a man of taste and learning is not, at least, an honest man, whatever frailties may attend him" (E-Sc, 170).

The Moral Refinement of the Middle Ranks

Hume assigned specific virtues to each of the three socioeconomic classes. Those in the lower class were most able to cultivate the virtues of "Patience, Resignation, Industry and Integrity," whereas the nobility were free to exercise the virtues of "Generosity, Humanity, Affability and Charity" (E-MSL, 546). Only those in the middle ranks, having acquired the most refined disposition and sentiments, and a suitable delicacy of taste, might enjoy the unique capacity to internalize the virtues of those both above and below their station, Hume asserted. Hence, among the middle class, he noted, "every moral Quality, which the human Soul is susceptible of, may have its Turn, and be called up to Action: And a Man may, after this Manner, be much more certain of his Progress in Virtue, than where his good Qualities lye dormant, and without Employment" (E-MSL, 546–47).

Hume offered numerous illustrations of how the middle ranks developed finer social virtues through their pursuit of industry, commerce, and the arts. First, he argued that people who are intellectually sophisticated tend to be, on average, more sociable. Once in possession of "a fund of conversation," they are no longer satisfied to live in solitude, away from their fellow citizens, like those in "ignorant and barbarous nations" (E-RA, 271). Instead, they take advantage of the opportunities for sociability created by a vibrant commercial culture and tend to rub shoulders with people from the far corners of the world and from all walks of life. Their commercial activities compel them toward conspicuous consumption, which in turn demands that they become connoisseurs of the latest fashion and advancements in the arts. Urbanization facilitated both the new sartorial culture and the new theatrical display of refinement. The middle ranks "flock into cities; love to receive and communicate knowledge; to show their wit or their breeding; their taste in conversation or living, in clothes or furniture" (E-RA, 271). This facilitates the exchange of idea and polishes people's conversations:

> Beside the improvements which [people] receive from knowledge and the liberal arts, it is impossible but they must feel an encrease of humanity, from the very habit of conversing together, and contributing to each other's pleasure and entertainment. (E-RA, 271)

That is, an effete culture combined with a developed commercial sociability tends to promote good manners and conviviality, the increase of "humanity" that completes the catena singled out in the title of this chapter.

Second, Hume argued, as the middle rank acquire by degrees more refined tastes, they are less likely to engage in overconsumption. The center of gravity of their customs and habits is such that they become far more likely to embrace the virtue of moderation. The higher pleasures in life — such as friendship, conversation, and study — become more appealing to them than engaging in an ever-escalating consumption of luxuries "because nothing is more destructive to true pleasure than such excesses" (E-RA, 271). Their more enduring "sense of honour and virtue," which tends to abound in "ages of knowledge and refinement," dampens their excessive pursuits of pleasure and avaricious love of money (E-RA, 276).[44]

As people become more refined, Hume argued, they shift from the pleasures of consumption and the body to the pleasures of the mind and the imagination.[45] At the close of the second *Enquiry*, Hume compared "the unbought satisfaction of conversation, society, study, even health and the common beauties of nature, but above all the peaceful reflection of one's own conduct," with "feverish, empty amusements of luxury and expense" (EPM, 82). There is, he declared, no comparison between these higher and lower pleasures. The first set are "really without price; both because they are below all price in their attainment, and above it in their enjoyment" (EPM, 82). The insertion of the adjective *unbought* makes clear that Hume wished to demarcate a realm that is not reducible to the marketplace. Not everything has a price; more important, it is those facets of life that are without price that matter most. Just as there is no need for property within the sphere of marriage — "what's mine is thine" — there are spheres of human activity and pleasure that cannot be measured in monetary terms. In a 1747 letter to his friend Lord Kames, Hume reflected that while he thoroughly enjoyed the luxuries he had encountered during his travels, should no further opportunities to indulge present themselves, he would "return very cheerfully to books, leisure, and solitude, in the country." He added that, "an elegant table has not spoilt my relish for sobriety; nor gaiety for study" (HL, 1:99–100). This quotation echoes his description of the refined man: "he lothes the sumptuous banquet, and prefers even the most abstracted study and speculation, as more agreeable and entertaining" (E-St, 152).

Hume's third proposition is that people in the middle ranks are more likely to develop deep and enduring friendships.[46] The capacity for friendship was a particularly important virtue to Hume. We know that he had reflected on

Aristotle's insight in the *Nicomachean Ethics* that one must strive to have the right number of friends, that one could have too many or too few (MEM, 518; E-PA, 447). Hume suggested that because those in the middle class encounter one another as equals, their friendships are not based on flattery, favors, or patronage. Instead, their equal status allowed them to form deep and harmonious bonds. Moreover, those who had developed a finely calibrated "delicacy of taste" shared a sophisticated sense of what pleases and amuses, thus increasing the probability of a deeper connection. While the aristocrats took pride in maintaining vast numbers of acquaintances and the lower sorts promiscuously mixed with anyone offering them a dram of hard liquor, or so Hume believed, those in the middle rank tended to be more discerning. They scrutinized people more carefully and settled on a smaller number of friends than those in the higher or lower stations. "One that has well digested his knowledge," Hume noted, "both of books and men, has little enjoyment but in the company of a few select companions. He feels too sensibly, how much all the rest of mankind fall short of the notions which he has entertained" (E-DT, 7).

A fourth claim by Hume is that those of the middle rank tend to forge a more stable polity. They are the staunchest protectors of both law and liberty. Hume stated emphatically that "laws, order, police, discipline; these can never be carried to any degree of perfection, before human reason has refined itself by exercise, and by an application to the more vulgar arts, at least, of commerce and manufacture" (E-RA, 273). In ignorant and unpolished ages, people are prone to "superstition, which throws the government off its bias [regular course], and disturbs men in the pursuit of their interest and happiness" (E-RA, 273). In modern commercial society, citizens conduct themselves with greater transparency and rationality; their actions are predictable and hence are more easily aligned with those who govern: "Knowledge in the arts of government naturally begets mildness and moderation, by instructing men in the advantages of humane maxims above rigour and severity, which drives subjects into rebellion" (E-RA, 273–74). As knowledge spreads, "the tempers of men are softened . . . [and their] humanity appears still more conspicuous" (E-RA, 274). As a result, the government could execute its authority with less cruelty, Hume contended.

Hume furthermore argued that military combat between commercial nations had become less barbaric and vicious. This contention did not, however, imply that people lost their martial valor in commercial nations. As such, Hume did not agree with republican theorists, including his fellow Scots Andrew Fletcher of Saltoun and Adam Ferguson, that commerce and luxury consumption diminish if not eradicate courage and honor.[47] Hume insisted that the soldiers in wealthier nations would be "undaunted and vigorous in defence of their country or their liberty" (E-RA, 274). If one looks to the "French and English, whose bravery is as uncontestable, as their love for the arts, and their assiduity in commerce," there is no reason to fear the diminution of the martial spirit (E-RA, 275).[48]

Industry and the refinement of the arts combined to add force to both body and mind, thus creating a population better equipped to defend their nation, Hume argued. While nations that Hume considered "ignorant and barbarous" (E-RA, 271) might cultivate bravery and brute strength in their warriors, refined and industrious nations abound with people who are more disciplined because of the work ethic. They therefore have a greater potential to learn all the complexities of modern warfare, whether sophisticated battlefield strategies or refined technologies of ballistics, navigation, or fortification. In nations lacking a habit of diligence and ingenuity, Hume asserted, their "labourers cannot encrease their skill and industry on a sudden," and "their soldiers must be as ignorant and unskilful as their farmers and manufacturers" (E-Co, 261). Although they may be courageous, "courage can neither have any duration, nor be of any use, when not accompanied with discipline and martial skill, which are seldom found among barbarous people" (E-RA, 274). Civilized combatants, by contrast, while not bred for the brutality of the battlefield or the man-of-war, nevertheless can put to good use their ability to read and to learn, and thus recognize the value of honor and service to king and country. As Hume noted:

> Anger, which is said to be the whetstone of courage, loses somewhat of its asperity, by politeness and refinement; a sense of honour, which is a stronger, more constant, and more governable principle, acquires fresh vigour by that elevation of genius which arises from knowledge and a good education. (E-RA, 274)

Finally, as part of the conclusion to the second *Enquiry*, Hume conjured up the ideal bourgeois subject of the future, whom he named Cleanthes. Hume described him as a man of "honour and humanity" from whom everyone could expect to encounter the most *"fair* and *kind* treatment" (EPM, 72). Not only was he virtuous, but he also enjoyed great professional success. He had assiduously studied law and already possessed great expertise in both "men and business." As if this were not enough, Cleanthes was also known as a jovial and entertaining figure. He kept the "gayest company" and was "the very life and soul" of any conversation, full of "wit and good manners" (EPM, 73). One person described Cleanthes in the following words: "So much gallantry without affectation; so much ingenious knowledge so genteelly delivered, I have never before observed in any one" (EPM, 73). Notwithstanding his "cheerful disposition," Cleanthes had developed a serene "countenance, and tranquility in his soul" (EPM, 73). The reason was that he had stoically endured "severe trials, misfortunes as well as dangers," conquering them with "his greatness of mind" (EPM, 73). Cleanthes is the "model of perfect virtue" (EPM, 73). He has none of the "monkish virtues," such as self-denial and solitude that are wisely "rejected by men of sense" (EPM, 73). These austere dispositions will "neither advance a man's fortune in the world, nor render him a more valuable member of society; neither qualify him for the entertainment of company, nor encrease his power of self-enjoyment" (EPM, 73). Cleanthes is virtuous precisely because he has adopted the habits and customs of commercial society, because his engagement with the world strikes the best possible balance between self-interest, moral sentiments, and reason.

In conclusion, Hume offered one of the most penetrating analyses of the mechanisms by which commercial societies channel human proclivities to promote wealth and virtue. He demonstrated that the prudent and industrious actions of those in the middle ranks strengthen the trends of sociability and political stability. The modern commercial age has a greater stock of trust and honesty, peace and order, or so Hume argued. Hume clearly valued material affluence and the sumptuous luxuries enjoyed by the bourgeoisie of his time, but of much greater significance was the claim that modern commerce in eighteenth century Europe spawned more refined and robust virtues than were found in prior eras.

Hume's "indissoluble chain" between industry, knowledge, and humanity captures elements of Montesquieu's principle of *doux commerce*. Insofar as the pursuit of commercial wealth forges refined social virtues, people engage more dispassionately, and a "gentle dominion over the breasts of men" ensues (EPM, 12). Commerce promotes not only industry and knowledge but also has the potential to foster the "happiness of mankind, the order of society, the harmony of families, [and] the mutual support of friends" (EPM, 12). It is this "mildness and moderation" that distinguishes "a civilized age from times of barbarity and ignorance" (E-RA, 273–74). In commercial societies, interests thus subdue the passions.

Mandeville had trumpeted the ideas that private vices become public virtues, that a strong self-interested pursuit of money or other gains could have unintended and beneficial consequences. These ideas were later incorporated into Adam Smith's concept of the "invisible hand," particularly as posited in his *Wealth of Nations* (WN, 1:456). Hume also had elements of the concept of unintended consequences in his account of the chain. He argued that there is a strong tendency for people freed from autocratic rule to organically form commercial societies and that the institutions therein incentivize people to engage in industry, commerce, and the arts and sciences. The impetus behind this process is self-interest — or more precisely, a desire to enjoy personal happiness — but one unintended consequence is that people become more orderly and predictable. While this argument falls considerably short of the Hayekian notion of spontaneous order, if only because Hume puts weight on power relations, a charitable reading of Hume positions him as a progenitor of Smith in the sense that public welfare is more effectively promoted indirectly by the pursuit of self-interest than by a direct or concerted action.[49]

Hume recognized that institutions take time to emerge and that they continue to evolve due to the emergent properties of individual and collective actions. In a moment of reflection and skepticism, Hume observed of his fellow Scots, "I doubt that our morals have not much improved since we began to think riches the sole thing worth regarding" (HL, 1:276). In his published work, Hume promoted the strong potential of commercial societies to continue on a progressive path for many generations to come. This is the sense in which Hume was an enthusiast for capitalism and the progress of humanity. Needless to say, some links in the chain might break. Indolence might become widespread or curiosity wane. Republics might dissolve as financial capital is exported or discredited. But there were so many tendencies that bolstered the path to improvement and, if only for this reason, there was much cause for optimism.

Hume found many indications of the upward trajectory in the moral sentiments and civility in the cities in which he lived — Edinburgh, London, and Paris — notwithstanding the evident scourge of poverty and disease among the lower classes. Suffering caused by the enclosure movement as well as England's engagement in the slave trade and the practice of slavery itself were additional reasons to proclaim that all was not perfect. Indeed, as Hume's essay on a utopia made clear, no country had yet established an ideal commonwealth (E-IPC). But Hume was clear that the means to shape a better society was a *philosophical* question, not a *political* one. For whatever may be the consequence of such a miraculous transformation of mankind, as would endow them with every species of virtue, and free them from every species of vice; this concerns not the magistrate" (E-RA, 280). The magistrate might be able to pit one vice against another, or find ways to speak directly to the interests of his citizens, but he could not legislate more ethical outcomes. The best course was an indirect one — namely, to foster industry, commerce, and the refinement of the arts and then let these pursuits work their magic silently and slowly on the habits and customs of the age.

CHAPTER 5

"Little Yellow or White Pieces"

Hume on Money and Banking

Over the course of his economic writings, David Hume identified a number of impediments to commercial progress that derived from martial ambitions, particularly the preoccupation among statesmen with stockpiling precious metals and issuing bonds in order to fund their imperial pursuits. He was particularly concerned about early modern European governments' frequent abuse of the monetary system, historically manifest as the devaluation or debasement of coins, or an overissuance of paper money. He hoped that if legislators gained a deeper understanding of the principles of money, they might be in a better position to serve the long-term interests of the nation. As a result, Hume devised his monetary theory with concrete policy recommendation in mind.

Hume was not the first to broach the central principles of the quantity theory of money, the specie-flow mechanism, or the multiplier effect triggered by an injection of money. But in many important respects, partly because his *Political Discourses* (1752) was so widely read and admired, Hume's name became synonymous with these reigning tenets of monetary theory. It could be argued that Hume put the capstone on a relatively intensive period of theorizing about money such that money was not restored to mainstream theory until the opening decades of the twentieth century, particularly with the work of Irving Fisher, Knut Wicksell, and John Maynard Keynes. It was not that no one wrote about money. Many did, notably Henry Thornton, David Ricardo, and William Stanley Jevons, but money was nonetheless relegated to the sidelines in the core texts of economics throughout the nineteenth century.

There are many challenges to interpreting Hume's treatment of money. Hume spread his ideas across a number of texts rather than collecting them into one coherent account. Hume offered some important passages on money in his *Treatise of Human Nature* (1739–40), in his second *Enquiry* (*An Enquiry concerning the Principles of Morals*, 1751), and in his *History of England* (1754–62). The primary analysis, however, is to be found in his *Political Discourses*, but there too, Hume's analysis is not confined to his essay entitled "Of Money." As Istvan Hont observed of Hume's monetary theory, "some of the most important arguments were cut up and fragmented among the essays."[1] These difficulties of interpreting Hume on money are compounded by his decision to publish his ideas in the short essay format made popular by Joseph Addison and Richard Steele's *Spectator*. The genre called for a "more easy Style & Manner" and valued wit and irony, which enhanced the reading experience but certainly did not make the interpretive process any easier.[2] It is particularly difficult to settle definitively Hume's position on banking and the issuance of paper currency more generally. There is reason to believe that he changed his mind in step with specific economic developments and actions of statesmen of his day. Indeed, Hume viewed it as a badge of honor for a philosopher to be willing to adjust and revise his ideas. He complained that this was a rare trait; all too often, he noted, "when a philosopher has once laid hold of a favourite principle, which perhaps accounts for many natural effects, he extends the same principle over the whole creation, and reduces to it every phænomenon, though by the most violent and absurd reasoning" (E-Sc, 159).

The Specie-Flow Mechanism

In Hume's mind, one of the most damaging policies of early modern states was to attract and hoard *specie*—gold and silver. While more bullion would in principle facilitate the conduct of war and diplomatic negotiations, the best way to strengthen the state, Hume argued, is to attract money indirectly by fostering domestic industry and commerce. As he asserted, it "is only the *public* which draws any advantage from the greater plenty of money; and that only in its wars and negociations with foreign states" (E-Mo, 281–82).[3]

England, like most other early modern European nations, lived in fear of a general scarcity of money.[4] Starting with the commercial crisis of the 1620s, leading thinkers such as Edward Misselden, Gerard Malynes, and Thomas Mun blamed the economic downturn on a dearth of circulating coin.[5] There simply was not enough money in circulation to carry out all desired transactions. To rectify this problem, a number of economic writers insisted that each nation should try to attract a quantity of money proportional to its level of economic activity and balance of trade. The aim should not be to accumulate as much money as possible; Spain a century before had amply demonstrated to the rest of the world the negative consequences of such pursuits.[6] There was thus an emerging recognition that each nation had its own unique optimal quantity of money. As William Petty declared, "Money is but the Fat of the Body-politick, whereof too much doth as often hinder its Agility, as too little makes it sick."[7]

Similar to Adam Smith, who would later lament that no complaint "is more common than that of a scarcity of money" (WN, 1:437), Hume insisted that trading nations should not fear that money would remain scarce for any considerable period. Nor should trading nations seek to amass more money than the level needed to circulate their commodities. He believed that there was an inexorable dynamic built into the very logic of the commercial world that creates a tendency for the world's gold and silver to gravitate toward the regions in which they are in greatest demand—that is, where economic activity is most abundant. For Hume, it was therefore a "groundless apprehension" to believe that it was possible for a nation to lose its money, even for a moment. Trade ensures that the requisite stock of gold and silver will flow to the nations that export more than they import. If the state focused its attention on industry and commerce, it did not have to be concerned about a shortage of money. "I should as soon dread," Hume wrote, "that all our springs and rivers should be exhausted, as that money should abandon a kingdom where there are people and industry" (E-BT, 309).

Hume is celebrated for discovering the so-called specie-flow mechanism, although he never coined the name. Thomas Mun, in *England's Treasure by Forraign Trade*, had already identified the core insight, but Hume significantly broadened and extended the analysis, offering a more sophisticated analytical framework. The argument for the specie-flow mechanism runs as follows: if a country amassed an excess of specie, as Spain did by the conquest of Mexico in the sixteenth century, then, ceteris paribus, its price level would rise, in accordance with the quantity theory of money. In turn, because domestic prices have become higher than before, citizens would prefer to import foreign goods sold at lower prices. But they would need to use specie to pay for those imports, and the money would thus flow out of the nation as quickly as it had come in. The result would be a return to the quantity of money commensurate with the actual or "real" level of economic production and trade. Hume drew an analogy between money and water: the specie washes up to shore, only to ebb away. At the global level, just as the oceans are always at sea level, so is the money: "All water, wherever it communicates, remains always at a level. . . . It is impossible to heap up money, more than any fluid, beyond its proper level" (E-BT, 312).

Hume thus identified a self-correcting mechanism grounded in the under-lying logic of trade and commerce that rectifies imbalances in the global distribution of bullion. If there is a glut or shortage of specie, then purchases of foreign goods will ensure that a balance is once again restored. If this mechanism does not transpire legally, then enterprising criminals will complete the process. It was this set of forces that took silver out of Spain in the sixteenth century, over the Pyrenees, where "all commodities could be sold in France for a tenth of the price" (E-BT, 312). This outflow of money transpired not-withstanding a law that imposed the death penalty on smugglers.[8]

Hume presented his version of the specie-flow mechanism in a series of thought experiments. In one of these, he made the radical assumption that four-fifths of the domestic money supply is eliminated overnight and then traced the consequences. He reasoned that the reduction in the money supply would immediately lower all prices and wages proportionately, and this would unleash a rapid increase in exports, which would result in an inflow of specie. "In how little time, therefore," he asked, "must this bring back the money which we had lost, and raise us to the level of all the neighbouring nations?" (E-BT, 311). The proper ratio is achieved, Hume concluded, when the nation loses "the advantage of the cheapness of labour and commodities; and the farther flowing in of money is stopped by our fulness and repletion" (E-BT, 311). Hume also carried out the analysis with the reverse process: a sudden in-crease in the domestic money supply, say, multiplied fivefold in a single night. All prices and wages would rise in proportion, making the nation's prices so high that "no neighbouring nations could afford to buy from us" (E-BT, 311). A rapid rise in imports would quickly drain the nation's coffers, and prices would fall until the money supply was restored to its previous level.

This chain of events would come about with an inexorable force. Con-sumers and producers across the land would respond promptly and predict-ably to price changes and bring about the chain of adjustments. The specie-flow mechanism overrides localized efforts by individuals, even those with regal power, to control the money supply. One might as well attempt to dam the oceans. The forces reside deep within human nature and garner strength from the actions of millions. There are always sufficient numbers of con-sumers to seek out the lower priced goods, whether domestic or foreign pro-duced, legally imported or smuggled, and there are always sufficient numbers of merchants to arbitrage price inequalities and thus bring prices in line with the effective demand. These economic forces operate with the same necessity as the forces posited in the natural sciences. As Hume pointed out, "We need not have recourse to a physical attraction, in order to explain the necessity of this operation. There is a moral attraction, arising from the interests and passions of men, which is full as potent and infallible" (E-BT, 313). Here again Hume elevates the nomothetic principles of the moral realm to those of the physical.

Hume employed the device of the thought experiment to isolate the mechanism at work and remove some of the impediments that would otherwise complicate the analysis. Insofar as his analysis is cast in a hypothetical world, it was intended to isolate a strong propensity for the global readjustment of gluts or shortfalls in specie. However, in the actual world, it would manifest itself only partially, due to a number of frictions—for example, the interference of foreign exchange ratios that are subject to the speculative activities of "money-jobbers" (E-Mo, 285). A number of modern scholars have criticized Hume for failing to recognize these frictions and incorporate them into the analysis.[9]

Paul Samuelson, most notably, argued that Hume grossly oversimplified the analysis.[10] One oversight was a failure to account for nontransportable goods, including most services; the mechanism depended critically on the fact that most disposable income was expended on commodities that were exportable. Another criticism was a neglect of the concept of demand elasticity as coupled with the interference of foreign exchange rates, a feature that came to be known as the Marshall-Lerner condition. Insofar as each good (corn or salt, for example) varies in terms of its elasticity of demand, a sudden inflation would unleash a heterogeneous pattern of adjustment in domestic consumption. The fact that foreign exchange ratios were also governed by speculation and independent market factors adds more complexity. It is far too simple to suppose that a sudden overnight inflation would be remedied by imports that would map, in either real or monetary terms, to the prior pattern of demand. Finally, Samuelson charged Hume with failing to discern the law of one price, and thus for failing to grasp that the lower price of a foreign good would immediately reduce the domestic price of the same good until they were equivalent.

For each of these charges, with a bit of charity, Hume could be exonerated. He recognized that services are part of each domestic economy and that the Netherlands thrived by exporting mercantile services (E-JT, 330). He also noted that there are nontransportable goods but argued that their prices would be connected through competition in the labor market to the prices of goods that are exported: "Even were there some Commodities of which no part is exported, the Price of Labour [wages] employ'd in them, cou'd not rise; for this high Price wou'd tempt so many hands to go into that Species of Industry as must immediately bring down the Prices" (HL, 2:94). Moreover, he understood the concept of demand elasticity and thus that at different manifest prices the quantity of an import would vary and yield different revenues (E-BT, 324–25).

Hume recognized the interference effects of "money-jobbers" and foreign exchange traders. He was also apprised of the importance of the devaluation of the currency based on shifting values between gold and silver and the consequences of this devaluation for foreign exchange rates. The English gold guinea, for example, that was created in 1663 and set at a value of twenty shillings, was revalued under Queen Anne to twenty-one shillings to accommodate the increasing value of gold relative to silver. Hume also recognized that coins are fungible. Moreover, there is an inherent equivalence between specie and paper bills that would not, in principle, impede the specie-flow mechanism. Hume considered the case when twelve million pounds of currency, from a total of thirty million, have been replaced with circulating paper notes. His view is that this makes no difference: "We are as careful to stuff the nation with this fine commodity of bank-bills and [ex]chequer-notes, as if we were afraid of being overburthened with the precious metals" (E-BT, 317). If the paper was removed, the trade balance is such that the nation would promptly attract the equivalent in specie until the nation was "full and saturate" (E-BT, 317). Foreign exchange markets were sufficiently responsive to accommodate paper substitutes and thus facilitate the flow of money and achieve a balance of trade.[11]

Filippo Cesarano has argued, in direct response to Samuelson, that Hume articulated a preliminary version of the law of one price.[12] The law was not explicitly posited, at least in English, until William Stanley Jevons, who named it the "law of indifference," but it was of critical importance to David Ricardo's theory of rent and thus a central proposition in classical economics by 1817.[13] In its simplest form, the law of indifference states that there cannot be two prices in a market for the same commodity. Strictly speaking, the law never holds, except trivially, and thus requires a number of qualifications. Hume was fully aware that the price of corn, for example, varied from region to region, and that wages in the American colonies were three times higher than British wages, so the law demanded that the boundaries of a market be stipulated. But what Hume brought to the analysis was the argument that via competition, the labor and capital markets would tend to induce uniform wages and profits and hence uniform final prices, particularly within a nation. Because a higher wage, as we saw in the earlier quotation, would tempt "hands to go into that Species of Industry," and because capital tends to migrate rapidly to sectors with a higher profit, these shifts would engender uniformity and thus mean that the cost of production for a given good was governed by forces that went beyond any specific sector. Prices would thus tend to be similar if not identical for the same good in markets across a given region, at least one in which laborers were willing to uproot in search of higher wages.

Hume makes plain that, while prices fluctuate because of supply and demand, the core or long-standing price is governed by the costs of production, the return to labor above all and to capital secondarily. Anne-Robert-Jacques Turgot, in a letter to Hume, distinguished between the "fundamental price" that correlates with the cost of production, especially the wages of the artisan, and the "current price" established by market conditions, "supply and demand."[14] Adam Smith would later posit a theory of price that distinguished between the "natural price" and the "market price" and, for the former, covered the returns to three factors of production: labor, capital, and land (WN, 1:74–77). But Hume made no acknowledgment of a rental payment that a producer might make, nor did he mention the cost of land or natural resources in the formation of a price. We know from his negative reaction to Smith, upon reading the *Wealth of Nations*, that Hume subscribed to a two-factor theory. "I cannot think," he wrote, "that the Rent of Farms makes any part of the Price of the Produce" (HL, 2:311).

Hume was clear that if either the wage rate or the profit rate fell in a nation, goods would become cheaper. He momentarily suggested that the two are inversely related—that a fall in the wage rate increases the profit rate and vice versa—but does not elevate this to a general rule (E-In, 302), as Ricardo would in his core text of 1817. But insofar as both the wage and profit rates depend on supply and demand conditions, and insofar as Hume grants a high degree of factor mobility, there is an emergent law of one price. Hume stated with great clarity: "The Tradesmen who work in Cloath, that is exported, cannot raise the Price of their Labour; because in that Case the Price of the Cloath wou'd become too dear to be sold in foreign Markets: Neither can the Tradesmen who work in Cloath for home Consumption raise their Prices; since there cannot be two Prices for the same Species of Labour. This extends to all Commodities of which there is any part exported, that is, to *almost every Commodity*" (HL, 2:94, emphasis added). This explanation makes clear that the price is governed by the cost of labor, the prevailing wage, and that "since there cannot be two Prices for the same Species of Labour," there is a strong tendency for the same cloth to command the same market price. Hume noted that wages tend to be sticky: "By what contrivance can he [the weaver] raise the price of his labour? The manufacturer who employs him, will not give him more: Neither can he, because the merchant, who exports the cloth, cannot raise its price, being limited by the price which it yields in foreign markets" (E-Ta, 347). Hume inserted in the 1768 edition of the essay "Of Taxes" that "no Labour in any commodities, that are exported, can be very considerably raised in the price, without losing the foreign market" (E-Ta, 636). The domestic labor market is sufficiently competitive to induce a uniform wage for the same type of labor. Hume here was broaching the strong interconnectedness of domestic and foreign demand for manufactured products such as cloth.

The most important point to underscore in response to Samuelson, however, is that Hume presented the specie-flow mechanism as a thought experiment in a counterfactual world. By abstracting from the complexities of the situation, his analysis of the adjustment process succeeded in isolating a strong propensity for the global equilibration of specie, coating the world much as the oceans do. Hume highlighted the sense in which the adjustment was triggered by the differential between the quantity of money and the extent of economic activity. It is evident, Hume asserted, "that the same causes, which would correct these exorbitant inequalities, were they to happen *miraculously*, must prevent their happening in the common course of nature, and must for ever, in all neighbouring nations, preserve money *nearly* proportionable to the art and industry of each nation" (E-BT, 312, emphasis added). Hume went on to make a more fine-grained observation that encompasses regional variations as well: it is "impossible for money to lose its level, and either to rise or sink beyond the proportion of the labour and commodities which are in each province" (E-BT, 313). Moreover, as a nation expands its commerce, the price differential between its provinces will diminish (E-PC, 354–55).

Hume believed he had good empirical support that demonstrated the transnational reallocation of specie. His mechanism could explain why, for example, Scotland had attracted money from England after the trade barriers were removed by the Act of Union in 1707. Could anyone doubt, Hume asked, that this increase resulted from anything but "an encrease of its art and industry?" (E-BT, 314). Moreover, had China been located closer to Europe, its industrious people, low wages, and resulting low prices would have attracted the bulk of Europe's New World silver (E-BT, 313). As Hume explained in a letter to James Oswald, "a Chinese works for three-halfpence a day, and is very industrious. Were he as near us as France or Spain, every thing we use would be Chinese, till money and prices came to a level; that is, to such a level as is proportioned to the numbers of people, industry, and commodities of both countries" (HL, 1:144). But because of the vast distance and insularity of China, as well as the monopolistic practices of the East India Company, there was no reason to fear that China "would drain us of the overplus of our specie" (E-BT, 313). In 1750, there was little trade between Europe and China. Hence, the specie-flow mechanism, while always dictating the underlying logic of currency readjustment, could be thwarted by various impediments, as Hume fully recognized.

In an exchange with Oswald two years prior to the publication of the *Political Discourses*, Hume corrected Oswald's misunderstanding regarding the quantity of money in each state: "I never meant to say that money, in all countries which communicate [trade], must necessarily be on a level, but only on a level proportioned to their people, industry, and commodities" (HL, 1:142–43). This proportionality was also true, Hume recognized, for specific regions within a nation; capital cities and seaports would attract "more men, more industry, more commodities, and consequently more money" (E-BT, 315). London had considerably more money in circulation than did any other region in Britain. As a result of this exchange with Oswald, Hume realized that he had to clarify his views, since others less informed might also mistakenly believe that he has ascribed equal quantities of money to each country. He therefore added a footnote: "It must carefully be remarked, that throughout this discourse, wherever I speak of the level of money, I mean always its proportional level to the commodities, labour, industry, and skill, which is in the several states. And I assert, that where these advantages are double, triple, quadruple, to what they are in the neighbouring states, the money infallibly will also be double, triple, quadruple" (E-BT, 315n). In sum, the specie-flow mechanism highlights the tendency for money to be drawn toward the most prosperous regions of the world. As a result, efforts to reroute or otherwise meddle with the flow of money are without just cause and tend to be ineffective in the face of the stronger pull of trade.

Adam Smith's views were not far from Hume's on this topic. Smith similarly subscribed to the notion that a region's level of economic activity dictates the extent to which it attracts money: "The value of goods annually bought and sold in any country requires a certain quantity of money to circulate and distribute them to their proper consumers, and can give employment to no more. The channel of circulation necessarily draws to itself a sum sufficient to fill it, and never admits any more" (WN, 1:441). Extant student notes from his lectures at Glasgow, published as the *Lectures on Jurisprudence*, indicate that Smith thought highly of Hume's insights. One student documented Smith as positing that "Mr. Hume published some essays . . . [in which] he proves very ingeniously that money must always bear a certain proportion to the quantity of commodities in every country; . . . Thus money and goods will keep near about a certain level in every country. Mr. Hume's reasoning is exceedingly ingenious" (LJ, 507).[15]

The Quantity Theory of Money

The widespread inflation experienced across Europe during the sixteenth century inspired some of the greatest minds, including Nicholas Copernicus and Jean Bodin, to investigate its causes. They each independently broached a version of the *quantity theory of money*—that is, that prices tend to go up in response to an increase in the quantity of money. They did not put it quite this way, but what was well recognized by everyone was that the same unit coin could not purchase as much cloth or corn as it had once been able to command. As Hume noted in his essay "Of Money," "a crown in Harry VII.'s time served the same purpose as a pound does at present" (E-Mo, 281).[16] This means that in England from 1500 to 1750, prices had risen fourfold. Hume also recognized that where silver is abundant, prices tend to be considerably higher. In the *Early Memoranda*, he recorded that "what costs 3 pence at Paris is sold for half a crown in Mexico" (MEM, 504). The core principles of the quantity theory of money were well established by the time Hume wrote, but there were still essential features about the interrelationship of money, prices, and commercial activity that were subject to debate.

One such question was whether an increase in the quantity of money has the power to augment the nation's commerce and industry. Some of the first theorists of credit money, later known as the Hartlib Circle, argued that an expansion in the amount of money in circulation has the power to vitalize commerce.[17] That is, writers such as William Potter, Cheney Culpeper, and Henry Robinson insisted that a properly managed paper currency, which they referred to as a "Token or Ticket," would enable people to carry out more transactions and thus augment the formation of wealth.[18] The campaign to establish a widely circulating credit currency eventually resulted in the founding of the Bank of England in 1694. The bank was chartered by the government, was capitalized by private financiers, and served as a source of funds for the Crown, issuing something akin to high-powered money. Through the circulation of its banknotes, albeit in large denominations available only to the wealthy, it alleviated the immense strain on the beleaguered metallic currency and, according to its proponents, facilitated further economic growth.

With the essay "Of Money," Hume entered the debate about the efficacy of money to generate additional output. With the help of the specie-flow mechanism, Hume had demonstrated that an increase in the quantity of money results in a temporary increase in prices and thus has no long-term effects on employment and trade. However, this mechanism only held true in the context of a thought experiment. In the actual world, an increase in the money supply might prove to be less neutral in its effects. Examining the historical record, Hume found that money and prices did not always move up and down in exactly the same proportion. In the prior 250 years, prices had increased three to four times while the amount of money in circulation had increased by significantly more than a factor of four (E-Mo, 292). The fact that prices had not increased at the same rate as the money supply could only be attributed to an increase in economic activity and output. Indeed, it seemed to Hume that an inflow of money might even have ignited some of that additional economic activity. He noted in a 1750 letter to Oswald, "I agree with you, that the increase of money, if not too sudden, naturally increases people and industry, and by that means may retain itself" (HL 1:143).[19]

The historical record indicated to Hume that, since the influx of gold and silver from the Americas began, industry had increased in "all the nations of Europe, except in the possessors of those mines" (E-Mo, 286). Spain and Portugal had acquired precious metals through conquest and mining, but then failed for the most part to achieve stable economic growth. The rest of the European nations, on the contrary, lacking access to the American mines and therefore only able to attract money through trade, experienced a boost to their economies as the foreign silver entered their borders. Hume described how in every such kingdom, "in which money begins to flow in greater abundance than formerly, every thing takes a new face: labour and industry gain life; the merchant becomes more enterprising, the manufacturer more diligent and skilful, and even the farmer follows his plough with greater alacrity and attention" (E-Mo, 286). To Hume, thriving nations that experienced a favorable balance of trade received an additional surge of growth due to the inflow of money. The same pattern, but in reverse, held for a nation in decline: as it lost its money due to its failing commerce and industry, the outflow of money exacerbated its economic decline. In both cases, the high wages of the thriving nation or the low wages of the declining one would serve to dampen the effect in accordance with the specie-flow mechanism. These observations raise a couple of key questions: Are there circumstances in which an increase in the quantity of money might override the negative effects that higher wages and prices have on the nation's international competitiveness? And, if so, is it possible for the government to manage judiciously the nation's money supply in a way that takes advantage of this pattern?

An Inflow of Money from Exports

To grasp Hume's argument about the compensating benefits of an inflow of money from trade, it is important to look carefully at several steps in the process: first, stipulate the channels by which the new money enters circulation; second, trace the effects of the new money on production and distribution; and third, ascertain the changes to wages and prices. It turns out, Hume noted, that a considerable time elapses before the "money circulates through the whole state, and makes its effect be felt on all ranks of people" (E-Mo, 286). He described that at first, "no alteration is perceived; by degrees the price rises, first of one commodity, then of another; till the whole at last reaches a just proportion with the new quantity of specie which is in the kingdom" (E-Mo, 286). Even though Hume believed that prices are relatively flexible, he recognized that the adjustment was not instantaneous. This account, therefore, differs markedly from his thought experiments used to motivate the specie-flow mechanism.

In his analysis of an inflow of money from trade, Hume had in mind a nation such as Britain, which had developed both its agrarian and manufacturing sectors and had a sophisticated system of monetized commerce. The various sectors of the economy were well integrated, and there were large numbers of shopkeepers and producers responding to fluctuations in inventories caused by a shift in aggregate demand. Hume often insisted that when a spirit of industriousness and ingenuity envelops a nation, it tends to spread into every sector of the economy. Inventions of new commodities and improvements in the production of existing commodities render the nation's tradable commodities more competitive abroad and thus lead to more exports. Hume noted: "The encrease of domestic industry lays the foundation of foreign commerce. Where a great number of commodities are raised and perfected for the home-market, there will always be found some which can be exported with advantage" (E-JT, 329). In a well-developed commercial society, merchants leave no opportunities for gain unexploited: "A variety of fine manufactures, with vigilant enterprising merchants, will soon draw money to a state, if it be any where to be found in the world" (E-In, 303). To further simplify this account, Hume initially ignored banking and international bills of exchange and focused exclusively on the flow of specie between countries. Credit instruments, as we will see, are examined after the core principles are clarified.

When additional money enters through trade, Hume explained, "it is not at first dispersed into many hands; but is confined to the coffers of a few persons, who immediately seek to employ it to advantage" (E-Mo, 286). The exporting manufacturers and merchants who receive the money will seek to invest it as soon as possible in order to further expand their production. This investment ensures that the money enters circulation through the hands of people who are dedicated to using their capital, ingenuity, and skills to first and foremost enrich themselves. Hume recognized that this scenario deviates from the specie-flow account, for which there are no principal agents or special beneficiaries. Normally there would be inflation, "if we consider only the influence which a greater abundance of coin has in the kingdom itself, by heightening the price of commodities" and reducing exports, since the "great plenty of money" has raised "the price of every kind of labour" (E-Mo, 286). But if the additional money is channeled effectively, there will be an increase in output before prices and wages fully adjust.

Hume described the sequence of events that follows an inflow of money from Cádiz, the coastal city that had replaced Seville as the entry port for Spanish galleons in the late seventeenth century, when the Guadalquivir River became difficult to navigate. The passage that commences with the arrival of specie from Spain—which we will call the *stimulus account*—has sparked much scholarly debate.[20] There is much at stake, since it appears to conflict with the specie-flow mechanism. While Hume maintains that some monetary phenomena are "easily accounted for," in the case of the stimulus account, Hume has put his finger on a more puzzling phenomenon and admits that it "is not easily to be accounted for" (E-Mo, 288, 286). How, in fact, can money in and of itself result in a genuine increase in output within a nation? If money is simply a system of representation, how does it penetrate into the realm of economic production? Hume unfolds a detailed account of the various steps by which money triggers additional economic activity. We will consider two different interpretations.

One, which Carl Wennerlind favors, emphasizes that the influx of money is the result of an export of manufactured goods, such as cloth.[21] The exported cloth found customers abroad because previous improvements in technique or technology had lowered the cost of production and thus allowed the producers to undersell the foreign competition. To meet the increase in foreign demand, the manufacturers increase production. Once the revenues from abroad are received at home, the exporting manufacturers directly reinvest the funds in their operations. Hume identified these persons and described their immediate actions as follows:

> Here are a set of manufacturers or merchants, we shall suppose, who have received returns of gold and silver for goods which they sent to Cadiz. They are thereby enabled to employ more workmen than for-

merly, who never dream of demanding higher wages, but are glad of employment from such good paymasters. (E-Mo, 286–87)

The manufacturers who receive the Spanish specie increase their demand for labor, which leads them to hire more workers. Wages stay the same at first, but as the manufacturer continues to export more goods and hire more workers, wages are soon bid up.

If workmen become scarce, the manufacturer gives higher wages, but at first requires an encrease of labour; and this is willingly submitted to by the artisan, who can now eat and drink better, to compensate his additional toil and fatigue. He carries his money to market, where he finds every thing at the same price as formerly, but returns with greater quantity and of better kinds, for the use of his family. (E-Mo, 287)

Workers are now paid more, but they must, in exchange, continue to produce at the new higher rate. Because wages and prices are still unchanged in the rest of the economy, the workers in the export sector, who are now receiving higher wages, enjoy an increase in real income. The workers are thus compensated for the increase in output that led to the rise in exports that initiated the whole process.

After workers in the exporting sector begin to buy additional goods and services with their newfound wealth, the new money starts making its way through the economy. As the producers of the goods purchased by the newly enriched workers see their inventories fall, they realize that there is now greater demand for their commodities and thus intensify their efforts. There is no indication that Hume believed that an increase in demand of this magnitude had the capacity to spark an improvement in knowledge, techniques, or technology, so the added production had to come from an intensification of industry—by producers working either harder or longer.[22] Hume describes the adjustment as follows:

The farmer and gardener, finding, that all their commodities are taken off, apply themselves with alacrity to the raising more; and at the same time can afford to take better and more cloths from their tradesmen, whose price is the same as formerly, and their industry only whetted by so much new gain. (E-Mo, 286–87)

Even though Hume does not explicitly note that the "farmer and the gardener" had hired hands and therefore that they would soon employ additional workers to help meet the increased demand, it is sensible to assume that this is what he had in mind and therefore that industry, wages, and prices increase in sector after sector. Along the way, as all prices have yet to adjust fully, every additional worker experiencing an increase in their nominal pay enjoys an increase in real wealth. Eventually, however, as the additional money circulates fully throughout the economy, prices adjust and the multiplier process comes to an end.[23] Hume thus concluded the foregoing oft-quoted passage by noting that it "is easy to trace the money in its progress through the whole commonwealth; where we shall find, that it must first quicken the diligence of every individual, before it encrease the price of labour" (E-Mo, 287).

Another interpretation, favored by Margaret Schabas, is based on a different understanding of why output increases in response to an inflow of money from abroad.[24] The workers in manufacturing, such as weavers, increase their work effort because their wages are paid by "good paymasters" (E-Mo, 287). This means they are paid on time and with well-minted coins, rather than with hammered coins, wooden tokens, or paper IOUs, as was customary at the time. While demand for labor had increased, wages persisted unchanged for the moment. Not only did the workers not expect a raise—they "never dream of demanding higher wages" (E-Mo, 287)—but they were pleased to have the additional work.

Hume granted that eventually wages and prices will be bid up, and that will put an end to the stimulus account, but he first located the growth—and this is critical—in an interval that precedes the increase in wages. The key stimulus is money, but it has the psychological effect of inspiring weavers, who are otherwise passive and not enterprising, to "willingly submit" to the increased demand for labor. Moreover, it is the labor that creates the increased output. In this respect, Hume adhered to the core principle later enshrined by the classical economists as the labor theory of value: a nation is rendered more powerful by its labor force; "trade and industry are really nothing but a stock of labour" (E-Co, 262).

The next step makes clear that the manufacturer of cloth inspired the weavers to work more intensively, thereby unleashing "an encrease of labour . . . that is willingly submitted to by the artisan" (E-Mo, 287). There are several ways to interpret this passage. If the weavers are paid by the piece, they will see their income rise with the augmented hours, even if the payment per bolt of cloth remains unchanged. Alternatively, the manufacturer, wishing to expand output, contracts more labor, but only if it is more productive than before, weaving with greater intensity by the hour or the day. The weavers in Hume's account are inclined to work more attentively because they find that the new coins settle their debts with the local shops and hence they are able to bring home better-quality goods. As Hume put it, the weaver "can now eat and drink better, to compensate his additional toil and fatigue" (E-Mo, 287). It was common practice for workers to run up a tab with their local providers, of "paying on tick," as the expression went.[25] With good silver coins in his pocket, the weaver is able to entice the grocer or butcher into selling him a better selection of goods: "He carries his money to market, where he finds every thing at the same price as formerly, but returns with greater quantity and of better kinds, for the use of his family" (E-Mo, 287). In this sense, the weaver's standard of living has improved both quantitatively and qualitatively.

The final step, again prior to an increase in prices or wages, is that the depleted inventories in the shops signal to the producers in the agrarian sector that there is an increased demand for their goods. Hume described what happens next: "The farmer and gardener, finding, that all their commodities are taken off, apply themselves with alacrity to the raising more; and at the same time [they] can afford to take better and more cloths from their tradesmen, whose price is the same as formerly, and their industry only whetted by so much new gain" (E-Mo, 287). Note that the price of cloth has not increased, and hence the wage is still the same for cloth producers as before the influx of specie.

To finish off the stimulus account, Hume ascribed an intensification of labor in the agrarian sector that also results in more output per unit of labor. Recall that he observed that "even the farmer follows his plough with greater alacrity and attention" (E-Mo, 286). Note as well that the farmers are able to purchase "better and more cloths" at the same price. How is this possible? Again, they are able to use bona fide coins rather than request credit in the shops, and again, because the payment is with silver, the providers are willing to sell the better-quality cloth for "ready money" (E-BT, 310). The critical source of the growth lies in the fact that money "quicken[s] the diligence of every individual, before it increase the price of labour [the wage]" (E-Mo, 287). The new specie vitalizes the local region; "every thing takes a new face: labour and industry gain life" (E-Mo, 286).

It is important that Hume points to "every individual." He had noted that the merchant becomes more enterprising and the manufacturer more skilled, as well as the farmers and weavers. Everyone is eventually swept up by the influx of the shipment of money from Spain. Although he does not specify exactly how prices rise, presumably shopkeepers respond to the excess demand. The rise in wages ensues in order that the workers maintain their customary standard of living. The initial surge of intensified labor only settles back to the normal level of activity when it becomes clear that the temporary increase in the real wage has been eliminated by inflation. There is an element of deception incorporated into Hume's account whereby a localized injection of money can temporarily inspire people to behave differently.

In our separate interpretations, the increased circulation of money causes more industry wherever it flows. It is not a pure monetary phenomenon but one that has real effects on economic activity. If we think of the initial increase in output, stemming from a general improvement in industry, commerce, and the arts and sciences in the thriving nation, as a stone thrown into a pond, the ripple effect consists of money and industry spreading outward in concentric circles, becoming weaker and weaker and ultimately petering out entirely. While Hume invoked water analogies in his monetary theory, he also referred to money more generally as a fluid. He might have also incorporated analogies from the doctrine of subtle fluids ascendant at the time. Benjamin Franklin, in 1747, circulated the single most widely read paper in natural science that year, in which the subtle fluid of electricity displayed the properties of diffusion, capacity, conservation, and vitalization. There is evidence that Hume knew about that work, and this might partly explain why each and every one of those properties were invoked by Hume in his monetary theory.[26]

The inflow of money from trade that sparked additional economic activity in the affluent nation would generate increases in wages and prices, which had the detrimental effect of eroding the advantages enjoyed by the exporting merchants. "It is true," Hume reflected, that "the English feel some disadvantages in foreign trade by the high price of labour, which is in part the effect of the riches of their artisans, as well as of the plenty of money: But as foreign trade is not the most material circumstance, it is not to be put in competition with the happiness of so many millions" (E-Co, 265). Hume considered the international competitive disadvantage a small price to pay for the improvement in the overall standard of living. In Hume's words, "that provisions and labour should become dear by the encrease of trade and money, is, in many respects, an inconvenience; but an inconvenience that is unavoidable, and the effect of that public wealth and prosperity which are the end of all our wishes" (E-Mo, 284).

Moreover, there was no reason to believe that the higher wages enjoyed in advanced commercial nations would put an end to the nation's economic growth, at least not for some time. Rich countries would still be able to develop new and better techniques that could enhance productivity in agriculture, mining, shipping, and manufacturing and thus maintain a downward pressure on prices.[27] Only after a considerable time passes would the higher wages have an effect on the nation's competitiveness. Eventually, the sectors in which the improvement in the arts and sciences have the least effect would begin to feel the brunt of higher wages and prices and would fail to be internationally competitive, which in turn would open up opportunities for poorer countries to gain a foothold in the global economy. As we will discuss further in chapter 6, the wage and price increases in rich countries constitute an important feature of the global transfer of wealth, ensuring that "the growth of trade and riches" will never be "confined entirely to one people" (E-Mo, 283).

It was clearly more beneficial to have a thriving economy in which money flowed in rather than a contracting economy in which money flowed out, as Hume observed: "A nation, whose money decreases, is actually, at that time, weaker and more miserable than another nation, which possesses no more money, but is on the increasing hand" (E-Mo, 288). He describes this scenario as follows: "The workman has not the same employment from the manufacturer and merchant; though he pays the same price for every thing in the market. The farmer cannot dispose of his corn and cattle; though he must pay the same rent to his landlord. The poverty, and beggary, and sloth, which must ensue, are easily foreseen" (E-Mo, 288–89). There is a sense in which the downward spiral accelerates. In these circumstances, nations "cannot expect to keep their gold and silver: For these precious metals will hold proportion to the former advantage" (E-BT, 325).

Hume thus concluded that there were certain favorable effects of an inflow of money that offset the negative impact on the nation's competitiveness caused by the increase in wages and prices. These benefits, however, should not be exaggerated. Recall that it was never Hume's intention to show that an addition to the money supply was a major source of economic growth but rather to investigate whether there were *any* conditions under which an increase in the money supply yielded favorable effects. This acknowledgment that an inflow of money has certain benefits should not alter our impression of Hume's overall agenda in "Of Money," which was to convince the legislator to leave the money alone and focus instead on upholding justice, promoting improvements in manufacturing, and fostering population growth. Hume declared, "The greater number of people and their greater industry are serviceable in all cases; at home and abroad, in private, and in public. But the greater plenty of money, is very limited in its use, and may even sometimes be a loss to a nation in its commerce with foreigners" (E-Mo, 283). As he remarked, "It is of no manner of consequence, with regard to the domestic happiness of a state, whether money be in a greater or less quantity" (E-Mo, 288).

Some commentators have suggested that Hume's "good policy of the magistrate" included the gradual expansion of the money supply (E-Mo,

288). We, however, find it much more convincing, given Hume's stimulus account and the context in which this "good policy" was discussed, that Hume meant that the government should be content to protect the institutions enabling the growth of commerce, industry, trade, and population.[28] As Hume made clear in his 1750 letter to Oswald, "my intention in the Essay ["Of Money"] was both to remove people's errors, who are apt, from chimerical calculations, to imagine they are losing their specie, though they can show in no instance that either their people or industry diminish; and also to expose the absurdity of guarding money otherwise than by watching over the people and their industry, and preserving or increasing them" (HL, 1:144). As a general rule, "the only way of keeping or increasing money is, by keeping and increasing the people and industry" (HL, 1:143).

Hume used the term *magistrate* generically, to mean a government authority. In his essay on the "perfect commonwealth," he defined the magistrate as an elected representative, with no salary, who oversees the "officers of the revenue in each county" (E-IPC, 520). The primary function of the magistrate was to uphold the law and ensure an efficient collection of taxes. De facto, at least in eighteenth-century Britain, the magistrate had no power over the quantity of specie in circulation. The local magistrate might find ways to enhance the health and well-being of the populace, or foster commerce and inventiveness, but as Hume has demonstrated, it is best to leave the money alone to be determined by underlying factors. He recognized certain circumstances in which money might leave the nation for noneconomic reasons, such as when the government pays a foreign ally or pays interest on the part of the national debt owned by foreign investors. These two drains constituted "violent and forcible methods of carrying away money" that had no bearing on the real balance of trade (E-BT, 325). If wars and the national debt were minimized or eliminated, the specie drain would end and the money would find "its way back again, by a hundred canals" (E-BT, 325). As a general maxim, Hume concluded, "a government has great reason to preserve with care its people and its manufactures. Its money, it may safely trust to the course of human affairs, without fear or jealousy" (E-BT, 326).

Debasement and Hoarding

Hume investigated whether changes in the money supply induced by other means than exports might also have positive effects on economic activity. One long-standing method of expanding the money supply was to *debase* the coins—that is, to remint and reissue them with the same nominal value but with a lower silver content. By diluting the silver and thus stretching the same quantity of metal over a greater number of coins, a debasement in effect injects money into the domestic economy. Hume claimed that the new coins "would probably purchase every thing that could have been bought by the old; the prices of every thing would thereby be insensibly diminished; foreign trade enlivened; and domestic industry, by the circulation of a great number of pounds and shillings, would receive some encrease and encouragement" (E-Mo, 288n). He noted that the success of such a recoinage was based on the false belief that the old and new coins retained their equivalences to other coins. "In executing such a project, it would be better to make the new [silver] shilling pass for 24 halfpence [copper coins], in order to better preserve the illusion, and make it be taken for the same" (E-Mo, 288n). Hume thus pointed to the important insight in monetary theory that the value of a coin is primarily determined by its face value, by what passes for legal tender. Coins trade on "the illusion" that they are worth more than the metal of which they are composed.

Hume pointed to "the frequent operations of the French king on the money" (E-Mo, 287). The French Crown was notorious for using debasement as a fiscal strategy (E-PC, 638). In the fourteenth century, it issued eighty-five separate legal proclamations to alter the seigniorage or to debase the currency.[29] Under Louis XIV, particularly during the latter part of his reign, the currency was debased or devalued dozens of times. According to Charles de Ferrère Du Tot, Hume noted, from 1683 until 1739, the French livre had lost its metallic value by 40 percent: "Silver was then at 30 livres the mark, and is now at 50" (E-Mo, 287). Hume also posited a universal principle: "It was always found, that the augmenting of the numerary value did not produce a proportional rise of the prices, at least for some time" (E-Mo, 287). The temporal lag was confirmed in France in 1715: "In the last year of Louis XIV money was raised three-sevenths, but prices augmented only one[-seventh]" (E-Mo, 287). Insofar as the nominal price of corn in France had stayed the same for more than fifty years, Hume declared, the real price had declined considerably. As a result, everyone had more bread on the table. Hume voiced skepticism about the accuracy of the figures, but "the general observation, that the augmenting of the money in France does not at first proportionably augment the prices, is certainly just" (E-Mo, 287n).

Tudor England endured a series of debasements that became known as the Great Debasement. However, the monetary alteration still recollected at the time Hume wrote was the 1696 recoinage, during which the coins were reminted with more, rather than less, silver. Isaac Newton and John Locke had famously favored calling in the silver coins, which had been damaged by clipping and hammering to the point that their content was 50 percent of the nominal value.[30] Newton, then warden of the mint, oversaw a massive operation whereby the coins were reissued at the old full-bodied standard. This measure cost the mint approximately two million pounds of silver and reduced the quantity of coins in circulation, triggering a significant deflation and economic downturn. The setback was temporary, however, as England soon recovered and prospered during Queen Anne's reign.

Hume was critical of the recoinage of 1696. He claimed that it would have been preferable to remint the coins with a lower silver content and preserve the illusion of the shilling's equivalence in market transactions to twelve pence: "Were all our money, for instance, recoined, and a penny's worth of silver taken from every shilling, the new shilling would probably purchase every thing that could have been bought by the old" (E-Mo, 288n). This injection of about 8 percent more shillings into the domestic economy would have prompted industry and trade, Hume believed. Nevertheless, Hume did not advocate debasement as a regular measure. The problem with frequent or unjustified debasements is that they undermine confidence in the value of money and thus wreak havoc with commercial contracts.

Hoarding, or taking money out of circulation, also alters the money supply and, prima facie, could be viewed in a positive light. As Hume pointed out, hoarding lowers prices and wages and thus tends to generate a favorable balance of trade (E-BT, 317). The hoarded specie also provides a storehouse of wealth in case of public emergencies. After the crash of 1720, the French tended to hoard their silver in the form of tankards, tableware, and ornaments: "Great quantities of plate are used in private houses; and all the churches are full of it" (E-BT, 317). French wages and prices were thus lower, even in comparison to a country with half the quantity of specie (E-BT, 317). The lack of credit, however, had dire consequences for French manufacturing and trade. As Hume acknowledged, Britain and the Netherlands, seeking to bring the silver into circulation, imposed a tax on silver plate and promoted the use of porcelain (E-BT, 318). Hume was strongly committed to any methods that would promote the "universal diffusion and circulation" of money (E-Mo, 294).

Hume also reflected on the creation of public hoards, "the gathering of large sums into a public treasure, locking them up, and absolutely preventing their circulation" (E-BT, 320). To him, such hoards were "destructive" of the nation's "industry, morals, and numbers of its people" (E-BT, 321). The problem was that "there [does not] seem to be any necessary bounds set, by the nature of things, to this practice of hoarding" (E-BT, 320–21). A "cunning, rapacious, frugal, and almost absolute monarch" could go to extreme lengths, as was the case when Henry VII hoarded 2.7 million pounds over twenty years, roughly three-fourths of the entire domestic money supply

(E-BT, 321). While public hoards lower prices and wages and thus improve the nation's international competitiveness, they are often detrimental as they provide the means for unscrupulous statesmen to launch "dangerous and ill-concerted projects" (E-BT, 321). The devastating Peloponnesian War was purportedly prolonged by the availability of such a hoard in ancient Athens. Building up a substantial treasury also exposed a nation to foreign invasions. The Swiss canton of Berne, for example, had attracted approximately four times the amount of money needed given the size of its economy. While Hume noted no detrimental effects on the economy, he worried that Berne might "soon become a prey to some of its poorer, but more powerful neighbours" (E-BT, 321).

Monetization

As noted in the *Treatise*, money is a critical agent for the spread of sociability; only in commercial societies are people as "serviceable to each other, as by nature they are fitted to become" (T, 334).[31] To reinforce this point, Hume outlined the steps by which an undeveloped region, such as the Scottish Highlands, undergoes monetization. People in such areas were often self-sufficient, and as a result, money had yet to enter into most "contracts and sales" (E-Mo, 292).[32] Most exchanges were conducted in kind and ambition for economic betterment was lacking. As Hume observed: "fancy has confounded [people's] wants with those of nature, [and] men, content with the produce of their own fields, or with those rude improvements which they themselves can work upon them, have little occasion for exchange, at least for money" (E-Mo, 291). Hume described their "rustic" ways: "The wool of the farmer's own flock, spun in his own family, and wrought by a neighbouring weaver, who receives his payment in corn or wool, suffices for furniture and cloathing" (E-Mo, 291). Even though there may have been several skilled artisans in the region—for example, a carpenter, a blacksmith, a tailor—they often accepted payments in kind rather than in money. Adam Smith would later remark that because of the inadequate monetization, Scottish villagers commonly used iron nails as substitutes for money (WN, 1:38). Because of the dearth of money, even the rent was paid "in commodities raised by the farmer" (E-Mo, 291). The landlords were generally content to live in "rustic hospitality," consuming only that which they received in kind from their tenants (E-Mo, 291). On rare occasions, they could bring a small surplus to nearby towns and use the proceeds to procure a few luxuries.

Hume believed that this situation was not sustainable and therefore that monetization would eventually take hold. The desire for more refined pleasures would prompt the transition away from simple exchange: "The tradesmen will not be paid in corn; because they want something more than barely to eat" (E-Mo, 291). The ambit of trade starts to exceed the parish, and the landlord moves to the capital or a foreign country and "demands his rent in gold and silver, which can easily be transported by him" (E-Mo, 291). As markets spread and diversify, "great undertakers [entrepreneurs], and manufacturers, and merchants, arise in every commodity; and these can conveniently deal in nothing but in specie" (E-Mo, 291). As the people depart from their rustic simplicity, "coin enters into many more contracts, and by that means is much more employed than in the former" (E-Mo, 291). The increased use of money stimulates the division of labor and the production of new types of commodities. Soon, Hume predicted, there will be "more exchange and commerce of all kinds, and more money [will enter] into that exchange" (E-Mo, 291). Hume thus anticipated the powerful claim that the division of labor is a function of the size of the market.

Hume insisted that money had to be thoroughly diffused into every corner of the nation to realize its full benefit to society. As Francis Bacon quipped, "money is like muck, not good unless it be spread."[33] Merchants served as the primary agents in this process, creating new channels for the diffusion of money by discovering unmet needs between neighboring provinces (E-In, 300). As money spreads, Hume explained, "industry and refinements of all kinds incorporate [money] with the whole state, however small its quantity may be: They digest it into every vein, so to speak; and make it enter into every transaction and contract. No hand is entirely empty of it" (E-Mo, 294). The key to the thorough monetization of a region is not necessarily a greater quantity of money. A nation with a limited supply of specie could simply "mix the gold or silver with a baser metal" (E-Mo, 290). Poor countries should thus not blame their poverty on a lack of money. Instead, Hume insists, the ill effects "supposed to flow from scarcity of money, really arises from the manners and customs of the people" (E-Mo, 290).

Another benefit of monetization is that it facilitates the government's collection of tax revenues. As Hume noted, when "men live in the ancient simple manner, and supply all their necessaries from domestic industry or from the neighbourhood, the sovereign can levy no taxes in money from a considerable part of his subjects" (E-Mo, 293). Cities like Edinburgh and Glasgow could not augment the Crown's coffers as much as "the whole state could, did gold and silver circulate throughout the whole [nation]" (E-Mo, 293). In such circumstances, the government had "little force even at home; and cannot maintain fleets and armies to the same extent, as if every part of it abounded in gold and silver" (E-Mo, 289). The government also benefited from the overall reduction in the price level generated by the "universal diffusion and circulation" of money. As such, the sovereign enjoys "a double advantage: He may draw money by his taxes from every part of the state; and what he receives, goes farther in every purchase and payment" (E-Mo, 294).

The appeal to the "double advantage" was surely meant to catch the eye of the king's ministers and prompt reforms. But there were no obvious expedients to achieve this end. There was no precedent for the state to facilitate the diffusion of money in peripheral regions still inclined to use barter transactions. "It is the simple manner of living which here hurts the public," Hume observed, "by confining the gold and silver to few hands" (E-Mo, 293). The best policy, in keeping with Hume's overarching liberalism, is to leave the money alone, allow it to flow freely and trust that the desires for luxuries and a higher standard of living will promote commercialization. The state might enact measures to facilitate certain industries, as Argyll did in protecting the linen industry and promoting banking. But the important principle for political leaders to grasp is that a nation is not weak "merely because it wants money. It appears, that the want of money can never injure any state within itself: For men and commodities are the real strength of any community" (E-Mo, 293). Hume thus established the principle that "the absolute quantity of the precious metals is a matter of great indifference. There are only two circumstances of any importance, namely, their gradual encrease, and their thorough concoction and circulation through the state" (E-Mo, 294).

Paper Money

The bulk of Hume's analysis in "Of Money" was focused on the circulation and diffusion of specie, rather than paper money. Considering the drawbacks of an increase in the quantity of money, it seemed unlikely that it would be in the nation's interest to multiply the money supply by issuing paper money, a form of money plagued by its own intrinsic inconveniences. Hume wrote, "There *appears* no reason for encreasing that inconvenience by a counterfeit money [paper bills], which foreigners will not accept of in any payment, and which any great disorder in the state will reduce to nothing" (E-Mo, 284, emphasis added). However, he added, "of this subject of paper credit we shall treat more largely hereafter" (E-Mo, 285). Hume circled back to this question and inquired as to whether an increase in the quantity of circulating paper money might also have some positive effects.

Paper money had become the dominant medium of exchange by 1752. Hume estimated that some 60 to 70 percent of transactions in Britain were conducted with paper bills. He also recognized that this was the medium that the government could most easily manipulate, issuing banknotes in the form of exchequer bills, annuities, and bonds. Although Hume underscored the fact that the materiality of money was of secondary concern, he acknowledged that paper money was often preferable to coin. In the late Middle Ages, European merchants initiated the practice of bills of exchange to avoid having to transport bullion across the open seas. The same reasons of safety and cost governed the use of paper notes within a nation. "It is true," he noted, "many people in every rich state, who having large sums of money, would prefer paper with good security; as being of more easy transport and more safe custody" (E-Mo, 284). While counterfeiting always posed a risk, it was outweighed by the greater risk of theft by pirates, highwaymen, or pickpockets.

Hume clearly recognized that paper money functioned perfectly well in advanced commercial societies, but he carefully pointed out that only certain types of paper money were desirable. One such possibility was to establish a public bank that issued paper notes fully backed by gold or silver reserves. This system would resemble the Bank of Amsterdam, which issued notes only on the security of 100 percent bullion reserves (E-Mo, 284). It thus issued *paper* money, but it did not create *credit* money. Hume offered a similar view in a letter to Lord Elibank: "Banks are convenient by the safe Custody & quick Conveyance of Money; but as to the Multiplication of Money, I question whether it be any Advantage either to an industrious or idle Country."[34] Since this bank would not alter the quantity of money in circulation but only its form, it did not warrant further consideration by Hume.

The most common method in the eighteenth century, whereby the government artificially increased the amount of money in the nation beyond the natural level dictated by its balance of trade, was by instituting a system of "banks, funds [government bonds], and paper-credit" (E-BT, 316). Hume described how these paper bills, which had been embraced by the English population during the previous fifty years, "render paper equivalent to money, circulate it throughout the whole state, make it supply the place of gold and silver, raise proportionably the price of labour and commodities, and by that means either banish a great part of those precious metals, or prevent their farther encrease" (E-BT, 316). He illustrated the effects of an introduction of paper bills by referring to an unnamed nation whose industry, commerce, and arts had attracted a stock of thirty million pounds. If this nation did not issue any paper credit, the entire money supply would be comprised of "real cash." But by introducing paper notes, "which circulate in the kingdom as money," the quantity of gold and silver would be reduced proportionally. Issue twelve million pounds in paper money, Hume speculated, and the same sum in specie would soon depart from the nation. Here, there is no mention of the possibility of a multiplier effect providing an extra spark to industry. Nothing, therefore, could be more shortsighted than to expand the money supply artificially by issuing paper money, as it imposed all the costs of an expansion of money without any of the benefits.

Hume thus concluded, at least tentatively, that an expansion of state-issued paper money was primarily negative: "We feel, by its means, all the ill effects arising from a great abundance of money, without reaping any of the advantages" (E-BT, 317).[35] However, he added a footnote to this claim, which further complicates the matter: "We observed in Essay III. ["Of Money"] that money, when encreasing, gives encouragement to industry, during the interval between the increase of money and rise of the prices. *A good effect of this nature may follow too from paper-credit*" (E-BT, 317n, emphasis added). Although he did not specify the exact process whereby the additional paper notes stimulated economic activity, we can only assume that he had in mind an account similar to the one with money flowing in from Cádiz. As some people receive additional money, they spend or invest, thus generating an employment effect, a wealth effect, and an increase in wages and prices. This seems to open up the possibility that the government could use paper money to stimulate the economy. Yet, in the same footnote, Hume cautioned, "but it is dangerous to precipitate matters, at the risk of losing all by the failing of that credit, as must happen upon any violent shock in public affairs" (E-BT, 317n). Hence, in principle, a government-issued paper currency could stimulate economic activity, but because the risks associated with this type of multiplication of the money supply, Hume voiced serious reservations. His position on state-issued paper money was thus similar to his views on debasement.

Hume's opposition to the government issuing paper money was grounded in the fact that there was no anchor or explicit limitation on how much money could be issued. Hume did not believe that the government had sufficient integrity to resist the temptation to use its note-issuing power to pay for its expenditures. He feared the government would therefore generate unnecessary inflation, prompting an outflow of gold and silver, thus weakening the domestic currency. As he remarked in a 1769 letter to Abbé Morellet, "Money must always be made of some materials, which have intrinsic value, otherwise it would be multiplied without end, and would sink to nothing" (HL, 2:204). In other words, money had either to be composed of a scarce material or to be secured by it. If the government is empowered to issue money without limit, the likelihood of instability is high. As George Caffentzis has emphasized, "the problem with paper currency [was] not that it violates some deep ontological, representational relations with commodities. It simply arises from the greater possibilities of 'abuse' due to its ease in iteration."[36] For example, the irredeemable paper notes issued in colonial

America, which passed "in all payments, by convention," might have continued to circulate without a problem, "had it not been abused by the several assemblies, who issued paper without end, and thereby discrediting the currency" (HL, 2:204).

Government-issued bonds, which had become "a kind of money, and pass as readily at the current price as gold or silver" (E-PC, 353), exhibited a similar mix of benefits and drawbacks. The unique advantage of these bonds was that they "furnish merchants with a species of money, that is continually multiplying in their hands, and produces sure gain" (E-PC, 353). Because of these bonds, wealth need no longer lie idle. Having access to an asset that paid a guaranteed rate of return but that could also be used in payments enabled merchants to trade on smaller profits, which yielded numerous benefits to the merchants and the nation. "The small profit of the merchant," Hume proceeded to point out, "renders the commodity cheaper, causes a greater consumption, quickens the labour of the common people, and helps to spread arts and industry throughout the whole society" (E-PC, 353).[37] These benefits, however, had to be considered in relation to the dangers associated with the mounting national debt, a topic we explore in further detail in chapter 6.

There were several methods, as Hume recognized, by which the government could expand the money supply: debasement, paper notes, and government bonds.[38] He insisted that paper money and government bonds had the capacity to serve as good substitutes for coins and that each method of creating more money brought some benefits along with its drawbacks. This was, of course, also the case for an inflow of money from trade. However, there were significant differences between an inflow from trade and increases in the quantity of money engineered by other means. First, an inflow of money from trade was the result of commercial prosperity. Even if the actual inflow of money triggered an increase in prices that would in turn diminish the nation's competitiveness abroad, this was a small price to pay for all the benefits associated with commercial prosperity. Second, an inflow of money from abroad did not normally alter the composition of the nation's money supply. An increase in paper money, conversely, would tend to lead to a substitution of paper money for silver coins, which would not necessarily have any detrimental *economic* effects but would diminish the nation's geopolitical clout. Third, while an inflow of money from abroad was always gradual and limited in quantity, publicly issued paper money could be multiplied endlessly. The inflow of specie from abroad and the ability of the nation to retain it were dictated by the balance of trade in manufactured and agrarian commodities. By contrast, because public paper money was not always backed by tangible assets, public officials might be tempted to finance the government's operations by printing additional money. Once they opted for this—and sooner or later they probably would—the stability of the nation's commercial architecture would be put in jeopardy. Finally, Hume noted that a temporary excess supply of specie in the nation would be readily corrected by global trade, whereas an unwarranted expansion of paper money did significant damage. He wrote in the 1768 edition of the *Political Discourses*:

> We may also remark, that this increase of prices, derived from paper-credit, has a more durable and more dangerous influence than when it arises from a great increase of gold and silver: Where an accidental overflow of money raises the price of labour and commodities, the evil remedies itself in a little time: The money soon flows out into all the neighbouring nations: The prices fall to a level: And industry may be continued as before; a relief, which cannot be expected, where the circulating specie consists chiefly of paper, and has no intrinsic value. (E-PC, 637)

Although paper money might continue to expand and circulate widely, the negative effects of an expansion of such money, Hume argued, outweighed the benefits.

Hume's views on paper money continued to evolve over the years. Perhaps inspired by the views of his interlocutor Robert Wallace, Hume became more favorably inclined toward paper money, at least certain types. In his *Characteristics of the Present Political State of Great Britain* (1758), Wallace insisted that merchants and consumers in advanced commercial nations must rely on a sophisticated credit money system; there simply was not enough metallic money in the world to mediate all desired transactions. Moreover, he noted that paper money has the capacity to stimulate economic activity. He wrote, "Industry stands sometimes in need to be *quickened*; and money is very serviceable for this purpose."[39] In a passage that bears a strong resemblance to Hume, Wallace argued that an inflow of money would lead "merchants and manufacturers" to increase their expenditures and prompt an increased demand for labor and capital investment. With the additional money, Wallace explained, "every one would be enabled to spend a little more, and to carry on his business better. By these means there would be every where more labour. Of course, the commodities, or *real* riches, which are quite *different* from *money*, would be greatly increased."[40] This effect would also follow from the expansion of paper notes. As long as banks are "settled by public authority under right regulations," they will be able to put money in the hands of people who will promote commerce and give "greater employment to the industrious."[41] The key was that the banks only issued notes on good security—"coin, bullion, lands, goods, and good debts"—to men of "integrity, prudence, and activity, or to men of substance."[42] Wallace recognized that there were indeed some drawbacks to paper money but argued that these were insignificant in comparison to its benefits. As long as paper money was issued within limits, it would always be beneficial to a nation insofar as it "supports and increases industry and useful labour."[43]

Hume significantly revised the essay "Of the Balance of Trade" in 1764, in particular with the insertion of two lengthy paragraphs outlining the benefits of an expansion in paper money. He announced that it must be "confessed, that, as all these questions of trade and money are extremely complicated, there are certain lights, in which this subject may be placed, so as to represent the advantages of paper-credit and banks to be superior to their disadvantages" (E-BT, 318). Although paper money, regardless of its type, raises prices and thus banishes specie from the nation, Hume remarked, "specie and bullion are not of so great consequence as not to admit of a compensation, and even an overbalance from the encrease of industry and of credit, *which may be promoted by the right use of paper-money*" (E-BT, 318, emphasis added). Like Wallace, Hume argued that the key criteria were that paper notes were issued on good security by and to men of probity and integrity. For that reason, Hume argued, only private banks should be allowed to expand the money supply by issuing paper notes.[44]

Since the passing of the Promissory Note Act in 1707, merchants had had the power to generate credit money by circulating personal debt instruments. This practice, Hume argued, was not only beneficial to merchants but also "favourable to the general commerce" (E-BT, 319). Private bankers similarly had the capacity to create money by extending loans on the security of their monetary reserves or other assets, such as land and inventories. Such loans, payable in notes, enabled merchants to monetize their assets and therefore to activate their otherwise dormant capital. The discounting of bills and the extension of loans by private banks were well-established operations in Britain, particularly in Scotland. Hume described how the banks in Edinburgh had come up with the "ingenious" practice of bank credit. Depending on a man's reputation and wealth, he could receive a line of credit from a bank. This meant that he could withdraw funds only as needed, to settle accounts with other merchants, and thus pay interest only on the money he had "in his hands" (E-BT, 319). Prior to this invention, a merchant would pay interest for a contracted loan whether or not he needed the funds at the time. But in this case, "his bank-credit costs him nothing except during the very moment, in which it is of service to him" (E-BT, 319). As Hume pointed out, "a merchant does hereby in a manner coin his houses, his household furniture, the goods in his warehouse, the foreign debts due to him, his ships at sea; and can, upon occasion, employ them in all payments, as if they were the current money of the country" (E-BT, 319). With this new type of credit, merchants could take advantage of profitable opportunities and need not worry about a temporary lack of liquidity (E-BT, 310).

The banks of Glasgow not only copied the system pioneered in Edinburgh but also discovered another method to increase liquidity, issuing banknotes with the unprecedented low denomination of ten shillings, roughly the weekly wage for a tradesman in Scotland. The ten-shilling notes in Scotland proved to be successful, and as Hume observed, passed as payments for "goods, manufactures, [and] tradesmen's labour of all kinds" (E-BT, 320). With the advent of five-shilling notes soon thereafter, the benefits of paper currency were evident across the ranks of urban Scotland. Nevertheless, concerns were voiced that credit was issued too liberally, that the credit system is precarious, and that Scotland would be drained of specie.

Hume issued cautionary words that the banking system was at risk, and his worries were prescient. The Ayr Bank, one of the largest banks in Scotland, founded in 1769 by Argyll, collapsed on June 22, 1772, due to the overextension of credit.[45] This collapse in turn sparked a much larger financial crisis, including a run on the Mansfield bank in Edinburgh, with withdrawals totaling about forty thousand pounds in a few days. It and the Coutts bank, which held Hume's savings, proved to be the only two to remain creditworthy. The banks in Newcastle, Norwich, and Bristol suspended payments, and the credit houses of London were severely impaired. As Hume remarked from Edinburgh in a letter to Adam Smith, "We are here in a very melancholy situation: Continual Bankruptcies, universal Loss of Credit, and endless Suspicions" (HL, 2:263). Hume was also deeply concerned about the effect on employment, noting that the Carron ironworks near Stirling might close and thousands of workers might lose their jobs.[46] He also worried about his friend John Adams, who had participated in the launch of the get-rich-quick Adelphi Scheme in London. It did not survive the panic of 1772. Hume thought it had been born "imprudently" and marveled that it had endured as long as it had (HL, 2:264).

Adam Smith shared Hume's view on the vulnerability of paper money. He argued that insofar as the "judicious operations of banking . . . enables the country to convert a great part of this dead stock into active and productive stock," paper money provides a "sort of wagon-way through the air" (WN, 1:321). The bank notes metaphorically float in the sky above the highway paved with bona fide gold and silver coins. If credit is overextended, if the notes soar too high, they will melt and dissolve like "the Daedalian wings" that came too close to the sun (WN, 1:321). How apt that the name of the first bank to bring home this lesson was a homonym for *air*. Hume, however, saw a silver lining in the 1772 collapse. In a correspondence with Smith, he observed, the collapse "will reduce people to more solid and less sanguine Projects, and at the same time introduce Frugality among the Merchants and Manufacturers" (HL, 2:264). If used prudently and cautiously, paper money had many virtues. Even though both privately and publicly issued money had the capacity to circulate widely, in the end, Hume primarily endorsed the former.

The Interest Rate

The Roman Catholic Church had condemned the practice of usury, and for much of premodern Europe, lending with interest was illegal. Thomas Aquinas acknowledged certain exceptions—for example, the practice of partnerships or the appeal to extrinsic titles—but argued that the practice of usury was unethical. In 1571, Queen Elizabeth I passed a law tolerating interest on loans in England provided the rate did not exceed 10 percent. In his *Early Memoranda*, Hume included several entries on interest rates in ancient Greece and Rome and also noted that in the United Provinces (the Netherlands), the interest rate fell from 14 percent to 4 percent by around the year 1600 (MEM, 513). About thirty years later, Thomas Mun expressed his envy of the Dutch rate of 3 percent. In 1691, John Locke issued a pamphlet on the interest rate opposing the measure before Parliament to lower the ceiling from 6 to 4 percent. By 1750, the legal ceiling in Britain had fallen to 5 percent, and the prevalent rate was closer to 3 percent, a sign of the efficiencies and size of capital markets.

Hume celebrated a low rate of interest because it facilitated borrowing by enterprising merchants, manufacturers, and entrepreneurs. But in his theoretical analysis, Hume positioned the interest rate more as an effect than a cause, and thus for the most part he believed it was best left unregulated. Until Hume, the prevailing doctrine regarded the interest rate as a monetary phenomenon, the price set by the market for lending and borrowing. Hume argued forcefully that the interest rate was only a price in a superficial sense: it was correlated with the supply and demand for loanable funds, but as in the case of the money supply, the interest rate was governed by nonmonetary factors that stem from human dispositions to accumulate capital that in turn are grounded in deeper propensities for risk or time.[47]

Hume's analysis of the interest rate draws on his appeal to the quantity theory of money. If a person goes to the bank to borrow money to build a house, the only effect of a general increase in the quantity of money is that the builder has to bring home a "greater load; because the stone, timber, lead, glass, &c. with the labour of the masons and carpenters, are represented by a greater quantity of gold and silver. But as these metals are considered chiefly as representations, there can no alteration arise, from their bulk or quantity, their weight or colour, either upon their real value or their interest" (E-In, 297). What matters is the share of resources a person seeks to borrow. That is what dictates the price of borrowing. Borrowing to build a house is therefore very expensive in a rude and uncultivated society but cheap in places where industry, commerce, and knowledge abound.

Hume posited three correlative features of financial markets. A low rate of interest occurs when there is at least one of the following: (1) low demand for loans, (2) large sums available for lending, and (3) low profits. These three "circumstances are connected together, and proceed from the encrease of industry and commerce, not of gold and silver" (E-In, 297). Hume explained the first two conditions by pointing out that in a thriving commercial society, there are fewer prodigal landowners seeking to borrow for nonproductive purposes, and there are more frugal merchants with large stocks of accumulated capital, which they can either invest themselves or lend to others. Furthermore, when commerce flourishes, the rivalry among the merchants would increase, and this rivalry, Hume believed, tends to force down the rate of profit. Hume articulated the process by which capital flows readily from one sector with a lower return to another where the perceived profit rate is higher, until the augmented supply brings that price down as well, rendering the profit rate uniform across the nation.

The most important insight Hume offered was his demonstration that the interest rate, which is readily visible via the banking system, is convergent on the profit rate. In a world of no liquidity frictions or monopolistic banking, the two rates might be almost identical, but at the very least there were strong forces to induce their convergence. The justification is located in individual investment decisions: "No man will accept low profits, where he can have high interests; and no man will accept of low interest, where he can have high profits" (E-In, 303). Because the banks are ever vigilant to make a profit and thus inclined to compete with one another for a larger share of the market for loanable funds, they will also be inclined to bring about a uniform interest rate. The profit rate, because of the risk and uncertainty of a capital investment, will always tend to be higher than the interest rate, but never much higher, for the reasons just articulated. No one would risk an investment if the rate of return from a bank deposit is higher, and vice versa.

With this piece of reasoning that implicitly appeals to the opportunity cost of capital, Hume also pointed to the strong tendencies to bring profit rates into uniformity and to equal the interest rate, particularly in a world with sophisticated capital markets. Capital will flow out of a nation if a higher return could be secured abroad. With sufficient time and global development, there would be a convergent international rate of interest. This was not the case in his day, however. He noted that Jamaica had a rate of 10 percent and Portugal a rate of 6 percent, as contrasted with 3 percent in Amsterdam or London (E-In, 296). China and France were hampered by unduly high rates. In support of his analysis, Hume pointed to the precommercial states of ancient Greece and Rome. With the brief exception when Augustus conquered Egypt and the interest rate fell to 4 percent, for most of the ancient world, interest rates rarely fell below 6 percent and were often closer to 12 percent (E-In, 305–6; MEM, 509–11).[48]

For Hume, the interest rate was thus a leading indicator of the economic development of a nation. He characterized it as the "barometer of the state," and added that "its lowness is a sign almost infallible of the flourishing condition of a people" (E-In, 303). Hume thus grasped that, like a barometer, the interest rate measures a phenomenon that is not, strictly speaking, observable; the economy is as invisible and ubiquitous as the atmosphere that surrounds the earth. Much as the barometer measures changes in atmospheric pressure and thus serves to forecast changes in weather patterns, rises or falls in the interest rate forecast a shift in economic output. By the 1740s, the barometer had become a household instrument among the well-to-do, and it unleashed a flurry of amateur recorders of the daily weather.[49] Likewise, in large cities such as Edinburgh and London, broadsheets and newspapers made available the schedule of interest rates on offer for various types of credit.

The analogy to a barometer is also apt because the earth's atmosphere, like capital, knows no national boundaries. Barometers provide local measurements that are most informative of local conditions, but in order to make informed judgments of broader patterns, as Alexander von Humboldt would with his notion of the isobar, one must branch out and look at larger regions. Hume's specie-flow mechanism conjured up the image of the monetary fluid, like the oceans, evenly distributed around the globe. Now his analogy to the barometer saw this fluid as evenly enveloped by an atmosphere of economic activity that, under ideal circumstances and sufficient time for capital accumulation, would also reach a global equilibrium.

To enlighten his readers who might mistake the interest rate as the price of gold and silver, Hume offered to "distinguish between a cause and a concomitant effect" (E-In, 304). His *Political Discourses* makes this point several times. The closing sentence of his essay "Of Money" highlights the common "fallacy" such that "a collateral effect is taken for a cause" (E-Mo, 294). Hume promoted the core theme that economic outcomes are caused by "manners and customs" that tend to evolve at a glacial pace (E-Mo, 294). The secular tendency of the interest rate to fall over the preceding few centuries was for Hume the best indication of the significant change in behavioral norms, the spirit of the modern age that makes everyone into a type of merchant, and where "no hand is entirely empty of [money]" (E-Mo, 294). As long as the government protects the fundamental institutions of commerce and facilitates the mobility of labor and capital, the interest rate will decline of its own accord.

In conclusion, Hume's account of money is arguably brilliant. It sheds new light on the relation between money and wealth, takes the quantity theory to an ever-greater degree of abstraction and generalization, and carefully clarifies the confusion surrounding paper money. Hume's specie-flow mechanism implies a global equilibrium that under perfect conditions would ensure that each nation has the optimal quantity of money to service its trade. If capital markets develop across the globe, there would also be a convergent interest rate, both within and among nations. Hume captured the sense in which money is neutral as a representation of the value of commodities and services in the market, but also the sense, given certain conditions, in which money penetrates the surface and stimulates additional economic activity, both an intensification of labor and an acceleration of commerce via the multiplier. The main virtue of money, however, is its ubiquity. If it is used in every transaction, it renders more efficient the markets for labor, capital, services, and commodities. Prices will tend to fall and almost everyone will enjoy a higher standard of living.

Hume's penetrating analysis of money strongly opposed the traditional practices of restricting the export of money. Money should be allowed to flow freely within and between nations. "To prohibit the exportation of money," he wrote to Oswald, "or the importation of commodities, is mistaken policy" (HL, 1:144). If imbalances emerged, Hume knew that arbitrageurs would correct them. Similarly, he believed that privately issued credit money functions best if left to its own devices. As long as private banks issued notes on good security, there was a built-in check against excessive liquidity. Hume was aware that there were no guarantees against an overextension of private credit and that financial meltdowns might occur, such as the one he witnessed in Scotland during the summer of 1772. But for the most part, private bank notes contributed substantially to the flourishing of commerce. The more serious problem stemmed from monetary interventions by the state, particularly government bonds. Although they served as useful substitutes for money, Hume believed that publicly issued bonds constituted a significant source of political instability.

Money came into being as a result of a gradual process of uncoordinated exchange and, once established, operated according to its own intrinsic principles. Inasmuch as Hume identified the significance of a variety of self-correcting mechanisms, money had achieved a considerable degree of autonomy from human agency. It had evolved into such a complex phenomenon, and was so deeply entrenched in human society, that interventions by individual citizens and politicians were largely impotent. In sum, people might attempt to channel or reduce the effectiveness of the specie-flow mechanism or the quantity theory of money, but they could not override the powerful forces at work. Money, for Hume, had a will of its own.

CHAPTER 6

"A Prayer for France"

Hume on International Trade and Public Finance

David Hume's paean to international trade as the means to induce global peace was in stark contrast to Britain's imperial endeavors. The scale of eighteenth-century warfare undertaken by the British was without precedent. The Seven Years' War (1756–63), in particular, spread to five continents and was essentially the first worldwide war. Britain's ascent to world power has been aptly described as a form of "war capitalism."[1] Ongoing efforts by the British to colonize distant regions led to the displacement or death of millions of indigenous peoples. During the eighteenth century, the volume of the transatlantic slave trade increased by a factor of five, reaching its peak in 1792, when more than one hundred thousand African captives were forced to endure the Middle Passage.[2] Britain alone shipped more than three million slaves across the Atlantic during the eighteenth century to toil on plantations growing sugar, tobacco, or cotton.[3]

War and slavery were undoubtedly subjects for debate in the Edinburgh clubs, London coffeehouses, and Parisian salons that Hume frequented. Moreover, Hume's occasional employments provided him with firsthand knowledge of the quotidian violence required to sustain Britain's overseas empire. Recall his youthful stint as a clerk to a merchant in Bristol, the center of England's sugar and slave trade, and in 1746, his participation in the aborted invasion of Lorient. Later in life, Hume once again entered the halls of imperial power, first as secretary to the British ambassador to France at the conclusion to the Seven Years' War and then as undersecretary of state in London.[4] In several of his writings, he declared his opposition to slavery, describing it as "cruel and oppressive" and suggesting that it was "as little advantageous to the master as to the slave" (E-PA, 383, 390n). Empires, he found "destructive to human nature; in their progress, in their continuance, and even in their downfal, which never can be very distant from their establishment" (E-BP, 340–41). And wars, he condemned as "attended with every destructive circumstance; loss of men, encrease of taxes, decay of commerce, dissipation of money, [and the] devastation by sea and land" (E-PC, 351). Hume was strongly opposed to the use of subjugation and conquest—press-gangs, slavery, and the appropriation of foreign territories—as the means to build wealth and power.[5]

When Hume wrote the *Political Discourses*, Britain's "jealousy and . . . hatred of France" was at a high pitch (E-BT, 315). In addition to the recent war between Britain and France, the two nations' mutual animosity had "occasioned innumerable barriers and obstructions upon commerce" (E-BT, 315). In 1748, while in Breda, Hume had witnessed firsthand the extent to which war harms trade. Remarking on both the economic depravity of Flanders and the bedraggled French soldiers, he confided to his brother, "I suppose the Loss of their Trade pinches them: So that there are some Hopes of a Peace" (HL, 1:118). He recorded the destruction of the region a few years later: "What immense treasures have been spent, by so many nations, in Flanders, since the revolution, in the course of three long wars? More money perhaps than the half of what is at present in Europe. But what has now become of it?" (E-BT, 325–26). Hume believed the situation would only worsen in the future, as powerful states resorted to the use of mercenaries to fight their wars and thereby drifted further into debt (E-BP, 341).

Hume thus witnessed that the loss of peace meant a diminution in trade, but he was equally drawn to the opposite causal inference, that trade fosters peace. If nations became interdependent in trade, and ministers grasped the full benefits of international commerce, he believed hostilities between nations would abate. Legislators and diplomats would be more inclined to let trade, not war, mediate international relations. Hume believed that a thriving overseas trade would not only solidify the indissoluble links between industry, knowledge, and humanity but also contribute toward making the world more enlightened and civil. He recognized that there was still much potential for economic development around the globe and that this would draw underdeveloped nations toward more civil and peaceful relations. As Hume insisted, nothing could be "more favourable to the rise of politeness and learning, than a number of neigbouring and independent states, connected together by commerce and policy" (E-RP, 119).

Most European legislators conceived of international trade as a zero-sum game, serving as war by other means. They looked "on the progress of their neighbours with a suspicious eye, to consider all trading states as their rivals, and to suppose that it is impossible for any of them to flourish, but at their expence" (E-JT, 328), Hume asserted. There were exceptions, however. In the *History of England*, Hume pointed to efforts to dismantle barriers to trade, notably the Act of Union that joined Scotland and England in 1707. Hume also praised the Russian czar Theodore Basilides, who argued in the late sixteenth century that "by the law of nations, [trade] ought to be common to all, . . . [and not] a monopoly for the private gain of a few" (HE, 4:376).[6] For the most part, however, the majority of rulers were inclined to foster trade wars and this, Hume believed, was the bane of modern commercial development. He denounced the tendency of one nation to be jealous of the prosperity of another, to think that one country's gain was the loss of another. Instead, he advocated a doctrine of unrestricted trade, on the principle that "the encrease of riches and commerce in any one nation, instead of hurting, commonly promotes the riches and commerce of all its neighbours" (E-JT, 328).[7] Hume directly attacked the prevailing adherence to protective trade measures. He argued that "a state can scarcely carry its trade and industry very far, where all the surrounding states are buried in ignorance, sloth, and barbarism" (E-JT, 328). Wherever open commerce and trade are preserved, Hume continued, "it is impossible but the domestic industry of every one must receive an encrease from the improvements of the others" (E-JT, 328).

Britain ought therefore to dismantle its protectionist policies, or face the prospect of reducing its neighbors to the "same state of sloth and ignorance that prevails in Morocco and the coast of Barbary" (E-JT, 331). Furthermore, if Britain persisted in its practice of restricting trade, its "domestic commerce . . . would languish for want of emulation, example, and instruction: And we ourselves should soon fall into the same abject condition, to which we had reduced [our neighbors]" (E-JT, 331). In a letter of March 4, 1758, to Lord Kames, Hume expressed his dismay at these restrictions: "This narrow spirit of nations, as well as individuals, ought carefully to be repressed. . . . My principle is leveled against the narrow malignity and envy of nations" (HL, 1:272). Hume's cosmopolitan appeal to unrestricted trade went far beyond the immediate interests he harbored for Britain's welfare, as his famous prayer for France makes clear:

> I shall therefore venture to acknowledge, that, not only as a man, but as a British subject, I pray for the flourishing commerce of Germany, Spain, Italy, and even France itself. I am at least certain, that Great Britain, and all those nations, would flourish more, did their sovereigns and ministers adopt such enlarged and benevolent sentiments towards each other. (E-JT, 331)

Although international trade, Hume recognized, would not put an end to envy and emulation, these passions could nevertheless be channeled toward more productive ends, fostering commerce and thereby expanding the ambit of peaceful relations.[8]

Hume realized how difficult it would be to establish a world of unrestricted trade. Adam Smith later noted, with a melodramatic tone, that the prospect of establishing a complete "freedom of trade" is "as absurd as to expect that an Oceana or Utopia should ever be established" (WN, 1:471). There were concrete practical reasons to uphold the system of customs and duties. For one, the facility by which customs could be charged as goods entered the country at a specific port makes it a particularly attractive means to raise state revenue.[9] Moreover, taxes on certain foreign goods might have favorable effects on domestic commerce. Hume mentioned two such instances: a tax on foreign brandy would shift demand to rum and thus promote production in the British colonies, and a tax on German linen would protect the infant linen industry at home (E-BT, 324). Once the domestic production reaches the point at which it can compete with foreign producers, Hume argued, these restrictions should be removed because the desire for profits by the entrepreneurs would provide sufficient incentive for its continuation. In the spirit of *laissez-faire*—a term devised by Pierre de Boisguilbert in 1704—Hume pointed out that "most of the arts and professions in a state are of such a nature, that, while they promote the interest of the society, they are also useful or agreeable to some individuals; and in that case, the constant rule of the magistrate, except, perhaps, on the first introduction of any art, is, to leave the profession to itself, and trust its encouragement to those who reap the benefit of it" (HE, 3:135).[10] Hume thus acknowledged the infant industry argument, but also that individual incentives would continue to drive trade and thus serve the good of the nation.

Hume hoped his theoretical principles would persuade legislators to dismantle both the monopolistic joint-stock companies and the extensive system of customs and duties. For the most part, he argued, trade restrictions "serve to no purpose but to check industry, and rob ourselves and our neighbours of the common benefits of art and nature" (E-BT, 324). Everyone would reap the benefits of gains from trade, much as they did in their local community if one person specialized in baking and the other in brewing. During the recent war with France, strategic trade restrictions were employed to inflict harm on the enemy, which forced the English to drink "worse liquor at a higher price" imported from Spain and Portugal. If trade channels were restored, Hume argued, "each new acre of vineyard planted in France, in order to supply England with wine, would make it requisite for the French to take the produce of an English acre, sown in wheat or barley" (E-BT, 315).

Here is the germ of an idea that would mature into the principle of *comparative advantage*.[11] It stipulates that even in the case where a country could produce two goods (in this instance, wine and corn) more efficiently, it ought to produce only the one in which it has a greater comparative advantage (wine) and import the other (corn). The land that would otherwise produce corn in France would be better switched to wine, to meet the demand in England for superior wines. As a result, France would more readily accept corn from England to meet its demand for bread.[12] Implicit in this idea is that more acreage in England would be sown with wheat or barley than would otherwise have been the case, and, as a result, its agrarian yield would also be augmented. More significant, even though in principle France could produce both wine and corn more efficiently than England, it was still more beneficial for France to concentrate on wine, the good in which it had a greater comparative advantage, and import English corn, than to produce both to meet domestic needs.

Hume noted that there was a strong bias in France against this outcome, and as a result, wine production was below capacity. Not only were the French under the grip "of the superior value of [their] corn, above every other product," but there were also "many edicts of the French king, prohibiting the planting of new vineyards, and ordering all those which are lately planted to be grubbed up" (E-BT, 315–16). The French also imposed trade barriers within their nation and, as a result, the peasant in Burgundy had wine but little bread. Hume cited Mareschal Vauban, who vehemently opposed the "absurd duties" that prevented the sale of wine from southern France into the north, from Languedoc to Normandy (E-BT, 316). In favor of his recommendation that France produce wine for export and import English corn, Hume noted that the additional transportation costs of shipping would be negligible, "that a few leagues more navigation to England would make no difference; or if it did, that it must operate alike on the commodities of both kingdoms" (E-BT, 316). Although England had been a net exporter of corn to France in the seventeenth century, that Hume could propose that the French import English corn in the 1750s is highly suggestive of the degree to which he was wedded to the international gains from trade and the reconfiguration of the production of goods in accordance with the different natural endowments found around the globe. It also explains in part his strong antipathy to the physiocrats, who privileged the production of corn above all other goods and who advocated against exporting French manufactured goods.

The Enrichment of the World

Hume's reflections on the long-term consequences of global trade were part of a broader discourse at the time, which Istvan Hont aptly labeled the "rich country–poor country debate."[13] It was predicated on the realization that international trade had differential effects, depending on the region or the degree to which manufacturing had taken hold. A nation that is primarily agrarian would develop and grow differently from a nation that had already established a substantial manufacturing sector. There were strong indications that the advanced manufacturing nations would sustain their positions of superior wealth far into the future, but perhaps not forever. Hume traced the long-term trajectory that ensued from these initial inequalities. He believed that, given enough time, manufacturing would spread around the globe and that this spread would also engender a more civilized moral and political order.

Hume posited a developmental path that bears some resemblance to the *stadial* theory of John Millar and Adam Ferguson.[14] In prehistoric times, Hume explained, once a community advances beyond subsistence hunting and fishing, it will begin to engage in agriculture, grazing animals, cultivating grains, or practicing a mixed form of husbandry (E-Co, 256). As the community prospers and surplus food is produced, an increasing number of people produce artisanal goods. At first, they produce "necessary manufactures," but over time, "the superfluous hands apply themselves to the finer arts, which are commonly denominated the arts of *luxury*" (E-Co, 256). This process transpired over centuries, if not millennia. Once the modern era arrived, a symbiotic developmental path emerged: "When a nation abounds in manufactures and mechanic arts, the proprietors of land, as well as the farmers, study agriculture as a science, and redouble their industry and attention. The superfluity, which arises from their labour, is not lost; but is exchanged with manufactures for those commodities, which men's luxury now makes them covet" (E-Co, 261). In this narrative, manufacturing unfailingly drives improvements in the agrarian sector. Hume emphasized, "The most natural way, surely, of encouraging husbandry, is, first to excite other kinds of industry, and thereby afford the labourer a ready market for his commodities, and a return of such goods as may contribute to his pleasure and enjoyment. This method is infallible and universal" (E-PA, 419–20).

Hume weighed in on the alternative path, whereby a region remains primarily agrarian, and "where manufactures and other arts are unknown and neglected" (E-PA, 419). He claimed that it is possible for such a nation to flourish for a period of time, citing Switzerland as an example: there one finds "the most skilful husbandmen, and the most bungling tradesmen, that are to be met with in Europe" (E-PA, 419). It is also the case that nations with warmer climates tend to resist development and remain at subsistence agriculture, Hume observed. In France, Italy, and Spain, because the soil is rich and the climate is warm, there are fewer incentives to invest in tools or new crops, and the peasants toil in much the same manner as their ancestors. Farming is an "easy art" that a single man can perform with two "sorry horses;" the only "art" in use is to leave the land fallow for a year and, as a result, the peasantry remain comparatively poor (E-Co, 266). In Burgundy, for example, the production of wine requires little more than the limbs of the peasants to crush the grapes. Hume estimated the capital outlay for the instruments at only twenty shillings. The lack of capital accumulation means that its "fine vineyards" are "cultivated by peasants, who have scarcely bread" (E-Co, 266–67).

Conversely, Hume continued, in England, where the soil is "coarse [and] must be cultivated at a great expense," farmers are compelled to work diligently, to undertake improvements, and to invest capital in the land (E-Co, 266). The fear of "slender crops" is unrelenting (E-Co, 266). As a result, they experiment and undertake more complex methods, introducing new techniques and investing in capital improvements. English farmers "must have a considerable stock, and a long lease," since it might take several years before they see a profit on their investment (E-Co, 266). His contrast between English farming and the Burgundy peasantry is perhaps overblown, but it serves his purpose of underscoring the central claim that the limitations of England's natural endowments prompt prudence and foresight, which in turn prompt the investment of capital and more roundabout methods of production. The end result is to induce greater specialization and economies of scale. Hume's observations were empirically sound. Right through the early modern period, more capital was invested in the agrarian sector in England than in manufacturing, and the average farm became larger and more specialized to meet the growing demand from towns and cities.[15]

As developing nations engaged actively in international trade, the array of goods in domestic markets soon expanded. The novel products from abroad inspired envy and inventiveness, stimulating the growth of domestic industries. In Hume's mind, "foreign trade has preceded any refinement in home manufactures, and given birth to domestic luxury" (E-Co, 263). Initially, countries would import commodities they were unable to produce on their own, but soon domestic manufacturers copied the arts and technologies used abroad. "Imitation," Hume suggested, "soon diffuses all those arts; while domestic manufactures emulate the foreign in their improvements, and work up every home commodity to the utmost perfection of which it is susceptible"

(E-Co, 264). Had it not been for the adoption and modification of foreign techniques and products during the previous two centuries, Hume argued, British agriculture and manufacturing would have remained "extremely rude and imperfect" (E-JT, 328). Hume generalized that "every improvement, which we [Britons] have since made, has arisen from our imitation of foreigners; and we ought so far to esteem it happy, that they had previously made advances in arts and ingenuity" (E-JT, 328). Much of the transfer is about knowledge, Hume asserted: "All the sciences and liberal arts have been imported to us from the south; and it is easy to imagine, that, in the first ardor of application, when excited by emulation and by glory, the few, who were addicted to them, would carry them to the greatest height, and stretch every nerve, and every faculty, to reach the pinnacle of perfection" (E-NC, 210).[16]

Given the momentum imparted on a country by its adoption of new luxuries and its embrace of a novel spirit of industriousness, was it possible that a prosperous country would continue on this path indefinitely, or would a saturation point be reached at some point in the distant future? One of Hume's first interlocutors, James Oswald, conveyed his opinion to Hume in a letter dated October 10, 1750: "The advantages of a rich countrey in this respect compared with the disadvantages of a poor one, are almost infinite," and therefore it is almost impossible for poor countries to catch up.[17] Hume viewed matters differently. He replied a month later, "I cannot agree with you that, barring ill policy or accident, the former [rich country] might proceed gaining upon the latter [the poor country] for ever. The growth of every thing, both in arts and nature, at last checks itself" (HL, 1:143).

In a letter to Lord Kames in 1758, Hume revisited this question, wondering "whether these advantages can go on, increasing *in infinitum* [*sic*], or whether they do not at last come to a *ne plus ultra*, and check themselves, by begetting disadvantages, which at first retard, and at last finally stop their progress" (HL, 1:271). The reason the rich country would not continue to dominate indefinitely, Hume thought, stemmed from rising wages and prices. As Hume explained, "We may reckon [that] the dear price of provisions and labour, . . . enables the poorer country to rival them, first in coarser manufactures, and then in those which are more elaborate" (HL, 1:271). The higher the wages and prices in the rich country, the easier it would be for the poor country to compete and eventually overtake the rich country in the global market. This explanation did not, however, imply that Hume preferred lower wages. As we saw in chapter 5, Hume argued that the benefits of higher wages outweigh the drawbacks of reduced international competitiveness, in both the short and the long term.

Hume anticipated the emergence of a division of labor between rich countries and poor countries, with the rich specializing in advanced manufacturing and the poor specializing in the production of "coarser" commodities. While Hume generally regarded manufacturing as more advanced than agriculture, he also acknowledged that there are some manufacturing sectors that are more sophisticated than others and some agricultural sectors in which art and technique matter more than in others.[18] Hume wrote to Oswald, "The rich country would acquire and retain all the manufactures, that require great stock and great skill; but the poor country would gain from it all the simpler and more laborious [manufactures]" (HL, 1:143). This was not, however, a static division, but one that would evolve over time, Hume explained. As producers in the poor country learned about the commodities they imported and then successfully imitated the technologies and techniques used to produce them, it would gain the capacity to produce the same commodities as competitively as the rich country. Even if the poor country's producers did not match the same level of skill, their lower wages would give them an advantage and enable them to sell them at a lower price. The time might very well come when the rich country would be forced to give up the production of those goods.

Initially, Hume observed, the manufacturers of the rich country are more competitive because of the size of their capital holdings. In the rich country, the "superior industry and . . . greater stocks, of which its merchants are possessed, . . . enable them to trade on so much smaller profits" (E-Mo, 283). However, the low wages in the poor countries serve as a magnet for capital investment and would prompt the emigration of capital from the richer nations. Hume had made note of *factor mobility* within a nation—that is, that both labor and capital would flow to places where the remuneration was higher. Looking toward the future, Hume predicted that manufacturers would "gradually shift their places, leaving those countries and provinces which they have already enriched, and flying to others, whither they are allured by the cheapness of provisions and labour" (E-Mo, 283). The flow of capital to underdeveloped regions might continue indefinitely, and the developing country might eventually suffer the same fate once its wages become too high, "banished by the same causes" (E-Mo, 283–84). There was no intrinsic end point to capital's capacity to cycle the globe. "There seems to be a happy concurrence of causes in human affairs," Hume submitted, "which checks the growth of trade and riches, and hinders them from being confined entirely to one people" (E-Mo, 283).

Hume thus envisioned a benign process of globalization whereby sector after sector migrated from rich to poor countries. For the former, it might mean a loss of industry and employment: "If strangers will not take any particular commodity of ours, we must cease to labour in it" (E-Co, 264). But, he quickly added, the "same hands will turn themselves towards some refinement in other commodities" (E-Co, 264). Workers who lose their employment certainly will feel the pain of economic dislocation, but Hume believed it would be a temporary hardship. As long as "the spirit of industry be preserved, it may easily be diverted from one branch to another; and the manufacturers of wool, for instance, be employed in linen, silk, iron, or any other commodities, for which there appears to be a demand" (E-JT, 330). The key is for the historically rich country to continue to foster a spirit of industry and ingenuity, thus enabling it to remain competitive and secure advancements in the manufacturing of novel goods.[19] As such, Hume endorsed the benefits of global competition. He concluded, "The emulation among rival nations serves rather to keep industry alive in all of them" (E-JT, 330).

This account raises the important question of how long the advanced manufacturing nation might retain its superior position. If capital could, in principle, leave the nation and move to other regions of the globe, surely this would spell the end of the supremacy of a nation such as Britain? The outcome is underdetermined, since the flourishing of new countries would potentially increase the demand for foreign goods, particularly if they were produced with considerable technical skill. Hume left open the possibility that once a country reached its peak, it would not necessarily decline. It might not grow further, but the flourishing of other nations ensured its place in the global order. The best example of this position, for Hume, was the Netherlands. It had reached its apogee by the middle of the seventeenth century but had continued to compensate for its relatively small size and lack of natural resources with a thriving export business as shippers and brokers. Hume noted that other nations in his day competed with the Netherlands for these services but that the superior skills of the Dutch, not to mention the increased demand that comes in the wake of international prosperity, might ensure that their nation's decline is "wholly eluded" (E-JT, 331).

Hume continued to debate these issues in 1758 with Lord Kames, who relayed to Hume some of the arguments broached by Josiah Tucker in an unpublished 1755 tract on trade and commerce. For Tucker, there was no evidence that "Trade and Manufactures" would flow from rich to poor countries as swiftly as a "Current of Air rushes from a heavier to a lighter Part of the Atmosphere, in order to restore Equilibrium."[20] Had this been the case, the rich country would have been "obliged by a Kind of Self-Defence to make War upon the poor one . . . in order . . . to prevent the fatal Consequences of losing its present Influence, Trade, and Riches."[21] Instead, much as Hume did, Tucker found the jealousy-of-trade doctrine grossly misleading. Looking right next door, he wrote, *"England* need not entertain any Jealousy against the Improvements and Manufactures of *Scotland*;—and on the other Hand, *Scotland*, without hurting *England*, will likewise increase in Trade, and be benefited both by its Example, and its Riches."[22] Similar to Hume, Tucker opposed efforts by rich countries to suppress their poor neighbors; there was no cause for trade wars, he believed.

Tucker acknowledged that the higher wages in the rich country consti-tuted a competitive disadvantage. However, this was only a minor inconve-nience in comparison to the long list of advantages enjoyed by rich countries. Tucker noted that the rich country enjoys "superior Wealth" acquired by its "long Habits of Industry," sophisticated systems of "Trade and Credit," its many shops and workhouses, the "great Variety of the best Tools and Im-plements in the various Kinds of Manufactures, and Engines for abridging Labour." Moreover, rich countries had the capacity to build better roads, canals, and harbors. The agrarian sector was also superior in many respects, due to enclosures, drainages, tools, and skilled husbandry, the result of long periods of "expensive trials."[23] While much of the "superior Skill and Knowl-edge" developed in rich countries would eventually be diffused throughout the world, poor countries would "always be found to keep at a respectful Distance behind . . . the richer Country."[24] According to Tucker, even with higher wages, rich countries could often produce goods more cost-effectively. Their superior "Quickness and Dexterity" make it "cheaper to give 2s. 6d. [two shillings and six pence] a Day in the rich Country to the nimble and adroit Artist, than it is to give only 6d. in the poor one, to the tedious, auk-ward [*sic*] Bungler."[25]

Hume granted the merits of Tucker's emphasis on "extensive commerce," pointing out in his letter to Lord Kames the contributions made by "great capital, extensive correspondence, skilful expedients of facilitating labour, dexterity, industry, &c." (HL, 1:271). Hume thus grasped the importance of specialization and the division of labor. He nevertheless insisted that no "one spot of the globe would engross the art and industry of the whole" (HL, 1:271). He opined, "It was never surely the intention of Providence, that any one nation should be a monopolizer of wealth" (HL, 1:271–72). Using an organic analogy, Hume claimed that "the growth of all bodies, artificial as well as natural, is stopped by internal causes, derived from their enormous size and greatness. Great empires, great cities, great commerce, all of them receive a check, not from accidental events, but necessary principles" (HL, 1:272).

The critical factor for the saturation of economic development—one that Hume elevated to the status of a "necessary principle"—is that knowledge reaches an upper bound in a given nation. In his essay "Of the Rise and Progress of the Arts and Sciences," Hume offers a long narrative of the intensification and remission of knowledge: "When the arts and sciences come to perfection in any state, from that moment they naturally, or rather necessarily decline, and seldom or never revive in that nation, where they formerly flourished" (E-RP, 135). While this proposition might at first seem "contrary to reason," Hume showed that at least in the realm of the liberal arts, there are plausible reasons to believe in an eventual decay (E-RP, 135).

First, he suggested that if there are too many great geniuses in a nation, a young man who is just starting out "naturally compares his juvenile exercises with these," and as he recognizes how far behind he is in the development of his skills, he "is discouraged from any farther attempts, and never aims at rivalship with those authors, whom he so much admires" (E-RP, 135). Hume concluded, "Admiration and modesty" naturally extinguish that "noble emulation" that is the "source of every excellence" (E-RP, 135). Second, Hume suggested that people are encouraged in their intellectual and artistic endeavors by praise and glory. A writer, for example, is motivated to pursue perfection by the memories of the applause she received for her previous works. But in a culture where the "posts of honour" are already occupied by writers who have reached perfection, a writer's first efforts will only be "coldly received by the public" (E-RP, 136). Hume therefore warned against importing too many great works from abroad, as it only served to suffocate the creativity of the nation's youth: "So many models of Italian painting brought into England, instead of exciting our artists, is the cause of their small progress in that noble art" (E-RP, 136). Hence, when knowledge and the arts reach a level that stifles further creativity and ingenuity, the nation falls into an irrevocable state of stagnation if not decline. Hume concluded that "the arts and sciences, like some plants, require a fresh soil; and however rich the land may be, and however you may recruit it by art or care, it will never, when once exhausted, produce any thing that is perfect or finished in the kind" (E-RP, 137).

Duncan Forbes dismissed this passage as only applicable to "literature and the fine arts" and argued that it therefore does not have direct bearing on economic development.[26] Notice, however, that Hume also included the sciences in his last organic metaphor. The more operative question is whether a nation must produce "perfect" knowledge to flourish in economic terms. Furthermore, in another essay, one that takes a larger time horizon, Hume suggested that the progress of knowledge might prove more cyclical than linear: "The arts and sciences, indeed, have flourished in one period, and have decayed in another, . . . yet in a succeeding generation they again revived, and diffused themselves over the world" (E-PA, 378). It is possible that Hume is contradicting himself. Alternatively, as Hont argued in response to Forbes, because Hume wanted to support his primary conclusion that the modern European population exceeded that in ancient Rome, he believed that the modern era had adopted a different pattern in its fostering of knowledge to the one found in the past.[27]

According to Hume, there are forces at work in modern commercial society which promote a steady improvement in practical and technical knowledge. People's insatiable demand for novelty inspires ingenuity and inventiveness. Domestic manufacturing might continue "till every person in the state, who possesses riches, enjoys as great plenty of home commodities; and those in as great perfection, as he desires; *which can never possibly happen*" (E-Co, 264, emphasis added). Because the desires of "opulent and skilful" people in rich countries are insatiable, the upward trajectory of economic growth may thus continue indefinitely (E-JT, 329). It is possible, however, that if the educated middle rank came to prefer nonpecuniary goods, such as poetry, friendship, and conversation, then the allure of luxuries might wane. But the desire for novelty per se would never disappear. As Hont observed, "the impossibility of satisfying all of commercial man's desires put the decline of the rich country [for Hume] beyond the finitude of time."[28] Insofar as Georgian Britain was far from reaching its economic apex, its progress in the arts and sciences, commerce, and manufacturing might continue for many generations, if not for many centuries.

The Economic Development of "Rude" and "Barbarous" Countries

Hume maintained that all commercial countries, rich as well as poor, would benefit from engaging in open commerce. Although poorer countries, such as Poland or Portugal, would lag behind, perhaps for centuries, they would nonetheless become wealthier by trading with richer countries, such as England or France. Within advanced nations, there were still underdeveloped regions, such as the Scottish Highlands or Lapland in northern Sweden. Hume wrote at length about the gradual development of these hinterlands and adhered strongly to the belief that the periphery in time would develop through trade with the prospering core of the nation. There is a strong degree of inertia in precommercial societies, however, that resists commerce and remains predominantly agrarian. As Hume argued: "In rude unpolished nations, where the arts are neglected, all labour is bestowed on the cultivation of the ground" (E-RA, 277). There is no middle class, just landlords and peasants. The former tend to be "petty tyrants" and are prone to feud with one another, such that there is either anarchy or despotism. The peasants are "necessarily dependent, and fitted for slavery and subjection;" they lack "knowledge in agriculture; as must always be the case where the arts are neglected" (E-RA, 277). There were, nonetheless, factors that would enable them to overcome this stagnation, Hume acknowledged. Because clans in the Scottish Highlands had established property rights, there was a system of justice in place that enabled such rudimentary communities to persist over time. But at some point, Hume believed, regardless of how satisfied the ruling barons were with their political power, they would become jealous of the wealth and splendor enjoyed in more refined societies and would seek to join commercial civilization. Once markets became monetized, it would not take long before the introduction of new commodities whetted people's appetites for more, launching them onto the same path of improvement as their neighbors to the south.

Matters were significantly different, however, among people who had never established a system of property rights. This lack of property would much restrict the potential for commercial growth and, as a result, Hume believed, these regions would remain poor and "barbarous" (E-RA, 271). Many of these regions were located in the tropics. Hume asked, provocatively, "What is the reason, why no people, living between the tropics, could ever yet attain to any art or civility, or reach even any police in their government, and any military discipline; while few nations in the temperate climates have been altogether deprived of these advantages?" (E-Co, 267). At first glance, the reasons stemmed from the hot and humid climate, which induced a languor and an inclination to be satisfied with sparse clothing and shelter, Hume asserted, and for this reason, there were few possessions to quarrel about and hence no need for policing and governance.[29] Drawing on Montesquieu's *Spirit of the Laws*, Hume also suggested that people in tropical regions more easily succumb to carnal pleasures:

> The heat in the southern climates, obliging men and women to go half naked, thereby renders their frequent commerce more dangerous, and inflames their mutual passions. . . . Nothing so much encourages the passion of love as ease and leisure, or is more destructive to it than industry and hard labour; and as the necessities of men are evidently fewer in the warm climates than in the cold ones, this circumstance alone may make a considerable difference between them. (E-NC, 213)

In opposition to Montesquieu, however, Hume tended to diminish the role of climate or physical conditions more generally.[30] The belief that people living "beyond the polar circles or between the tropics, are inferior to the rest of the species, and are incapable of all the higher attainments of the human mind," Hume maintained, could be better explained by economic and political factors than by their adverse climates (E-NC, 207). Moreover, people of similar climates did not always exhibit the same characteristics. To Hume, it was obvious that, notwithstanding a similar climate, people in France, Greece, Egypt, and Persia exhibited "gaiety," while the Spaniards, Turks, and Chinese were known for their "gravity" and "serious comportment" (E-NC, 208).

It was in the context of exploring different national characters that Hume added his infamous footnote about people of African descent. Hume proclaimed, "I am apt to suspect the negroes to be naturally inferior to the whites" (E-NC, 208n). He continued, "There never was a civilized nation of any other complexion than white, nor even any individual eminent either in action or speculation. No ingenious manufactures amongst them, no arts, no sciences" (E-NC, 629). Hume made this judgment, that there were no "symptoms of ingenuity," looking to Africans living in Europe and the colonies (E-NC, 208n). Hume granted the possibility that "low people [in Europe], without education, will start up amongst us, and distinguish themselves in every profession" (E-NC, 208n). Moreover, he claimed that, among the "most brute and barbarous of the whites"—Hume cited the ancient Germans or modern Tartars—there are always some people who can rise to some sort of eminence. Africans, however, are excluded from this potentiality, or so Hume suggested. In the same footnote, he dismissed the widespread esteem for the Jamaican polymath Francis Williams, who had attended the University of Cambridge. Hume wrote, "in Jamaica, indeed, they talk of one negroe as a man of parts and learning; but it is likely he is admired for slender accomplishments, like a parrot, who speaks a few words plainly" (E-NC, 208n).[31] Hume then concluded, based on what he regarded as sound reasoning, "Such a uniform and constant difference could not happen, in so many countries and ages, if nature had not made an original distinction between these breeds of men" (E-NC, 208n).

Hume appears to have slightly revised his thinking on the potential of nonwhites achieving better outcomes, perhaps as a result of his discussions with Denis Diderot, Comte de Buffon, and Benjamin Franklin. In the last edition of his *Essays*, which was published posthumously and so we cannot be certain was faithful to Hume's intentions, the "never" was changed to a "scarcely." Hume thus granted the possibility that while still infrequent, there may be nonwhite peoples who might attain the status of a civilized nation (E-NC, 629). However, given that the more categorical claim endured in print for some twenty-five years, it seems more likely that Hume strongly adhered to a belief in the inferiority of people other than his own. Yet, to the extent that he meant to shift from a polygenetic view of race to one in which all the world's people are part of the same race, he seems to suggest that it is at least conceivable for people of African descent to prosper.[32] While the French naturalist Buffon opined that Africans who were transferred to Paris, fed French food, and exposed to French education would become white again in about ten generations, Hume thought the path forward would require a shift in economic culture.[33]

For people in the tropics to advance, as Hume understood that term, they had to develop a more sophisticated material culture and thereby establish a system of property rights. Once such a system was established, they too would find themselves motivated to engage in hard work, buying and selling, as well as trying to come up with new methods to increase productivity. Hume recognized that people "naturally prefer ease before labour, and will not take pains if they can live idle" (E-Ta, 344). However, when a culture of consumption has given rise to a new work ethic, "by necessity, they have been inured to [labor], they cannot leave it, being grown a custom necessary to their health, and to their very entertainment" (E-Ta, 344). That said, societies in the tropics had a long journey to travel before they were ready to embrace a taste for luxuries and sober industry. For Hume, their consumer culture was such that "you may obtain any thing of the Negroes by offering them strong drink; and may easily prevail with them to sell, not only their children, but their wives and mistresses, for a cask of brandy" (E-NC, 214).

It is possible that Hume witnessed the use of slaves while visiting Berwick-upon-Tweed as a young child or while living in Edinburgh at the age of ten. The numbers were low; about one hundred domestic slaves worked in wealthy households in mid-eighteenth-century Scotland. While in Bristol, however, a twenty-three-year-old Hume would have gained detailed information regarding the slave trade and the practice of plantation slavery. Hume's *Early Memoranda* makes references to the sugar trade in the Caribbean and notes that there "are 20,000 Blacks in Antigua alone." He also comments on the oscillation in the value of shares in the Royal Africa Company (MEM, 505–6).[34] In his fifties, Hume also purportedly extended a considerable loan (four hundred pounds) to a person he knew was involved in the plantation business.[35] As Emma Rothschild points out, Hume also had several close friends and acquaintances "connected, indirectly or directly, to the Atlantic slave economy."[36]

Despite his racist views and his apparent lack of discomfort fraternizing with people engaged in colonial commerce, for Hume, slavery was never legitimate, not even during a transitional period.[37] Although he did not participate in the abolitionalist movement, he was consistently opposed to slavery on both moral and economic grounds. While the majority of his remarks on slavery were drawn from his readings and reflections on ancient texts, there is little doubt that he intended his interventions to be understood in the context of his day. He argued that one of the main reasons why ancient Greeks and Romans were less happy and virtuous than modern Europeans stemmed from their prevalent practice of slavery. Hume recognized that peasants and serfs lack various freedoms, but he insisted that "domestic slavery [is] more cruel and oppressive than any civil subjection whatsoever" (E-PA, 383). In addition to the violence, overwork, and suffering of the slaves, Hume also argued that the institution of slavery destroyed the moral fiber of society by turning masters into oppressors, that their "little humanity" and "unbounded dominion" serves only to "disgust us" (E-PA, 383–84). By being socialized "amidst the flattery, submission, and low debasement of his slaves," a typical slave owner becomes "a petty tyrant" (E-PA, 384).[38] Indeed, the "remains of ancient slavery" presently found in the American colonies, "would never surely create a desire of rendering it more universal" (E-PA, 383).

Despite Hume's reprehensible comments about people of African descent, he viewed slavery as a violation of human rights and integrity. In the second *Enquiry*, Hume addressed the tendency of people in power to subjugate those they perceive as weak. He outlined a version of Aristotle's justification for slavery, suggesting that creatures who are inferior in both body and mind are not equipped to possess property, enjoy other rights, or participate in the system of justice: there must therefore be "absolute command on the one side, and servile obedience on the other" (EPM, 18). While he agreed with Aristotle that animals ought to be subjugated on such grounds, he lamented that this dogma led to a systematic mistreatment of fellow human beings. He thought that British colonizers had tended to treat indigenous populations as animals and had therefore lost sight of "all restraints of justice, and even of humanity, in our treatment of them" (EPM, 18).[39]

Hume's analysis of the economics of slavery led him to conclude that it was both expensive and inefficient. He proclaimed that "from the experience of our planters, slavery is as little advantageous to the master as to the slave, wherever hired servants can be procured" (E-PA, 390n). Slavery is in fact more expensive than wage labor because in addition to the obligation to "cloath and feed" the slaves, the slave master must also pay the purchasing price of the slave. Free laborers only have to be paid enough to cover their bare necessities. Because slaves often died young—Hume estimated that the "stock of slaves" in the West Indies declined by 5 percent per year—the owners frequently had to replenish their "stock" at considerable expense (E-PA, 389–90n). Slavery was also more expensive than wage labor because "the fear of punishment will never draw so much labour from a slave, as the dread of being turned off and not getting another service, will from a freeman" (E-PA, 390n). Adam Smith would similarly point out that "work done by freemen comes cheaper in the end than that performed by slaves" (WN, 1:99).

In his essay "Of the Populousness of Ancient Nations," Hume argued that slavery tended to hinder population growth. A growing population, however, was considered one of the best indications of a prospering nation, by both Hume and his contemporaries. For this reason alone, Hume believed that the population of modern Europe much exceeded that of ancient Rome at its height. One of the reasons the Roman population was lower than it might otherwise have been was its widespread adoption of slavery, Hume argued, pointing out that most slave owners segregated their male and female slaves so as to prevent reproduction. He acknowledged that this seemed counter-intuitive, that a slave owner might seem rather to encourage the propagation of his slaves "much as that of his cattle" (E-PA, 386).[40] Hume exemplified his argument by referring to how costly it is to rear a child before he or she can enter the workforce. He remarked that "to rear a child in London, till he could be serviceable, would cost much dearer, than to buy one of the same age from Scotland or Ireland; where he had been bred in a cottage, covered with rags, and fed on oatmeal or potatoes" (E-PA, 387). As a result, London recruited about five thousand adults per year (E-PA, 388). Moreover, as Hume pointed out, if Londoners were not free to bear offspring, then the number of newcomers would have to increase to meet the demand for labor. Because "great numbers" of ancient slaves were manumitted every year or enjoyed the "privileges and indulgences" associated with being "born and bred in the family," Hume insisted that the "masters would not be fond of rearing many of that kind" (E-PA, 388–89). The ancient slave owners would thus "discourage the pregnancy of the females, and either prevent or destroy the birth" (E-PA, 388).[41] The racist views held by Hume were far from uncommon during the eighteenth century. His position on these matters serves as a potent reminder that the Enlightenment arguments for liberty and progress did not apply in the same way to all the peoples of the world.

Public Finance and the Pacification
of the Commercial World

For commerce to envelop the globe and spread its benefits far and wide, hostility and warfare between nations must also abate. Hume hoped that his arguments for economic globalization would convince political leaders to shift their legislative focus from war to commerce. But he was well aware that theoretical principles only held so much sway over the minds of men, at least in the short run. Additional initiatives therefore had to be undertaken to reduce warfare between nations. To Hume, there was one immediate policy change that the government must undertake: eliminate or drastically reduce the system of public credit, one of the primary methods that governments used to pay for war.

Hume viewed modern warfare as far less cruel and brutal than wars fought in antiquity.[42] But it was still destructive of life and land, and it was increasingly costly in monetary terms (E-PC, 351). While Hume hoped that there would come a time when international relations were mediated primarily by trade and diplomacy, he recognized that there would always be some rulers zealous to expropriate wealth through conquest.[43] Louis XIV was an excellent example, and Hume commended Great Britain for having had the courage to oppose his imperial ambitions. Hume remarked, "In the three last of these general wars, Britain has stood foremost in the glorious struggle; and she still maintains her station, as guardian of the general liberties of Europe, and patron of mankind" (E-BP, 635). With a nod to the long-standing doctrine of *bellum justum*, Hume asserted that "our wars with France have been begun with justice, and even, perhaps, from necessity" (E-BP, 339). But the cost escalated as both nations became increasingly irrational in their respective pursuits of power. Hume argued that the British retaliations "have always been too far pushed from obstinacy and passion" and proved to have been as "imprudent" as the ambitions of the French (E-BP, 339). According to Hume, the Nine Years' War (1688–97) ought to have been concluded in 1692, the War of the Spanish Succession (1701–13) in 1709, and the War of the Austrian Succession (1740–48) in 1743, about five years earlier than it did (E-BP, 339). Because Britain was crippled with debt, Hume observed, the settlement of the war in 1748 was "more pernicious to the Victors than to the Vanquished" (NHL, 235). The most costly war of them all, the Seven Years' War (1756–63), was unwarranted from the start, Hume believed, contending that it resulted from "the most frivolous Causes" and was "fomented by some obscure designing Men, contrary to the Intentions of the two Kings, the two Ministries, even the Generality of the two Nations" (NHL, 235). Hume, in the strongest words possible, called for the immediate settling of the debt and the elimination of the practice of issuing government bonds. If not, he feared that the British constitution might be undone and civil society destroyed.

The modern system of public credit, formed in the 1690s, was controversial from the very start. Various commentators criticized the size, design, and securitization of the debt, as well as the destabilizing effects it had on the balance of power that had been struck between the Crown and Parliament, on the one hand, and the landed and moneyed classes, on the other. In the 1730s, Lord Bolingbroke was one of the severest critics of public credit, both of the institution in general and of its management by the prime minster Robert Walpole in particular. The intrinsic weaknesses of the system were many. In Bolingbroke's eyes, the new financial architecture rested on a foundation of oppressive land taxes, legitimized the practice of stockjobbing, unduly empowered the owners of government bonds, created a powerful political force in the Bank of England, and infused British society with corruption and vice.[44] The debt forged a self-propelling dynamic between the bondholders and the military establishment, at the expense of the landowners and merchants.[45] Landowners were squeezed by land taxes, and merchants found their profits curtailed by customs and excise taxes, which were used to service the debt. The national debt was thus a sure way to undermine both political expediency and commercial advancement. Bolingbroke waxed nostalgically about the olden times, when Englishmen embraced economy, probity, and simple manners, and valued honor over vanity.[46] His proposed solution was to install on the throne a "Patriot King," who would reform the culture and practice of government, reduce the power and influence of money, instill a spirit of public frugality and, crucially, abolish once and forever the institution of public credit.[47]

The system of public credit continued to generate heated debate. In the aftermath of the War of the Austrian Succession, one anonymous pundit's *An Essay on Publick Credit* (1748) extolled the benefits of bond issuance, insisting that "to this *Public Credit* may principally be ascrib'd those superior Blessings, which are self-evident to every honest Enquirer, which our Ancestors never did enjoy."[48] Over the fifty years since the system of public credit had commenced, the author argued, Britain's domestic and foreign trade had prospered, the nation's fleets had become stronger, the interest rate had fallen, and the value of property increased.[49] Hume agreed that Britain had thrived since the Glorious Revolution—indeed, without precedent—but it had done so in spite of the system of public credit. The pattern Hume observed was one of mounting interest payments with each major conflict. The greatest increase came with the Seven Years' War, during which the debt almost doubled.[50]

The Whig prime minister George Grenville voiced concerns that Britain must commit to a policy of public frugality and higher taxes to settle the debt. Although they shared Grenville's conviction that the national debt should be paid off, a faction within the Whig Party called the Patriot Whigs advocated that the government should pursue a policy of lower taxes and find the means to stimulate economic growth so that sufficient revenues would be generated to pay down the debt.[51] Hume found both policies inadequate.

Hume expressed profound dismay for the future of Britain as it became increasingly mired in debt. To borrow on future earnings to finance warfare was, in Hume's view, a sure way to court disaster. Hume's most developed thinking on this topic can be found in the essay "Of Public Credit," but the record shows that he was preoccupied with government debt for much of his life. The problem is identified in his *Early Memoranda*, in correspondence that transpired over some thirty years, and in several of his essays, starting with "Of Civil Liberty" in 1741 and ending with his last essay, "Of the Origin of Government," written in 1776. Hume undertook a substantial revision of his essay "Of Public Credit" in 1764 and made further changes in the editions of 1768 and 1770.[52]

Despite his vehement dislike of public credit, Hume acknowledged, in his customarily noncategorical way, that there were also some benefits. First, the bonds issued to raise funds for the government provided merchants with a type of money that paid a secure rate of return, enabling them to trade on smaller profits. Lower profits put downward pressure on interest rates, which meant easier access to credit and hence the potential to increase investment and commercial activity more generally. The availability of a secure, government-backed form of investment also made it more likely that wealthy merchants would remain in London. Instead of retiring to the countryside and investing their earnings in the land, they might continue in business and enjoy the returns from both their mercantile endeavors and their bond holdings, which in turn would abate the outflow of capital from London and thus, ceteris paribus, augment the manufacturing sector. Moreover, because bondholders tended to favor political stability, if only to ensure that paper wealth was secure, they provided a crucial safeguard against sedition and rebellion. Hume argued: their "property is the most precarious of any; and will make them fly to the support of the government, whether menaced by Jacobitish violence or democratical frenzy" (E-PC, 355), as in the Wilkes riots of 1768.

Hume acknowledged these benefits of public credit but nevertheless found that there is "no comparison between the ill and the good which result from [the issuance of public debt]" (E-PC, 354). He advanced five reasons why public credit, in principle, was destructive to "the whole *interior* œconomy of the state" and would likely result in state bankruptcy and eventual tyranny (E-PC, 354). "First," he argued, "It is certain, that national debts cause a mighty confluence of people and riches to the capital, by the great sums, levied in the provinces to pay the interest" (E-PC, 354). In principle, Hume celebrated urbanization provided that it followed from the development of trade and industry and fed on the symbiotic exchange between town and country. Although many observers feared that London was already over-sized, Hume thought its size was an inconvenience that could be tolerated be-cause it induced a greater volume of trade and more liquid financial markets. Urbanization triggered by the redistribution of wealth from landed men to the rentier class, however, impeded the natural progression of opulence and thus created power imbalances that were potentially destructive.[53] Addition-ally, in one of the last editions of his essays, Hume added that the gathering of too many people in a relatively small area tends to incite political instability. In his eyes, there was a genuine danger of people becoming "factious, muti-nous, seditious, and even perhaps rebellious" (E-PC, 355). Fortunately, the national debt provided its own remedy, in that the bondholders would tend to bolster the status quo and support the existing government.

The second drawback to the system of public credit, as Hume saw it, was that government bonds drive out specie from the country. Because bonds circulated throughout the economy as a kind of money, they tended to raise prices for all goods and labor and therefore trigger an outflow of money. But, since bonds were not accepted abroad as money abroad, and gold and silver coins would exit from the nation's circulation, which in turn weakened the government in its public negotiations with other nations. As we discussed in the previous chapter, Hume believed that the "increase of prices, derived from paper-credit, has a more durable and a more dangerous influence than when it arises from a great increase of gold and silver" (E-PC, 637).

The third major economic disadvantage of the national debt pointed out by Hume was that the taxes instituted to service the interest on the debt would suffocate commerce. If the tax falls on a segment of the population that can convince employers to compensate them with higher wages, the country is weakened by the loss of international competitiveness that follows from increased wages and higher prices. But if the tax falls on the poorer and disenfranchised segment of the population, who do not have the bargaining power to pass on the tax to their employers, their miserable condition wors-ens, a case of "oppression on the poorer sort" (E-PC, 355). This is one of the rare instances when Hume showed concern for the lower class, although he did not elaborate further.

A fourth disadvantage Hume posited was that "foreign" bondholders might transmit the interest payments to their home countries. This, in essence, amounted to a direct transfer of wealth from British taxpayers to foreign interests, which might shift the economic center of gravity in Europe. Wealthy "men, who have no connexions with the state, who can enjoy their revenue in any part of the globe in which they chuse to reside," pose a threat to national stability (E-PC, 357), Hume believed.

The fifth drawback on Hume's list was that the national debt might transform the British class structure. Instead of wealth gravitating toward the industrious merchants, improving landowners, and entrepreneurial manufacturers, the system of taxation channeled the nation's wealth into the hands of "idle" bondholders and thus would "give great encouragement" to their "useless and unactive life" (E-PC, 355). Such men often ended up living as prodigals "in the capital or in great cities" and would "sink into the lethargy of a stupid and pampered luxury, without spirit, ambition, or enjoyment" (E-PC, 357–58). The rentier class was different from the enterprising middle rank, who by contrast, when gathering in cities, "love to receive and communicate knowledge, to show their wit or their breeding; their taste in conversation or living; in clothes or furniture" (E-RA, 271). As the owners of the government debt become all the richer, the landowners and merchants, bereft of their gains from land improvement and trade, become despondent and lose much of their wealth and political influence.

If nothing were done, Hume prognosticated, the national debt might turn the nation's social hierarchy upside down, so that in five hundred years, "the posterity of those now in the coaches [the aristocrats], and of those upon the boxes [the footmen], will probably have changed places" (E-PC, 357). Although Hume was for the most part not an enthusiast for the old landed elites, he spoke to "the dignity and authority of the landed gentry and nobility" and the fact that they were "much better rooted" than the rentier class (E-PC, 364n). He also warned about the effects that a world turned upside down might have on the stability of politics: "Adieu to all ideas of nobility, gentry, and family" (E-PC, 358). Without the aristocracy, who had traditionally provided the military upper ranks, this future world meant that "no expedient remains for preventing or suppressing insurrections, but mercenary armies: No expedient at all remains for resisting tyranny: Elections are swayed by bribery and corruption alone: And the middle power between king and people being totally removed, a grievous despotism must infallibly prevail" (E-PC, 358).

The Perils of Public Credit

These five disadvantages identified by Hume that plagued the system of public credit not only threatened the collapse of Britain's hard-earned constitution but also exposed the nation to the threat of foreign invasion. The central problem as Hume saw it stemmed from the lack of built-in discipline to restrain the government's tendency toward overissuance. Hume complained that the practice "of contracting debt will almost infallibly be abused, in every government. It would scarcely be more imprudent to give a prodigal son a credit in every banker's shop in London, than to impower a statesman to draw bills, in this manner, on posterity" (E-PC, 352). Hume remarked, "It is very tempting to a minister to employ such an expedient, as enables him to make a great figure during his administration, without overburthening the people with taxes, or exciting any immediate clamours against himself" (E-PC, 352). Prudent politicians who employ restraint are rare; most prefer to mortgage future generations. As Hume observed, the tendency to overvalue the present is a "great weakness" that is "incurable in human nature" (E-OG, 38).

The most obvious solution to the problem of the burgeoning debt would be to raise taxes to pay it off. Unfortunately, given Britain's fiscal situation, this option was not available. At the close of the War of the Austrian Succession, when Hume wrote the first edition of his essay "Of Public Credit," the government allocated close to half of its tax revenues to service the interest on the debt that had grown from 48 million pounds in 1738 to 78 million pounds in 1749.[54] The next and more costly conflict, the Seven Years' War, put an even greater strain on the public's finances. Before the war, the government had already exhausted what Hume viewed as the more benign excise taxes on non-essential commodities. Because such goods have a relatively elastic demand, the payment of the tax appears to be voluntary and over time tends to become invisible as it is "confounded with the natural price of the commodity" (E-Ta, 345).[55] With the war, the state had to resort to more pernicious forms of taxation, notably increased land taxes. In a thought experiment, Hume imagined that land would be taxed at eighteen or nineteen shillings on the pound (E-PC, 357). It was also likely that the state would be forced to impose a number of arbitrary taxes as emergency measures, which constituted severe "punishments on industry" (E-PC, 345). The inevitable outcome would be widespread poverty and deprivation: "The seeds of ruin are here scattered with such profusion as not to escape the eye of the most careless observer" (E-PC, 357). England was thus faced with a stark choice: "either the nation must destroy public credit, or public credit will destroy the nation" (E-PC, 360–61).

In the 1710s, the British and French, respectively, had pursued what appeared at the time to be an ingenious method to lighten the burden of the debt. They chartered a set of joint-stock companies and gave them exclusive rights to certain colonial trades. Once formed, the South Sea Company in England and the Mississippi Company in France were instructed to purchase the outstanding and highly discounted government bonds in exchange for shares. Investors were enticed to accept the bargain on prospective dividends and appreciating company stocks.[56] Initially, this massive debt-for-equity swap seemed brilliant. In one fell swoop, the national debt had been removed from the government's balance sheet and investors were pleased to see the value of their stock increase. But speculation and overissuance proved to be the undoing of these schemes. In the matter of a few weeks in 1720, most of the value of the Mississippi Company shares and a significant portion of the South Sea Company shares evaporated, leaving investors with huge losses.

France was traumatized by the experience and did not reinstate a comparable system of public credit until after the French Revolution. The collapse in England was not nearly so dire and, notwithstanding the widespread suspicion of such schemes, the credit system rebounded rather quickly.[57] However, by the time Hume wrote the *Political Discourses*, the debt had once again ballooned. With each war, the government had borrowed more and more, so that by the end of the Seven Years' War, the debt was once again of unfathomable proportions. There was no guarantee that some version of the schemes developed in the 1710s would not be tried again. Hume speculated that, "when the nation becomes heartily sick of their debts, and is cruelly oppressed by them, some daring projector may arise with visionary schemes for their discharge. And as public credit will begin, by that time, to be a little frail, the least touch will destroy it, as happened in France during the regency [1715–23]; and in this manner it will *die of the doctor*" (E-PC, 361).[58] In France, the doctor's name was John Law, and in England, his name was John Blunt.

A more likely scenario, Hume believed, was that the nation would not do anything and hence would continue down its path of mounting debt, careening toward the brink of disaster. As the bulk of the nation's wealth was transferred to the idle bondholders, commerce and industry would soon suffocate and leave the nation weak and impoverished. The nation would then become vulnerable to both civil unrest and foreign invasion. The government could try to stave off an invasion by financing the nation's defense through taxes on bondholders. To the extent that this was even feasible, it would only provide a temporary fix, as the population was so weakened by the languor and inactivity generated by the demise of industry, commerce, and the arts. Soon, a conquest by a foreign power would become all but inevitable. And, once such a conquest was completed, not only would people's property be at the mercy of the invading power, but the public debt would not be serviced or the principal paid down, resulting in "the *violent death* of our public credit" (E-PC, 365). It would be the end of the constitution and national sovereignty.

For Hume, the best option for the government was to declare a national bankruptcy and thus pursue the "*natural death* of public credit" (E-PC, 363). As the debt kept on mounting and the government introduced more and more taxes, eventually there would come a day when it would be impossible for the government to meet its obligations. This day would most likely come at a moment when the state desperately needed additional money—for example, during "wars, defeats, misfortunes, and public calamities" (E-PC, 361–62). In such cases, the legislator had few options. Instead of using tax revenues to service the existing debt, it would use the money to deal with the pressing crisis. It would seize the money "under the most solemn protestation . . . of being immediately replaced," knowing full well that such promises were hollow. In actuality, the entire system of public credit, "already tottering, falls to the ground, and buries thousands in its ruins" (E-PC, 363). The state has effectively declared itself bankrupt and those who thought their bonds secure find themselves empty-handed.

While such a government default would surely be "calamitous" for the thousands of people who owned government bonds—Hume estimated the figure to be around seventeen thousand people—it was in Hume's view a small price to pay to ensure "the safety of millions" (E-PC, 364). Even though a default constituted a serious violation of one species of private property, he believed it was the best way to uphold the system of justice, prevent a significant increase in taxes, and fend off an eventual invasion. Hume was not optimistic that the government would prioritize this task wisely and that "millions may be sacrificed for ever to the temporary safety of thousands" (E-PC, 364). He feared that Members of Parliament, all men of means who either owned bonds themselves or had close ties to bondholders, would rather uphold the system of public credit than undertake the measures he recommended.

At the heart of the problem of the mounting public debt was the difficult question of whether certain types of property (landed, mercantile, or equities) should be prioritized over others (government bonds). As he discussed in the *Treatise* and the second *Enquiry*, the respect for private property rights constituted the fundamental condition for justice. The reason private property rights are so useful to society is because they incentivize industry and commerce, the foundation of moral and material improvement. While property in land, commodities, and financial securities clearly promote these ends, government bonds tend to promote the exact opposite. In providing rich and idle bondholders with a steadily growing share of the country's wealth, public bonds slowly sapped the spirit of industriousness, ingenuity, and inventiveness and left the nation in misery. For that reason, it was perfectly compatible with Hume's philosophical convictions for him to advocate the eradication of one form of private property to protect the economy on the whole.

Hume, however, feared that a voluntary bankruptcy would not put a definitive end to public credit, that the practice of bond issuance would quickly be reinstated. After the collapse, the government would find ways to devise new debt instruments or disguise the ones used previously. Investors, he believed, would be fooled into subscribing to new lending schemes, even with the recent collapse still fresh in their minds. As Hume remarked in this context, most people were such "dupes" that even though they had just experienced a government default, it would not take long before they would once again start lending to the government, and public debts would rise again. Even though people are mostly governed by what they see or experience, Hume believed, in the realm of credit, expectations matters more. They are thus susceptible to promises, schemes, and allurements. Hume added, "Mankind are, in all ages, caught by the same baits: The same tricks, played over and over again, still trepan them" (E-PC, 363). He argued that "a prudent man, in reality, would rather lend to the public immediately after we had taken a spunge to our debts, than at present," since the state is still more "opulent" and reliable than any given individual (E-PC, 363–64). Over the long run, the public debt would rise, only to collapse once more.

Hume argued that the proximate cause of public debt was war and not commerce per se. Nevertheless, there was an indirect link. Excessive indebtedness was correlated with overseas expansion and imperialism that required the protection of the navy. Insofar as military might was thus integral to the protection of trading networks, Hume was not optimistic about the prospects of a more peaceful world. He sincerely hoped that nations would come to their senses and resist imperial conquests, but he knew full well that this was improbable. The best practice, he believed, would be to anticipate these expenses and build a reserve of funds during peacetime, a practice that had been followed by the ancients (E-PC, 349). It was partly for this reason that he advocated the formation of a standing army, rather than the common practice of ad hoc militia formed in response to conflict. A standing army would induce realistic estimates and prudential habits of saving to cover the costs required for military services. As the increase in global trade and commerce would enhance the political clout of merchants and manufacturers, who were also in a better position to know how destructive wars could be on commerce, they would only engage in war when absolutely necessary. As the ongoing migration of economic opportunity and enrichment continued to envelop the world, or so Hume believed, he remained hopeful that opportunities for peace would increase with time.

Although the collapse of the system of public credit was not imminent, it nonetheless was likely to transpire at some point. Hume noted in a letter to William Strahan in 1771 that "I can forsee nothing but certain and speedy Ruin Either to the Nation or to the public Creditors" (HL, 2:237). In another letter to Strahan the same year, he added that the public debt would "bring on inevitable Ruin, and with a Certainty which is even beyond geometrical, because it is arithmetical" (HL, 2:245).[59] Hume's fear of the public debt stayed with him until the end of his life. Whereas the ancients had proclaimed that to "reach the gift of prophecy," it was necessary to be infused with a certain "divine fury or madness," Hume asserted that when it came to predicting the future of the public debt, "no more is necessary, than merely to be in one's senses, free from the influence of popular madness and delusion" (E-PC, 365). Hume's intentions were to disperse the clouds of confusion and in their place provide the government with a set of straightforward and rigorous principles that would guide it toward the path of commercial development and political stability.

The Ideal Constitution

In his last years, not long before he died, Hume wrote one more essay. "Of the Origin of Government" offered numerous reflections pertaining to the relationship between constitutional politics and commerce. His analysis of the trade-offs between liberty and authority and between commerce and military conquest also considered which type of government—civilized monarchy or republic—was best suited to manage commercial nations. Although most of his commentary on constitutional politics suggests a preference for republics, Hume also saw merit in constitutional monarchies. Fundamentally, he believed, the responsibility of government is to protect the system of private property rights. We should therefore, he declared, "look upon all the vast apparatus of our government, as having ultimately no other object or purpose but the distribution of justice" (E-OG, 37).[60] He reduced all the members of the polity, "kings and parliaments, fleets and armies, officers of the court and revenue, ambassadors, ministers, and privy-counsellors," and "even the clergy" to one single role—namely, "to administer justice" (E-OG, 37). His assertion also subsumes the fact that these men must, at all times, respect and adhere to these principles.

In a well-governed society, people have the freedom to pursue their own economic interests and in the process contribute to the nation's wealth. The richer the nation, the easier it is for the government to tax its citizens. A symbiotic relationship thus existed between the state and its citizens; as Hume observed, "as private men receive greater security, in the possession of their trade and riches, from the power of the public, so the public becomes powerful in proportion to the opulence and extensive commerce of private men" (E-Co, 255). The growth of trade and commerce, grounded in individual self-interest, meant that governments did not have to introduce "any violent change in their principles and ways of thinking" (E-Co, 260). The "best policy" of the government was therefore to "comply with the common bent of mankind" (E-Co, 260) and accept men's passions and motivations, and "animate them with a spirit of avarice and industry, art and luxury" (E-Co, 263). This was the preferred way to ensure that "industry and arts and trade" would thrive and thereby "encrease the power of the sovereign as well as the happiness of the subjects" (E-Co, 260).

The question of whether a monarchy or a republic is better suited to govern commercial societies therefore boils down to which kind of government is most likely to protect property and thus enable commerce to expand. He believed that people who enjoy success in commercial societies, the middle rank of men, were most likely to be content with "their part in society" and therefore have an interest in protecting it (T, 344). Hume thus viewed them as the "best and firmest basis of public liberty." He wrote:

> [The middle rank] submit not to slavery, like the peasant, from poverty and meanness of spirit; and having no hopes of tyrannizing over others, like the barons, they are not tempted, for the sake of that gratification, to submit to the tyranny of the sovereign. They covet equal laws, which may secure their property, and preserve them from monarchial, as well as aristocratical tyranny. (E-RA, 277–78)

A government of the middle ranks was more likely not only to protect property but also to properly manage money, taxes, and international trade. A republican government, in particular, was also less likely to pursue empire by the sword, as it realized that geopolitical prominence could best be sustained through thriving manufacturing and commerce. As Hume noted, republics are more advantageous because they provide incentives for people to make themselves "*useful*," by "industry, capacity, or knowledge," while monarchies encouraged people to be "*agreeable*," by "wit, complaisance, or civility" (E-RP, 126). Moreover, Hume argued, "in a republic, the candidates for office must look downwards, to gain the suffrages of the people" (E-RP, 126). In a monarchy, by contrast, the men of government cultivate "polite arts" and "refined tastes" since they must "turn their attention upwards, to court the good graces and favour of the great" (E-RP, 126). Honor is most valued in a monarchy, whereas the commercial virtues of industry, honesty, and probity loom large in a republic. In monarchies, "birth, titles, and place, must be honoured above industry and riches" (E-CL, 93). Republican governments thus seemed to Hume better suited to safeguard and to govern commercial societies.

Hume, however, qualified this position. In addition to his observation that civilized monarchies had proven capable of strictly upholding property and thus maintaining justice, Hume believed that monarchies were better suited to handle the mounting problem of the public debt. Because Members of Parliament were committed, on principle and self-interest, to uphold the government's commitment to its creditors, they were unlikely to adopt Hume's recommendation for a voluntary bankruptcy.[61] An enlightened monarch, on the other hand, who was not beholden to or under the influence of an electorate, might have the freedom to orchestrate a bankruptcy, if necessary. Hume cautioned, however, that the defaulting monarch had to voluntarily reduce the punitive tax rate to restore a flourishing commerce.[62]

Hume also maintained that monarchies are better equipped to put an end to political factions. Republics were, in his mind, "extremely delicate and uncertain" because of the party strife they engendered (E-PG, 64). There is thus a fundamental contradiction implicit in republics. As Knud Haakonssen points out, "the very engine of civilized living, namely freedom under law, found its most refined protection in a system of political liberty which inevitably harboured forces which could become destructive of that engine."[63] Hume asked, while "there is no doubt, but a popular government may be imagined more perfect than absolute monarchy, or even than our present constitution," to what extent can we "expect that any such government will ever be established in Great Britain, upon the dissolution of our monarchy?" (E-BG, 52). He continued this line of thought and declared that because such a "fine imaginary republic" was unlikely to transpire in Britain, "I should rather wish to see an absolute monarch than a republic in this island" (E-BG, 52).

In conclusion, Hume offered an ambitious account of the complex conditions that link international relations with economic development. By convincing governments around the world to abandon the jealousy-of-trade doctrine and instead promote unrestricted commerce among merchants, he hoped that global prosperity and peace would ensue. He did not believe that wars would ever fully disappear, however, only that foreign trade would serve as a moderating influence on national rivalries. Abbé de Saint Pierre's proposal for a permanent elimination of intrastate warfare through the formation of a "republic of sovereigns," or Immanuel Kant's subsequent plan for a federation of free states, thus differed markedly from Hume's more qualified position.[64] Moreover, because the very idea of closing borders to promote peace was anathema to Hume's vision for commercial cosmopolitanism, he would have discredited Johann Gottlieb Fichte's proposition for a "Closed Commercial State."[65] Instead, Hume agreed with his friend Benjamin Franklin, whom he praised as America's "first philosopher," that commerce had the power to pacify states, more than ever before (HL, 1:357). They both would have concurred with Jeremy Bentham, who proclaimed that all plans for commercial cosmopolitanism "in the past were premature [because] they were put forth before the spirit of enlightenment had spread sufficiently to allow people to recognize the community of interest that exist among nations. This will not be accepted before the science of political economy is understood by the general public."[66] Hume was an important part of this trajectory to enlighten the public about the science of economics and thus to render the world, at least theoretically, a safer, wealthier, and happier place to live.

CHAPTER 7

"Our Most Excellent Friend"

Hume's Imprint on Economics

In 1975, Milton Friedman, when asked to assess what economists had achieved in monetary theory in the previous twenty-five years, replied that the better question to pose would be: What has been learned in the two hundred years since David Hume? The answer, he concluded, was very little: "We have advanced beyond Hume in two respects only: first, we have now a more secure grasp on the quantitative magnitudes involved; second, we have gone one derivative beyond Hume."[1] Robert Lucas, in his Nobel Memorial Prize lecture of 1995, singled out Hume's efforts as the "beginnings of modern monetary theory."[2] Neither Friedman nor Lucas is an expert historian of economics, so they may not have known that there were others in the eighteenth century who pointed to the nonneutrality of money or articulated the specie-flow mechanism, but because of Hume's prominence in general, he is the one credited with these ideas.[3] Hume, however, put the capstone on an important chapter of monetary analysis, as subsequent commentators fully acknowledged. Treatises on monetary theory and practice continued to be issued, but money waned into insignificance in the core *Principles* texts during the first half of the nineteenth century.[4] It was only in the early twentieth century, with Knut Wicksell, Irving Fisher, and John Maynard Keynes, that money was restored to center stage. Their respective tributes to Hume also ensured that his insights into money are still remembered and valued to this day.

Hume's legacy, however, much exceeds that of monetary theory. There is no modern philosopher who could outshine Hume with respect to the philosophical foundations of economic analysis. Adam Smith constructed a moral psychology, but he was strongly indebted to Hume's insights on sympathy and the complex chain of pride and esteem that it engenders between rich and poor. If Smith had not destroyed his treatises on justice and political philosophy, it is possible that he would have rivaled Hume in that area, but he was certainly no equal in the fields of epistemology or metaphysics. John Stuart Mill is the only other philosopher who might hold a candle to Hume in terms of significant contributions to economics, epistemology, and ethics.[5] Mill's *System of Logic* (1844) offers a lengthy analysis of the moral sciences, and his *Principles of Political Economy* (1848) reaches beyond the fundamentals of pure theory to forge a "social philosophy" in the spirit of liberal utilitarianism. The core tenets of Mill's ethics and political philosophy, however, are a natural extension of Hume. And in the case of metaphysics—at which Hume excelled—Mill's one major work, *An Examination of Sir William Hamilton's Philosophy* (1865), has fallen into oblivion. Mill's contributions to ethics are still the most appreciated part of his philosophical writings, and in that respect he is better paired with Smith than with Hume in terms of his philosophical breadth. Hume is without equal among philosopher-economists; to grasp the full compass of his economic analysis demands a careful reading of his entire oeuvre and a concerted effort to situate his economics within his philosophical tenets.

Virtually every prominent British economist of the nineteenth century read and admired David Hume for his ethics, epistemology, or economics. Hume is cited by Jeremy Bentham, Thomas Robert Malthus, James Mill, David Ricardo, John Ramsey McCulloch, and John Stuart Mill, as well as by the early neoclassical economists William Stanley Jevons and Francis Ysidro Edgeworth. Insofar as a case could be made that Hume's imprint on nineteenth-century economics is significant, however, it is primarily via Adam Smith, who embedded many Humean principles in his *Wealth of Nations*, arguably the most influential book in the annals of economics.

Classical political economy was the dominant discourse for almost a century. After it was overturned by the Marginal Revolution of the 1870s that established neoclassical economics as the reigning paradigm, Hume's and Smith's standing within economics declined. Conversely, the relative eclipse of Hume's philosophical tenets during the first half of the nineteenth century ended by the 1870s. The neo-Kantian movement that dominated German philosophy from roughly 1870 to 1914 drew attentive readers of Immanuel Kant back to Hume.[6] Evolutionary thinking also embraced Hume's secularism. In 1879, Thomas Henry Huxley—Charles Darwin's "bulldog"—wrote one of the first books on Hume's epistemology that bolstered Huxley's new concept of "agnosticism."[7] In ethics, a leading text by Henry Sidgwick, *Method of Ethics* (1874), bolstered by Ernest Albee's *History of Utilitarianism* (1902), made plain that Hume had one foot firmly planted on the path that Bentham subsequently trod.[8] Most of all, by the early twentieth century, Hume had been anointed the patron saint of logical positivism, for his fact/value distinction and for his admonition to commit to the flames every single metaphysical assertion for containing "nothing but sophistry and illusion."[9] His consistently empiricist analyses of space and time, for example, were of seminal importance for Albert Einstein.[10] Furthermore, Hume's problem of induction became standard fare for Anglophone analytic philosophy. Bertrand Russell, A. J. Ayer, and Karl Popper paid homage to Hume for his brilliance in articulating the problem, and efforts to grapple with it continue unabated.[11]

The two economists who brought Hume back into mainstream discourse, Keynes and Friedrich Hayek, were both philosopher-economists who had a deep admiration for Hume.[12] Keynes, together with Piero Sraffa, discovered and subsequently published an important manuscript, Hume's *Abstract* to the *Treatise of Human Nature*, written while Hume was completing Book 3 of the *Treatise*, on property and contracts.[13] Hayek published an essay specifically on Hume and referred to him in several of his major books.

Hume inspired two distinct lines of economic theory: the centrist or left-leaning liberals and the right-leaning libertarians. The liberal admirers of Hume, emanating out of Keynes, include Paul Samuelson, Arthur Lewis, Amartya Sen, and Paul Krugman. The libertarian followers, emanating out of Hayek, include Friedman, James Buchanan, Douglass North, and Vernon Smith. All of the aforementioned are winners of the Nobel Memorial Prize in Economics and can thus be taken to represent the practices and beliefs of countless others in the discipline of economics. We will briefly canvass their respective appeals to Hume and thus bolster the view that a Humean thread can be detected in both traditions. We attribute this reach among economists stretching back to the early twentieth century to the depth and breadth of Hume's thought. Hume defies ready classification; he was in part a skeptic and in part a builder of knowledge; he was in part a stoic and in part an epicurean; he was in part a republican and in part a monarchist; he was at times a Whig and at other times a Tory. In short, Hume is difficult if not impossible to pigeonhole. His versatility was such that his ideas appealed to economists across the political spectrum, from Hayek to Krugman. Even in the field of ethics, he was neither a full-fledged utilitarian nor a clear adherent of virtue theory.[14] To make sense of this, we will trace Hume's legacy in economics and philosophy from his time up to the present.

Adam Smith's Relationship with Hume

Adam Smith (1723–90), especially the young Smith, was an attentive reader of everything his fellow Scot Hume wrote. Smith had clandestinely read Hume's *Treatise* while a student at Oxford (1742–46), until his college tutors confiscated the book because it was censored by the church. Presumably Smith knew the author's name from his beloved professor Francis Hutcheson. Hume had corresponded with Hutcheson starting in 1739 and requested that he read a draft of Book 3 of the *Treatise* before it was published in 1740. There is one letter from Hume to Hutcheson of March 4 1740 that mentions that Hume's bookseller had sent a copy of the *Treatise* (Books 1 and 2) to a Mr. Smith (HL, 1:37). J. Y. T. Grieg, the editor of the correspondence, argues that this Mr. Smith was Adam Smith because Smith was a student under Hutcheson at the time. As Grieg points out, "it was Hutcheson's practice to set his students to make abstracts of new philosophical works as they appeared" (HL, 1:37). Although this might have been another Smith, the probability is low, given the philosophical acumen required to understand the *Treatise* and to please Hutcheson. There is also a debate that it was Smith and not Hume who wrote the *Abstract* now placed at the end the *Treatise*, but the current position is that this was by Hume.[15] Whatever the case, the main point to underscore is that Smith knew Hume's first major philosophical work in his formative years.

Because Hume had published his monumental *Treatise* before the age of thirty, and because he was eleven years older, Hume has aptly been called Smith's "mentor."[16] There is also a pronounced similarity to their basic tenets in both economics and philosophy. At the most general level, they are closely aligned in their commitment to empiricism, secularism, and Enlightenment ideals. Both Hume and Smith drank from the same intellectual well, studying not only Hutcheson but also Thomas Hobbes, John Locke, Lord Shaftesbury, Bernard Mandeville, George Berkeley, and Montesquieu, among others. Of the leading schools in natural philosophy, they clearly sided with the Newtonians over the Cartesians or Leibnizians. Hume and Smith moved in the same circles and exchanged ideas regularly with the same leading intellects of Scotland, England, and the Continent. Even before they met circa 1750, they had several friends in common, and as their own friendship deepened, their circle of close friends grew apace. The specific propositions advanced by Smith, both where he agreed with Hume and, of equal significance, where he disagreed, indicate an influence that is immense and inestimable.

Hume's *Treatise* infused all of Smith's works, particularly manifest in their shared mission to develop a science of human nature. Ian Simpson Ross marshals evidence to support the view that Smith's early lectures in Edinburgh, starting in 1748 before he and Hume had met, were forged in response to Hume's *Treatise*, particularly Book 3.[17] Knud Haakonssen also argues that Smith wrote in direct reaction to Hume.[18] Eric Schliesser highlights Smith's critical appropriation of Hume's theory of property.[19] There are also several essays by Smith—on sensory perception, the origin of language, and the history of science—that reflect ideas drawn directly from the *Treatise*.

Like Hume, Smith maintained that we can never know that a given scientific theory is true, and may even be deviating further from the true configuration of physical nature, but in the moral sciences we have insights into human behavior that enable us to grasp that a given theory is preposterous and thus we are more likely to know whether we are on the right path or not. Both Hume and Smith appealed to introspection as an additional resource in their efforts to forge the foundations of the science of human nature and the manner by which we construct ideas and draw inferences more generally. And both men devised a system of ethics that commenced with the sympathetic regard, from which emanated the realignment of moral sentiments and the bolstering of sociability. Their respective systems of ethics, in the tradition of Hutcheson, were essentially secular, although Smith's "invisible hand" might appeal to a providential order.[20] They each resisted a full-blown subscription to either virtue theory as it had been bequeathed from the Hellenic period, or to a consequentialist system of ethics. To a significant degree, Hume and Smith walked a common road that shortly thereafter branched into the two distinct systems of moral philosophy associated with Kant and Bentham, respectively.

The two Scots developed an analysis of the human species that invoked modes of thinking drawn from natural history, in the sense that moral and cultural conventions are contingent on material conditions and evolve over time. They eschewed essentialism and embraced a more plastic view of human nature. National characters, for example, were fluid insofar as they emerged from sympathetic ties with family and those in close proximity. Taxonomy is an important part of the natural history of humankind. Hume and Smith were both inclined to classify or catalog virtues, economic practices, and political regimes, and to think of them in evolutionary terms. Both used much the same methodology in their economics, laying out general principles and illustrating them with empirical facts, from either historical or contemporary sources. Both Hume and Smith believed that the science of economics had many lawlike propositions that could be linked together into a broader theory of economic development and distribution. Both appreciated the utilitarian consequences of the modern commercial era but also discerned the potential for social decay and anomie.

The friendship between Hume and Smith commenced in 1749 or 1750 and endured right up to Hume's death.[21] One of Hume's last letters—written on August 23, 1776, just two days before he died—was to Smith, and he signed it, "Adieu My dearest Friend" (HL, 2:335–36). Smith recorded in his published letter shortly after Hume died that Hume was to be remembered as "our most excellent, and never to be forgotten friend."[22] Their correspondence indicates that they had countless face-to-face meetings, particularly in the 1750s, of which almost no record survives. Smith burned most of his letters and manuscripts on the eve of his own death. But we do know that Hume sent Smith drafts of his *Dissertations* and the *Dialogues* and asked for feedback on subsequent editions of the *Essays* and *The History of England*. Smith sent Hume drafts of each of his two books and kept him abreast of specific essays, such as his "History of Astronomy," that he intended Hume to shepherd into print as his literary executor. They also kept each other informed of current events, political intrigues, favorite books, and personal challenges.

Their letters speak to a close rapport in which candid advice was given freely, although Hume was more prone to teasing Smith, albeit affectionately. For example, Hume wrote to Smith, after reading *The Theory of Moral Sentiments* (1759), that the book had the misfortune to be much applauded by the public and that "nothing, indeed, can be a stronger presumption of falsehood than the approbation of the multitude" (HL, 1:305). In that same lengthy letter, Hume kept Smith in suspense, twice recording interruptions due to visitors at the door, before finally offering the rather backhanded praise that "it may prove a very good Book" (HL, 1:306). Hume, however, later published a critical review of Smith's first book, and the next edition of *The Theory of Moral Sentiments* (1761) engaged some of those objections. Hume thus insinuated some of his ideas even more deeply into that great work.[23]

Hume took issue with Smith's asymmetrical account of sympathy in *The Theory of Moral Sentiments* of 1759. For Hume, sympathy ought to extend equally toward people one likes or dislikes. He suggested that Smith incorporate this change of view in a subsequent edition, but Smith did not. Both, however, endorsed the view that people are repelled by poverty and sympathize with the rich. Moreover, this predilection to admire wealth fosters human industry, even though it does not yield genuine well-being. Hume sought to guide merchants to embrace honor over wealth, since he believed that doing so would serve the commercial system far better in the long run. He also discerned, as Smith did, that wealth is always vulnerable to decay and that riches do not prevent personal suffering. As Smith aptly noted, riches might protect one from the "summer showers" but not the "winter storms" of genuine affliction (TMS, 183). The lottery of life is such, Hume had observed, that "all men are equally liable to pain and disease and sickness" (EPM, 55n33).

While both used sympathy as the cornerstone of their respective theory of ethics, there are some significant differences between Hume and Smith on their construal of the sympathetic regard. Hume's account of sympathy, as we saw, is more congenital; sympathy for others springs forth without the same degree of cognitive work that Smith ascribes to the sympathetic regard. There is more room for imagination in Smith's articulation of the mechanism, in both people's efforts to put themselves in the shoes of another and their efforts to conjure up what they might feel were they not only in that person's predicament but that person as well. But Smith also emphasized the extent to which human beings fall short of a perfect sympathetic stance, and the inscrutability of other minds that means that people are each confined to a subjective and hence inaccurate estimation of the pain or pleasure of others. There is a greater degree of subjectivity in Smith. Each person mistakenly registers the state of others—the mother overreacts to the cries of her infant, for example, or, more extremely, a bereaved person sympathizes with the dead buried underground—such that human sympathy is never perfectly aligned, notwithstanding the post facto corrective judgment of the impartial spectator. Hume lacked the adjustment process that Smith articulated, one of achieving concord even if it falls short of perfect unison. Smith's account of sympathy incorporates more cognitive steps that engage the imagination.

Despite these differences, there is considerable overlap on the role sympathy plays in bolstering economic ranks and activities. This overlap might partly account for the similarities in their economics, since it was in the 1750s that they spent the lion's share of their time together. Insofar as Hume and Smith became friends at least two years before 1752, there is also the possibility that Smith helped shape the ideas in Hume's *Political Discourses*. Because there is no correspondence between them before September 1752, however, this causal link proves difficult to establish. Moreover, Hume had begun thinking about economics well before 1750. The trip to the Continent in 1748 and Hume's reading of Montesquieu's *Spirit of the Laws* (1748) seem to have been the more proximate inspirations for the *Political Discourses*. Hume recollected in *My Own Life* that he had composed the second *Enquiry* and the *Political Discourses* at the same time, in seclusion at Ninewells, in the autumn of 1749. Most probably, this composition preceded his first contact with Smith, although he may have heard about the gifted young philosopher, recently returned from Oxford, from one or more of their mutual acquaintances, such as James Oswald or Lord Kames.

One puzzling fact is that Hume and Smith offer different publication dates for the *Political Discourses*. In the *Wealth of Nations*, Smith claims that Hume's *Political Discourses* appeared in 1751 or 1752 (WN, 1:325), whereas we know that it did not appear until January 1752. This claim could be taken to mean that Smith had seen drafts or preprints of the work prior to publication. Hume made a similar slip with the publication date of his second *Enquiry*, recollecting in *My Own Life* (written in 1776) that it was published at the same time as the *Political Discourses* in 1752.[24] Moreover, because the second *Enquiry* was published in London, but the *Political Discourses* in Edinburgh, this may have confused matters even more because of different calendars.[25] We will probably never be able to tell for certain whether Smith's offer of two dates for the publication was made to accommodate the calendar reform or because he in fact had read a draft and left his mark on Hume's economics.

Whatever the fact of the matter, there appears to be strong evidence that Smith knew Hume's work well around the time of its release and admired it sufficiently to convince a colleague at the University of Glasgow, James Wodrow, to read Hume's *Political Discourses* and to consider Hume for a vacant post.[26] Although Smith's initial appointment at the University of Glasgow in October 1751 was as professor of logic, he also assumed the task of lecturing on jurisprudence because the professor of moral philosophy, Thomas Craigie, had fallen ill and resigned the following year. In 1752, Smith was appointed Craigie's successor and lectured on moral and political philosophy, among other subjects, until he left Glasgow in 1764. Because we have two sets of student lecture notes, we know that Smith wove much economic analysis into his courses on jurisprudence and moral and political philosophy.[27] We also know that Smith delivered a lecture on "some of Mr David Hume's Essays on Commerce" to the newly founded Literary Society of Glasgow on January 23, 1752, just weeks after the *Political Discourses* was published.[28] Less than a year after the publication of the *Political Discourses*, Hume asked Smith for his reactions for a subsequent edition. In a letter of September 24, 1752, the first surviving letter between them that we have, Hume wrote to Smith:

> I am just now diverted for a Moment by correcting my Essays moral & political, for a new Edition. If any thing occur to you to be inserted or retrench'd, I shall be obligd to you for the Hint. In case you shou'd not have the last Edition by you, I shall send you a Copy of it. (HL, 1:168)

The fact that Hume, as far as we can tell, asked no one else for such feedback that year is indicative of his high regard for Smith and of the fact that Smith was already well versed on the subject of economics. Again, we do not know what "hints" Smith offered, but it is likely there were some.

Although Smith took up an appointment at the University of Glasgow in 1751, he went to Edinburgh frequently throughout the 1750s, in order to take part in the gatherings of the Edinburgh Philosophical Society and later the Select Society that he formed with Hume in 1754. This gives us reason to believe that Smith was in regular contact with Hume for much of that decade, while Hume was composing his *History of England* and Smith his *Theory of Moral Sentiments*. While there were other sources that inspired Smith's economic thought in the late 1750s and 1760s—Richard Cantillon, James Steuart, Anne-Robert-Jacques Turgot, and François Quesnay—Hume clearly played a critical part in Smith's intellectual genesis. Smith's first biographer, Dugald Stewart, offered the judgment that "the *Political Discourses* of Mr. Hume were evidently of greater use to Mr. Smith, than any other book that had appeared prior to his lectures [of 1755]."[29] We concur with this judgment. Smith was not friendly toward Steuart or his work, and while there are ideas drawn from the other three aforementioned, they do not compare with the strong imprint of Hume.

One important link between Hume and Smith is their mutual friendship with James Oswald of Dunnikier, who held several high offices in both Scotland and England, overseeing trade policy and naval defense. Smith's father had died while young Adam was still in the womb, and Oswald's father had served as executor of the will and as the man most responsible for rearing Adam to adulthood. His son James and Adam Smith attended the same school in Kirkaldy and formed a strong bond in their youth that endured for a lifetime. We are less certain when Hume first met James Oswald, but we know that in 1744, Hume was Oswald's houseguest in Kirkaldy and that they discussed the "oeconomy" of the navy (HL, 1:58). Their first exchange of letters in 1747 indicates a close bond; Hume, for example, worried out loud about a French invasion of Britain given the recent military triumphs in the Netherlands, and he expressed fears that this might "prove the last Parliament, worthy the name, we shall ever have in Britain" (HL, 1:106). A second letter disparages stockjobbers for clogging the wheels of trade (HL, 1:109). Finally, the Hume correspondence of 1750 indicates that Oswald helped Hume sharpen and clarify his analysis of the mechanism by which money prompts additional economic activity (HL, 1:142–44). Even in the 1760s, Hume maintained a close friendship, seeing Oswald three or four times a week until a falling out over religion in the spring of 1767. It is to Smith that Hume turned for comfort and vindication regarding the altercation, but

Smith refused to take sides and, characteristically, remained on good terms with both men (HL, 2:142–43).

Notwithstanding a close friendship spanning more than twenty years, there was as much cautionary reserve between Hume and Smith as there was tenderness. There are a few exchanges that record failed rendezvous in Edinburgh and in Paris, and, it seems, the fault lay with Smith for reneging on the arrangements. In a letter to Smith of February 8, 1776, Hume relayed in an uncompromising tone that he wants a visit: "Your Chamber in my House is always unoccupied: I am always at home: I expect you to land here" (HL, 2:308). As Ross notes, "Smith returned Hume's friendship warmly, though he never fell in readily with Hume's schemes to gain his company."[30] Smith came through, however, in the last few months of Hume's life. He intercepted Hume in Morpeth, on his brief trip to Bath for medical treatment, on April 23, and visited Hume in the last month of his life, in August 1776 (HL, 2:315n1).[31]

Smith had sent Hume a copy of the *Wealth of Nations* shortly after it was published, from London, and Hume read it immediately. His letter to Smith of April 1, 1776, was full of praise but also included candid reactions regarding points of disagreement on certain core matters (HL, 2:311–12). The letter is suggestive of prior conversations of which we have no record, and the belief on Hume's part that he might still persuade Smith to change his mind. In a letter from London of May 3, 1776, Hume relayed to Smith that he had heard much approbation expressed of the *Wealth of Nations* but also that "many People think particular Points disputable" (HL, 2:317).[32] Hume let Smith know that he himself was one of those people and that "these points will be the Subject of future Conversation between us" (HL, 2:317). Again, we have no record, but it is likely that they discussed economics when they met in August. There was, in sum, a complex give-and-take between them, as one might expect for a close friendship that endured for twenty-five years between two unmarried and childless men of considerable philosophical brilliance yet relatively modest means, who as Scots were still made to feel inferior in a world dominated by the English and French.

By the 1760s, both philosophers had become considerably more celebrated in learned circles, Hume for his *Essays* and *History of England*, and Smith for his *Theory of Moral Sentiments*. In the *Wealth of Nations*, Smith recorded for posterity that Hume was "by far the most illustrious philosopher and historian of the present age" (WN, 2:790). Smith also expressed much admiration in his widely circulated account of Hume's death, praising him for facing the end with courage and equanimity. Smith stated that Hume, on the whole, exemplified "a perfectly wise and virtuous man" (HL, 2:452). But Smith suffered for these associations. In a letter of October 26, 1780, Smith bemoaned that his brief account of Hume's death had generated "ten times more abuse than the very violent attack I had made upon the whole commercial system of Great Britain. So much for what relates to my Book [the *Wealth of Nations*]."[33] Smith's prudential considerations to safeguard Hume's reputation by refusing to publish the *Dialogues* backfired on him. By praising the character of Hume, an infidel, he incurred the wrath of clerics and pundits who wanted Hume's name sullied once and forever. By 1790, however, the *Wealth of Nations* was widely accepted as the authoritative text it has remained to this day, and Smith's associations with Hume only enhanced rather than harmed his reputation.

Smith's Economics

Albert Hirschman portrays Smith as the "end of a vision," as breaking away from the views of his predecessors, including Hume, who believed in the benign if not beneficial consequences of capitalism.[34] Smith's disclaimer that his economics constituted a "very violent attack" was sincerely put. Smith believed that colonialism never paid; it inflicted a searing wound on both the dominant and oppressed nations. Smith was openly hostile to the mercantile system, for its purported predilection to stockpile specie and foster monopolistic enterprises. Merchants are cast in a more suspicious light than in Hume's texts, for colluding to keep wages low and prices high. They also tend to undermine political stability by representing interests that diverge from the agrarian sector and thus undercut, in Smith's view, the natural progress of opulence.

The geopolitical order had changed during the twenty-four years that separated the *Political Discourses* and the *Wealth of Nations*. Although Britain had triumphed militarily against France, it was in the process of losing to the rebelling American colonists. Hume discerned that a break was imminent and declared himself a supporter. Smith could see that with its abundant fertile land, modern technology, and—above all—rapid population growth, it was only a matter of time before the new republic across the Atlantic would become the center of the world economy. With this notion partly in mind, the closing sentence of the *Wealth of Nations* alerts Britain to "accommodate her future views and designs to the real mediocrity of her circumstances" (WN, 2:947). Smith completed Hume's train of thought that there is a tendency for every rich nation to reach its apogee only to be surpassed by another.[35]

Smith drew heavily on Hume but rarely cited him. Indeed, he rarely cited anyone, and the six references to Hume in the *Wealth of Nations* put Hume in a league of his own: there are only three references to Quesnay, two to Locke, one to Cantillon, and none to Steuart or Turgot. Four of the six references to Hume are in Smith's analysis of money and banking. The received view bequeathed by Jacob Viner was that Smith had quietly dissented from Hume's two key propositions. Smith allegedly did not agree with Hume about the nonneutrality of money or the specie-flow mechanism. Frank Petrella corrected Viner's interpretation of Smith, pointing to Smith's *Lectures on Jurisprudence*, which offers a full endorsement of the specie-flow mechanism.[36] Petrella also argues that Hume's account of the effects of an injection of new money is also implicit in some of Smith's analysis, although not with the same clarity. Even if the published outcome was not a ringing endorsement of Hume, the specie-flow mechanism lived on in mainstream discourse and was clearly an important stepping-stone for Smith's analysis.[37]

In his monetary theory, Smith, like Hume, discounted the material composition of money and appreciated the complex layering of monetary issues that stemmed from degrees of credit and of liquidity. Smith wanted, like Hume, to keep banknotes redeemable in specie or land but was willing to accept that, as commerce expands, modern banking might increase its rate of exposure with respect to fractional reserve lending. Like Hume, Smith drew a sharp distinction between public and private banknotes and, also like Hume, worried that the government lacked the discipline to restrain its issuance of paper currency. Smith also believed that private notes needed to be regulated. One safeguard Smith advocated was to issue notes no lower than five pounds, since this was a denomination that would normally exceed what common tradesmen would handle and thus would ensure that only the wealthier and presumably more prudent merchants would hold private banknotes.

As James A. Gherity has shown, Smith had developed his views on the subject of paper money in two pamphlets of 1763, one entitled *Memorial with Regard to the Paper Currency of Scotland* and the other *Thoughts concerning Banks, and the Paper Currency of Scotland*.[38] They were written in response to a banking crisis of 1762–64 that had been attributed to a shortfall of liquidity. Smith's pamphlets advocated the Scottish system that fostered competitive banking, in contrast to the monopoly of the Bank of England. In the *Wealth of Nations*, however, Smith bent over backward to favor the monopoly of the Bank of England. Scholars have long puzzled over this seeming contradiction without reaching a full resolution.[39] Smith also readily accepted the Royal Mint as the sole producer of coins. Smith wanted the banks and monetary authority to be strong, and that demanded legal measures. He recommended a no-default clause on the redemption into specie so that banks could not stall when notes were presented. He also famously advocated a ceiling to the legal interest rate of 5 percent, another measure that appears to violate his more famous stance in favor of unregulated markets. One explanation on offer is that Smith knew all too well that prudence was never in sufficient supply to ensure the stability of the banks.

Smith thus shared Hume's admiration for the innovative steps taken by the Scottish system of banking, while voicing concerns about the potential for the overextension of credit. Smith maintained that, since the founding of the first public bank in Edinburgh, the Bank of Scotland in 1695, and the Royal Bank in 1727, Scottish trade and industry had grown "very considerably" (WN, 1:297). Some reports assigned a growth factor of four. Smith claimed that the proportion is unknowable, but it is certainly significant, and the efficacy of the new banks is not to be doubted. Smith also observed that, since the beginning of the eighteenth century, "provisions never were cheaper in Scotland than in 1759, though, from the circulation of ten and five shilling bank notes, there was then more paper money in the country than at present [i.e., 1776]" (WN, 1:324).

Notwithstanding this economic prosperity, both Hume and Smith expressed worries about the rise of an idle rentier class and the inequities this development would induce. They both articulated the prediction that in the event of a collapse of public credit, the majority of the population would be beholden to a small but powerful group of financiers. Hume and Smith each recognized that credit markets tend to create an imbalance in power such that modest lenders and borrowers are more likely to be at the mercy of those with large capital sums. Smith expressed much faith in the frugal predilections of ordinary people, and thus he blamed any credit fiascos on the misconduct of the extravagant expenditures by landlords, bankers, and politicians (WN, 1:345–47).

Smith is commonly viewed as one of the first writers in the history of economics to pay full attention to the plight of the lower echelon of society. His assertion that "no society can surely be flourishing and happy, of which the far greater part of the members are poor and miserable" (WN, 1:96) sounds tautological, but was novel for its time, since "society" was often directed exclusively to those who were well-heeled. Before Smith, or so the received view goes, the "lower orders" were depicted as passive or averse to labor, and they would only work hard if wages were kept low, under what came to be known as the doctrine of the "utility-of-poverty."[40] But Hume also advocated high wages and recognized the marginal utility of income, that a shilling meant far more to a poor person than to someone with wealth. His interest in stimulating growth paid attention to the population as a whole, and in that respect Smith was not as original as is commonly maintained.

We may never know whether Smith influenced the final drafts of Hume's *Political Discourses*, but we do know that Hume played a critical role in the genesis of Smith's *Wealth of Nations*. It draws on Hume's positions on trade policy, fiscal policy, and money and banking. In it Smith also gave a resounding endorsement of Hume's position on the interest rate (WN, 1:354), one that opposed the received view, which attributed the secular decline of the interest rate to the influx of silver and gold from the Spanish colonies. Smith agreed with Hume that the interest rate reflected deeper and nonmonetary features of the world, dispositions toward frugality and investment, and the accumulation and distribution of capital. In Smith's estimation, it had become the received view: "This notion, which at first sight seems so plausible, has been so fully exposed by Mr. Hume, that it is, perhaps, unnecessary to say any thing more about it" (WN, 1:354). Smith also adhered to the law of the falling rate of profit, an idea he may well have first gleaned from reading Hume.[41]

Both Hume and Smith provide empirical support for the secular decline of the interest rate, from 10 percent under Elizabeth I, when usury was first legalized, to roughly 3 percent in their day. Both saw the interest rate as a leading indicator of capital accumulation, and so they made it all the more salient in their efforts to promote a picture of economic relations. The capital stock is a product of what Smith called "sober people"—that is, those who abstain from prodigal spending (WN, 1:357). Like Hume, he believed that such predilections become habitual and deeply ingrained the longer they manifest profitable results. He thus accepted with Hume that the low interest rate is a reflection of human dispositions that have taken hold in modern commercial states; the observation that Spain had a vast supply of specie but lacked entrepreneurial dispositions served as ample proof that interest rates would not decline simply because of an abundance of money (E-In, 306).

In sum, while Hume and Smith differed in some fundamental respects—Hume was more sanguine about the future of humankind than Smith was—it is clear that Hume was a critical point of departure for Smith's own economic thinking. Modern commerce will, on the whole, elevate our benevolent tendencies even if, as Smith worried out loud, it might corrupt those in power. Smith was more inclined than Hume was to see conflict and colonization as an integral facet of overseas trade, and Smith was more explicit that the capitalist system feeds on vanity and greed and necessarily "oppresses" the lower classes (WN, 1:267). But Smith's debt to Hume, philosophical and personal, was profound and pervasive, and in that sense, Hume's legacy in economics was sustained long after 1776.

Hume's Reception on the Continent

During Hume's life, his *Political Discourses* was translated into French four times—twice in 1754, once in 1758–60 (as part of his collected works), and once in 1767—as well as twice into both German and Italian, and once into both Swedish and Portuguese. The first translation, by Abbé Jean-Bernard Le Blanc in 1754, did far more than circulate Hume's economics on the Continent. As Loïc Charles has documented, Le Blanc's peritextual comments gave a distinctive French rendering of Hume's economics, injecting ideas drawn from the circle of savants led by Vincent de Gournay.[42] Hume's promotion of luxuries, trade, and manufacturing bolstered French economic thought and policy at the time. As intendant of trade starting in 1751, Gournay also sought to erase the memory of John Law's unfortunate experiment with credit and to promote the British system of banking as a means to stimulate foreign trade. As a result, the Gournay circle downplayed Hume's caveats regarding paper bills and public debt. Le Blanc's translation inspired many new texts on the science of commerce in the 1750s and 1760s. For example, the philosophe François Véron de Forbonnais, a notable ally of Gournay, issued both the *Élémens du commerce* (1754) and *Principes et observations oeconomiques* (1767), and both were heavily indebted to Le Blanc's translation of Hume.

Jean Lerond d'Alembert and Denis Diderot, whom Hume befriended during his stint in Paris, brought into being one of the most important publications of the Enlightenment: the seventeen-volume *Encyclopédie, ou dictionnaire raisonné des sciences, des arts et des métiers* (1751–72). It featured a diagram of the tree of knowledge whereby the moral sciences were positioned as a prominent branch that spawned the subordinate sciences of natural jurisprudence, politics, and economics. It also included many entries on economic thought. Montesquieu, Turgot, and Jean-Jacques Rousseau were contributors to the *Encyclopédie*, as were Forbonnais on "Commerce" and "Espèces", and Quesnay on "Fermiers" and "Grains." These were Quesnay's first publications in the field of economics (1756–57) and have come to be seen as the seed that germinated physiocratic thought, best instantiated in his *Tableau économique* (1758). More significant, the instigators of the *Encyclopédie* valued practical and artisanal knowledge as much as they did philosophical and included many illustrations of people at work in ateliers, minting coins, or making pins. This choice of illustrations reflects Hume's own emphasis on the economic importance of manufacturing and practical knowledge.

There is little to no evidence that Hume influenced the work of Rousseau, although, as Ryu Susato has recently argued, there are some similar positions on money and luxury.[43] Rousseau was only one year younger than Hume but claimed not to have read Hume's work in the early 1750s, at least before his primary works on political philosophy and economics were published, and there is also no indication that he revised his thoughts because of his later exchanges with Hume in the 1760s. There was a brief period of mutual admiration between the two men that started in 1762 and ended in 1765 with hostile denunciations. James Harris speculates that there is some chance that Hume had read Rousseau's 1750 *Discourse on the Sciences and Arts* and absorbed it into his own essay "Of Luxury" (1752), which he renamed "Of Refinement in the Arts."[44] We consider this possibility unlikely, however, because Hume was generally inclined to cite his sources at least once, and there is no mention of Jean-Jacques Rousseau in his work.[45] Rousseau's first foray into economics, *Discourse on Political Economy* (1755), was clearly indebted to Montesquieu. Rousseau had written on luxury and taxation in a number of his works, and his *Social Contract* endures as a part of the canon in political philosophy, but he did not leave an enduring mark in the history of economics.

Anne-Robert-Jacques Turgot (1727–81) is one of the most prominent contributors to eighteenth-century French economics. He devoted most of his life to the study of economics and the promotion of trade, but he also achieved high office in the French government, as the controller-general of finance, albeit for just two years (1774–76). Turgot was on cordial terms with both the Gournay circle and the physiocrats but never formally joined either group. He was perceived as more closely allied with the latter group, but when Gournay died, Turgot penned the official *Éloge de Vincent de Gournay* (1759). Turgot and Hume met several times, and their correspondence suggests fruitful exchanges. Turgot had read Hume's work with care, and this attention is manifest in his most important work on economics, first issued in 1766 as lectures entitled *Réflexions sur le formation et distribution des richesses*. It develops more fully Hume's brief gesture to capital accumulation and the role of the entrepreneur.

Hume's *History of England* was widely appreciated in France. Hume had sent a copy to Paul-Henri Thiry, baron d'Holbach, one of the more powerful members of the Parisian salons, who facilitated a wide embrace of Hume upon his arrival in 1763. A translation of Hume's volume on the Stuarts, undertaken first by Le Blanc and completed by Abbé Prévost, appeared in 1760, and a translation by Octavie Gichard (known as Madame Belot) of two more volumes, on the Tudors and the Plantagenets, was released in 1765 (HL, 1:258n2, 1:415n). Hume's work found a sizable following among thinkers of a conservative bent, both before and after the French Revolution. Hume's emphasis on gradual and constitutional reforms in his account of English history proved seminal. Laurence Bongie claims that Hume's interpretation of seventeenth-century England became "an integral part of the French historical consciousness" that fomented the ruptures of 1789.[46]

François Quesnay first read Hume at age sixty-two, when he decided to pursue economics as part of his greater mission to preserve the health of the French Crown. In dialogue with the Marquis de Mirabeau in July 1757, they forged the doctrine of physiocracy. In 1756, Mirabeau had published a treatise entitled *L'ami des hommes ou Traité de la population* that made considerable use of Hume's ideas on population, luxury consumption, and taxation (HL, 1:257). Hume admired Mirabeau and, in correspondence with Le Blanc in 1757, admitted, perhaps with false modesty, to some uncertainty about his principles but more significantly to a willingness to change his mind if and when he were to receive a copy of Mirabeau's work (HL, 1:258–61). But Mirabeau's promotion of a "patriotic agriculture" that allied him with physiocracy would not have appealed to Hume, and there is no evidence that Hume's declaration to change his mind, at least due to Mirabeau, ever came to pass.[47]

There are few signs of a Humean imprint on Quesnay. Indeed, the physiocratic privileging of the agrarian sector, the doctrines of *le bon prix* (high prices for grains), high interest rates (10 percent), the doctrine of a single tax, and the strong restriction of the export of artisanal goods directly negate the teachings of David Hume. We also noted that Hume did not appreciate the degree of abstraction embedded in Quesnay's *Tableau*. One of the only clear points of overlap is their respective effort to delineate a nascent version of the multiplier. It is possible that Hume's account in "Of Money" prompted similar lines of thinking in Quesnay, but there is no record of this. We also have no indication that Hume and Quesnay met or corresponded, although Hume went to Versailles in 1763 when both were renowned, so it is not out of the question. Smith's high regard for Quesnay in the early 1770s stemmed from meetings in 1766, but we have little record of their conversations. The evidence is stronger that Hume may have met up with some of Quesnay's contemporaries, notably those who reflected on the scientific standing of their discourse, such as Mercier de la Rivière or Dupont de Nemours, if only because they had left Versailles and were friends with Mirabeau and Turgot.[48]

Both Milan and Naples had flourishing groups of savants who concentrated on the study of economics, such as Cesare Beccaria and Pietro Verri. The best known at the time, Ferdinando Galiani, had issued his three-volume *Della moneta* (*On Money*) in 1751, just a year before Hume's *Political Dis-*

courses. There is no evidence that Hume knew the Italian work before it went to press, but Hume and Galiani may have met in their mature years, since Galiani lived in Paris from 1759 to 1769 and also frequented the salons. They were both contemptuous of the physiocrats, but only Galiani put his criticisms into print, with the *Dialogues sur le commerce des blés* (1770).[49] Hume's library contains a copy of this work, and, given its wide popularity, it is likely that Hume had read it before he died. John Robertson has identified important parallels between Hume and Galiani as theorists in peripheral and developing nations, Scotland and the Kingdom of Naples, dominated by much richer and more powerful monarchies, England and Spain, respectively.[50] Galiani evinced a similar historical sensibility to Hume, and was also committed to a secular and scientific analysis of economic phenomena.

In 1847, Eugène Daire edited a collection of works by prominent economists that included Hume, Forbonnais, Franklin, Condorcet, and Étienne Bonnot de Condillac and that was available in every major library on the Continent.[51] This volume kept Hume in the canon, since French remained the primary language in the republic of letters. Two economists on opposite ends of the political spectrum, Karl Marx and Carl Menger, each read Daire's collection. Marx found Hume too conservative for his taste but appreciated Hume's skeptical and irreligious sentiments and made use of his insights on money and the interest rate.[52] Although Menger read Hume, he does not cite him in his core works, but his disciple Eugene Böhm-Bawerk does, drawing on similar topics that Marx had singled out.[53] Menger's son, Karl Menger, was a close associate of the Vienna Circle, and one of its founders, Otto Neurath, was actively engaged in economics, both the theory and the application; both appreciated Hume. Their respective work infiltrated the next generation who wrote on philosophy and economics, notably Karl Popper and Ludwig Lachman. Hume's reach into Austrian economics was primarily as a philosopher, specifically as a reductionist and empiricist. Hume's economic writings were carefully read and absorbed by two of the leading Austrians of the twentieth century: Joseph Schumpeter and Friedrich Hayek.

Late Eighteenth-Century and Nineteenth-Century Anglophone Economics

David Hume was much admired by some of the leading figures in the newly formed United States of America. Hume had befriended Benjamin Franklin in Edinburgh in 1759 and visited him often at his home on Craven Street in central London from 1767 to 1769. Hume and Franklin assisted each other in publishing their respective works. Hume, for example, invited Franklin to publish an article on lightning rods for the proceedings of the Edinburgh Philosophical Society that Hume edited, and Franklin "promised" to publish an edition of the *Essays* in America (HL, 2:258).[54] Although the first American edition of Hume's *Essays* was not issued until 1817, they proved immensely popular, appearing in magazines and college libraries, and sold widely.[55] Hume's economic thought seeped into Franklin's economic texts, particularly his work on population. Franklin served as the first American ambassador to France and was thus instrumental in planting Humean political ideals among the French republicans.[56]

The leading American statesmen Alexander Hamilton (of Scottish ancestry), James Madison, and Thomas Jefferson read and absorbed Hume's *Essays* and *History of England*, albeit with varying degrees of appreciation. Hamilton was the only one to acknowledge Hume favorably, in his work on governance and on money. In his design of the capital markets and banking systems of the new republic, Hamilton leaned heavily on Hume's economic theory. Madison was silent on Hume in print, but we know that there was a deep influence, as scholars have found in the *Federalist Papers*, particularly number 10, wherein he addressed the significance of the commercial system.[57] The young Jefferson was an attentive reader of Hume's economics and history, but circa 1810 he became a vocal opponent—primarily, it seems, on religious grounds. In his vision for economic development, Jefferson was a strong advocate of the agrarian sector, and he found Hume's emphasis on commerce and manufacturing distasteful.[58] Several scholars, most notably J. G. A. Pocock, have shown the extent to which Humean moral and political philosophy, whether in a positive or negative light, was embedded in the ideology of antebellum America.[59] Hume's early endorsement of the right to quit colonial rule was not lost on the young republicans, nor were his efforts to join population growth with economic prosperity. The colony that declared its independence the year Hume died had the fastest recorded birthrate in the literate world, with population doubling at a rate of approximately every twenty-five years.

The prominent British economists of the pre-Victorian era, Jeremy Bentham and Thomas Robert Malthus, were careful readers of Hume's works. Bentham was particularly drawn to Hume's ethics and was explicit about his debt to Hume on the importance of the principle of utility in an early work, *A Fragment on Government* (1776). Bentham stated that when he read Hume's *Treatise*, he "felt as if the scales had fallen" from his eyes and that he "learned to see that *utility* was the test and measure of all virtue."[60] While Bentham is renowned for promoting utilitarianism, he was also a major contributor to economics. His influence on the circle he frequented—that of Malthus, James

Mill, and David Ricardo—has been increasingly appreciated.[61] Malthus made considerable use of Hume's lengthy essay on population, in part because both men had challenged the work of Robert Wallace. Malthus engaged Hume on specific details, particularly on epidemics and on the question of slavery and its alleged impediment to the birthrate.[62]

With the notable exception of John Stuart Mill in the 1830s and 1840s, most contributors to political economy were disinclined to probe into the psychological and ethical foundations of economics as developed by Hume and Smith. This disinclination is most apparent in Ricardo's *Principles of Political Economy and Taxation* (1817), without doubt the most influential single text in economics of the first half of the nineteenth century. It is mute on the subject of the proximate causes of economic agency and also makes no reference to Hume or Smith on moral psychology. Ricardo's primary adversary was Smith for his economic analysis. Ricardo exposed a number of fallacious arguments that had become canonical since 1776—for example, that an increase in wages would necessarily result in inflation. Ricardo assigned dominant motives to each of the three separate classes of landowners, laborers, and capitalists but did not unpack those ascriptions nor reduce them to individual motives, let alone psychological states. Ricardo was drawn to what later became known as *macroeconomics*—that is, the distribution of the national product and the long-term tendencies for the returns to the three factors of production: land, labor, and capital. Ricardo offered methodological maxims, to posit universal laws that he claimed have the same binding necessity as physics and to strive for analytical clarity and rigor, but there is little overt attention to methodological or ethical questions. Ricardo, however, had a much wider range of interests than is reflected in his *Principles*. His intellectual genesis and earlier writings, not to mention his parliamentary addresses toward the end of his life, indicate a considerable interest in Enlightenment natural and social philosophy.[63]

More to the point, Ricardo had read Hume's *Political Discourses* with care by 1811, or perhaps sooner, since we know that he had cultivated interests in political economy while still working as a stockbroker in the first decade of the nineteenth century. He referred to Hume's insights on money, the specie-flow mechanism, and the interest rate in two early works, *The High Price of Bullion* (1810) and a *Reply to Mr. Bosanquet's Practical Observations on the Report of the Bullion Committee* (1811), and again in a parliamentary speech of May 24, 1819.[64] He also quoted, in a set of unpublished notes, Hume's famous passage about money arriving from Cádiz. He disagreed with Hume, however, claiming that Hume was "erroneous" to maintain that a decreasing quantity of money would induce poverty.[65] In his *Essay on Profits*

(1815), a work treated as a sketch for the *Principles*, Ricardo acknowledged Hume's monetary analysis and its absorption by Malthus.[66] Finally, in a letter to James Mill of December 18, 1817, Ricardo confessed, "I admire exceedingly the ingenuity with which Hume shews from Locke's doctrines that we have no proof of the existence of external objects. . . . Your view I observe of the manner in which mankind become acquainted with the idea of a Supreme Being is much the same as that of Hume."[67] This remark suggests that Ricardo had also pondered Hume's *Treatise*, as well as read the *Natural History of Religion*, for which there are additional references.[68] In sum, there is evidence of a strong appreciation for Hume, both his economics and his metaphysics, woven into the corpus of Ricardo's work.

Hume was best known in the nineteenth century for his *History of England*. It was reprinted over one hundred times and made widely available in Britain, France, and the United States. His stock in philosophy fell, however, notwithstanding the deep admiration expressed by both Bentham and Kant.[69] For the most part, philosophy moved toward idealism and romanticism under the beacon of G. W. F. Hegel, Johann Gottlieb Fichte, and Friedrich Wilhelm Joseph von Schelling, and this school of thought demanded strong allegiances.[70]

Economics also became doctrinal in the first half of the nineteenth century. Jean-Baptiste Say and his cohort known as the *ideologues* were subject to the gravitational pull of system building, a stance that was orthogonal to Hume's commonsense empiricism.[71] As a result, Hume was partially eclipsed for much of nineteenth-century philosophy and economics. Everyone read him and cited him, but the influence was mostly indirect, via Smith, Bentham, and Malthus. Hume is most cited in monetary theory, notably by the leading contributor of the period, Henry Thornton, who developed some of Hume's ideas on paper currency.[72] Overall, however, Hume's more episodic approach to economics did not resonate well with the system-building predilections of the leading classical economists. Notwithstanding the continuation of British empiricism with John Stuart Mill and John Herschel, among others, Hume was relegated to the periphery of mainstream British philosophy. Mill, for example, believed that Thomas Reid had solved Hume's problem of induction, and it was only with T. H. Green in 1878 that Hume's problem became widely known.[73] Hume may have left more of an imprint on Mill's economics. We know from his *Autobiography* that Mill had studied Hume's *Essays* in his formative years, and an annotated copy of Hume's *Essays* was found among Mill's personal collection in Avignon, where he lived for the last decade of his life.[74]

Only after the Marginal Revolution of the 1870s did Hume's name become prominent again. It was a time as well for soul-searching on the methods and ethical foundations of economics. John Neville Keynes, William Stanley Jevons, and Henry Sidgwick in their respective writings took up philosophical topics drawn from Hume, as did Alfred Marshall, who was the doyen of the economics profession at the turn of the twentieth century. Marshall's *Principles of Economics* (1890) lays out the discipline with a distinctly Humean tone, noting the importance in reflecting on the difficult task of finding enduring principles, and emphasizing the value of an evolutionary approach.[75] Among the early neoclassical economists, Francis Ysidro Edgeworth was the most avid devotee of Hume, particularly in his work on probability and decision theory.[76] Edgeworth, professor of political economy at Oxford University, was editor of the single most prominent periodical in Britain, the *Economic Journal*. Edgeworth's work also resonated well with A. C. Pigou, who became professor of economics at Cambridge University when Alfred Marshall retired in 1908. Both Edgeworth and Pigou were careful students of moral philosophy, including the landmark work of Sidgwick, and in that sense they fall within the tradition set out by Hume and Smith.

By the early twentieth century, Hume's work was widely available in the United States.[77] The *Political Discourses* came back into print in 1906 as part of the popular and inexpensive Walter Scott Publishing Company's library catalog. It included a short introduction by William Bell Robertson, who underscored the importance of viewing Hume as an economist in close contact with Adam Smith.[78] In addition to the twelve original essays of 1752, it included Smith's account of Hume's life and seven more essays on political philosophy. Both Thorstein Veblen and Irving Fisher, two of the most prominent economists at the time, displayed an interest in Hume.[79] Another major American economist of the period, John R. Commons, identified parallels between the Institutionalism that he helped found and Hume's evolutionary account of economics.[80] Wesley Clair Mitchell covered Hume's contributions in his *Types of Economic Theory: From Mercantilism to Institutionalism* (1949), while his various *Essays*, particularly the set entitled *The Backward Art of Spending Money* (1937) suggest a careful reading and absorption of Hume.[81] American institutionalism, as developed by Commons and Mitchell, drew heavily on the pragmatism of Charles Sanders Peirce, William James, and John Dewey. They endorsed a strong evolutionary and secular set of beliefs and wove Hume's social philosophy into the mix. Pragmatism was also developed in Britain, particularly at Cambridge University by the economist-philosopher Frank Ramsey, who was a close associate of John Maynard Keynes.[82] The strong allegiance to empiricism among this circle at Cambridge meant that Humean ideals were kept in full view.

Libertarian Heritage

More than any other economist or philosopher, Hume was Friedrich Hayek's "constant companion and sage guide."[83] In an essay of 1966 on Mandeville, Hayek wrote, "I do not intend to pitch my claim on behalf of Mandeville higher than to say that he made Hume possible. It is indeed my estimate of Hume as perhaps the greatest of all modern students of mind and society which makes Mandeville appear to me so important."[84] In his lengthy essay of 1963 on Hume, Hayek praised Hume above all for developing the philosophical foundations for economics. Hayek singled out Hume's analysis of property and justice and recommended that readers start with the second *Enquiry* and work their way back to the *Treatise*. He proclaimed Hume "the greatest legal philosopher whom Britain produced before Bentham."[85] He much appreciated Hume's command of emergent properties and the realization that individual actions are relatively nonsensical unless treated collectively as a group.

There are numerous references to Hume in two of Hayek's larger works, the *Constitution of Liberty* (1960) and the three-volume *Law, Legislation and Liberty* (1973–79), as well as his writings on money and his more popular *Road to Serfdom* (1944).[86] As the tribute to the front page of *The Fatal Conceit: The Errors of Socialism* (1988) makes plain—"the rules of morality are not the conclusions of our reason"—Hayek was particularly taken with Hume's efforts to subordinate reason in his account of ethical judgment.[87] Hayek also took inspiration from Hume, in conjunction with Mandeville and Smith, on the idea of a spontaneous and emergent market order.[88] Hayek foregrounded the analysis of markets as systems of information, and in that respect, he drew on Hume's semiotic interpretation of prices, as well as his emphasis on the importance of local and tacit knowledge.[89]

In general, libertarians believe that the private sector should provision most if not every economic resource. Accordingly, libertarians eschew government interference with economic processes, the control of markets and trade practices, even the issuance of money or other securities such as annuities. In that respect, they differ from Hume, who saw a clear role for the government, including property rights, the mint, and the provisioning of public goods such as military defense. But the leading twentieth-century libertarians share with Hume certain predilections, particularly the emphasis on individual freedom and the value of knowledge in fostering economic development. They also welcome Hume's efforts to circumscribe reason but retain the power and relative autonomy of the human mind to forge a representation of the world.

Milton Friedman was an avid student of the history of ideas, both philosophy and economics. Hume played an important role in his intellectual schooling, both in epistemology and in the analysis of money. Friedman probably first encountered Hume's writings on economics in the course he took with Jacob Viner at the University of Chicago while pursuing his master's degree, which he completed in 1933. Viner had an encyclopedic command of the history of economics and, as we noted, had argued that Smith had dissented from Hume on the specie-flow mechanism. Friedman's "helicopter drop" is a thought experiment in the same tradition, and there are many interesting parallels to Hume's overnight and radical alteration of the money supply. Friedman would also have learned from Viner about Hume's passage on the arrival of money from Cádiz that demonstrated how an injection of money could engender economic activity. This seed planted by Hume germinated the Friedmanian doctrine of monetarism that eventually garnered its author the Nobel Memorial Prize in Economics in 1976.

Friedman's historical skills are evident in his masterful account, with Anna Jacobson Schwartz, of American monetary theory and practice. Because of his historical sensibility, he was interested in the legal and institutional setting of economic growth and in that respect shared Hume's evolutionary orientation.[90] Friedman also wrote the most influential paper in the philosophy of economics of the twentieth century, "The Methodology of Positive Economics" (1953).[91] It argues that good explanations stem from general and abstract propositions that are, strictly speaking, false. Friedman thus endorses an instrumentalist view of scientific truth that resonates well with Hume's. According to Friedman's paper, theoretical constructs in economics need not be veridical as long as they generate sound predictions. Propositions that build upon sense impressions will always lose veracity as we embark on general claims. Moreover, insofar as all knowledge is subject to revision, the most we can hope for are well-corroborated laws. Friedman downplayed the goal of truth in economic theory and foregrounded the importance of practical applications and predictions. Whatever the merits of Friedman's methodology, he displayed a remarkable understanding of the contingent nature of scientific explanations and the sense in which sound explanations are driven not by truth but by versatile and capacious concepts. If one aims at true descriptions, one straitjackets the inquiry and the explanations are less fecund. If one aims rather at representations that are abstracted from the details of the world and thus, strictly speaking, false, the explanations engendered are more likely to be of value both at present and for spawning future lines of investigation. For the most part, Hume and Friedman were both allied with this instrumentalist tradition.

Friedman paid tribute to Hume on a number of occasions—for example, at the start of his article "The Role of Monetary Policy" or in his entry on the "Quantity Theory of Money" for the *New Palgrave Dictionary of Economics*.[92] As Friedman recognized, Hume was one of the first observers to see the national stock of money as a function of output and thus broach the question of the optimal quantity of money. In his thought experiments, Hume gave the price level unprecedented flexibility, but in the real world, Hume recognized that wages and hence prices are sticky. Both Hume and Friedman treated the velocity of money as stable except in times of crisis. Habits and customs also form a natural basis for Friedman's *permanent-income hypothesis*—to wit, that agents forge consumption patterns based not on transitory income but rather on long-term expectations of earnings. In this respect, too, Friedman held beliefs that appear similar to Hume's. Human dispositions are sluggish and resistant to change, not because of foresight or a long rate of temporal discounting, but because human beings are creatures of habit.

More recent libertarian economists, notably James Buchanan, Douglass North, and Vernon L. Smith—all winners of the Nobel Memorial Prize in Economics—also manifest ideas that drew inspiration from Hume.[93] They saw Hume as a progenitor for the important insight by which a small number of rules can unintentionally result in robust institutions that shape significant economic outcomes. Buchanan linked Hume's insights from Book 3 of the *Treatise* to Michael Polanyi's analysis of spontaneous order.[94] He also appealed to Hume's specific propositions about excise taxes and public debt.[95] North rarely cited Hume, but others have argued that there is a strong similarity and that it is highly probable that North studied Hume during the course of his university education.[96] North discerned the implicit rules of human behavior that forge cooperation as an unintended consequence. He famously foregrounded the importance of institutions, defined as a set of rules, and approached economics in historical terms. Because there are transaction costs, stubborn inefficiencies, and imperfect foresight, economic institutions play a critical part and result in path dependencies. Vernon L. Smith, while renowned as a pioneer in experimental economics, has developed a substantial number of publications on conventions and rules in economics that draws directly on the Scottish Enlightenment. He pays tribute to Hume's probing study of human nature in several of his publications, including his Nobel Memorial Prize lecture, and study of rationality.[97] There is, in sum, considerable indebtedness to Hume among modern libertarian economics.

Liberal Heritage

The *liberal* heritage in economics is here defined in the sense of a commitment to both individual rights and the redistribution of wealth and income. There is in general a willingness to promote government action for the provision of public goods, to promote fiscal policies and guide the path of trade and commerce. All economists favor unrestricted trade, at least in principle, so that is a position that applies equally to libertarians and liberals. There are, however, significant differences between the two schools of thought. Libertarians seek to dismantle the government in many traditional spheres, and they put much conviction in the potential for order emerging organically from existing institutions. Liberals, by contrast, tend to introduce controls from the seat of power and thus leave themselves open to the charges of both suboptimal efficiencies and paternalist social policies. Both groups view the rights to various freedoms—association, belief, and expression—as sacrosanct, but the liberal group puts weight on the view that individuals are not sui generis. Rather, they recognize that individuals are the products of social norms that are subject to collective forces that undergo gradual evolution.

Hume had many liberal predilections, such as a strong allegiance to individual flourishing and the efficacy of markets, but also an eye toward the building of sound and just institutions that would shape people's dispositions and reconfigure their ascriptions of ethical norms. Hume understood that human beings tend to cling to their inherited beliefs rather than undertake radical shifts, and for the most part he leaned toward an approach based on gradual and subtle rather than surgical actions. But as we saw, Hume believed that the government could help promote the growth of population, achieve a more equitable system of taxes, and promote the general well-being of its populace. It could provide more education and thus reduce if not eliminate religious superstitions and idolatry (E-IPC, 519–27). And it could, as was already evident in Britain, form a less pious and austere society, one that was more licentious. The liberal tradition that stems from Hume found much purchase among twentieth-century adherents.

John Maynard Keynes was of monumental significance in the development of modern economics; some scholars speak of a "Keynesian revolution."[98] The main thrust of his *General Theory of Employment, Interest and Money* (1936) is to disclose at the macroeconomic level that the purported self-correcting mechanism of the market tends to break down. A slump such as the Great Depression might persist indefinitely. Keynes argued that leadership from the government, particularly massive investments in infrastructure such as Franklin Delano Roosevelt's New Deal of 1933–36, might be the only viable solution. Fiscal tools tend to be a more effective than monetary policy to counteract serious and persistent downturns. The monetary authority might induce more stability in a healthy economy, but in one that has broken down and resulted in massive unemployment, efforts to lower the interest rate and engage in monetary easing would have no further effect on investment.

Keynes was a leading voice in restoring money to the center of economic theory, albeit with an emphasis on liquidity preferences and the manner by which money is invested into capital. Keynes recognized that different forms of money lent themselves to different purposes, as forms of liquid capital or as instruments for speculation. Although Hume's primary emphasis was on the money supply, he also recognized these types of demand. In his remarks about merchants and their novel practices with banking and credit instruments, Hume posited three types of liquidity demand—namely, the transactionary, precautionary, and speculative functions that Keynes would later identify and foreground (E-BT, 319). Hume also attended to the importance of inventories in the chain of events by which a monetary injection alters economic output. In the passage of the money arriving from Cádiz, a critical step is when the farmers and gardeners notice that inventories are depleted (E-Mo, 287). Keynes would feature inventories as offering important signals in his analysis of business cycles and thus developed further an idea broached by Hume. We know Keynes read this passage in Hume because he cited it in his *General Theory* and also offered the judgment that Hume hovered somewhere between the mercantilists and classical economists.[99]

Keynes read and critiqued Hume's epistemology in considerable detail. Hume's insights into analogical and inductive inferences form a central part of Keynes's one purely philosophical work, his *Treatise on Probability* (1921). Keynes makes about a dozen references to Hume in that work, and his critical concept of weight, whereby additional data bolster the veracity of a given proposition, was directly indebted to Hume's analysis of testimony.[100] Both Hume and Keynes were reluctant to assign quantitative measures to empirical ascriptions of probability, other than more or less, in part because they recognized the inherent difficulties of treating events as identical and hence as equiprobable.[101] Although Keynes did not formally ally himself with logical positivism, his close association with Bertrand Russell and A. J. Ayer meant that he was well acquainted with the strong reductionism and empiricism that Hume espoused.

If a society is to attain greater freedoms, it must also strive for more enlightenment, Keynes argued. Both John Stuart Mill and John Maynard Keynes referred to the "Art of Living" as an informed set of pursuits, one that feeds on the cultivation of the intellect and an engagement with aesthetic pursuits. This state of being could only come to pass if there was ample leisure time and hence widespread economic prosperity. Keynes thus articulated a vision similar to the one offered by Hume, and John Stuart Mill, that the end point of individual flourishing is such that enlightened citizens would cultivate higher-order pleasures such as friendship or poetry rather than the purchase of luxuries or the pursuit of mindless games.[102] The quotation that serves as the epithet to our book finds Hume identifying an enlightened and nonpecuniary path to happiness. Keynes's essays put much emphasis on the prospect of technological advancement such that ordinary citizens might enjoy more leisure time and cultivate their minds. Education, especially in the arts, was of paramount importance. Keynes took an active role in linking the state with cultural development, notably serving as the first chair of the Arts Council of Great Britain in 1946, shortly before he died. Hume's vision for human flourishing championed innovations in the arts, such as his endorsement of the production and distribution of the play *Douglas* by his good friend John Home. Ernest Mossner goes so far as to suggest that Hume's paean to *Douglas* at the start of his *Four Dissertations* (1757) was nothing less than "the Scottish Declaration of Literary Independence."[103] In short, Hume's promotion of literature, theater, and new social mores blends seamlessly into Keynes's strong appeal to cultivate the arts, such as Keynes himself enjoyed with the Bloomsbury circle and his wife, the ballerina Lydia Lopokova.[104]

After Keynes, the baton of liberalism passed to Paul Samuelson, who shone as the leading mind in mathematical economics of the mid-twentieth century and who sought to extend the life of Keynesianism in opposition to the monetarist policies of Milton Friedman. Samuelson had pursued the undergraduate program in the Great Books at the University of Chicago, and it specifically included a section in term three of his first year on the Scottish Enlightenment where he would have been exposed to some of Hume's texts. Samuelson reminisced at age seventy about knowing Hume as "a great reductionist," a stance he claims commenced as an undergraduate. But it is not clear what he meant by this fleeting remark.[105] Hume's sensory empiricism is reductionist in spirit, as is his account of personal identity. There are building blocks to all knowledge, simple impressions and ideas, and combinatorial methods for retrieving and rearranging these with the machinery of the mind. Samuelson famously urged that the term *utility* be purged from economic discourse and mounted in its place the weak and strong axioms of revealed preferences. In this respect, he opted to shift away from propositions about the working of the mind and look only at manifest actions. Hume's predilections were different, insofar as he emphasized the importance of intentions, the memory, and the imagination in forging human activities.

As a doctoral student at Harvard, at age twenty, Samuelson came under the sway of Joseph Schumpeter, who later wrote the definitive text on the history of economics of the twentieth century, published posthumously as *A History of Economic Analysis* (1954). It was most likely in Schumpeter's courses that Samuelson developed a passion for the history of economics and most likely encountered Hume's *Political Discourses*. Samuelson also wrote many reminiscences on leading economists, as well as articles analyzing the economics of, for example, Ricardo and Marx. Samuelson wrote two articles specifically on Hume's specie-flow mechanism, in 1971 and 1980.[106] As we saw, Samuelson was critical of Hume, for failing to follow through on several technical implications of the mechanism. Nevertheless, Samuelson bestowed much time and attention trying to understand Hume's writings on economics and philosophy and in that respect undoubtedly absorbed some of his ideas.

Among living liberal economists, Paul Krugman singles out Hume's first *Enquiry* as one of the most influential books he read as an undergraduate student.[107] Hume served to steer him away from dogma, and toward a skeptical empiricism that he claims has guided him in his economics to this day. Krugman continues to pay tribute to Hume on a regular basis, as do others in the liberal tradition who investigate the overlap of philosophy and economics, notably Ken Binmore and Robert Sugden. There are several other mainstream economists—Edmund Phelps, for example—who point to Hume's influence on his efforts to understand the links between knowledge formation and economic growth.[108] Because Hume's works are now a permanent feature of the philosophical canon, the probability is high that influential economists would have read these in their formative years.

In the field of economic development, Arthur Lewis—a prominent liberal contributor—gleaned much from Hume's analysis.[109] Among living economists on development, Amartya Sen has also donned Hume's mantle. As professor of economics and philosophy at Harvard University, he exemplifies the tradition that reaches back to Hume that keeps in full view the philosophical dimensions of economics. In one of his most famous essays, "Rational Fools" (1977), Sen strongly resembles Hume for his insights into the benign ways in which people tend to act for the greater good, often reflexively. Sen appeals to people's own personal experiences of extensive honesty, respect, and truth telling to strangers as a means to demonstrate the shortcomings of rational choice theory. He thus highlights the ethical context to many human actions and the extent to which principled or civil acts of "commitment" undercut the axiom of self-interest and result in counterpreferential behavior. Sen's land-mark philosophical work, *The Idea of Justice* (2009), does more than pay lip service to Hume and positions his analysis in a direct line leading up to John Rawls, who was also an avid reader of Hume. Sen has been a leading voice for restoring the ethical content of economics and expanding its purview to prompt economists to reflect more broadly on human well-being.[110]

Did David Hume promote economic liberalism? Hume certainly anchored economic production and distribution in a respect for property rights, one of the more robust claims of economic liberalism.[111] He also favored disman-tling unnecessary restrictions on commercial freedoms, both individual and collective, and generally favored competition at the expense of Crown privi-leges or monopolies. As part of his liberal predilections, he also addressed the question of whether the existing system tended to reduce or enhance un-warranted inequality, arguing that a "too great disproportion [of wealth] among the citizens weakens any state. Every person, if possible, ought to enjoy the fruits of his labour, in full possession of all the necessaries, and many of the conveniences of life" (E-Co, 265). Furthermore, with a gesture toward the principle of diminishing marginal utility of income, he asserted that "wherever we depart from this equality, we rob the poor of more satisfac-tion than we add to the rich" (EPM, 20). He repeated this insight in his *Politi-cal Discourses*. In his essay "Of Commerce" he stated, "No one can doubt, but such an equality is most suitable to human nature, and diminishes much less from the *happiness* of the rich than it adds to that of the poor" (E-Co, 265).

At one point, Hume speculated about a world in which all of nature's "presents" would be equally divided among everyone, in which case, "every individual would enjoy all the necessaries, and even most of the comforts of life" (EPM, 20). Notwithstanding these remarks, Hume did not advo-cate complete equality or endorse taking empowered steps in this direction. Rather, he positioned political stability over appeals to inequality, and he col-lapsed justice to a system of property rights. It was also important to Hume never to eliminate a social hierarchy. He welcomed the expansion of the middle class and the values it espoused, but he believed that inequality was critical to provide the necessary incentives to industry. As Hume observed, such "ideas of *perfect* equality . . . would be extremely *pernicious* to human society" (EPM, 20). Hume also considered property rights to be of critical importance as a source of pride and well-being. There is a strong conserva-tive streak in Hume that foregrounds the importance of the slow evolution of social norms and institutions.

Aspirations for an Enlightened World

Hume sought a stable and ever-improving world guided above all by the new commercial middle class. He waxed poetic that the person in "merchandize or manufacture" is "like the sun, an inferior minister of providence . . . [who] invigorates, and sustains the surrounding world" (EPM, 9–10). He regarded commerce as a life-affirming activity, radiating prosperity like the sunshine; to him, commerce and trade provided food and clothing and guided the "ignorant and slothful [toward] skill and industry" (EPM, 9). Furthermore, if any group was to advance and safeguard liberty, Hume argued, it was the class that would later be known as the bourgeoisie. The seeds within the commercial world sown by enterprising merchants were potent and, if given the right soil and nutrients, would inevitably grow and spread their benefits around the globe.

Virtue, for Hume, takes much effort to cultivate and augment. The man of business, however, was fortunately engaged in daily interactions that tested his moral mettle and was thus in a position to strengthen his character. Not everyone, of course, is honest or honorable, but the tendencies to these ends are stronger than the converse, Hume believed. Even if an opportunity for fraud or theft presents itself, the honest person will tend to stay within the law: "The antipathy to treachery and roguery is too strong to be counterbalanced by any views of profit or pecuniary advantage. Inward peace of mind, consciousness of integrity, a satisfactory review of our own conduct; these are circumstances very requisite to happiness, and will be cherished and cultivated by every honest man, who feels the importance of them" (EPM, 82). Happiness for Hume could only be sustained if grounded in a genuine accountability to one's self. In this respect, the virtuous person perceives what the less virtuous do not. In Hume's view, virtue requires constant attention and the shoring up of goodness; it is something one has to practice and keep readily in view; good deeds and good offices are critical to the mission of social advancement.

Wisdom, for Hume, comes from grasping that there is a significant difference between wealth and happiness: "Who admires not Socrates; his perpetual serenity and contentment, amidst the greatest poverty and domestic vexations; his resolute contempt of riches" (EPM, 63). But one could be virtuous and wealthy at the same time, Hume asserted. Hume's hypothetical perfect son-in-law, Cleanthes, "a man of business and application," also "preserves a perpetual serenity on his countenance, and tranquillity in his soul" (EPM, 73). Conversely, Hume related the fable of a recently deceased miser opting to swim the river Styx rather than pay the boatman Charon his fee for crossing. Possible punishments—chaining him to Prometheus or assisting Sisyphus—were ruled out as not severe enough. The only consequence sufficiently punitive, in Hume's account, was to return the miser back to earth "to see the use his heirs are making of his riches" (E-Av, 572).

Hume imparted a narrative that captures an underlying "economy of esteem."[112] In his own autobiographical account he remarked that he was more pleased to acquire a "rising reputation" from his scholarship than "to be born to an estate of ten thousand [pounds] a year." (E-MOL, xxxvi). He also throws into the mix that his cheerful disposition is partly due to nature and partly to nurture. In Book 3 of the *Treatise of Human Nature*, Hume devoted a section to "Natural Abilities" and emphasized that these abilities can be enhanced or diminished under various circumstances. For example, "good sense and genius beget esteem," while "wit and humour excite love" (T, 388). In this same section, Hume explored the many factors that might not only forge the most virtuous character but also carry a person "farthest in any of his undertakings . . . for business." The list is long but includes industry, application, and frugality (T, 389).

Hume was clear that people's lives have more setbacks than advances, that pains tend to outweigh pleasures (E-DT, 4). He advised his readers to prepare themselves for adversity and to strive for security and tranquillity, best achieved with friendship and esteem. The paradox of acquiring wealth is that one must be always fearful of its disappearance; these insecurities prey upon the mind. Hume thus offered much wisdom on the economic dimensions of the pursuit of happiness and the prospects for reducing inequalities. The best goods in life—friendship, good health, and equanimity—are nonpecuniary. Not only are these goods acquired outside the marketplace, but their value is immeasurable: "What comparison, I say between these, and the feverish, empty amusements of luxury and expence? These natural pleasures, indeed, are really without price; both because they are below all price in their attainment, and above it in their enjoyment" (EPM, 82). These nascent utilitarian judgments resonate well with the cultivation of people's benevolent dispositions. One's love for one's family and community is testament to the ability to subordinate self-love and, in some instances, to find joy in the happiness of another even if there is no gain for oneself.

In the spring of 1776, Hume, by then seriously ill, made his last journey to England, to Bath for a medical cure. His companion was his good friend John Home, who later recorded some of the conversations from the trip. Because Home was known to have an excellent memory, there is reason to believe the following anecdote is authentic.[113] Home recollected an exchange during which Hume speculated about what would happen if he ruled one kingdom, while Home and their friend Adam Ferguson served as princes of adjacent states. Hume would pursue "projects of cultivating, improving, and civilizing mankind by the arts of peace."[114] Because Home and Ferguson did the opposite, and invested heavily in building their respective armies, they would each overspend and "be continually in want of money, whilst he [Hume] would have his finances in excellent condition, his magazines well filled, and naval stores in abundance."[115] Hume joked that to secure lasting peace, he would give a subsidy to either Home or Ferguson to wage war against the other, which would defeat them both and leave Hume as the "master of all three kingdoms."[116] Home recollected that this was "so like David's manner of playing with his friends, I fell into a fit of laughing, in which David joined; and the people that passed us certainly thought we were very merry travelers."[117] Hume's imaginary ascent to benevolent dictator speaks to his enduring optimism that prudential actions would insure a peaceful world. What is less clear is that, were he to return to see the results, would he still be laughing?

ACKNOWLEDGMENTS

Our paths first crossed in 1999, at the annual meetings of the History of Economics Society, and a few years later we organized a workshop on Hume's economics, held at Barnard College in May 2003. This event brought together about a dozen scholars on the subject, many of whom contributed to our co-edited volume, *David Hume's Political Economy* (Routledge, 2008). We were heartened by its reception and the evident swell of interest in Hume's economics. We next coauthored an article on Hume, for the *Journal of Economic Perspectives* (2011), and within a couple of years decided to coauthor this monograph. With hindsight, we can see that the seeds of this project were first planted in 1999, when we were both beginning to immerse ourselves in Hume scholarship, but the bulk of the writing of this book has transpired over the past few years. We like to think that because there was much back-and-forth, the whole is greater than the sum of the parts.

In addition to our one coauthored article and coedited book, we have each published several more articles or book chapters on Hume's economics. We decided, however, to write afresh and not recycle past material. This book builds on our previous work but is not, as some books tend to be, a reissuing of past publications. Indeed, one of the things we treasure most about Hume is that we keep discovering new ideas and insights about his economics. There seems to be no end, in fact. We found, in the course of writing this, that several interesting leads had to be confined to a single sentence or footnote, or we would never finish. There is still much to explore on the subject: Hume on slavery, on the economic status of women, on the religious context of economics, on patterns of consumption, on contractual obligations, and so on and so forth.

The research for this book was generously funded by a number of agencies. Margaret Schabas wishes to acknowledge the support of the Social Sciences and Humanities Council of Canada, the Ludwig Lachmann Foundation, the Max Planck Institute for the History of Science, the Peter Wall Institute, and the Hampton Fund and Dean of Arts at the University of British Columbia. Carl Wennerlind wishes to acknowledge the support of the Davis Center for Historical Studies at Princeton University, ACLS, Wenner-Gren Foundation, INET, and the Barnard College Provost Office.

We are thankful for the help of countless librarians and archivists who helped us with our research, first and foremost at our home institutions, Columbia University and the University of British Columbia. Our efforts to track down sources related to this project took us to the British Library, the National Library of Scotland (St. Clair Papers), and the Huntington Library. We also used collections at the University of Edinburgh, the University of St. Andrews (Istvan Hont Papers), McGill University (David Hume Collection), Harvard University (Baker Library), and Princeton University (Firestone Library). We thank the private owner for permission to reproduce the portrait as the frontispiece to this book and William Zachs for assistance in locating this painting.

We have many people to thank who have directed us to various sources or helped us sort out our thoughts, and we apologize up front if any names are not recorded here. We were fortunate to have had conversations and valuable exchanges with some of the leading scholars in the field who have since passed away, notably Istvan Hont, Nicholas Phillipson, Ian Simpson Ross, and Andrew Skinner. Other senior scholars from whom we have benefited are Tony Aspromorgous, Peter Baldwin, Tom Beauchamp, Christopher Berry, George Caffentzis, Sheila Dow, Roger Emerson, Knud Haakonssen, André Lapidus, Antoin Murphy, David Raynor, and Tatsuya Sakamoto.

For specific insights or modifications, we thank Donald Ainslie, Tim Alborn, Fredrik Albritton-Jonsson, John Berdell, Richard van den Berg, Mauro Boianovsky, Deborah Brown, Bruce Caldwell, Dan Carey, Loïc Charles, Paul Cheney, Annie Cot, Angela Creager, Craig Fraser, Stephen Gaukroger, Jerry Gaus, Michael Gill, Martin Giraudeau, James Harris, Dan Hausman, Kevin Hoover, Onur Ulas Ince, Ann Levey, Harro Maas, Mary Morgan, Craig Muldrew, Arnaud Orain, David Owen, Steve Pincus, Sophus Reinert, Malcolm Rutherford, Amy Schmidt, David Schmidtz, John Shovlin, Phil Stern, Richard Sturn, Felix Waldman, Andre Wakefield, Ray Weintraub, Richard Whatmore, and Christine Zabel.

We would also like to take the opportunity to thank respective colleagues (past and present) either at the University of British Columbia or at Barnard

College and Columbia University: in particular, David Armitage, Robert Brain, Susanna Braund, Chris Brown, Mary Chapman, Charly Coleman, Will Deringer, Mauricio Drelichman, Mukesh Eswaran, Pierre Force, Sima Godfrey, Martha Howell, Ed Hundert, Joel Kaye, Dorothy Ko, William Koty, Andrew Lipman, Perry Mehrling, Adam Morton, Angela Redish, Paul Russell, Lisa Tiersten, Rhea Tregebov, Adam Tooze, and Aaron Zubia. We also thank our student research assistant, Sophie Wilkowske. And we much appreciate the patience and encouragement of our editor at the University of Chicago Press, Priya Nelson, as well as her editorial assistant, Dylan Montanari, and our production editor, Tamara Ghattas. We would also like to pay tribute to the excellent work of our copy editor, Lori Meek Schuldt.

We especially wish to acknowledge and heartily thank Monica Miller, who helped in more ways than can be remembered. Finally, we dedicate this book to our respective children: Margaret to her son, Joel; and Carl to his son, Langston, and daughter, Selma. They light up our lives.

NOTES

See the bibliography for full citations of
sources cited by author and date in the notes.

Introduction

1. See the section Abbreviations and Modifications at the beginning of the book for a complete list of abbreviations used parenthetically in the text and their corresponding sources.
2. The observation of Hume's "applause" was made by his learned correspondent Alison Cockburn and cited in Mossner 1980, 567. On the geography of the European enlightenment, see R. Porter and Teisch 1981.
3. Cited in Burton (1820) 1849, 45.
4. See, for example, the work of Parfit 1984, Korsgaard 1996, and Dennett 1996.
5. In 2009, a general survey of more than three thousand active Anglophone philosophers placed Hume as their favorite, both for teaching and for scholarship; see D. Garrett 2015, 334. Judging from the success of *Hume Studies* and the appeal to Hume scholarship in general, Hume garners more scholarly attention than Thomas Hobbes, John Locke, or John Stuart Mill.
6. It was only with the edition edited by Eugene F. Miller that the title *Essays, Moral, Political, and Literary* was first introduced, albeit with some fidelity to Hume's title for his initial set of essays of 1741–42 title, *Essays, Moral and Political* (1987). Miller's variorum edition is based on the 1777 version, but as Knud Haakonssen (1994) points out, we cannot know for certain whether the posthumous changes were faithful to Hume's wishes. As a result, he uses the 1772 edition for his selection of essays.
7. A fourth translation of the essays, by J.-B. Merian and J. B. R. Robinet, was published as part of the five-volume set *Œuvres philosophiques de Mr D. Hume* (see Hume 1758–60).
8. Steuart (1767) 1966, 2:343. Some of the other languages were Italian, German, and Swedish.
9. Quoted in Shovlin 2008, 203. The first translation by Jean-Bernard Le Blanc (Hume 1754a) includes substantial peritextual material that connected Hume's ideas to the French debates on luxury and trade. See Charles 2008. On receiving

a copy in 1755, Hume graciously wrote to Le Blanc, "it gives me great Satisfaction to find my Sense so justly preserved, and at the same time embellish'd by the Propriety & Elegance of your Expressions" (HL, 1:228). Hume kept a close eye on the French reactions to his work, corresponding several times with Le Blanc, Anne-Robert-Jacques Turgot, and André Morellet, who each defended his stance on luxury in opposition to Gabriel Bonnot de Mably, the Marquis de Mirabeau, and the Marquis de Saint-Lambert.

10. Quoted in Charles 2008, 201n43.
11. Charles 2008, 181. On the influence of the 1767 translation, see Charles 2008, 194–95. Smith's work did not begin to make its mark until the 1790s. See Tribe 1988, 133–48.
12. Hume considered dedicating his first *Enquiry* to Argyll; see HL, 1:113. On the infant industry tribute, see Emerson 2008, 13–14.
13. Quoted in E. Miller 1987, xvii.
14. The term "worldly philosopher" was coined by Robert Heilbroner (1953).
15. See Sen 1987, 2009; Hausman and McPherson 2006. We use "ethical" in the broadest sense, to include appeals to behavioral assumptions, moral judgments, and the implications for justice and fairness.
16. Stroud 1977; Baier 1991.
17. D. Garrett 1997; Russell 2008.
18. Harris 2015.
19. See Hume (1745) 1967; Hume 1751b. Hume wrote an anonymous political satire in 1761 that was never adequately identified in his lifetime. David Raynor argues convincingly that it is *Sister Peg*, a work that had mistakenly been attributed to John Millar. See Raynor 1982.
20. See Schabas, forthcoming.
21. See McArthur 2007.
22. See Waldman 2014, 109–11.
23. The date of Hume's *Early Memoranda* (MEM) is under dispute, but not its pronounced orientation toward economic questions. Ernest Mossner, who first edited this document, argued that the inscriptions range from 1729 to 1740 (see Mossner 1948, 492–94), while James Harris submits, based on arguments by at least three other scholars, especially Tatsuya Sakamoto, that the most probable dating for all three sections is the early 1740s (see Harris 2015, 509n11). More recently, Mazza and Mori (2016) argue that most of the entries predate the *Treatise*. Insofar as Hume cites the work of Du Tot early in section 3 (1738 in French and 1739 in English), it is highly probable that the bulk of the economic observations were registered after 1738. Hume does not cite Melon, so this suggests he only read him at some point in the 1740s.
24. This same insight prompted David Ricardo to discredit Smith and issue his groundbreaking two-factor theory of prices in his *Principles of Political Economy and Taxation* (1817). There is no reason to believe that Ricardo knew about Hume's letter, although he had read Hume's published work while formulating his tracts on money and could extract from Hume a cost theory of price that establishes the primacy of wages and profits.
25. See, for example, Wennerlind 2001, G. Davis 2003, Rotwein 2007, Sturn 2004, and Sakamoto 2016.

26. For an overview of Hume on causation and reasons to endorse the first *Enquiry* as a more mature account of the phenomenological realism of causes, see Strawson 1989 and Beebee 2015.

27. Forbes (1975, 87) acknowledged at the start of his book that he lacks expertise in economics and thus excluded it in his treatment of Hume's politics. McArthur (2007) has remedied this imbalance.

28. See Schabas 2014a.

29. See Diaye and Lapidus 2005a; 2005b.

30. See Hirschman 1977, 31–42.

31. Hume submits that "the lives of men depend upon the same laws as the lives of all other animals; and these are subjected to the general laws of matter and motion" (E-Su, 582). And because animals, he argues, have no immortal souls, we must entertain the same of humans, if only because of the strong anatomical resemblance (E-IS, 597).

32. Gaskin (2009, 506) argues that Hume's efforts to motivate a "secular, this-worldly, utilitarian morality . . . [was] revolutionary thought of ever widening application."

33. Quoted in Gay (1966) 1977, 24. Voltaire marveled at the mixture of faiths—he cites Muslim, Jewish, Presbyterian, Anabaptist, Anglican, and Quaker—among the brokers in the London stock exchange. As he (Voltaire [1734] 1961, 26) remarked, the stock exchange was a place "more venerable than many a court," where promises were honored and humankind served. All of them "reserve the name of infidel for those who go bankrupt."

34. See Stockton 1976; Wennerlind 2002; Phillipson 2011; Wei 2017.

35. See, for example, A. Brewer 1995, 1997; Berdell 1996; Mokyr 2009. Slack (2015) argues that English reformers embraced the idea of "improvement" during the seventeenth century, but this is not the same as identifying the dynamics of economic growth.

36. Locke wrote extensively on money, trade, and credit, but not the dynamics of growth. For Locke, markets played a passive role in the creation of wealth.

37. See Schatz 1902; Deleule 1979; Baldi 1983; Sakamoto 1995. The languages are German, French, Italian, and Japanese.

38. See J. Robertson 2005; W. Henderson 2010; and Wei 2017.

39. For more details on the use of the term *œconomy* in the early modern period, see Schabas 2005, 4–5.

40. See Lapidus 2010; 2011; 2019.

41. See Sugden 2005 for Hume's formal models; Vanderschraaf 1998, Hardin 2007, and Binmore 2011 for Hume as a nascent game theorist; and Palacios-Huerta 2003 and Diaye and Lapidus 2005a and 2005b for Hume's implicit appeals to rational assessments of time.

42. On Hume's temporal dimensions, see Schabas 2008b.

43. See Montesquieu (1748) 1989, 338; Hirschman 1977, 60. In 1734, while living in Reims, Hume observed in his commerce with the French that they displayed a "real Politeness" and "Softness of Temper" (HL, 1:20).

44. On Hume's evolutionary sensibility, see Schabas 2009.

45. See Foucault (1966) 1994.

Chapter 1

1. Mossner 1980, 245.
2. He interrupted the life of the scholar to accompany St. Clair on a diplomatic mission in 1748 that lasted the entire year.
3. Hume sent the manuscript to a mathematician friend, Philip Stanhope, who persuaded Hume to withdraw it from publication, and Hume concurred: "there was some Defect in the Argument or in its perspicuity" (DP, xxiii).
4. See Wootton 2009, 447–48.
5. As Mossner observes, "the current of Hume's life ran far from smooth. Its course was troubled by a series of bitter disappointments and frustrations" (Mossner 1980, 230).
6. See Mossner 1980, 268; Harris 2015, 265–89.
7. Mossner 1980, 391; 36.
8. Quoted in Mossner 1980, 272.
9. Emerson 2009, 43.
10. R. Porter and Teisch 1981.
11. Harris 2015, 444.
12. Harris 2015, 440.
13. The term *scientist* was not coined until 1833. See Snyder 2011, 3, 297–98.
14. See Hume and Munro (1754–71) 2002, 1:v–vi; Schabas 2001, 421–22.
15. Emerson (2009, 177) records that from 1720 to 1799, some fourteen thousand students attended anatomy lectures at the University of Edinburgh, taught successively by Munro I, his son Munro II, and his grandson Munro III.
16. For a general overview, see Boantza 2013.
17. Rothschild 2009, 415.
18. The age of eleven was the one on record among Hume scholars, including Mossner, but has been corrected to age ten. This confusion is due partly to the fact that a signature for matriculation comes in the second year of studies and partly from the fact that Scotland adopted the Gregorian calendar in 1600 while England waited until September 1752.
19. Hume's professor William Scot had edited Grotius, *The Rights of War and Peace*. We know Hume read Bayle by 1727 and Spinoza by 1737 because he registers this in letters to Michael Ramsay (HL, 1:12; see also Mossner 1980, 626–27) and because they are each cited numerous times in the *Treatise*. Hume also corresponded with Pierre Desmaizeaux, a friend and editor of Bayle's works, exiled in London (HL, 1:29). See Mossner (1980, 39–51) and Harris (2015, 35–77), for details on Hume's education at Edinburgh and the Dutch legacy.
20. Had Hume stayed one more year, he would have studied with of one of the most eminent British mathematicians of the eighteenth century, Colin Maclaurin (1698–1746), who started teaching at the University of Edinburgh in the autumn of 1725 and became the leading voice for Newtonian philosophy (Grabiner 1998).
21. Barfoot 1990, 155; see also Emerson 2009, 82.
22. The first Section of Hume's *Early Memoranda* (most likely 1729) is entitled *Natural Philosophy*, and the first entry reads that "a Ship sayls always swiftest when her Sides yield a little" (MEM, 499). He also cites Mareschal de Vauban, a renowned contributor to fortification (MEM, 510). Most of the entries on commercial data are to be found in the third section, most likely written in the 1740s. Hume's essays

also refer to the mathematical improvements to ship design by Christiaan Huygens (E-IPC, 513) and the contributions of Vauban on taxes (E-BT, 316).

23. Kawashima 2004.

24. Rothschild 2009, 407.

25. Hume also left some books to his sister, but since she had no children, she most likely united them with the collection that her nephew inherited. See D. Norton and M. Norton 1996.

26. The dearth of philosophical texts suggests that much of the collection was built after he composed the *Treatise* and turned more of his attention toward politics and economics. We do know that sometime in or before 1740, Hume had read works by Josiah Child, Johann De Witt, Jacques Savary des Brûlons, and Sir William Temple, because they are registered in his *Early Memoranda* (MEM, 498–99).

27. Rothschild (2009, 431) claims that since commercial pursuits were still derogated in Scotland, and Hume was a gentleman, it was unusual for someone of his station to undertake this position.

28. J. Y. T. Greig, the editor of *The Letters of David Hume*, tentatively assigned Cheyne as the recipient, and Harris has reinforced this assertion. Mossner, on the other hand, argues that it was Arbuthnot. See HL, 1:12; Harris 2015, 76–77; and Mossner 1980, 84–88.

29. In his autobiography, written in 1776, Hume represents his Bristol sojourn less positively than his youthful letters suggest at the actual time. He states that because of his poor health and "slender fortune," he "was tempted, or rather forced, to make a very feeble trial for entering into a more active scene of life" (E-MOL, xxxiii). Hume misremembers other details in "My Own Life"—for example, that he did not receive a salary when serving as librarian for the Advocates Library.

30. Defoe (1724–26) 1971, 362.

31. Waldmann 2014, 65–69.

32. Reinert 2011, 125; Charles 2008, 185–86.

33. Defoe (1724–26) 1971, 363.

34. Mandeville (1924) 1988, 1:343. Hume offered a variant of this inconsistent behavior by noting that two Europeans meeting in China would embrace. Gill 2000 traces Hume's observation back to Mandeville.

35. Mossner 1980, 90; Waldmann 2014.

36. Jacob Vanderlint (1734, 141) estimated that the cost of maintaining a family with four children and maidservant in the middle station amounted to twelve shillings a day.

37. One explanation is offered in Hume's *Treatise*, when he states that "nothing is more usual than for men of good families, but narrow circumstances, to leave their friends and country. . . . We shall be unknown, say they, where we go, . . . and our poverty and meanness will by that means sit more easy upon us" (T, 209). The editors claim that Hume was referring to himself and that a subsequent letter confirms this (T, 503n17).

38. See Pluche (1746) 2003, 282–87.

39. I. Ross 2008, 38–39. See also Shovlin 2007. It is possible that Hume had read some of the economic writings of Colbert.

40. Alison Gopnik (2009) has argued that Hume would have conversed with one of the more renowned Jesuits at La Flèche, Charles François Dolu, who had previ-

ously lived in northeastern India and been exposed to Buddhism. There is no mention of Buddhism, however, in Hume's *Natural History of Religion*. He makes note of beliefs held by many other faiths, including Hinduism, Zoroastrianism, and Islam.

41. The question of whether Hume read a draft of Cantillon's *Essai* has been heavily debated and is unlikely to be resolved. There are, as Wennerlind (2008) points out, some clear similarities in their respective monetary theories. But Hume may have absorbed Cantillon indirectly or arrived independently at these ideas. Larrère (1992) argues that Montesquieu drew on Cantillon, and we know Hume read Montesquieu in 1748. Anthony Brewer (1992) argues that Hume learned about Cantillon from reading Malachy Postlethwayt's *Universal Dictionary of Trade and Commerce*, which contained reprints of parts of the *Essay*. As van den Berg (2012b;2017) points out, however, the *Dictionary* was released after Hume had completed his *Political Discourses*, and it did not include Cantillon on money. Furthermore, Postlethwayt did not acknowledge his source when he plagiarized from Cantillon, and the material constitutes less than 1 percent of the overall content of the *Dictionary*. It remains a matter of speculation whether Hume read Postlethwayt, even after 1752. Mirabeau (1756) cites Cantillon extensively, and we know Hume read Mirabeau, but there is no evidence that Hume revised his ideas because of a post-1756 knowledge of Cantillon gained indirectly from Mirabeau.

42. For the entry on Cantillon, see D. Norton and M. Norton 1996, 83. They argue that a substantial portion of the library dates back to David Hume's own collection.

43. Richard van den Berg (2012a, 2012b) has tracked down Cantillon's manuscripts, and he argues that the publication and reception of Cantillon's work is far more complicated than previous authors have recognized. In the end, he sides with Antoin Murphy (1986). The likelihood that Hume had read Cantillon before 1752 is very low. See also Sabbagh 2016.

44. Mossner 1958, 32.

45. Mossner 1962, 446.

46. Hume puzzled over the settlement for the rest of his life. A record of a conversation with his friend, the writer John Home, on April 30, 1776, makes clear that Hume still believed that the French, irrationally, gave up too much power in the peace treaty of 1748 (Home 1976, 22–23).

47. For a rendition of the appointment as judge advocate, see Mossner 1980, 191–92.

48. For a brief summary of the emotional toll that this war had on Hume, see Mossner 1980, 202. On the court martials, see Waldmann 2014, 112–27.

49. Hume later wrote an account of this episode, "Descent on the Coast of Brittany," to challenge the account by Voltaire. See Mossner 1980, 200.

50. German unification had been broached first by Tacitus and later by Leibniz. Whether Hume knew of these specific sources at the time is difficult to ascertain. The epithets to Books 1 and 2 of the *Treatise* are by Tacitus, and Hume makes reference to the *Histories* and the *Art of Prudence* but not *Germania*. Hume also cites Leibniz on logic (T, 408), but it is highly improbable that he knew his political works.

51. Mossner 1980, 218–19.

52. I. Ross 2008, 43.

53. London had adopted silk production before the Revocation of the Edict of Nantes.

Thomas Mun ([1664] 1968, 11), writing in the 1620s, estimated some fourteen thousand workers in the silk industry of Spitalfields. But the influx of Huguenots much expanded the industry. In 1750, England imported 600,000 pounds of raw and thrown silk to be woven. See R. Porter 1991, 365.

54. Rothschild 2011.

55. The full title of Hume's pamphlet is *A True Account of the Behaviour and Conduct of Archibald Stewart, Esq., Late Lord Provost of Edinburgh: In a Letter to a Friend* (1748). Stewart was exonerated.

56. Pocock 1975.

57. On his name change, see Mossner 1980, 90. Hume's first volume on the early Stuarts was entitled *The History of Britain* (1754). Because sales were poor outside of Edinburgh, he changed the title.

58. The Seven Years' War ended in 1763, but Hume did not sell his shares (HL, 1:371).

59. Mossner 1980, 410.

60. Rothschild 2009, 417. In 1766, Hume suffered some losses and transferred his equities into annuities (HL, 2:7).

61. Harris 2015, 169–74.

62. In his introduction to the Cambridge edition of Hume's political and economic essays, Haakonssen (1994, xxviii–xxx) highlights the centrality of factionalism and its potential undoing of political stability for Hume.

63. Hume reminisced that "there is, however, a real satisfaction in living at Paris, from the great number of sensible, knowing, and polite company with which that city abounds above all places in the universe. I thought once of settling there for life" (E-MOL, xxxix).

64. Cockayne 2007, 245–46.

65. Cowan 2012.

66. Vickery 2009.

67. Mokyr 2009, 167, 172, 199.

68. In 1699, Parliament overturned an agreement dating back to 1283 that set the daily price of fish in London, and circa 1760, additional reforms were introduced to reduce prices. See Westerfield (1915) 1968.

69. R. Porter 1991, 217, 370, 372.

70. The *Gentleman's Magazine* frequently published price charts (for example, of corn) for London and the provinces. The London price tended to be on the lower end of the scale. See Schabas 1994, 123.

71. See McKendrick, Brewer, and Plumb 1984; De Vries 2008.

72. There is a long-standing debate on this subject. See Hoppit 2017.

73. For a reproduction of the full text, see Dimand 2008, 178–79. The original, in Hume's handwriting, can be found in the National Library of Scotland (MS 2618, 53–54).

74. For more on Hume's friendship with Pinto, see I. Ross 2008, 45–46. For a general account of Isaac de Pinto, see Cardoso and Nogueira 2005.

75. For a discussion of Hume's sympathetic regard for the Jewish people, see Baier 2010, 25.

76. Mossner 1980, 639–40.

77. Emerson 2008, 19.

78. Emerson 2008, 12–13.

79. Mossner 1980, 146; Rothschild 2009.
80. Schaffer 1997.
81. Bonnyman 2012.
82. Mokyr (2009, 15) notes that in 1700, about 28 percent of households were shop-keepers, traders, or artisans and that "an astonishingly low figure" of 32 percent of the labor force worked primarily in agriculture.
83. See also Goodspeed 2016.
84. See Raynor 1998.
85. Home 1976, 16.
86. Mossner 1980, 600.
87. Mossner 1980, 642.

Chapter 2

1. Smith (1980) offered insights into epistemology in his essays on the history of physics and the history of astronomy, and he briefly engaged the science of political economy (WN, 1:428). Other reflections can be found in Turgot 1750 and Du Pont de Nemour 1768. See Redman 1997.
2. This unifying theorem was achieved in the 1950s with the general equilibrium theory of Kenneth Arrow and Gerard Debreu. See Weintraub 1974.
3. Steuart (1767) 1966, 2.
4. For insights regarding new phenomena in the history of science, see Hacking 1983. On the paucity of new phenomena in economics, see Schabas 1995; Boumans 2007.
5. In the second edition of his book on scientific revolutions, Thomas Kuhn (1970) coined the term "disciplinary matrix" to replace his earlier term "paradigm" and noted that it was particularly suitable in the case of smaller groups of like-minded practitioners.
6. See Bruni and Porta 2003.
7. See Stigler 1986; Daston 1988; Sylla 2003.
8. See Raynor 1980.
9. Quesnay (1758) 1958; 1962. On the visual sense in which Quesnay devised his "picture" of the economy, see Charles 2003.
10. Hoppit 2006. See also Hutchison 1988, 239–40; van den Berg 2017.
11. The precise count comes to 3,563 titles by 1,856 different authors, from 1700 to 1789. See Théré 1998.
12. Derringer 2018.
13. We cannot know for certain that Pluche had these books in 1734 or that Hume read them at the time, but Pluche cites Savary in his passages on commerce published in 1746. See Pluche (1746) 2003, 284.
14. Postlethwayt 1751–55. See van den Berg 2017.
15. Postlethwayt 1757. It would take another half century (1804) before Thomas Robert Malthus was appointed as the first British chair in political economy. Adam Smith, in his lectures on jurisprudence at the University of Glasgow in the 1750s included many of the core principles of Book 1 of his *Wealth of Nations*.
16. Mun (1664) 1968, 83–86.
17. For a contrary view, see Derringer 2018.
18. Daston 2011, 83. See also Harkness 2007; Terrall 2014.

19. Hume refers to the discovery by an unnamed philosopher of the "laws and forces" governing the planets (EHU, 11).
20. For more on Hume's complicated regard for Newton, see De Pierris 2006; Hazony and Schliesser 2016.
21. The claim that Hume was the Newton of the moral sciences is long-standing. See, for example, Capaldi 1975; Finlay 2007.
22. Reill 2005; Gaukroger 2010.
23. See Garber 1992 for more details on Descartes's emphasis on geometry and his counterintuitive laws of mechanics. Newton has three laws of motion, but only the second law stipulates mechanical action.
24. Hume's specie-flow mechanism is a good example of a conservation principle in economics. On the topic more generally, see Mirowski 1984.
25. Rosenberg 1993.
26. For more details on Hume's mental machinery, see D. Garrett 1997; Owen 2009.
27. Descartes 1911 (1637), 81.
28. On Hume on free will, see Pitson 2016. On applications to Hume's economics, see Sugden 2005; Lapidus 2010, 2011.
29. This predilection might be bolstered all the more by Hume's skepticism regarding the ascription of personal identity; because individuals reduce down to bundles of sensations or properties that are in persistent flux, there is less reason to position the individual as the primary analytical unit (T, 164–71).
30. Forbes 1975, 105; Schabas 2007.
31. Hume's "contagion" is not dissimilar to the appeal John Searle (1995) makes for collective intentionality as the motivation of robust social facts.
32. A leading economist, Mancur Olson (1996, 3), observed that "the market typically eliminates opportunities for supranormal returns: big bills aren't often dropped on the sidewalk, and if they are, they are picked up very quickly." Recent empirical studies, however, support the opposite outcome; contrived experiments leaving wallets with small amounts of cash inside have ascertained that the majority of wallets are returned to the owner with the sum intact. None of the studies, however, have experimented with a "purse full of gold." See, for example, Dufwenberg and Gneezy 2000.
33. See Read and Richman 2007 on the debate over the "New Hume" that endorses veridical causation.
34. For a complete list, see Fleischacker 2004, 41.
35. Hume did not offer an explanation. However, one of the worst volcanic eruptions in human times transpired in mid-February 1600, at Huaynaputina in Peru. The European harvests were severely affected by the resulting ash and drop in temperature. This does not line up with Hume's ascription of January 1600 unless one takes into account the calendar reform (1752 lost over a month). This seems the only reasonable explanation of what is otherwise a peculiar phenomenon.
36. See W. Henderson 2010.
37. Hume provided details about prices for cloth and food in the "Appendix to the Reign of James I" in his *History of England* and drew comparisons to mid-eighteenth-century London (HE, 5:138–40). He also noted that the navy allotted eight pence per day to feed a sailor while in port (HE, 5:140).
38. Quoted and translated from the Latin by Volckart (1997, 435).

39. For a more detailed analysis see Velde 2012; Derringer 2018.
40. Redish 2000. In his letter to Adam Smith upon reading the *Wealth of Nations*, Hume cited more recent data on the seigniorage extracted at the French mint, drawn from Jacques Necker, the finance minister to Louis XVI. Hume had a more reliable figure than Smith did, which again suggests that Hume had a sustained interest in securing an accurate estimate of French purchasing power. See HL, 2:312.
41. We surmise that Hume meant Joseph Pâris-Duverney. French surnames often had multiple spellings at the time.
42. See Schabas 1994, 123n9.
43. Quoted in Hutchison 1988, 49. See pp. 46–48 for an analysis of the King-Davenant law of demand.
44. In his first *Enquiry*, Hume refers to the circulation of blood in frogs and fish, the same two creatures Harvey used to universalize his principle (EHU, 79, 166). Even if Hume never read the original text by Harvey, or read it with care, he would have absorbed the gist of the argument from reading Descartes's *Discourse on Method*, and we know that he read Descartes while writing the *Treatise*.
45. See Foley 1973 for the received view and Charles 2003 for the new interpretation that the zigzag was partly inspired by Grolier's pinball game. Charles grants that both attributions hold, Harvey as the general source of circulation and Grolier for the zigzag configuration.
46. For a general overview of La Mettrie, Buffon, and Hume, see Gaukroger 2010, 389–420. Hume much admired Buffon; on their friendship, see Mossner 1980, 480.
47. In his *Second Treatise*, Locke ([1690] 1988, 293) observed that land was so abundant that a newcomer to Spain might help himself to barren land for cultivation without a legal deed.
48. Massey 1991, 293. We can only speculate as to how Hume came to excel at devising thought experiments, but his personal library included works by Galileo as well as Robert Boyle's debate with Thomas Hobbes on the vacuum. Hume may have reacted adversely to Boyle, who was central to the early modern movement to conjoin theology with natural science and who voiced dissent from the practice of thought experiments. We know Hume read Boyle as a student at the University of Edinburgh. See Barfoot 1990. On Boyle more generally, see Gaukroger 2010, 30–32.
49. Schabas 2008a.
50. Schabas 2018b.
51. Good examples in twentieth-century economics are the consumption-loan model by Paul A. Samuelson and the model for lemons by George Akerlof. Both models had important policy implications as well: Samuelson for social security and Akerlof for health care. For a philosophical analysis of these models, see Hausman 1992.
52. Hont 2005, 30–33.
53. On Hume's absorption of Melon (1738) that may have commenced in Reims, see Ross 2008, 37–40; Harris 2015, 152–53.
54. See the editorial comments in Hume's *Treatise* (T, 461n5). De Moivre's ideas were featured in Chamber's *Cyclopædia* (1728). See Stigler 1986, 85. On Hume's knowledge of Pascal before 1739, see D. Norton and M. Norton 1996, 42.

55. Stigler 1986, 225–26.
56. Stewart 1994, 167. This indirect reference to Arbuthnot's findings could be used to weigh in favor of Arbuthnot as the recipient of Hume's heartfelt letter of 1734 (HL, 1: 12–18).
57. See Stigler 1986, 226; T. Porter 1986. They claimed that since more boys were born than girls, but young men died more frequently, this meant that the numbers were equal at the time of marriage. This was used as an example of God's design.
58. Hacking 1978.
59. For a Bayesian reading of Hume's *Dialogues*, see Salmon 1978; Cartwright 1978. For an account of Hume's knowledge of Bayesianism, see Raynor 1980.
60. See Daston 1988; Sylla 2003.

Chapter 3

1. Hirschman 1977.
2. Mandeville first published part 1 of the *Fable of the Bees* in 1714 and revised it multiple times. Following in the wake of the South Sea Bubble, it was the 1723 edition that sparked the most outrage and gained the largest readership. He issued part 2 in 1729, and the two were combined into one volume in 1733. See Kaye (1924) 1988, xxxiii–xxxvii; Hundert 1994, 6–15.
3. Stafford (1997) has collected a number of the reactions to Mandeville.
4. Montesquieu (1748) 1989, 338.
5. See Sheehan and Wahrman (2015), who group Hume with Smith on the existence of a self-organizing mechanism that turns a local chaotic disorder into an aggregate stable order.
6. Magri 2015, 301.
7. For recent interpretations on Hume on sympathy, see Cohon 2008; Taylor 2015b.
8. Phillipson 1993, 307.
9. Others in this group are Nicholas Barbon and Mandeville; see J. Robertson 2005, 259; Harris 2009; Zubia 2019.
10. On the benefits of specialization by trade in the philosophical literature of the Scottish Enlightenment, see Berry 2013, 66–78.
11. Annette Baier (2010, 21–34) offers an enlightening analysis of Hume's account of the reasons to repay a loan, as broached at the start of part 2, Book 3 of the *Treatise* (T, 308).
12. See Hardin (2007) for an extensive account of how Hume's elaboration on social conventions can be seen as a game theoretic analysis.
13. Baier (2010) shows that in his later work, in particular the *History of England*, Hume introduces appeals to fairness and reciprocity.
14. Several commentators lament Hume's narrow definition of justice. See, for example, Hiskes 1977; Raphael 2001; Baier 2010.
15. Taylor 2015b, 193.
16. D. Norton 2009a.
17. See Haakonssen 1981, 39; Hundert 1994, 44; J. Robertson 2005, 272, 286.
18. See Phillipson 2011, 7–8.
19. See Besser-Jones 2006.
20. Jacob Vanderlint popularized the sense in which money has a linguistic component in his *Money Answers All Things* (1734). James Steuart also underscored the treat-

ment of money as a set of symbols or signs that represent promises; see Steuart (1767) 1966, 212–13. For accounts of money and language, see Caffentzis 1989; Woodmansee and Osteen 1999.

21. Aristotle discerned that a price is a ratio of exchange between two goods and that exchange is always of goods that are unalike. Expediency enables the comparison and hence the formation of a price. "Although things so different [as two commodities] cannot become commensurate in reality, they can become commensurate enough in relation to our needs" (Aristotle 1985, 131).

22. See Shell 1995; Wennerlind 2001.

23. Strictly speaking, it was a "counter," a wooden or metal round piece that resembles a coin and was used as a substitute if silver coins were scarce. See NHR, 151.

24. Davenant 1698, 38.

25. Defoe 1710, 6. The Dutch had a term—*windhandel*, or trading in the wind—when credit was used. See De Marchi and Harrison 1994.

26. Defoe 1710, 6. For a discussion of Defoe's understanding of credit, see Sherman 1996; L. Brown 2001; Wennerlind 2011a.

27. K. Moore 2016.

28. Dimand 2008.

29. Hume also added that money is "none of the wheels of trade: It is the oil which renders the motion of the wheels more smooth and easy" (E-Mo, 281).

30. Berkeley 1725, 9. The practice of describing money as a "ticket" or "token" can be traced back to William Potter (1650), one of the earliest writers to propose that modern commercial societies can function perfectly well with a credit currency. For a discussion of Berkeley, see Caffentzis 2000; of Potter, see Wennerlind 2011a.

31. Montesquieu (1748) 1989, 401.

32. See Pocock 1975.

33. See Venning 1976; Stockton 1976; Wennerlind 2002; Wei 2017.

34. See, for example, Neeson 1993; Wrightson 2000.

35. Gurney 2013.

36. Rees 2016.

37. Jan de Vries (2008) has named the trend that Hume recognized during his lifetime the "industrious revolution."

38. Perhaps due to the Wilkes Riots of 1770 and the fear he would be misinterpreted, Hume deleted this passage in the last two editions of 1770 and 1777.

39. Richard Steele famously argued in the *Spectator* in 1711 that any artificial bolstering of wages would serve as "Wages of Idleness," as it enables people to survive by performing less labor than they otherwise would have. See A. Ross 1982, 452.

40. A. Young 1771, 361. For a discussion of the phrase "utility of poverty," see Furniss 1920.

41. Locke 1695, 100.

42. See Kelly 1991; Caffentzis 1989; Levenson 2009; Wennerlind 2011a.

Chapter 4

1. This observation was made in 1711, the year Hume was born. See Mandeville 1988, 1:138–39.

2. See Berry 2006, 291.

3. While enclosures were first introduced in the sixteenth century to take advantage

of higher prices on wool, there were frequent enclosure acts passed by Parliament right up into the nineteenth century. See Hoppit 2017.

4. George Wallace, as quoted in P. Jones 1983, 99. See also Buchan 2003; Broadie 2007.

5. See Emerson 1973, 2009; Berry 2013.

6. See Rothschild 2008.

7. Wennerlind 2011b; Schabas 2014a.

8. Mossner 1980, 394. This was unusual since few London coffeehouses were owned or frequented by women. See Cowan 2005, 246.

9. Mossner 1980, 448–55. By and large, these women were aristocrats. Nevertheless, they provided a model for how previously disenfranchised groups could gain a voice and serve to enlarge the sphere of polite discourse.

10. Roy Porter (1991, 25) provides a colorful account of the voice of women in the eighteenth century and notes that in London, "society ladies . . . were much less submissive."

11. On Hume's views on women, see Baier 1994; Guimarães 2015; La Vopa 2017.

12. Locke (1690) 1988, 291.

13. Locke 1997, 184. See also Hundert 1972; Hundert 1974; M. Marshall 2000.

14. See Thomas 1964, 52–57.

15. Adam Smith would reinforce this judgment: "The man whose whole life is spent in performing a few simple operations, . . . [who] has no occasion to exert his understanding, . . . naturally loses, therefore, the habit of such exertion, and generally becomes as stupid and ignorant as it is possible for a human creature to become" (WN, 2:782).

16. See J. Brewer and Porter 1994; M. Berg 2005.

17. See Wrightson 2000; see also the classic statement by Polanyi 1944.

18. See De Marchi and Morgan 1994.

19. See Hoppit 1987, 6.

20. The strong antipathy toward the abuses committed by certain middlemen survived into the eighteenth century, as witnessed by the anonymous tract, discussed in E. P. Thompson (1993, 196), titled *An Essay to prove that Regrators, Engrossers, Forestallers, Hawkers, and Jobbers of Corn, Cattle, and other Marketable Goods are Destructive of Trade, Oppressors to the Poor, and a Common Nuisance to the Kingdom in General* (1719).

21. For discussions of early modern mercantile life in the British Empire, see Hancock 1995; Gauci 2007.

22. Mun (1664) 1968, 8. For a broader discussion of mercantile knowledge, see Leng 2014.

23. Addison's *Spectator* article is reprinted in A. Ross 1982, 437.

24. Quoted in A. Ross 1982, 437.

25. Quoted in A. Ross 1982, 437.

26. Quoted in A. Ross 1982, 437.

27. Defoe (1726) 1987, 132.

28. Defoe (1726) 1987, 133. See also L. Brown 2001 for a broader discussion of Lady Credit.

29. Quoted in Raynor 1998, 22.

30. See Hont 2006.

31. Fénelon 1994.
32. Helvétius (1759) 1807, 21. Hume contested this argument explicitly, pointing rather to the "ill modeled government" of ancient Rome (E-RA, 276).
33. Melon (1738, 174), for example, claimed that luxury is "always relative to Time, and to Persons" and "what was Luxury in the days of our Fathers, is now very Common; and what is Luxury among us, will not be so, to our Posterity." For a general discussion of the eighteenth-century debates on luxury, see Sekora 1977; Berry 1994; Hont 2006. For a discussion of Hume's treatment of luxury, see Cunningham 2005; Susato 2015; Trentmann 2016.
34. As Susato (2015, 98) points out, "the enjoyment of luxury should be regarded as a condition favourable to the maintenance of morals. Although [Hume] calls these pleasures not 'virtuous' but just 'innocent,' he considers that they can foster a new form of morality in commercial and refined nations."
35. Mossner 1980, 447.
36. Mandeville 1988, 1:129.
37. Smith went one step further and argued that people parade riches first and foremost to be admired: "It is the vanity, not the ease, or the pleasure, which interests us [in displaying our wealth]. But vanity is always founded upon the belief of our being the object of attention and approbation. The rich man glories in his riches, because he feels that they naturally draw upon him the attention of the world," and this increases the sympathy of others below his station (TMS, 50–51).
38. Hume succeeded, with the aid of Lord Hertford, in securing Burney the appointment as musician to Louis XV. See Mossner 1980, 501.
39. See, for example, P. Smith and Findlen 2002; Harkness 2007; Slack 2015.
40. Gillispie 1993.
41. Fox 2010.
42. Jacob (1997) emphasizes the view that knowledge developed for practical purposes, while Mokyr (2009) foregrounds the cultural significance of science in prompting economic growth.
43. See Kula 1986; Wise 1995.
44. Gatch 1996, 179.
45. Hume here drew on the tradition of polite discourse forged by Shaftesbury, Addison, and Steele. See L. E. Klein 1984; A. Brewer 1995. For these three men, the "pleasures of the imagination," to use Addison's famous phrase, were morally superior to the "pleasures of the flesh." Addison quoted in A. Ross 1982, 27.
46. Silver 1990. Hume had read Aristotle's *Ethics*, which offers many interesting reflections on friendship (EPM, 107).
47. See Berry 2013, 162–72. This debate ensued in the wake of the Jacobite conflicts. In his efforts to save his friend Archibald Stewart, who had lost Edinburgh to the Highlanders in 1745 and who faced court martial, Hume in 1748 also appeared to have endorsed the republican view that civil society tends to lessen the martial spirit. For example, he wrote that "when Men have fallen into a more civilized Life, & have been allowed to addict themselves entirely to the Cultivation of Arts and Manufactures, the Habit of their Mind, still more than that of their Body, soon renders them Unfit for the Use of Arms and gives a different Direction to their Ambition" (Hume 1748, 6–7). These claims, however, may be attributed to expediency: Hume wrote in order to save the life of his friend, and he was successful. Just a few years later, in the *Political Discourses*, Hume towed a different line.

48. Adam Smith was more worried than Hume was about the decline of the martial spirit among modern Europeans and, in emulation of the Romans, advocated gymnastics as an essential part of the school curriculum (WN, 2:785–88).
49. Sheehan and Wahrman 2015, 9.

Chapter 5

1. Untitled and undated essay, Hont Papers.
2. Quotation in Waldmann 2014, 41. See Reinert 2015, 73–75, for a discussion of the challenge of interpreting the meaning of texts that employ wit and irony.
3. Elsewhere he similarly asserted that it is "only in our public negociations and transactions with foreigners, that a greater stock of money is advantageous" (E-BT, 316).
4. See, for example, Muldrew 1998; Wennerlind 2011a; Desan 2014.
5. See Misselden 1622, 1623; Malynes 1622, 1623; Mun (1664) 1968.
6. Magnusson (1994) dispelled the myth that seventeenth-century thinkers mistook gold for wealth. More recent discussions of mercantilism demonstrate that it was a complex and sophisticated body of thought and practice; see Pincus 2012; Stern and Wennerlind 2014.
7. Petty (1691) 1899, 113.
8. Drelichman and Voth 2014.
9. Duke 1979; Mayer 1980.
10. Samuelson 1971, 1980.
11. Oswald pointed this out to Hume in his letter of October 10, 1750. See Rotwein 2007, 196 (which mistakenly gives the date of 1749).
12. Cesarano 1998.
13. Jevons 1957, 91 (added to the second edition of 1879). On his strong commitment to a single market price for commodities such as corn, see Ricardo 1951b, 67–73.
14. The letter of March 25, 1767, is translated by Rotwein 2007, 211.
15. The extent to which Smith agreed with Hume's thinking on money is a long-debated topic. See, for example, Vickers 1959; Eagly 1970; Wennerlind 2000.
16. A pound is twenty shillings, a crown is five shillings, and a shilling is twelve pence.
17. Wennerlind 2011a.
18. Potter 1650, iv. George Berkeley (1725, 7) echoed this insight: "whether the true idea of money . . . be not altogether that of a ticket or a counter." See Caffentzis 2000.
19. Hume later reiterated this point in a 1758 letter to Lord Elibank: "There seems to be some Foundation for the common Opinion, that the Encrese of Money encreases the Price of Commodities; tho' it ought not be suppos'd that the one Encrease is always exactly propotion'd to the other. The Encrease of the Money encreases the Demand; but if the Encrease of the Demand encreases as much the Industry, the Price will remain the same; and this Encrease of Industry will always have place in some Degree." Quoted in Mossner 1962, 441–42.
20. See, for example, Duke 1979; Mayer 1980; Perlman 1987; Cesarano 1998; Paganelli 2006. For our respective interpretations, see Wennerlind 2005; Schabas 2008b.
21. Wennerlind 2005. Wennerlind's reading is in many ways compatible with Hont 1983, but it differs in that Wennerlind argues that the influx of money occurs in a rich country, not a poor and underdeveloped country, as Hont claims.

22. Duke 1979, 577.
23. The use of the word *multiplier* is anachronistic, but the gist of Hume's analysis resembles that of the multiplier, albeit without specifying details, such as the marginal propensity to consume.
24. See Schabas 2008b.
25. "Tick" is short for *ticket* and was used by the mid-seventeenth century to denote a credit account with a shop. As Mokyr (2009, 373) points out, "credit was omnipresent in eighteenth-century Britain. . . . Local tradesmen and shopkeepers gave customers personal credit."
26. Schabas 2001.
27. Both Cesarano (1998, 182) and Skinner (2009, 404) recognize that Hume situated the multiplier process in a secular trend of commercial prosperity.
28. For further elaboration, see Wennerlind 2001; 2005.
29. J. Kaye 1998.
30. See Kelly 1991; Carey 2013; Desan 2014.
31. Gatch (1996, 169) points out that, for Hume, money "must become the mediator of social relations because a society actuated on Humean psychological principles would otherwise be an entropic one."
32. Caffentzis 2005.
33. Bacon 1625, 85.
34. David Hume to Lord Elibank, April 6, 1758, reprinted in Mossner 1962, 441.
35. Hume, in a 1749 letter to Montesquieu, stated that "paper has the same inconveniences as coined money, and none of its advantages" (HL, 1:136, as translated by Rotwein [2007, 188]).
36. Caffentzis 2001, 326.
37. Hume developed a similar argument in his 1749 letter to Montesquieu (HL, 1:133–38).
38. The state also issued annuities, lotteries, and exchequer notes.
39. Wallace 1758, 16–17.
40. Wallace 1758, 18.
41. Wallace 1758, 18.
42. Wallace 1758, 20, 28.
43. Wallace 1758, 34. He acknowledged that foreigners will not readily accept paper money in transactions, but as long as they are willing to take the nation's goods, it does not matter. It is also the case that an increase in paper money will generate inflation, but since this inflation is accompanied by an increase in industry and wealth, the increases in prices and wages are small "disadvantages, or rather natural consequences." Indeed, he noted, "it is only by encreasing *industry* and *consumption*, that bank-notes increase these prices" (Wallace 1758, 29). And, since credit "is *absolutely necessary* to an extensive commerce," the inconveniences of higher prices should not deter the proper use of paper money (Wallace 1758, 27).
44. Hume may also have responded to Prime Minister George Grenville's act of 1764 that banned the use of paper money in all private and public transactions in the colonies south of New England.
45. See Goodspeed 2016.
46. Hume gave the figure of ten thousand workers at Carron, but we have on good authority that the number was closer to one thousand. It was, however, one of the

largest employers in Britain and produced a variety of iron goods, such as cannons, and cauldrons.

47. Hume offered insights into both of these. See Diaye and Lapidus 2012.
48. See Homer and Sylla 2005.
49. See Golinski 2007.

Chapter 6

1. Beckert 2014.
2. These figures are for the entire European slave trade, of which Britain was the leading perpetrator. See Eltis et al. 1999. See also Zahedieh 2010.
3. K. Morgan 2000, 10. To compare, the population of England in 1750 was 5.9 million (Wrigley and Schofield 1981, 614–15).
4. Although these last assignments came in the 1760s, after the publication of the *Political Discourses*, his experiences shaped the revisions of his economic writings, for the 1770 and 1777 editions.
5. For general discussions of Enlightenment thinking and empire, see Reinert 2011; Muthu 2012.
6. For more examples, see Wei 2017.
7. Rothschild (2009, 413) describes Hume's interventions on the subject of international trade as a "eulogy" to open commerce and communication.
8. The French philosopher Abbé de Raynal (1798, 508), who met Hume in the 1760s, observed that "whatever advantage one nation may derive from another in trade, becomes a motive of industry and emulation to both: in war, on the contrary, the injury affects both; for plunder, fire and sword can neither improve lands, nor enrich mankind." For a discussion of commerce over conquest, see Shovlin 2018.
9. As a result, smuggling was widespread at the time. See, for example, Frykman 2014; Kwass 2014.
10. On Boisguilbert, see Faccarello 1999.
11. Hont was the first to see that Hume broached the principle of comparative advantage, a discovery that would later be attributed to David Ricardo. See Hont 2005, 68–70; 2008, 312–14.
12. Hume observed that France imported corn from Greece in times of scarcity (E-PA, 462).
13. While Hume was neither the first nor the last person to contribute to this debate, his nuanced interventions were widely recognized at home and abroad. See Hont 1983; 2005, 69.
14. See Meek 1976; Berry 2013.
15. Mokyr 2009, 171–97.
16. Maxine Berg (2004), in part drawing on Hume, highlights the importance of global interconnectedness for the stimulus of learning and knowledge.
17. Quoted in Rotwein 2007, 194. There are conflicting dates for the Oswald letter. Rotwein, we believe, was in error to register it as 1749. We have adopted Grieg's date of 1750.
18. Hume to Elibank, April 6, 1758, reprinted in Mossner 1962, 442.
19. Hont (2008, 313) suggests that Hume emphasized the development of knowledge, or "human capital," and not "the increasing of productivity through a technical division of labor and the development of labor-saving machinery." Berdell

(1996), with whom we agree, argues that both insights were present in Hume, that he emphasized the importance of both theoretical and practical knowledge for the advancement of manufacturing, and this dual knowledge took the form of creating new goods, better techniques and organization, or more-refined tools and machines.

20. Tucker 1774, 17–18. The 1755 tract, entitled *The Elements of Commerce and Theory of Taxes*, became part of his *Four Tracts on Political and Commercial Subjects* (1774).
21. Tucker 1774, 19.
22. Tucker 1774, 22.
23. Tucker 1774, 30.
24. Tucker 1774, 31.
25. Tucker 1774, 34.
26. Forbes 2015, 315. Susato (2015, 215) criticizes Forbes's position and argues that Hume believed in the eventual demise of rich countries.
27. Hont 1983, 288n.
28. Hont 1983, 274.
29. Hume illustrated this notion by referring to indigenous peoples of the Americas: "an *Indian* is but little tempted to dispossess another of his hut, or to steal his bow, as being already provided of the same advantages; and as to any superior fortune, which may attend one above another in hunting and fishing, 'tis only casual and temporary, and will have but small tendency to disturb society" (T, 345–46).
30. On Hume's analysis of national character, see Ainslie 1995.
31. Francis Williams was known as an accomplished poet and mathematician. When Williams was denied membership in the Royal Society of London, which met at Crane Court, on account "of his complexion," Hume's adversary, James Beattie, wrote that "the vulgar, indeed, used sometimes to jeer and insult him in the streets; but such philosophers as Mr. Hume, and those of Crane Court, might have known, that souls are of no colour, and that no one can tell, on viewing a casket, what jewel it contains." Quoted in Caretta 2003, 214. Another critic of Hume, James Ramsey, wrote, "I trust his assertion, which certainly was made without any competent knowledge of the subject, will appear to have no foundation, either in reason or nature." Quoted in Popkin 1980, 264. Popkin added that Ramsay declared that had Hume been a slave on a plantation, he "probably would not have exhibited very much sign of civilized behavior" (Popkin 1980, 264).
32. For a discussion of Hume's revision of the footnote, see Immerwahr 1992; A. Garrett 2000; Morton 2002; Valls 2005; Whelan 2009. Winthrop Jordan (1968, 253) strongly condemns Hume for articulating the case for black inferiority "more boldly than anyone." For additional remarks by Hume on race, see E-PG, 59.
33. Popkin 1980, 252.
34. See Mazza and Mori 2016, 15.
35. Waldmann 2014, 65–69. Hume recognized that the modern merchant was not limited by geography but looked for lucrative opportunities wherever they could be found around the globe. For example, he noted that "an East-India merchant . . . is not without concern about what passes in Jamaica" (T, 275).
36. Rothschild 2008, 94.

37. Although Melon (1738, 87) opposed slavery, he argued that there were certain circumstances under which slave labor could turn slaves into "good Subjects."
38. Montesquieu ([1748] 1989, 246) observed, similarly, that a master contracts "all sorts of bad habits" as he becomes "accustomed to failing in all the moral virtues, because he grows proud, curt, harsh, angry, voluptuous, and cruel."
39. See Kuflik 1998.
40. Hume acknowledged that the "comparison is shocking between the management of human creatures and that of cattle; but being extremely just, when applied to the present subject" (E-PA, 387).
41. See, for example, Bush-Slimani 1993; J. Morgan 2004. Londa Schiebinger (2004; 2017) documents the extensive knowledge that enslaved women in the Caribbean had of botanical abortifacients used to terminate pregnancies resulting from rape by the slave owners.
42. For Hume's comparison of modern and ancient warfare, see "Of Refinement in the Arts" (E-RA, 274) and "Of the Populousness of Ancient Nations" (E-PA, 407).
43. See, for example, Glossop 1984; Whelan 1995; Van de Haar 2008.
44. Kramnick 1968.
45. Du Rivage 2017, 25.
46. See Armitage 1997.
47. Bolingbroke 1997, 223–94.
48. Anonymous 1748, 10. Isaac de Pinto's *Traité de la Cirulation et du Crédit* (1771) also brings out the benefits of public credit.
49. Anonymous 1748, 10.
50. Hont (2005, 340n) reports that the debt rose from 74 million to 133 million pounds.
51. See Pincus 2016.
52. For a detailed analysis of these revisions, see Hont 2005, 340–44.
53. Hume depicted Londoners as "the Barbarians who inhabit the Banks of the Thames." Quoted in Mossner 1980, 390.
54. Du Rivage 2017, 25.
55. A good example is a tax on malt and beer. Hume recommended that the tax be "moderate" (E-Ta, 342).
56. Sperling 1962; Antoin Murphy 1997.
57. Hoppit 2002.
58. We believe Eugene F. Miller's footnote (E-PC, 361n) is incorrect in assigning the years 1643–61, and we side with the interpretation of Hont (2005, 335), who read this as a reference to John Law.
59. For additional letters by Hume on public credit, see Laursen and Coolidge 1994, 145.
60. Neil McArthur (2007, 77) points out that "the primary duty of the civilized state, then, is to provide security to commerce but otherwise to stay out of its way." Knud Haakonssen (2009, 366) notes that Hume believed that "in a society where the government, for whatever reason, is restrained from doing much more than securing these things, a spirit of enterprise and individualism will tend to predominate."
61. North and Weingast 1989.
62. Hont 2005, 345.

63. Haakonssen 2009, 367–68.
64. Kant (1795) 1983. For a discussion of Hume's views on commerce and war, and the quote by Saint Pierre, see Manzer 1996.
65. Fichte 2012. See Nakhimovsky 2011.
66. Bentham quoted in Kapossy, Nakhimovsky, and Whatmore 2017, 2.

Chapter 7

1. Friedman 1975, 177.
2. Lucas (1996, 661) provides a detailed analysis of Hume.
3. See Sekine 1973 and Antoin Murphy 2009 on eighteenth-century contributors to monetary theory.
4. John Stuart Mill ([1848] 1965 3:506), for example, claimed that, "there is nothing more insignificant in the economy than money."
5. For an overview of Mill, see Skorupski 1989; 1998.
6. Kant ([1783] 1902, 7) famously credited Hume for awakening him from his "dogmatic slumber."
7. Huxley (1879) 2011. Mossner (1980, 483–86) remarks on Hume's agnosticism and unwillingness to identify with atheism.
8. Darwall 1994. Albee (1901) classified Shaftesbury and Hutcheson as utilitarians.
9. The last few lines of Hume's first *Enquiry* took on an iconic meaning for the logical positivists (EHU, 123).
10. J. Norton 2010.
11. See Ayer 1936; Howson 2000; L. Henderson 2018.
12. See Dow (2009) on the strong appreciation for Hume by Keynes and Hayek.
13. Keynes 2013, 28:373–90. Hayek (1938) argues that Keynes was wrong to suggest that Adam Smith had written the Abstract.
14. For placing Hume in a utilitarian tradition, see Blackburn 1993. For interpretations of Hume as a virtue theorist, see Hursthouse 1999; Abramson 2015. For a reading of Hume's ethics as "indirect utilitarianism," see Sayre-McCord 1995, 281.
15. See Raynor 1993; D. Norton 2009b, 25n.
16. Haakonssen 2006, 4.
17. I. Ross 1995, 83, 97. Hutcheson may have assigned Hume's *Treatise* to Smith while he was a student at Glasgow in 1739–40.
18. Haakonssen (1981, 2) suggests, "It was Hume's speculations about justice which put the decisive questions in answer to which Smith developed a whole new foundation of a system of natural jurisprudence."
19. Schliesser 2017, 82–92.
20. On the ambiguity of Smith's concept of the invisible hand, see, for example, J. Davis 1990; Rothschild 2001.
21. On their close and enduring friendship, see Schliesser 2003; Rasmussen 2017.
22. A. Smith 1987, 220. The letter by Smith of August 26, 1776, was sent to Hume's publisher, William Strachan, and published in March 1777 with Hume's short autobiography "My Own Life" (E-MOL).
23. See Raynor 1984; Haakonssen 2006b, 3.
24. Beauchamp (1998, xxiv) gives a detailed account of Hume's ascription of the date of publication. The second *Enquiry* was first published in July 1751 but was not

given an advertisement until November or December of that year. Because Hume made revisions, the inserted leaf for these additional changes is dated January 1752. The *Political Discourses* was completed by September 1751 (NHL, 28).

25. There is the added complexity of the adoption of the Gregorian calendar by the English on January 1, 1752. Under the Julian system, 1752 would not have commenced until March 25. The Scots, however, had already shifted to the January 1 custom of marking the New Year in 1600. In Scotland, it was unequivocally 1752 in January when Hume's book was released, but in England, the situation was less transparent.

26. I. Ross 1995, 111–14.

27. These are the *Lectures on Jurisprudence* (LJ).

28. I. Ross 1995, 113.

29. Quoted in I. Ross 1995, 272.

30. I. Ross 1995, 114.

31. Even in one of his last letters to Smith, Hume could not resist a brief reprimand in the postscript, noting the "strange blunder" by Smith in sending his prior letter by "the Carrier" (HL, 2:336).

32. In a letter to his publisher, William Strahan, Hume wrote, "Dr Smith's Performance is another excellent Work that has come from your Press this Winter; but I have ventured to tell him, that it requires too much thought to be as popular as Mr Gibbon's" (HL 2:314).

33. Smith 1987, 251. Smith worried that Hume's nephew might not honor the will and the burden of publishing the *Dialogues* would then fall on Smith's shoulders once more. But Hume's nephew brought the *Dialogues* into print in 1779, much to Smith's relief.

34. Hirschman underscores Smith's dissent from the Montesquieu-Steuart vision to which Hume subscribed. He also, however, notes that Hume's *History of England* was influential in prompting Smith to dissent. See Hirschman 1977, 100–113, esp. 102.

35. See Pocock 1979; Fleischacker 2003.

36. Petrella 1968.

37. Wennerlind 2000.

38. Gherity 1994.

39. See Viner 1927; Checkland 1975; Gherity 1994.

40. Furniss 1920.

41. Smith motivates the law differently than Hume, however, arguing that the rate would decline as capital amassed into larger sums, not because of increased rivalries or the efficiencies of capital flow per se.

42. Charles 2008. Gournay's full name is Jacques-Claude-Marie Vincent de Gournay.

43. Susato 2019. See Hont 2015 for an account of common and opposing themes in Rousseau and Smith on the politics of commercial societies.

44. Harris 2015, 561n36.

45. Hume cited one Rousseau in his *Essays*, but it is a Swiss poet, Jean-Baptiste Rousseau, who died in 1741 (E-RA, 127n).

46. Bongie 2000, 196–97.

47. Hont 2008, 274–78.

48. On French economic thought during this period, see Shovlin 2007; Sonenscher 2007; Cheney 2010; Terjanian 2013.
49. Galiani boasted in a letter to Mme d'Épinay, "I was the first man of some intelligence who dared to tear the mask from the economists [physiocrats] and to show them up for what they are, a fanatical mob whose purpose is sedition" (quoted in Hutchison 1988, 266). Mossner (1980, 480) suggests Galiani knew Hume.
50. J. Robertson (2005) develops a compelling case. See also Reinert 2018, 186.
51. See Condillac 1997, 59. Daire collaborated with Gustave Molinari.
52. Marx 1963–71.
53. Böhm-Bawerk 1891.
54. Franklin's 1771 article is in Hume and Munro (1754–71) 2002, vol. 3. On the lightning rod controversy, see Cohen 1990.
55. Spencer 2002.
56. See Bongie 1965; Riskin 1998, 333–36; Riskin 2002.
57. See, for example, Adair 1957; Adair 1998; Wilson 1989; Fleischacker 2002; Spencer 2002.
58. McCoy 1980.
59. Pocock 1985.
60. Bentham (1776) 1988, 51n1–2.
61. See Winch 1996; Sigot 2001.
62. Some of the prominent references to Hume in the works of Bentham, Steuart, and Malthus appear in Feiser 1999 1:125–28, 1:270–72, 2:229–54, 2:361–72.
63. We know that Ricardo read, for example, the writings of John Locke, George Berkeley, Thomas Reid, Dugald Stewart, William Paley, William Playfair, and Charles Lyell. See Ricardo 1951f, vol. 11.
64. For *The High Price of Bullion*, see Ricardo 1951c, 90; for *Reply to Mr. Bosanquet's Practical Observations on the Report of the Bullion Committee*, see Ricardo 1951c, 163; for the May 24, 1819, parliamentary speech, see Ricardo 1951e, 12. Le Maux (2014, 965) argues that Hume was a progenitor to the currency school that Ricardo helped spawn.
65. Ricardo 1951e, 524.
66. According to Ricardo (1951d, 36–37), Hume observed that "a rise of prices, has a magic effect on industry."
67. Ricardo 1951d, 36.
68. Ricardo 1951a, 197; Ricardo 1951f, 10:395, 399. As a dissenter, first a Jew and then, upon marriage, a Quaker, Ricardo championed religious toleration and would have found much inspiration in Hume's writings on the subject.
69. The introduction to Kant's *Prolegomena to Any Future Metaphysics* ([1783] 1902, 7) remarks that Kant, upon reading Hume, had awakened from a "dogmatic slumber." Much of the book revolves around Hume's analysis of causation.
70. Beiser 1987.
71. Forget 1999.
72. Antoin Murphy 2009; Arnon 2011, 114–19.
73. Skorupski (1998, 7) maintains that both James Mill and John Stuart Mill were hostile to Hume and favored the "non-sceptical naturalistic tradition to which Reid belongs. Skorupski (1989, 170) argues that Hume's problem of induction "hardly

figured at all in nineteenth-century British philosophy before T. H. Green's revival of Hume."

74. Robson and Stillinger 1981, 70, 673.

75. See A. Marshall (1890) 1920.

76. There are over a dozen references to Hume in Edgeworth's papers on probability and economics, and they reflect a solid command of Hume. See Mirowski 1994, 457.

77. Hume 1906. Spencer (2005, 283–99) offers a detailed tracking of the early publishing and presence of Hume's works in American libraries and private collections.

78. See W. B. Robertson 1906. William Bell Robertson had written two books on economics circa 1905 and publicized them on the title page of this edition of Hume's *Political Discourses*.

79. On Veblen's appreciation of Hume, see Edgell and Tilman 1989. On Fisher and his recognition of Hume on the interest rate as a nonmonetary phenomenon, see Dimand 2013.

80. Chapter 4 of his book *Institutional Economics: Its Place in Political Economy* was entitled "Hume and Peirce." See Commons 1934, 140–57.

81. See Mitchell (1949) 1967–69; (1937) 1950.

82. On pragmatism in general, see Misak 2004. On British pragmatism, see Misak 2016.

83. Hayek 1960, 420n9; see Burgin 2015, 112.

84. Hayek 1991a, 95–96.

85. Hayek 1991b, 104.

86. See Hayek 1960; 1973; 1976; 1979; 1944.

87. Hayek (1988) 2017, 3.

88. See Livingston 1991; Caldwell 2003.

89. Hayek 1945. On Hume on local knowledge, see Schabas 2018a.

90. Friedman and Schwartz 1963.

91. By 1990, this article had been cited 2,500 times. By 2020, according to Google Scholar, the number has grown to about 7,000. See Hausman 1992, 162; Hands 2010.

92. See Friedman 1968; 1989.

93. For a discussion of the selection of these winners, see Offer and Söderberg 2016.

94. On Polanyi's economic thought, see Nye 2011, 145–82.

95. See Buchanan 1999; Buchanan 2000; Buchanan and Tullock 2018.

96. See Furubotn and Richter 1997; Levi and Weingast 2019.

97. V. Smith 2007, 2008.

98. The term was popularized as the title of a book by Lawrence R. Klein, released in 1947.

99. According to Keynes ([1936] 1973, 343n), Hume "had a foot and a half in the classical world. For Hume began the practice amongst economists of stressing the importance of the equilibrium position as compared with the ever-shifting transition towards it, though he was still enough of a mercantilist not to overlook the fact that it is in the transition that we actually have our being."

100. See Keynes 1921; Meeks 2003; Runde and Mizuhara 2003.

101. On Hume's rich insights into probability and resistance of a frequentist stance, see Hacking 1978. On Keynes on probability, see Schabas 1998.

102. On Mill's concept of the "Art of Living," see Mill (1848) 1965, 756. Keynes ([1931] 1965, 368) proposed that in a century, citizens of prosperous countries might cultivate "the art of life itself" and use their leisure wisely. See also Keynes (1931) 1965, 312–18, for his appreciation of Hume's views on individual flourishing.
103. Quoted in Mossner 1943, 66.
104. On Keynes's participation in the group of artists and writers in Bloomsbury, see Goodwin 2006.
105. See Backhouse 2017, 29–30.
106. Samuelson 1971; 1980.
107. Krugman 2011a.
108. Phelps 2013, 101.
109. Boianovsky 2018.
110. See Sen 1977, 2009. Sen issued a serious of articles that grappled with some of the conceptual and methodological questions at the very heart of mainstream economics. A nontechnical account of the ethical dimensions of economics can be found in Sen 1987, 1993.
111. Economic liberalism is a species of the broader doctrine of liberalism, for which multiple and conflicting definitions abound. See Anderson 1999; Gaus and Courtland 2018.
112. The phrase is from Brennan and Pettit 2005.
113. See D. Norton 1976, 4.
114. Home 1976, 24.
115. Home 1976, 24.
116. Home 1976, 25.
117. Home 1976, 25.

BIBLIOGRAPHY

Abramson, Kate. 2015. "What's So 'Natural' about the Natural Virtues?" In Ainslie and Butler, *Cambridge Companion to Hume's Treatise*, 333–68.

Adair, Douglass. 1957. "'That Politics May Be Reduced to a Science': David Hume, James Madison, and the Tenth Federalist." *Huntington Library Quarterly* 20 (4): 343–60.

———. 1998. *Fame and the Founding Fathers: Essays by Douglass Adair*. Indianapolis: Liberty Fund.

Ainslie, Donald C. 1995. "The Problem of the National Self in Hume's Theory of Justice." *Hume Studies* 21 (2): 289–314.

———. 2015. "Hume and Moral Motivation." In Ainslie and Butler, *Cambridge Companion to Hume's Treatise*, 283–300.

Ainslie, Donald C., and Annemarie Butler, eds. 2015. *The Cambridge Companion to Hume's Treatise*. New York: Cambridge University Press.

Albee, Ernest. 1901. *A History of English Utilitarianism*. London: George Allen and Unwin.

Anderson, Elizabeth. 1999. "What Is the Point of Equality?" *Ethics* 109 (2): 287–337.

Andrews, David R. 1999. "Continuity and Change in Keynes's Thought: The Importance of Hume." *European Journal of the History of Economic Thought* 6 (1): 1–21.

Anonymous. 1748. *An Essay upon Publick Credit, in a Letter to a Friend. Occasioned by the Fall of Stocks*. London: H. Carpenter.

Appleby, Joyce O. 1978. *Economic Thought and Ideology in Seventeenth-Century England*. Princeton, NJ: Princeton University Press.

Aristotle. 1985. *Nicomachean Ethics*. Translated by Terence Irwin. Indianapolis: Hackett.

Armitage, David. 1997. Introduction to Bolingbroke, *Political Writings*, vii–xxiv.

———. 2000. *The Ideological Origins of the British Empire*. Cambridge: Cambridge University Press.

Arnon, Arie. 2011. *Monetary Theory and Policy from Hume and Smith to Wicksell: Money, Credit, and the Economy*. Cambridge: Cambridge University Press.

Ayer, Alfred Jules. 1936. *Language, Truth and Logic*. New York: Norton.

———. 1980. *Hume: A Very Short Introduction*. Oxford: Oxford University Press.

Backhouse, Roger E. 2017. *Founder of Modern Economics: Paul A. Samuelson*. Vol. 1, *Becoming Samuelson, 1915–1948*. New York: Oxford University Press.

Bacon, Francis. 1625. *The Essayes or Counsels, Civill and Morall*. London.

Baier, Annette C. 1991. *A Progress of Sentiments: Reflections on Hume's Treatise*. Cambridge, MA: Harvard University Press.

———. 2010. *The Cautious Jealous Virtue: Hume on Justice*. Cambridge, MA: Harvard University Press.

Bailey, Alan, and Dan O'Brien, eds. 2015. *The Bloomsbury Companion to Hume*. First published 2012 as *The Continuum Companion to Hume* by Continuum Press.

Baker, Keith M. 1962. "An Unpublished Essay of Condorcet on Technical Methods of Classification." *Annals of Science* 18 (2): 99–123.

Baldi, Marialuisa. 1983. *David Hume nel Settecento italiano: Filosofia ed economia*. Florence: La Nuova Italia Editrice.

Barfoot, Michael. 1990. "Hume and the Culture of Science in the Early Eighteenth Century." In *Studies in the Philosophy of the Scottish Enlightenment*, edited by M. A. Stewart, 151–90. Oxford: Oxford University Press.

Beauchamp, Tom L. 1998. "Introduction: A History of the Enquiry on Morals." In *An Enquiry concerning the Principles of Morals*, by David Hume, edited by Tom L. Beauchamp, xi–lxxx. Oxford: Oxford University Press.

Beckert, Sven. 2014. *Empire of Cotton: A Global History*. New York: Alfred A. Knopf.

Beebee, Helen. 2015. "Causation and Necessary Connection." In Bailey and O'Brien, *Bloomsbury Companion to Hume*, 131–45.

Beiser, Frederick C. 1987. *The Fate of Reason: German Philosophy from Kant to Fichte*. Cambridge, MA: Harvard University Press.

Ben-David, Joseph. 1971. *The Scientist's Role in Society: A Comparative Study*. Chicago: University of Chicago Press.

Bentham, Jeremy. (1776) 1948. *The Principles of Morals and Legislation*. New York: Haffner.

———. (1776) 1988. *A Fragment on Government*. Edited by J. H. Burns and Ross Hart. Cambridge: Cambridge University Press.

Berdell, John. 1995. "The Present Relevance of Hume's Open-Economy Monetary Dynamics." *Economic Journal* 105 (432): 1205–17.

———. 1996. "Innovation and Trade: David Hume and the Case for Freer Trade." *History of Political Economy* 28 (1): 107–26.

———. 2002. *International Trade and Economic Growth in Open Economies: The Classical Dynamics of Hume, Smith, Ricardo and Malthus*. Cheltenham, UK: Edward Elgar, 2002.

Berg, Maxine. 2004. "In Pursuit of Luxury: Global History and British Consumer Goods in the Eighteenth Century." *Past and Present* 182: 85–142.

———. 2005. *Luxury and Pleasure in Eighteenth-Century Britain*. Oxford: Oxford University Press.

Berkeley, George. 1725. *The Querist, Containing Several Queries, Proposed to the Consideration of the Public*. Dublin.

Berry, Christopher J. 1994. *The Idea of Luxury: A Conceptual and Historical Investigation*. Cambridge: Cambridge University Press.

———. 2006. "Hume and the Customary Cause of Industry, Knowledge, and Humanity." *History of Political Economy* 38 (2): 291–317.

———. 2008. "Hume and Superfluous Value (or the Problem with Epictetus' Slippers)." In Wennerlind and Schabas, *David Hume's Political Economy*, 49–64.

———. 2013. *The Idea of Commercial Society in the Scottish Enlightenment*. Edinburgh: Edinburgh University Press, 2013.

Besser-Jones, Lorraine. 2006. "The Role of Justice in Hume's Theory of Psychological Development." *Hume Studies* 32 (2): 253–76.

Binmore, Ken. 2011. *Rational Decisions*. Princeton, NJ: Princeton University Press.

Blackburn, Simon. 1993. "Hume on the Mezzanine Level." *Hume Studies* 19 (2): 273–88.

Boantza, Victor D. 2013. *Matter and Method in the Long Chemical Revolution*. Farnham, UK: Ashgate.

Böhm-Bawerk, Eugen von. 1891. *The Positive Theory of Capital*. Translated by William Smart. London: Macmillan. First published 1891.

Boianovsky, Mauro. 2018. "When the History of Ideas Meets Theory: Arthur Lewis and the Classical Economists on Development." *History of Political Economy* 50 (1): 172–90.

Bolingbroke, Henry St. John. 1997. *Political Writings*. Edited by David Armitage. Cambridge: Cambridge University Press.

Bongie, Laurence L. 2000. *David Hume: Prophet of the Counter-Revolution*. 2nd ed. Indianapolis: Liberty Fund. First published 1965 by Clarendon Press (Oxford).

Bonnyman, Brian. 2012. "Agrarian Patriotism and the Landed Interest: The Scottish 'Society of Improvers in the Knowledge of Agriculture,' 1723–1746." In *The Rise of Economic Societies in the Eighteenth Century: Patriotic Reform in Europe and North America*, edited by Koen Stapelbroek and Jani Marjanen, 26–51. London: Palgrave.

Boumans, Marcel. 2007. "Invariance and Calibration." In *Measurement in Economics: A Handbook*, edited by Marcel Boumans, 231–48. Amsterdam: Elsevier.

Boyd, Richard. 2008. "Manners and Morals: David Hume on Civility, Commerce, and the Social Construction of Difference." In Wennerlind and Schabas, *David Hume's Political Economy*, 65–85.

Brennan, Geoffrey, and Philip Pettit. 2005. *The Economy of Esteem*. Oxford: Oxford University Press.

Brewer, Anthony. 1992. *Richard Cantillon: Pioneer of Economic Theory*. London: Routledge.

———. 1995. "The Concept of Growth in Eighteenth-Century Economics." *History of Political Economy* 27 (4): 609–38.

———. 1997. "An Eighteenth-Century View on Economic Development: Hume and Steuart." *European Journal of the History of Economic Thought* 4 (1): 1–22.

Brewer, John. 1988. *The Sinews of Power: War, Money and the English State, 1688–1783*. Cambridge, MA: Harvard University Press.

———. 1995. "'The Most Polite Age and the Most Vicious': Attitudes towards Culture as a Commodity, 1660–1800." In *The Consumption of Culture, 1600–1800: Image, Object, Text*, edited by Ann Bermingham and John Brewer, 341–61. London: Routledge.

Brewer, John, and Roy Porter, eds. 1994. *Consumption and the World of Goods*. London: Routledge.

Broadie, Alexander, ed. 2003. *The Cambridge Companion to the Scottish Enlightenment*. Cambridge: Cambridge University Press.

———. 2001. *The Scottish Enlightenment: The Historical Age of the Historical Nation*. Edinburgh: Birlinn.

Brown, John. 1757. *An Estimate of the Manners and Principles of the Times*. London: Printed for L. Davis, and C. Reymers.

Brown, Laura. 2001. *Fables of Modernity: Literature and Culture in the English Eighteenth Century*. Ithaca, NY: Cornell University Press.

Bruni, Luigino, and Pier Luigi Porta. 2003. *"Economia civile* and *pubblica felicità* in the Italian Enlightenment."* In Schabas and De Marchi, *Oeconomies in the Age of Newton*, 361–85.

Bruni, Luigino, and Robert Sugden. 2000. "Moral Canals: Trust and Social Capital in the Works of Hume, Smith, and Genovesi." *Economics and Philosophy* 16 (1): 21–45.

Buchan, James. 2003. *Crowded with Genius: The Scottish Enlightenment: Edinburgh's Moment of the Mind*. New York: Harper Collins.

Buchanan, James M. (1958) 1999. *Public Principles of Public Debt: A Defense and Restatement*. Vol. 2 of *The Collected Works of James M. Buchanan*. Indianapolis: Liberty Fund.

———. (1975) 2000. *The Limits of Liberty: Between Anarchy and Leviathan*. Vol. 7 of *The Collected Works of James M. Buchanan*. Indianapolis: Liberty Fund.

Buchanan, James M., and Gordon Tullock. (1962) 2018. *The Calculus of Consent: Logical Foundations of Constitutional Democracy*. Vol. 3 of *The Collected Works of James M. Buchanan*. Indianapolis: Liberty Fund. First published 1962 by University of Michigan Press.

Buffon, Georges-Louis Leclerc, Comte de. 1749–76. *L'histoire naturelle, générale et particulière*. 15 vols. Paris: De l'imprimerie royale.

Burgin, Angus. 2015. *The Great Persuasion: Reinventing Free Markets since the Depression*. Cambridge, MA: Harvard University Press.

Burton, John Hill, ed. (1820) 1849. *Letters of Eminent Persons Addressed to David Hume*. Edinburgh: William Blackwood and Sons.

———. (1846) 1986. *Life and Correspondence of David Hume*. 2 vols. Edinburgh: William Tait.

Bush-Slimani, Barbara. 1993. "Hard Labour: Women, Childbirth and Resistance in British Caribbean Slave Societies." *History Workshop Journal* 36 (1): 83–99.

Butler, Joseph. 1726. *Fifteen Sermons Preached at the Rolls Chapel*. London: W. Botham.

Byon, Jiwon. 2017. "Thomas Henry Huxley's Agnostic Philosophy of Science." PhD diss., University of British Columbia.

Caffentzis, C. George. 1989. *Clipped Coins, Abused Words, and Civil Government: John Lock's Philosophy of Money*. Brooklyn, NY: Autonomedia.

———. 2000. *Exciting the Industry of Mankind: George Berkeley's Philosophy of Money*. Dordrecht, Neth.: Springer.

———. 2001. "Hume, Money, and Civilization; Or, Why Was Hume a Metallist?" *Hume Studies* 27 (2): 301–35.

———. 2005. "Civilizing the Highlands: Hume, Money, and the Annexing Act." *Historical Reflections / Réflexions Historiques* 3 (1): 169–94.

———. 2008. "Fiction or Counterfeit? David Hume's Interpretations of Paper and Metallic Money." In Wennerlind and Schabas, *David Hume's Political Economy*, 146–67.

Caldwell, Bruce. 2004. *Hayek's Challenge: An Intellectual Biography of F. A. Hayek*. Chicago: University of Chicago Press.

Cantillon, Richard. (1755) 2001. *Essay on the Nature of Commerce in General*. Translated by Henry Higgs (1931), with an introduction by Anthony Brewer. New Brunswick, NJ: Transaction Publishers.

Capaldi, Nicholas. 1975. *David Hume: The Newtonian Philosopher*. Boston: Twayne.

Cardoso, José Luís, and António de Vasconcelos Nogueira. 2005. "Isaac de Pinto (1717–87): An Enlightened Economist and Financier." *History of Political Economy* 37 (2): 263–92.

Carey, Daniel. 2013. "Locke's Species: Money and Philosophy in the 1690s." *Annals of Science* 70 (3): 1–24.

Carretta, Vincent. 2003. "Who Was Francis Williams?" *Early American Literature* 38 (2): 213–37.

Cartwright, Nancy. 1978. "Comments on Wesley Salmon's 'Science and Religion.'" *Philosophical Studies* 33 (2): 177–83.

Cary, John. 1695. *An Essay on the State of England in Relation to Its Trade, Its Poor, and Its Taxes*. Bristol: W. Barry.

Cesarano, Filippo. 1998. "Hume's Specie-Flow Mechanism and Classical Monetary Theory: An Alternative Interpretation." *Journal of International Economics* 45 (1): 173–86.

Charles, Loïc. 2003. "The Visual History of the *Tableau Économique*." *European Journal of the History of Economic Thought* 10 (4): 527–50.

———. 2004. "The *Tableau Économique* as Rational Recreation." *History of Political Economy* 36 (3): 445–74.

———. 2008. "French 'New Politics' and the Dissemination of David Hume's *Political Discourses* on the Continent." In Wennerlind and Schabas, *David Hume's Political Economy*, 181–202.

Checkland, Sydney G. 1975. *Scottish Banking: A History, 1695–1973*. Glasgow: Collins.

Cheney, Paul. 2008. "Constitution and Economy in David Hume's Enlightenment." In Wennerlind and Schabas, *David Hume's Political Economy*, 223–42.

———. 2010. *Revolutionary Commerce: Globalization and the French Monarchy*. Cambridge, MA: Harvard University Press.

Child, Josiah. 1693. *A New Discourse of Trade*. London: John Everingham.

Cockayne, Emily. 2007. *Hubbub: Filth, Noise, and Stench in England, 1600–1770*. New Haven, CT: Yale University Press.

Cohen, I. Bernard. 1990. *Benjamin Franklin's Science*. Cambridge, MA: Harvard University Press.

Cohon, Rachel. 2008. *Hume's Morality: Feeling and Fabrication*. Oxford: Oxford University Press.

Commons, John R. 1931. "Institutional Economics." *American Economic Review* 21 (December): 648–57.

———. 1934. *Institutional Economics: Its Place in Political Economy*. New York: Macmillan.

Condillac, Étienne Bonnot, abbé de Vasconcelos. (1776) 1997. *Commerce and Government Considered in their Mutual Relationship*. Translated and with an introduction by Shelagh Eltis and Walter Eltis. Cheltenham, UK: Edward Elgar.

Cowan, Brian. 2005. *The Social Life of Coffee: The Emergence of the British Coffeehouse*. New Haven, CT: Yale University Press.

———. 2012. "Public Spaces, Knowledge, and Sociability." In *Oxford Handbook of the History of Consumption*, edited by Frank Trentmann, 251–66. Oxford: Oxford University Press.

Cunningham, Andrew S. 2005. "David Hume's Account of Luxury." *Journal of the History of Economic Thought* 27 (3): 231–50.

D'Alembert, Jean le Rond. (1963) 1995. *Preliminary Discourse to the Encyclopedia of Diderot*. Translated by Richard N. Schwab. Chicago: University of Chicago Press. First published 1751.

Daire, Eugène, ed. 1847. *Mélanges d'économie politique*. Paris: Guillaumin.

Darwall, Stephen. 1994. "Hume and the Invention of Utilitarianism." In Stewart and Wright, *Hume and Hume's Connexions*, 58–82.

Daston, Lorraine. 1988. *Classical Probability in the Enlightenment*. Princeton, NJ: Princeton University Press.

———. 2011. "The Empire of Observation, 1600–1800." In *Histories of Scientific Observation*, edited by Lorraine Daston and Elizabeth Lunbeck, 81–113. Chicago: University of Chicago Press.

Davenant, Charles. 1698. *Discourses on the Publick Revenues, and on the Trade of England*. London.

———. 1699. *An Essay upon the Probable Methods of making a People gainers in the Ballance of Trade*. London.

———. 1715. *An Account of the Trade between Great-Britain, France, Holland, Spain, Portugal, Italy, Africa, Newfoundland, &c*. London.

Davis, Gordon F. 2003. "Philosophical Psychology and Economic Psychology in David Hume and Adam Smith." *History of Political Economy* 35 (2): 269–304.

Davis, J. Ronnie. 1990. "Adam Smith on the Providential Reconciliation of Individual and Social Interests: Is Man Led by the Invisible Hand or Misled by a Sleight of Hand?" *History of Political Economy* 22 (2): 341–52.

Defoe, Daniel. 1710. *An Essay upon Publick Credit*. London.

———. (1724–26) 1971. *A Tour through the Whole Island of Great Britain*. London: Penguin.

———. (1726) 1987. *The Complete English Tradesman*. Gloucester, UK: Allan Sutton.

Deleplace, Ghislain. 2017. *Ricardo on Money: A Reappraisal*. Abingdon, UK: Routledge.

Deleule, Didier. 1979. *Hume et la naissance du liberalism économique*. Paris: Aubier Montaigne.

De Marchi, Neil, and Paul Harrison. 1994. "Trading 'in the Wind' and with Guile: The Troublesome Matter of the Short Selling of Shares in Seventeenth-Century Holland." In De Marchi and Morgan, *Higgling*, 47–65.

De Marchi, Neil, and Mary S. Morgan, eds. 1994. *Higgling: Transactors and Their Markets in the History of Economics*. Durham, NC: Duke University Press.

Demeter, Tamás. 2012. "Hume's Experimental Method." *British Journal for the History of Philosophy* 20 (3): 577–99.

Dennett, Daniel C. 1996. *Consciousness Explained*. Boston: Little, Brown.

De Pierris, Graciela. 2006. "Hume and Locke on Scientific Methodology: The Newtonian Legacy." *Hume Studies* 32 (2): 277–329.

Derringer, William. 2018. *Calculated Values: Finance, Politics, and the Quantitative Age*. Cambridge, MA: Harvard University Press.

Desan, Christine. 2014. *Making Money: Coin, Currency, and the Coming of Capitalism*. Oxford: Oxford University Press.

Descartes, René. (1637) 1911. *Discourse on the Method of Rightly Conducting the Reason and Seeking for the Truth in the Sciences*. In *The Philosophical Works of Descartes*, vol. 1. Translated by Elizabeth S. Haldane and G. R. T. Ross. Cambridge: Cambridge University Press.

De Vries, Jan. 2008. *The Industrious Revolution: Consumer Behavior and the Household Economy, 1650 to the Present*. Cambridge: Cambridge University Press.

Diaye, Marc-Arthur, and André Lapidus. 2005a. "A Humean Theory of Choice of which Rationality May be One Consequence." *European Journal of the History of Economic Thought* 12 (1): 89–111.

———. 2005b. "Why Rationality May Be a Consequence of Hume's Theory of Choice." *European Journal of the History of Economic Thought* 12 (1): 119–26.

———. 2012. "Pleasure and Belief in Hume's Decision Process." *European Journal of the History of Economic Thought* 19 (3): 355–84.

———. Forthcoming. "Decision and Time from a Humean Point of View." *European Journal of the History of Economic Thought*.

Diderot, Denis. 1992. *Political Writings*. Edited by John Hope Mason and Robert Wokler. Cambridge: Cambridge University Press.

Dimand, Robert W. 2008. "David Hume on Canadian Paper Money." In Wennerlind and Schabas, *David Hume's Political Economy*, 168–80.

———. 2013. "David Hume and Irving Fisher on the Quantity Theory of Money in the Long Run and the Short Run." *European Journal of the History of Economic Thought* 20 (2): 284–304.

Dow, Sheila C. 2002. "Interpretations: The Case of David Hume." *History of Political Economy* 34 (2): 399–420.

———. 2009. "David Hume and Modern Economics." *Capitalism and Society* 4 (1): 1–31.

Drelichman, Mauricio, and Hans-Joachim Voth. 2014. *Lending to the Borrower from Hell: Debt, Taxes, and Default in the Age of Philip II*. Princeton, NJ: Princeton University Press.

Dufwenberg, Martin, and Uri Gneezy. 2000. "Measuring Beliefs in an Experimental Lost Wallet Game." *Games and Economic Behavior* 30 (2): 163–82.

Duke, Michael. 1979. "David Hume and Monetary Adjustment." *History of Political Economy* 11 (4): 572–87.

Du Pont de Nemours, Pierre Samuel. 1768. *De l'origine et des progrès d'une science nouvelle*. Paris: Desaint.

Du Rivage, Justin. 2017. *Revolution against Empire: Taxes, Politics, and the Origins of American Independence*. New Haven, CT: Yale University Press.

Du Tot, Charles de Ferrère. 1739. *Political Reflections on the Finances and Commerce of France*. London: A. Millar. First published 1738 as *Réflexions politiques sur les finances et le commerce* by Frères Vaillant and N. Prevôst (The Hague).

Eagly, Robert V. 1970. "Adam Smith and the Specie-Flow Doctrine." *Scottish Journal of Political Economy* 17 (1): 61–68.

Edgell, Stephen and Rick Tilman. 1989. "The Intellectual Antecedents of Thorstein Veblen: A Reappraisal." *Journal of Economic Issues* 23 (4): 1003–26.

Edgeworth, Francis Ysidro. 1925. *Papers Relating to Political Economy*. 3 vols. New York: Burt Franklin.

Elibank, Patrick Murray, Lord. 1758. *Thoughts on Money, Circulation, and Paper Currency*. Edinburgh: Hamilton, Balfour, and Neill.

Elmslie, Bruce. 1995. "Retrospectives: The Convergence Debate between David Hume and Josiah Tucker." *Journal of Economic Perspectives* 9 (4): 207–16.

Eltis, David, Stephen D. Behrendt, David Richardson, and Herbert S. Klein, eds. 1999. *The Trans-Atlantic Slave Trade: A Database on CD-ROM*. Cambridge: Cambridge University Press.

Emerson, Roger L. 1973. "The Social Composition of Enlightened Scotland." *Studies in Voltaire and the Eighteenth Century* 114:291–329.

———. 1995. "The 'Affair' at Edinburgh and the 'Project' at Glasgow: The Politics of Hume's Attempts to Become a Professor." In Stewart and Wright, *Hume and Hume's Connexions*, 1–22.

———. 2008. "The Scottish Contexts for David Hume's Political-Economic Thinking." In Wennerlind and Schabas, *David Hume's Political Economy*, 10–30.

———. 2009. *Essays on David Hume, Medical Men and the Scottish Enlightenment: Industry, Knowledge and Humanity*. Farnham, UK: Ashgate.

Faccarello, Gilbert, ed. 1998. *Studies in the History of French Political Economy: From Bodin to Walras*. London: Routledge.

———. 1999. *The Foundations of Laissez-Faire: The Economics of Pierre de Boisguilbert*. Translated by Carolyn Shread. London: Routledge. First published 1986 as *Aux origines de l'économie politique libérale: Pierre de Boisguilbert* by Éditions Anthropos (Paris).

Fausten, Dietrich. 1979. "The Humean Origin of the Contemporary Monetary Approach to the Balance of Payments." *Quarterly Journal of Economics* 93 (4): 655–73.

Feiser, James, ed. 1999. *Early Responses to Hume's Moral, Literary and Political Writings*. 2 vols. Bristol: Thoemmes Press.

Fénelon, François de Salignac de la Mothe-. 1994. *The Adventures of Telemachus, Son of Ulysses*. Edited and translated by Patrick Riley. Cambridge: Cambridge University Press. First published 1699 as *Les aventures de Télémaque*.

Ferguson, Adam. (1767) 1966. *An Essay on the History of Civil Society*. Edited by Duncan Forbes. Edinburgh: Edinburgh University Press.

Fichte, Johann Gottlieb. 2012. *The Closed Commercial State*. Translated by Anthony Curtis Adler. Albany: State University of New York Press. First published 1800 as *Der geschlossene Handelsstaat: Ein philosophischer Entwurf als Anhang zur Rechtslehre und Probe einer künftig zu liefernden Politik* by Cotta (Tübingen).

Finlay, Christopher J. 2004. "Hume's Theory of Civil Society." *European Journal of Political Theory* 3 (4): 369–92.

———. 2007. *Hume's Social Philosophy*. London: Continuum.

Fleischacker, Samuel. 2002. "Adam Smith's Reception among the American Founders, 1776–1790." *William and Mary Quarterly* 59 (4): 897–924.

———. 2003. "The Impact on America: Scottish Philosophy and the American Founding." In Broadie, *Cambridge Companion to the Scottish Enlightenment*, 316–37.

———. 2004. *On Adam Smith's Wealth of Nations: A Philosophical Companion*. Princeton, NJ: Princeton University Press, 2004.

Foley, Vernard. 1973. "An Origin of the *Tableau Économique.*" *History of Political Economy* 5 (1): 121–50.

Fontaine, Philippe. 1997. "Identification and Economic Behavior: Sympathy and Empathy in Historical Perspective." *Economics and Philosophy* 13 (2): 261–80.

Forbes, Duncan. 1975. *Hume's Philosophical Politics*. Cambridge: Cambridge University Press.

Forbonnais, François Véron de. 1754. *Élémens du commerce*. 2nd ed. 2 vols. Leiden, Neth.

Force, Pierre. 2003. *Self-Interest before Adam Smith: A Genealogy of Economic Science*. Cambridge: Cambridge University Press.

Forget, Evelyn. 1999. *The Social Economics of Jean-Baptiste Say: Markets and Virtue*. London: Routledge.

Foucault, Michel. (1966) 1994. *The Order of Things: An Archaeology of the Human Sciences*. New York: Vintage. Reprint of 1970 edition published by Random House (New York), a translation of *Les Mot et les choses*, first published in 1966 by Editions Gallimard (Paris).

Fox, Celina. 2010. *The Arts of Industry in the Age of Enlightenment*. New Haven, CT: Yale University Press.

Franklin, Benjamin. (1729) 1959. *A Modest Inquiry into the Nature and Necessity of a Paper-Currency*. In *The Writings of Benjamin Franklin*. Edited by L. W. Larabee and W. J. Bell Jr. New Haven, CT: Yale University Press.

———. (1762) 1771. "Letter from Dr. B. Franklin to D. Hume, Esq., on the Method of Securing Houses from the Effects of Lightning." In *Essays and Observations, Physical and Literary, Read before a Society in Edinburgh*, vol. 3, edited by David Hume and Alexander Munro II. Edinburgh: John Balfour, 129–41.

Friedman, Milton. 1953. "The Methodology of Positive Economics." In *Essays in Positive Economics*. Chicago: University of Chicago Press, 3–45.

———. 1968. "The Role of Monetary Policy." *American Economic Review* 58 (1): 1–17.

———. 1975. "Discussion in the Symposium of 25 Years after the Rediscovery of the Quantity Theory of Money: What Have We Learned?" *American Economic Review* 65 (2): 176–79.

———. 1989. "Quantity Theory of Money." In *The New Palgrave Dictionary of Economics: Money.*, 2nd ed., edited by J. Eatwell, M. Milgate, and P. Newman, 1–40. London: Macmillan; New York: Norton. First published 1987.

Friedman, Milton, and Anna Jacobson Schwartz. 1963. *A Monetary History of the United States, 1867–1960*. Princeton, NJ: Princeton University Press.

Frykman, Niklas. 2014. "Pirates and Smugglers: Political Economy in the Red Atlantic." In Stern and Wennerlind, *Mercantilism Reimagined*, 218–38.

Furniss, Edgar. 1920. *The Position of the Laborer in a System of Nationalism: A Study in the Labor Theories of the Later English Mercantilists*. New York: Houghton Mifflin.

Furubotn, Eirik G., and Rudolf Richter. 1997. *Institutions and Economic Theory: The Contribution of the New Institutional Economics*. Ann Arbor: University of Michigan Press.

Galiani, Ferdinando. 1751. *Della moneta*. Naples.

Garber, Daniel. 1992. *Descartes' Metaphysical Physics*. Chicago: University of Chicago Press.

Garrett, Aaron. 2000. "Hume's Revised Racism Revisited." *Hume Studies* 26 (1): 171–77.

Garrett, Don. 1997. *Cognition and Commitment in Hume's Philosophy*. New York: Oxford University Press.

———. 2015. *Hume*. New York: Routledge.

Gaskin, J. C. A. 2009. "Hume on Religion." In Norton and Taylor, *Cambridge Companion to Hume*, 480–513.

Gatch, Loren. 1996. "To Redeem Metal with Paper: David Hume's Philosophy of Money." *Hume Studies* 22 (1): 169–91.

Gauci, Perry. 2007. *Emporium of the World: The Merchants of London, 1660–1800*. London: Bloomsbury.

Gaukroger, Stephen. 2010. *The Collapse of Mechanism and the Rise of Sensibility: Science and the Shaping of Modernity, 1680–1760*. New York: Oxford University Press.

Gaus, Gerald, and Shane Courtland. 2018. "Liberalism." In *Stanford Encyclopedia of Philosophy*. Stanford University, 1997–. Article published November 28, 1996; last modified January 22, 2018. https://plato.stanford.edu/entries/liberalism/.

Gauthier, David. 1979. "David Hume, Contractarian." *Philosophical Review* 88 (1): 3–38.

Gay, Peter. 1969. *The Enlightenment: An Interpretation, The Science of Freedom*. New York: Norton. Originally published by Alfred A. Knopf.

Gee, Joshua. 1729. *The Trade and Navigation of Great-Britain Considered*. Glasgow.

Gervaise, Isaac. 1720. *The System or Theory of the Trade of the World*. London: H. Woodfall.

Gherity, James A. 1994. "The Evolution of Adam Smith's Theory of Banking." *History of Political Economy* 26 (3): 423–41.

Gill, Michael. 2000. "Hume's Progressive View of Human Nature." *Hume Studies* 26 (1): 87–108.

Gillispie, Charles C. 1993. *A Diderot Pictorial Encyclopedia of Trades and Industry: Manufacturing and the Technical Arts in Plates Selected from L'Encyclopedie*. New York: Dover.

Glossop, R. J. 1984. "Hume and the Future of the Society of Nation." *Hume Studies* 10 (1): 46–58.

Golinski, Jan. 2007. *British Weather and the Climate of Enlightenment*. Chicago: University of Chicago Press.

Goodspeed, Tyler Beck. 2016. *Legislating Instability: Adam Smith, Free Banking, and the Financial Crisis of 1772*. Cambridge, MA. Harvard University Press.

Goodwin, Craufurd D. 2006. "The Art of an Ethical Life: Keynes and Bloomsbury." In *The Cambridge Companion to Keynes*, edited by Roger E. Backhouse and Bradley W. Bateman, 217–36. Cambridge: Cambridge University Press.

Gopnick, Alison. 2009. "Could David Hume Have Known about Buddhism?" *Hume Studies* 35 (1–2): 5–28.

Grabiner, Judith V. 1998. "'Some Disputes of Consequence': Maclaurin among the Molasses Barrels." *Social Studies of Science* 28 (1): 139–68.

Graeber, David. 2011. *Debt: The First 5,000 Years*. Brooklyn, NY: Melville House.

Gray, John. 1990. "Hayek, the Scottish School, and Contemporary Economics." In *The Scottish Contribution to Modern Economic Thought* edited by Douglas Mair, 249–62. Aberdeen: Aberdeen University Press.

Greig, J. Y. T. 1931. *David Hume*. London: Jonathan Cape.

Griswold, Charles L. Jr. 1999. *Adam Smith and the Virtues of Enlightenment*. Cambridge: Cambridge University Press.

Grüne-Yanoff, Till, and Edward F. McClennen. 2008. "Hume's Framework for a Natural History of the Passions." In Wennerlind and Schabas, *David Hume's Political Economy*, 86–104.

Guimarães, Lívia. 2015. "Hume and Feminism." In Bailey and O'Brien, *Bloomsbury Companion to Hume*, 319–31.

Gurney, John. 2013. *Gerrard Winstanley: The Digger's Life and Legacy*. London: Pluto Press.

Haakonssen, Knud. 1981. *The Science of a Legislator: The Natural Jurisprudence of David Hume and Adam Smith*. Cambridge: Cambridge University Press.

———. 1994. Introduction to *David Hume: Political Essays*, edited by Knud Haakonssen, xi–xxx. Cambridge: Cambridge University Press.

———, ed. 2006a. *The Cambridge Companion to Adam Smith*. Cambridge: Cambridge University Press.

———. 2006b. "Introduction: The Coherence of Smith's Thought," in Haakonssen, *Cambridge Companion to Adam Smith*, 1–21.

———. 2009. "The Structure of Hume's Political Theory." In Norton and Taylor, *Cambridge Companion to Hume*, 341–80.

Haakonssen, Knud, and Donald Winch. 2006. "The Legacy of Adam Smith." In Haakonssen, *Cambridge Companion to Adam Smith*, 366–94.

Hacking, Ian. 1978. "Hume's Species of Probability." *Philosophical Studies* 33 (1): 21–37.

———. 1983. *Representing and Intervening*. Cambridge: Cambridge University Press.

Hamowy, Ronald. 1987. *The Scottish Enlightenment and the Theory of Spontaneous Order*. Carbondale: Southern Illinois University Press.

Hancock, David. 1995. *Citizens of the World: London Merchants and the Integration of the British Atlantic Community, 1735–1785*. Cambridge: Cambridge University Press.

Hands, D. Wade. 2010. "Did Milton Friedman's Methodology License the Formalist Revolution?" *Journal of Economic Methodology* 10 (4): 507–20.

Hankins, Thomas L. 1985. *Science and the Enlightenment*. New York: Cambridge University Press.

Hardin, Russell. 2007. *David Hume: Moral and Political Theorist*. New York: Oxford University Press.

Harkness, Deborah E. 2007. *The Jewel House: Elizabethan London and the Scientific Revolution*. New Haven, CT: Yale University Press.

Harris, James A. 2009. "The Epicurean in Hume." In *Epicurus in the Enlightenment*, edited by Neven Leddy and Avi S. Lifschitz, 161–81. Oxford: Voltaire Foundation.

———. 2015. *Hume: An Intellectual Biography*. Cambridge: Cambridge University Press.

Hausman, Daniel M. 1992. *The Inexact and Separate Science of Economics*. Cambridge: Cambridge University Press.

Hausman, Daniel M., and Michael S. McPherson. 2006. *Economic Analysis, Moral Philosophy, and Public Policy*. 2nd ed. Cambridge: Cambridge University Press.

Hayek, Friedrich A. 1932. *Prices and Production*. London: Routledge, 1931.

———. 1938. "Review of *An Abstract of a Treatise of Human Nature* by David Hume, J. M. Keynes, P. Sraffa." *Economica* 5 (19): 364–65.

———. 1944. *The Road to Serfdom*. London: Routledge.

———. 1945. "The Use of Knowledge in Society." *American Economic Review* 35 (4): 519–30.

———. 1960. *The Constitution of Liberty*. Chicago: University of Chicago Press.

———. 1973. *Law, Legislation and Liberty: Rules and Order*. Vol. 1. London: Routledge.

———. 1976. *Law, Legislation and Liberty: The Mirage of Social Justice*. Vol. 2. Chicago: University of Chicago Press.

———. 1979. *Law, Legislation and Liberty: The Political Order of Free People*. Vol. 3. Chicago: University of Chicago Press.

———. (1988) 2017. *Fatal Conceit: The Errors of Socialism*. Edited by W. W. Bartley III. In *The Collected Works of F. A. Hayek*, vol. 1, Bruce Caldwell, gen. ed. New York: Routledge.

———. 1991a. "Dr. Bernard Mandeville (1670–1733)." In Hayek, *Trend of Economic Thinking*, 79–100.

———. 1991b. "The Legal and Political Philosophy of David Hume (1711–1776)." In Hayek, *Trend of Economic Thinking*, 101–17.

———. 1991c. *The Trend of Economic Thinking: Essays on Political Economists and Economic History*. Edited by W. W. Bartley III and Stephen Kresge. In *The Collected Works of F. A. Hayek*, vol. 3, Bruce Caldwell, gen. ed. Chicago: University of Chicago Press.

———. (1976) 1999. *Good Money, Part II: The Standard*. Edited by Stephen Kresge. In *The Collected Works of F. A. Hayek*, vol. 6, Bruce Caldwell, gen. ed. Chicago: University of Chicago Press.

Hazony, Yoram, and Eric Schliesser. 2016. "Newton and Hume." In Russell, *Oxford Handbook of Hume*, 673–707.

Heilbroner, Robert. 1953. *The Worldly Philosophers: The Lives, Times and Ideas of the Great Economic Thinkers*. New York: Touchstone.

Helvétius, Claude-Adrien. (1758) 1807. *De l'esprit or, Essays on the Mind, and Its Several Faculties*. Translated by William Mudford. London: M. Jones. First published 1758 as *De l'esprit*.

Henderson, Leah. 2018. "The Problem of Induction." *Stanford Encyclopedia of Philosophy*. Stanford University, 1997–. Article published March 21. https://plato.stanford.edu /entries/induction-problem/.

Henderson, Willie. 2010. *The Origins of David Hume's Economics*. London: Routledge.

Heydt, Colin. 2007. "Relations of Literary Form and Philosophical Purpose in Hume's Four Essays on Happiness." *Hume Studies* 33 (1): 3–19.

Hill, Christopher. 1967. *Reformation to Revolution, 1530–1780*. Harmondsworth, UK: Penguin.

———. 1984. *The World Turned Upside Down: Radical Ideas During the English Revolution*. Harmondsworth, UK: Penguin.

Hirschman, Albert O. 1977.*The Passions and the Interests: Political Arguments for Capitalism before Its Triumph*. Princeton, NJ: Princeton University Press.

Hiskes, Richard. 1977. "Has Hume a Theory of Social Justice?" *Hume Studies* 3 (2): 72–93.

Hobbes, Thomas. (1651) 1996. *Leviathan*. Edited by Richard Tuck. Cambridge: Cambridge University Press.

Home, John. 1976. *A Sketch of the Character of Mr. Hume* and *Diary of a Journey from Morpeth to Bath, 23 April–1 May 1776*. Edited by David Fate Norton. Edinburgh: Tragara Press.

Homer, Sidney, and Richard Sylla. 2005. *A History of Interest Rates*. 4th ed. Hoboken, NJ: John Wiley and Sons.

Hont, Istvan. 1983. "The 'Rich Country–Poor Country' Debate in Scottish Classical Political Economy." In Hont and Ignatieff, *Wealth and Virtue*, 271–316.

———. 2005. *Jealousy of Trade: International Competition and the Nation State in Historical Perspective*. Cambridge, MA: Belknap Press of Harvard University Press.

———. 2006. "The Early Enlightenment Debate on Commerce and Luxury." In *The Cambridge History of Eighteenth-Century Political Thought*. Edited by Mark Goldie and Robert Wokler. Cambridge: Cambridge University Press, 379–418.

———. 2008. "The 'Rich Country–Poor Country' Debate Revisited: The Irish Origins and French Reception of the Hume Paradox." In Wennerlind and Schabas, *David Hume's Political Economy*, 243–323.

———. 2015. *Politics in Commercial Society: Jean-Jacques Rousseau and Adam Smith*. Edited by Béla Kapossy and Michael Sonenscher. Cambridge, MA: Harvard University Press.

Hont, Istvan, and Michael Ignatieff, eds. 1983. *Wealth and Virtue: The Shaping of Political Economy in the Scottish Enlightenment*. Cambridge: Cambridge University Press.

Hont Papers. n.d. Intellectual History Archive, University of St. Andrews Library, Fife, Scotland.

Hoppit, Julian. 1987. *Risk and Failure in English Business 1700–1800*. Cambridge: Cambridge University Press.

———. 1990. "Attitudes to Credit in Britain, 1680–1790." *Historical Journal* 33 (2): 305–22.

———. 2002. "The Myths of the South Sea Bubble." *Transactions of the Royal Historical Society* 12:141–65.

———. 2006. "The Contexts and Contours of British Economic Literature, 1660–1760." *Historical Journal* 49 (1): 79–110.

———. 2017. *Britain's Political Economies: Parliament and Economic Life, 1660–1800*. Cambridge: Cambridge University Press.

Howson, Colin. 2000. *Hume's Problem: Induction and the Justification of Belief*. Oxford: Oxford University Press.

Hume, David. (1745) 1967. *A Letter from a Gentleman to his Friend in Edinburgh*. Edinburgh: Edinburgh University Press.

———. 1746–47. Notebooks, Hume Papers, MSS. 25867–91. National Library of Scotland, Edinburgh.

———. (1747) 1846. "Descent on the Coast of Brittany." In *Life and Correspondence of David Hume*. Vol. 1. Edited by John Hill Burton. Edinburgh.

———. 1748. *A True Account of the Behaviour and Conduct of Archibald Stewart, Esq; Late Lord Provost of Edinburgh, In a Letter to a Friend*. London.

———. (1751a) 1998. *A Dialogue*. In *An Enquiry concerning the Principles of Morals*. Edited by Tom L. Beauchamp. Oxford: Oxford University Press.

———. 1751b. *Petition of the Grave and Venerable Bellmen, Or Sextons, of the Church of Scotland, To the Honourable House of Commons*. London.

———. 1752. *Political Discourses*. Edinburgh: A. Kincaid and A. Donaldson.

———. 1754a. *Discours politiques de monsieur Hume*. 2 vols. Translated and edited by Abbé Jean-Bernard Le Blanc. Amsterdam: Lambert.

———. 1754b. *Discours politiques de M. David Hume*. Translated by Elézéar Mauvillon. In 1756–58. *Discours Politiques*, 5 vols., edited by J. Schreuder. Amsterdam: J. Schreuder and P. Mortier.

———. 1755. *Discours politiques de monsieur Hume*. 2 vols. Edited by M. Groell. Translated by Abbé Jean-Bernard Le Blanc. Dresden.

———. 1758–60. *Œuvres philosophiques de Mr D. Hume*. 5 vols. Translated by J.-B. Merian and J. B. R. Robinet. Amsterdam: J. H. Schneider.

———. 1767. *Essais dur le commerce; le luxe; l'argent; l'intérêt de l'argent; les impôts; le crédit public, et la balance du commerce*. Lyon and Paris.

———. 1841. *Letters of David Hume and Extracts from Letters Referring to Him*. Edited by Thomas Murray. Edinburgh: Adam and Charles Black.

———. 1874–75. *David Hume: The Philosophical Works*. 4 vols. Edited by T. H. Green and T. H. Grose. London: Longman.

———. 1906. *Hume's Political Discourses*. Edited by William Bell Robertson. London and New York: Walter Scott Publishing.

———. 2007. *David Hume: Writings on Economics*. Edited and with an introduction by Eugene Rotwein; and with new introduction by Margaret Schabas. New Brunswick, NJ: Transaction. First published 1955.

Hume, David, and Alexander Munro II, eds. (1754–71) 2002. *Essays and Observations, Physical and Literary, Read before a Society in Edinburgh*. 3 vols. Edinburgh: John Balfour. Reprinted and edited by Paul B. Wood. Bristol: Thoemmes Continuum.

Hundert, E. J. 1972. "The Making of Homo Faber: John Locke between Ideology and History." *Journal of the History of Ideas* 33 (1): 3–22.

———. 1974. "The Achievement Motive in Hume's Political Economy." *Journal of the History of Ideas* 35 (1): 139–43.

———. 1994. *The Enlightenment's Fable: Bernard Mandeville and the Discovery of Society*. Cambridge: Cambridge University Press.

Hursthouse, Rosalind. 1999. "Virtue Ethics and Human Nature." *Hume Studies* 25 (1–2): 67–82.

Hutcheson, Francis. (1725) 2008. *An Inquiry into the Original of Our Ideas of Beauty and Virtue*. Edited by Wolfgang Leidhold. Indianapolis: Liberty Fund.

———. (1755) 2009. *A System of Moral Philosophy*. Edited by Knud Haakonssen. Indianapolis: Liberty Fund.

Hutchison, Terence. 1988. *Before Adam Smith: The Emergence of Political Economy, 1666–1776*. Oxford: Basil Blackwell.

Huxley, Thomas Henry. (1879) 2011. *Hume*. Cambridge: Cambridge University Press.

Ignatieff, Michael. 1984. *The Needs of Strangers*. London: Chatto and Windus.

Immerwahr, John. 1992. "Hume's Revised Racism." *Journal of the History of Ideas* 53 (3): 481–86.

Ince, Onur. 2018. "Between Commerce and Empire: David Hume, Colonial Slavery, and Commercial Incivility." *History of Political Thought* 39 (1): 107–34.

Israel, Jonathan. 2010. *A Revolution of the Mind: Radical Enlightenment and the Intellectual Origins of Modern Democracy*. Princeton, NJ: Princeton University Press.

Ito, Seiichiro. 2011. "The Making of Institutional Credit in England, 1600–1688." *European Journal of the History of Economic Thought* 18 (4): 487–519.

Jacob, Margaret C. 1997. *Scientific Culture and the Making of the Industrial West*. New York: Oxford University Press.

Jacobson, Anne Jaap, ed. 2000. *Feminist Interpretations of David Hume*. University Park: Pennsylvania State University Press.

Jevons, William Stanley. 1957. *The Theory of Political Economy*. 5th ed. London: Macmillan. First published 1871.

Jones, Norman. *God and the Moneylenders: Usury and Law in Early Modern England*. Oxford: Basil Blackwell, 1989.

Jones, Peter. 1983. "The Scottish Professoriate and the Polite Academy, 1720–46." In Hont and Ignatieff, *Wealth and Virtue*, 89–118.

———, ed. 2005. *The Reception of David Hume in Europe*. Bristol: Thoemmes-Continuum.

Jonsson, Fredrik Albritton. 2013. *Enlightenment's Frontier: The Scottish Highlands and the Origins of Environmentalism*. New Haven, CT: Yale University Press.

Jordan, Winthrop. 1968. *White over Black: American Attitudes toward the Negro, 1550–1812*. Chapel Hill: University of North Carolina Press.

Kames, Henry Home, Lord. (1751) 2005. *Essays on the Principles of Morality and Natural Religion*. Edited by Mary Catherine Moran. Indianapolis: Liberty Fund.

Kant, Immanuel. (1783) 1902. *Prolegomena to Any Future Metaphysics That Can Qualify as a Science*. Translated by Paul Carus. La Salle, IL: Open Court.

———. (1795) 1983. "To Perpetual Peace: A Philosophical Sketch." In *Perpetual Peace and Other Essays*. Translated by Ted Humphrey. Indianapolis: Hackett.

Kapossy, Béla, Isaac Nakhimovsky, and Richard Whatmore, eds. 2017. *Commerce and Peace in the Enlightenment*. Cambridge: Cambridge University Press.

Kawashima, Yukihiko. 2004. "Hume on Fluxions." *Journal of Tokyo International University* 70: 163–82.

Kaye, F. B. (1924) 1988. Introduction to Mandeville, *Fable of the Bees*, xvii–cxlvi.

Kaye, Joel. 1998. *Economy and Nature in the Fourteenth Century: Money, Markets Exchange, and the Emergence of Scientific Thought*. Cambridge: Cambridge University Press.

Kelly, P. H. 1991. "General Introduction: Locke on Money." In *Locke on Money*, vol. 1, edited by P. H. Kelly. Oxford: Clarendon Press.

Keynes, John Maynard. 1921. *A Treatise on Probability*. London: Macmillan.

———. 1930. *A Treatise on Money*. 2 vols. London: Macmillan.

———. 1930. "Economic Possibilities for Our Grandchildren." In *Essays in Persuasion*, 358–73.

———. (1931) 1965. *Essays in Persuasion*. New York: Norton. First published by Macmillan (London).

———. (1936) 1973. *The General Theory of Employment, Interest and Money*. Vol. 7 of *The Collected Writings of John Maynard Keynes*. Edited by Donald E. Moggridge. London: Macmillan, for the Royal Economics Society.

———. (1971–89) 2013. *Social, Political and Literary Writings*. Vol. 28 of The *Collected Writings of John Maynard Keynes*. Edited by Donald E. Moggridge. London: Macmillan, for the Royal Economics Society.

Keynes, John Maynard, and Piero Sraffa. 1938. Introduction to *An Abstract of a Treatise of Human Nature, 1740. A Pamphlet hitherto unknown by David Hume*. Cambridge: Cambridge University Press.

Klein, Lawrence E. 1984. "The Third Earl of Shaftesbury and the Progress of Politeness." *Eighteenth-Century Studies* 18 (2): 186–214.

Klein, Lawrence R. 1947. *The Keynesian Revolution*. New York: Macmillan.

Koerner, Lisbet. 1999. *Linnaeus: Nature and Nation*. Cambridge, MA: Harvard University Press.

Korsgaard, Christine M. 1996. *Creating the Kingdom of Ends*. Cambridge: Cambridge University Press.

Kramnick, Isaac. 1968. *Bolingbroke and His Circle: The Politics of Nostalgia in the Age of Walpole*. Ithaca:, NY Cornell University Press.

Krugman, Paul. 2011a. "An Interview with Paul Krugman: Inspiration for a Liberal Economist." *Browser*, June 20, 2011.

———. 2011b. "Models, Plain and Fancy." *New York Times*, February 2, 2011.

———. 2012. "How We Know the Earth is Old." *New York Times*, November 20, 2012.

Krugman, Paul R., Maurice Obstfeld, and Marc Melitz. 2018. *International Economics: Theory and Policy*. 11th ed. New York: Pearson.

Kuflik, Arthur. 1998. "Hume on Justice to Animals, Indians and Women." *Hume Studies* 24 (1): 53–70.

Kuhn, Thomas S. 1970. *The Structure of Scientific Revolutions*. 2nd ed. Chicago: University of Chicago Press.

Kula, Witold. 1986. *Measures and Men*. Translated by R. Szreter. Princeton, NJ: Princeton University Press.

Kwass, Michael. 2014. *Contraband: Louis Mandrin and the Making of a Global Underground*. Cambridge, MA: Harvard University Press.

Laidler, David. 1991. "The Quantity Theory Is Always and Everywhere Controversial—Why?" *Economic Record* 67 (4): 289–306.

Lapidus, André. 2010. "The Valuation of Decision and Individual Welfare: A Humean Approach." *European Journal of the History of Economic Thought* 17 (1): 1–28.

———. 2011. "The Possibility of a Welfare Policy in a World of Emotion-Driven Individuals: A Humean Point of View." In *Freedom and Happiness in Economic Thought and Philosophy: From Clash to Reconciliation*, edited by R. Ege and H. Igersheim, 212–28. Abingdon, UK: Routledge.

———. 2019. "David Hume and Rationality in Decision-Making: A Case Study on the Economic Reading of a Philosopher." In *The Individual and the Other in Economic Thought*, edited by R. Ege and H. Igersheim, 270–90. Abingdon, UK: Routledge.

Larrère, Catherine. 1992. *L'invention de l'économie au XVIIIe siècle: Du droit naturel à la physiocratie*. Paris: Presses Universitaire de France.

Laursen, John Christian, and Greg Coolidge. 1994. "David Hume and Public Debt: Crying Wolf?" *Hume Studies* 20 (1): 143–49.

La Vopa, Anthony J. 2017. *The Labor of the Mind: Intellect and Gender in Enlightenment Culture*. Philadelphia: University of Pennsylvania Press.

Law, John. (1705) 1966. *Money and Trade Considered, with a Proposal for Supplying the Nation with Money*. New York: Augustus M. Kelley.

Le Maux, Laurent. 2014. "Cantillon and Hume on Money and Banking: The Foundations of Two Theoretical Traditions." *Journal of Economic Surveys* 28 (5): 956–70.

Leng, Thomas. 2014. "Epistemology: Expertise and Knowledge in the World of Commerce." In Stern and Wennerlind, *Mercantilism Reimagined*, 97–116.

Levenson, Thomas. 2009. *Newton and the Counterfeiter: The Unknown Detective Career of the World's Greatest Scientist*. Boston: Houghton Mifflin Harcourt.

Levi, Margaret, and Barry Weingast. 2019. "Douglass North's Theory of Politics." *Political Science and Politics* 52 (2): 213–17.

Levy, David, and Sandra J. Peart. 2004. "Sympathy and Approbation in Hume and

Smith: A Solution to the Other Rational Species Problem." *Economics and Philosophy* 20 (2): 331–49.

Li, Ming-Hsun. 1963. *The Great Recoinage of 1696 to 1699*. London: Weidenfeld and Nicolson.

Livingston, Donald W. 1984. *Hume's Philosophy of Common Life*. Chicago: University of Chicago Press.

———. 1991. "Hayek as Humean." *Critical Review* 5 (2): 159–77.

Locke, John. (1690) 1988. *Two Treatises of Government*. Edited by Peter Laslett. Cambridge: Cambridge University Press.

———. 1695. *Further Considerations concerning Raising the Value of Money, Wherein Mr. Lowndes's Arguments for It in His Late Report concerning an Essay for the Amendment of the Silver Coins, Are Particularly Examined*. London: Printed for A. and J. Churchill.

———. *Locke on Money*, 2 vols. Edited by P. H. Kelly. Oxford: Clarendon Press.

———. 1997. *Locke: Political Essays*. New York: Cambridge University Press.

Lucas, E. Robert, Jr. 1996. "Nobel Lecture: Monetary Neutrality." *Journal of Political Economy* 104 (4): 661–82.

Magnusson, Lars. 1994. *Mercantilism: The Shaping of an Economic Language*. London: Routledge.

Magri, Tito. 2015. "Hume's Justice." In Ainslie and Butler, *Cambridge Companion to Hume's Treatise*, 301–32.

Malthus, Thomas Robert. (1798) 1989. *An Essay on the Principle of Population*. 2 vols. Edited by Patricia James. Cambridge: Cambridge University Press. Variorum edition of 1803; first published 1798.

Malynes, Gerard. 1622. *Consuetudo, vel Lex Mercatoria, or The Ancient Law-Merchant*. London.

———. 1623. *The Center of the Circle of Commerce: Or, A Refutation of a Treatise Intitled The Circle of Commerce, or The Ballance of Trade, Lately Published by E. M.* London.

Mandeville, Bernard. (1924) 1988. *The Fable of the Bees, or Private Vices, Publick Benefits*. 2nd ed. 2 vols. Edited by F. B. Kaye. Indianapolis: Liberty Fund. Reprint of second edition published by Clarendon Press (Oxford). First edition of vol. 1 first published 1714, second edition of vol. 1 in 1732; first edition of vol. 2 first published in 1729 (London). Page references are to the 1988 edition.

Mankin, Robert. 2005. "Can Jealousy be Reduced to a Science? Politics and Economics in Hume's *Essays*." *Journal of the History of Economic Thought* 27 (1): 59–70.

Manzer, Robert A. 1996. "The Promise of Peace? Hume and Smith on the Effects of Commerce on Peace and War." *Hume Studies* 22 (2): 369–82.

Marciano, Alain. 2006. "David Hume's Model of Man: Classical Political Economy as "'Inspired.'" *Political Economy* 64 (3): 369–86.

Marshall, Alfred. (1890) 1920. *Principles of Economics*. 8th ed. London: Macmillan. First published 1890.

Marshall, M. G. 2000. "Luxury, Economic Development, and Work Motivation: David Hume, Adam Smith, and J. R. McCulloch." *History of Political Economy* 32 (3): 631–48.

Marx, Karl. 1963–71. "Hume: Fall of Profit and Interest Dependent on the Growth of Trade and Industry." In *Theories of Surplus-Value*, vol. 1, translated by Emile Davis. Moscow: Progress Publishers.

Massey, Gerald J. 1991. "Backdoor Analyticity." In *Thought Experiments in Science and Philosophy*, edited by Tamara Horowitz and Gerald J. Massey, 285–96. New York: Rowman and Littlefield.

Massie, Joseph. 1760. *A Representation concerning the Knowledge of Commerce as a National Concern; Pointing out the Proper Means of Promoting such Knowledge in this Kingdom*. London: Payne.

Mayer, Thomas. 1980. "David Hume and Monetarism." *Quarterly Journal of Economics* 95 (1): 89–102.

Mazza, Emilio, and Gianluca Mori. 2016. "'Loose Bits of Paper' and 'Uncorrect Thoughts': Hume's Early Memoranda in Context." *Hume Studies* 42 (1–2): 9–60.

McArthur, Neil. 2007. *David Hume's Political Theory: Law, Commerce, and the Constitution of Government*. Toronto: University of Toronto Press.

McCoy, Drew. 1980. *The Elusive Republic: Political Economy in Jeffersonian America*. Chapel Hill: University of North Carolina Press.

McGee, Robert. 1989. "The Economic Thought of David Hume." *Hume Studies* 15 (1): 184–204.

McKendrick, Neil, John Brewer, and J. H. Plumb. 1984. *The Birth of a Consumer Society: The Commercialization of Eighteenth-Century England*. London: Harper Collins.

Meek, Ronald L. 1962. *The Economics of Physiocracy: Essays and Translations*. London: Allen and Unwin.

———. 1976. *Social Science and the Ignoble Savage*. Cambridge: Cambridge University Press.

Meeks, Gay Tulip. 2003. "Keynes on the Rationality of Decision Procedures under Uncertainty: The Investment Decision." In *The Philosophy of Keynes's Economics: Probability, Uncertainty, and Conventions*, edited by Jochen Runde and Sohei Mizuhara, 18–35. London: Routledge.

Melon, Jean-François. 1738. *A Political Essay upon Commerce*. Translated by David Bindon. Dublin: Philip Crampton. First published 1734 as *Essai politique sur le commerce*.

Merrill, Thomas W. 2015. *Hume and the Politics of Enlightenment*. New York: Cambridge University Press.

Mill, John Stuart. (1836) 1967. "On the Definition of Political Economy and on the Method of Investigation Proper to It." In *Essays on Economics and Society*. In *Collected Works of John Stuart Mill*. Vol. 4, edited by John M. Robson. Toronto: University of Toronto Press.

———. (1848) 1965. *Principles of Political Economy*. In *Collected Works of John Stuart Mill*, vols. 2–3, edited by John M. Robson. Toronto: University of Toronto Press.

———. (1873) 1981. *Autobiography and Literary Essays*. In *Collected Works of John Stuart Mill*, vol. 1, edited by John M. Robson and Jack Stillinger. Toronto: University of Toronto Press.

Millar, John. (1771) 2006. *The Origin of the Distinction of Ranks*. Edited by Aaron Garrett. Indianapolis: Liberty Fund.

Miller, David. 1974. "The Ideological Backgrounds to Conceptions of Social Justice." *Political Studies* 22 (4): 387–99.

Miller, Eugene F. 1987. Foreword and "Editor's Note" to *David Hume: Essays, Moral, Political and Literary*, edited by Eugene F. Miller, xi–xviii; xix–xxvii. Indianapolis: Liberty Classics.

Miller, Jon Charles. 2013. "Hume's Citation of Strabo and the Dating of the Memoranda." *Hume Studies* 39 (2): 197–202.

Mirabeau, Victor Riqueti, Marquis de. 1756. *L'ami des homes, ou Traité de la population.* 3 vols. Avignon.

Mirowksi, Philip. 1984. "The Role of Conservation Principles in Twentieth-Century Economic Theory." *Philosophy of the Social Sciences* 14 (4): 461–73.

———, ed. 1994. *Edgeworth on Chance, Economic Hazard, and Statistics.* Lanham, MD: Rowman and Littlefield.

Misak, Cheryl J., ed. 2004. *Cambridge Companion to Peirce.* Cambridge: Cambridge University Press.

———. 2016. *Cambridge Pragmatism: From Peirce and James to Ramsey and Wittgenstein.* Oxford: Oxford University Press.

Misselden, Edward. 1622. *Free Trade. Or, the Meanes to Make Trade Florish,* 2nd ed. London: Simon Waterson.

———. 1623. *The Circle of Commerce, or The Ballance of Trade, in Defence of Free Trade.* London: Nicholas Bourne.

Mitchell, Wesley Clair. (1937) 1950. *The Backward Art of Spending Money and Other Essays.* New York: August M. Kelly.

———. (1949) 1967–69. *Types of Economics Theory: From Mercantilism to Institutionalism.* 2 vols. Edited by Joseph Dorfman. New York: Augustus M. Kelly.

Mokyr, Joel. 2009. *The Enlightened Economy: An Economic History of Britain, 1700–1850.* New Haven, CT: Yale University Press.

Monroe, Arthur Eli. (1923) 1966. *Monetary Theory before Adam Smith.* New York: Augustus M. Kelley.

Montesquieu, Charles de Secondat. (1748) 1989. *The Spirit of the Laws.* Edited and translated by Anne M. Cohler, Basia Carolyn Miller, and Harold Samuel Stone. Cambridge: Cambridge University Press.

Moore, James. 1994. "Hume and Hutcheson." In Stewart and Wright, *Hume and Hume's Connexions,* 23–57.

Moore, Katie A. 2016. "America's First Economic Stimulus Package: Paper Money and the Body Politic in Colonial Pennsylvania, 1715–1730." *Pennsylvania History: A Journal of Mid-Atlantic Studies* 83 (4): 529–57.

Morgan, Jennifer L. 2004. *Laboring Women: Reproduction and Gender in New World Slavery.* Philadelphia: University of Pennsylvania Press.

Morgan, Kenneth. 2000. *Slavery, Atlantic Trade and the British Economy, 1660–1800.* Cambridge: Cambridge University Press.

Morton, Eric. 2002. "Race and Racism in the Works of David Hume." *Journal on African Philosophy* 1 (1). https://www.africaknowledgeproject.org/index.php/jap/article/view/6.

Moss, Laurence S. 1991. "Thomas Hobbes's Influence on David Hume: The Emergence of a Public Choice Tradition." *History of Political Economy* 23 (4): 587–612.

Mossner, Ernest Campbell. 1943. *The Forgotten Hume: Le Bon David.* New York: Columbia University Press.

———. 1948. "Hume's Early Memoranda, 1729–40: The Complete Text." *Journal of the History of Ideas* 9 (4): 492–518.

———. 1958. "Hume at La Flèche, 1735: An Unpublished Letter." *University of Texas Studies in English* 37: 30–33.

———. 1962. "New Hume Letters to Lord Elibank, 1748–1776." *University of Texas Studies in Literature and Language* 4 (3): 431–60.

———. 1980. *The Life of David Hume*. 2nd ed. Oxford: Clarendon Press.

Muldrew, Craig. 1998. *The Economy of Obligation: The Culture of Credit and Social Relations in Early Modern England*. Basingstoke, UK: Palgrave.

Mun, Thomas. (1664) 1968. *England's Treasure by Forraign Trade*. Fairfield, NJ: Augustus M. Kelly.

Murphy, Anne L. 2009. *The Origins of the English Financial Revolution: Investment and Speculation before the South Sea Bubble*. Cambridge: Cambridge University Press.

———. 2014. "Financial Markets: The Limits of Economic Regulation in Early Modern England." In Stern and Wennerlind, *Mercantilism Reimagined*, 263–81.

Murphy, Antoin E. 1986. *Richard Cantillon: Entrepreneur and Economist*. Oxford: Oxford University Press.

———. 1997. *John Law: Economic Theorist and Policy-Maker*. Oxford: Oxford University Press.

———. 2009. *The Genesis of Macroeconomics: New Ideas from Sir William Petty to Henry Thornton*. Oxford: Oxford University Press.

Muthu, Sankar, ed. 2012. *Empire and Modern Political Thought*. Cambridge: Cambridge University Press.

Nakano, Takeshi. 2006. "'Let Your Science be Human': Hume's Economic Methodology." *Cambridge Journal of Economics* 30 (5): 687–700.

Nakhimovsky, Isaac. 2011. *The Closed Commercial State: Perpetual Peace and Commercial Society from Rousseau to Fichte*. Princeton, NJ: Princeton University Press.

Neeson, J. M. 1993. *Commoners: Common Right, Enclosure and Social Change in England, 1700–1820*. Cambridge: Cambridge University Press.

North, Douglass C. 1981. *Structure and Change in Economic History*. New York: Norton.

———. 1990. *Institutions, Institutional Change, and Economic Performance*. Cambridge: Cambridge University Press.

North, Douglass C., and Barry R. Weingast. 1989. "Constitutions and Commitment: The Evolution of Institutions Governing Public Choice in Seventeenth-Century England." *Journal of Economic History* 49 (4): 803–32.

Norton, David Fate. 1976. Introduction to *A Sketch of the Character of Mr. Hume and Diary of a Journey from Morpeth to Bath, 23 April–1 May 1776*, by John Home. Edited by David Fate Norton. Edinburgh: Tragara Press.

———. 1993a. *The Cambridge Companion to Hume*. Cambridge: Cambridge University Press.

———. 1993b. "Hume, Human Nature, and the Foundations of Morality." In D. Norton, *Cambridge Companion to Hume*, 148–81.

———. 1993c. "More Evidence That Hume Wrote the *Abstract*." *Hume Studies* 19 (1): 217–22.

———. 2009a. "The Foundations of Morality in Hume's *Treatise*." In D. Norton and Taylor, *Cambridge Companion to Hume*, 270–310.

———. 2009b. "An Introduction to Hume's Thought." In D. Norton and Taylor, *Cambridge Companion to Hume*, 1–39.

Norton, David Fate, and Mary J. Norton, eds. 1996. *The David Hume Library*. Edinburgh: National Library of Scotland.

Norton, David Fate, and Jacqueline Taylor, eds. 2009. *The Cambridge Companion to Hume*. 2nd ed. Cambridge: Cambridge University Press.

Norton, John D. 2010. "How Hume and Mach Helped Einstein Find Special Relativity." In *Discourse on a New Method: Reinvigorating the Marriage of History and Philosophy of Science*, edited by Mary Domski and Michael Dickson, 359–86. Chicago: Open Court.

Nye, Mary Jo. 2011. *Michael Polanyi and His Generation: Origins of the Social Construction of Science*. Chicago: University of Chicago Press.

Offer, Avner, and Gabriel Söderberg. 2016. *The Nobel Factor: The Prize in Economics, Social Democracy, and the Market Turn*. Princeton, NJ: Princeton University Press.

Olson, Mancur Jr. 1996. "Big Bills Left on the Sidewalk: Why Some Nations Are Rich, and Others Poor." *Journal of Economic Perspectives* 10 (2): 3–24.

Olson, Richard. 1975. *Scottish Philosophy and British Physics, 1750–1880*. Princeton, NJ: Princeton University Press.

Owen, David. 1999. *Hume's Reason*. Oxford: Oxford University Press.

———. 2009. "Hume and the Mechanics of Mind: Impressions, Ideas, and Association." In Norton and Taylor, *Cambridge Companion to Hume*, 70–104.

———. 2016. "Reason, Belief, and the Passions." In Russell, *Oxford Handbook of Hume*, 333–55.

Paganelli, Maria Pia. 2006. "Hume and Endogenous Money." *Eastern Economic Journal* 32 (3): 533–47.

———. 2007. "'The Good Policy of the Magistrate': Deflation as a Policy Option in David Hume's Economics Essays." *History of Economic Ideas* 15 (3): 9–25.

Palacios-Heurta, Ignacio. 2003. "Time-Inconsistent Preferences in Adam Smith and David Hume." *History of Political Economy* 35 (2): 241–68.

Parfit, Derek. 1984. *Reasons and Persons*. Oxford: Oxford University Press.

Pâris-Duverney, Joseph. 1740. *Réflexions politiques sur les Finances*. 2 vols. The Hague: Vaillant and N. Prevost.

Penelhum, Terence. 2009. "Hume's Moral Psychology." In Norton and Taylor, *Cambridge Companion to Hume*, 238–69.

Perlman, Morris. 1987. "Of a Controversial Passage in Hume." *Journal of Political Economy* 95 (2): 274–89.

Perrot, Jean-Claude. 1992. *Une histoire intellectuelle de l'économie politique, XVIIe–XVIIIe siècle*. Paris: École des Hautes Études en Sciences Sociales.

Petrella, Frank. 1968. "Adam Smith's Rejection of Hume's Price-Specie-Flow Mechanism: A Minor Mystery Resolved." *Southern Economic Journal* 34 (3): 365–74.

Pettit, Philip. 2008. *Made with Words: Hobbes on Language, Mind, and Politics*. Princeton, NJ: Princeton University Press.

Petty, William. (1691) 1899. *Verbum Sapienti*. London. In *The Economic Writings of Sir William Petty*. 2 vols. Edited by C. H. Hull. Cambridge: Cambridge University Press.

Phelps, Edmund. 2013. *Mass Flourishing: How Grassroots Innovation Created Jobs, Challenge, and Change*. Princeton, NJ: Princeton University Press.

Phillipson, Nicholas. 1993. "Politics and Politeness in the Philosophy of David Hume." In *Politics, Politeness, and Patriotism*. Edited by Gordon Schochet, 305–18. Washington, DC: Folger Library.

———. 2010. *Adam Smith: An Enlightened Life*. New Haven, CT: Yale University Press.

———. 2011. *David Hume: The Philosopher as Historian*. Rev. ed. New Haven, CT: Yale University Press.

Pincus, Steve. 2012. "Rethinking Mercantilism: Political Economy, the British Empire, and the Atlantic World in the Seventeenth and Eighteenth Centuries." *William and Mary Quarterly* 69 (1): 3–34.

———. 2016. *The Heart of the Declaration: The Founders' Case for an Activist Government*. New Haven, CT: Yale University Press.

Pinto, Isaac de. 1771. *Traité de la circulation et du crédit*. Amsterdam.

———. 1774. *An Essay on Circulation and Credit, in Four Parts; and a Letter on the Jealousy of Commerce*. Translated by S. Baggs. London.

Pitson, Tony. 2016. "Hume, Free Will, and Moral Responsibility." In Russell, *Oxford Handbook of Hume*, 380–400.

Pluche, Noël-Antoine. (1746) 2003. "Spectacle of Nature." In *Commerce, Culture, and Liberty: Readings on Capitalism before Adam Smith*, excerpted, translated, and edited by Henry C. Clark, 282–87. Indianapolis: Liberty Fund.

Pocock, J. G. A. 1975. *The Machiavellian Moment: Florentine Political Thought and the Atlantic Republican Tradition*. Princeton, NJ: Princeton University Press.

———. 1979. "Hume and the American Revolution: The Dying Thoughts of a North Briton." In *McGill Hume Studies*, edited by D. F. Norton, N. Capaldi, and W. L. Robinson, 325–42. San Diego: Austin Hills Press.

———. 1985. *Virtue, Commerce, and History: Essays on Political Thought and History, Chiefly in the Eighteenth Century*. Cambridge: Cambridge University Press.

Poirier, Jean-Pierre. 1993. *Lavoisier: Chemist, Biologist, Economist*. Translated by Rebecca Balinski. Philadelphia: University of Pennsylvania Press.

Polanyi, Karl. 1944. *The Great Transformation*. Toronto: Farrar and Rinehart.

Poovey, Mary. 2008. *Genres of the Credit Economy: Mediating Value in Eighteenth- and Nineteenth-Century Britain*. Chicago: University of Chicago Press.

Popkin, Richard H. 1970. "Hume and Isaac de Pinto," *Texas Studies in Literature and Language* 12 (3): 417–30.

———. 1980. *The High Road to Pyrrhonism*. Edited by Richard A. Watson and James E. Force. San Diego: Austin Hill Press.

Porter, Roy. 1991. *English Society in the Eighteenth Century*. Rev. ed. London: Penguin.

Porter, Roy, and Mikuláš Teich, eds. 1981. *The Enlightenment in National Context*. Cambridge: Cambridge University Press.

Porter, Theodore M. 1986. *The Rise of Statistical Thinking*. Princeton, NJ: Princeton University Press.

———. 2003. "The Social Sciences." In *From Natural Philosophy to the Sciences: Writing the History of Nineteenth-Century Science*, edited by David Cahan, 254–90. Chicago: University of Chicago Press.

Porter, Theodore M., and Dorothy Ross, eds. 2003. *The Cambridge History of Science*. Vol. 7, *The Modern Social Sciences*. Cambridge: Cambridge University Press.

Postlethwayt, Malachy. 1751–55. *Universal Dictionary of Trade and Commerce*. London: John and Paul Knapton.

———. 1757. *Great Britain's True System*. London: Millar, Whiston, White, and Samdby.

Potter, William. 1650. *The Key of Wealth: Or, a New Way, for Improving of Trade*. London.

Prinz, Jesse. 2016. "Hume and Cognitive Science." In Russell, *Oxford Handbook of Hume*, 777–92.

Quesnay, François. (1758) 1958. "Tableau économique." In *Textes annotés*, vol. 2 of *François Quesnay et la physiocratie*. 2 vols. Edited by Jacqueline Hecht. Paris: Institut National d'Etudes Démographiques.

———. 1962. "The Tableau Économique." In Meek, *Economics of Physiocracy*, 108–202.

Raphael, D. D. 2001. *Concepts of Justice*. Oxford: Oxford University Press.

Rashid, Salim. 1984. "David Hume and Eighteenth-Century Monetary Thought: A Critical Comment on Recent Views." *Hume Studies* 10 (2): 156–64.

Rasmussen, Denis C. 2017. *The Infidel and the Professor: David Hume, Adam Smith, and the Friendship That Shaped Modern Thought*. Princeton, NJ: Princeton University Press.

Raynal, Guillaume Thomas François, Abbé. 1798. *A Philosophical and Political History of the Settlements and Trade of the Europeans in the East and West Indies*. 6 vols. Translated by J. O. Justamond. London: A. Strahan.

Raynor, David. 1980. "Hume's Knowledge of Bayes's Theorem." *Philosophical Studies* 38 (1): 105–6.

———, ed. 1982. *Sister Peg: A Pamphlet hitherto unknown by David Hume*. Cambridge: Cambridge University Press.

———. 1984. "Hume's Abstract of Adam Smith's *Theory of Moral Sentiments*." *Journal of the History of Philosophy* 22 (1): 51–79.

———. 1993. "The Authorship of the *Abstract* Revisited." *Hume Studies* 19 (1): 213–15.

———. 1998. "Who Invented the Invisible Hand?" *Times Literary Supplement* August 14, 1998, 2.

Read, Rupert, and Kenneth A. Richman, eds. 2007. *The New Hume Debate*. Rev. ed. London: Routledge.

Redish, Angela. 2000. *Bimetallism: An Economic and Historical Analysis*. Cambridge: Cambridge University Press, 2000.

Redman, Deborah A. 1997. *The Rise of Political Economy as a Science: Methodology and the Classical Economists*. Cambridge, MA: MIT Press.

Rees, John. 2017. *The Leveller Revolution: Radical Political Organization in England, 1640–1650*. London: Verso.

Reid, Thomas. 1764. *An Inquiry in the Human Mind, on the Principles of Common Sense*. Edinburgh.

Reill, Peter H. 2005. *Vitalizing Nature in the Enlightenment*. Berkeley: University of California Press.

Reinert, Sophus. 2011. *Translating Empire: Emulation and the Origins of Political Economy*. Cambridge, MA: Harvard University Press.

———. 2015. "The Way to Wealth around the World: Benjamin Franklin and the Globalization of American Capitalism." *American Historical Review* 120 (1): 61–97.

———. 2018. *The Academy of Fisticuffs: Political Economy and Commercial Society in Enlightenment Italy*. Cambridge, MA: Harvard University Press.

Ricard, Samuel. 1700. *Traité général du commerce*. 3 vols. Amsterdam: Paul Marret.

Ricardo, David. 1951. *The Works and Correspondence of David Ricardo*. 11 vols. Cambridge: Cambridge University Press.

———. 1951a. *Letters: 1816–18*. Vol. 7 of Ricardo, *Works and Correspondence*.

———. 1951b. *On the Principles of Political Economy and Taxation*. Vol. 1 of Ricardo, *Works and Correspondence*. First published 1817; 3rd ed. 1821.

———. 1951c. *Pamphlets and Papers, 1809–1811*. Vol. 3 of Ricardo, *Works and Correspondence*.

————. 1951d. *Pamphlets and Papers, 1815–1823*. Vol. 4 of Ricardo, *Works and Correspondence*.

————. 1951e. *Speeches and Evidence*. Vol. 5 of Ricardo, *Works and Correspondence*.

————. 1951f. *Biographical Miscellany*. Vol. 10 of Ricardo, *Works and Correspondence*.

Richards, R. D. 1958. *The Early History of Banking in England*. London: Franc Cass.

Riskin, Jessica. 1998. "Poor Richard's Leyden Jar: Electricity and Economy in Franklinist France." *Historical Studies in the Physical and Biological Sciences* 28 (2): 301–36.

————. 2002. *Science in the Age of Sensibility*. Chicago: University of Chicago Press.

Robertson, John. 1983. "The Scottish Enlightenment at the Limits of the Civic Tradition." In Hont and Ignatieff, *Wealth and Virtue*, 137–78.

————, ed. 1995. *A Union for Empire: Political Thought and the Union of 1707*. Cambridge: Cambridge University Press.

————. 2005. *The Case for the Enlightenment: Scotland and Naples, 1680–1760*. Cambridge: Cambridge University Press.

Robertson, William Bell. 1906. Introduction to *Hume's Political Discourses*, edited by William Bell Robertson. London and New York: Walter Scott Publishing, vii–xxvii.

Rosenberg, Alex. 1993. "Hume and the Philosophy of Science." In Norton, *The Cambridge Companion to Hume*, 64–89. Cambridge: Cambridge University Press.

Ross, Angus, ed. 1982. *Selections from the* Tatler *and the* Spectator. Harmondsworth, UK: Penguin.

Ross, Ian Simpson. 1979. *Lord Kames and the Scotland of His Day*. Oxford: Oxford University Press.

————. 1995. *The Life of Adam Smith*. Oxford: Oxford University Press.

————. 2008. "The Emergence of David Hume as a Political Economist: A Biographical Sketch." In Wennerlind and Schabas, *David Hume's Political Economy*, 31–48.

Rostow, W. W. 1990. *Theories of Economic Growth from David Hume to the Present: With a Perspective on the Next Century*. Oxford: Oxford University Press, 1990.

Rothschild, Emma. 2001. *Economic Sentiments: Adam Smith, Condorcet, and the Enlightenment*. Cambridge, MA: Harvard University Press.

————. 2008. "David Hume and the Seagods of the Atlantic." In *The Atlantic Enlightenment*, edited by Susan Manning and Francis D. Cogliano, 81–96. London: Routledge.

————. 2009. "The Atlantic Worlds of David Hume." In *Soundings in Atlantic History: Latent Structures and Intellectual Currents, 1500–1830*, edited by Bernard Bailyn and Patricia Denault, 405–48. Cambridge, MA: Harvard University Press.

————. 2011. *The Inner Life of Empires: An Eighteenth Century History*. Princeton, NJ: Princeton University Press.

Rothschild, Emma, and Amartya Sen. 2006. "Adam Smith's Economics." In Haakonssen, *Cambridge Companion to Adam Smith*, 319–65.

Rotwein, Eugene. 2007. Introduction to *Writings on Economics: David Hume*, edited by Eugene Rotwein, ix–cxi. New Brunswick, NJ: Transaction.

Rousseau, Jean-Jacques. 1987. "Discourse on Political Economy." In *Jean-Jacques Rousseau: The Basic Political Writings*. 2d ed. Edited and translated by Donald A. Cress. Indianapolis: Hackett. First published in 1755 as *De l'économie politique*.

Runde, Jochen, and Sohei Mizuhara, eds. 2003. *The Philosophy of Keynes's Economics: Probability, Uncertainty, and Convention*. London: Routledge.

Rusnock, Andrea A. 1999. "Biopolitics: Political Arithmetic in the Enlightenment." In

The Sciences in Enlightened Europe, edited by William Clark, Jan Golinski, and Simon Schaffer, 49–68. Chicago: University of Chicago Press.

Russell, Paul. 1985. "Hume's *Treatise* and Hobbes's *The Elements of Law*." *Journal of the History of Ideas* 46:51–63.

———. 1995. *Freedom and Moral Sentiment: Hume's Way of Naturalizing Responsibility*. Oxford: Oxford University Press.

———. 2008. *The Riddle of Hume's Treatise: Skepticism, Naturalism, and Irreligion*. Oxford: Oxford University Press.

———, ed. 2016. *The Oxford Handbook of Hume*. Oxford: Oxford University Press.

Rutherford, Malcolm. 1994. *Institutions in Economics: The Old and the New Institutionalism*. Cambridge: Cambridge University Press.

Sabbagh, Gabriel. 2016. "Cantillon in French and English. Two Editions by Richard van den Berg and Antoin E. Murphy: New Facts and Hypotheses." *Contributions to Political Economy* 35 (1): 91–126.

Sabl, Andrew. 2012. *Hume's Politics: Coordination and Crisis in the History of England*. Princeton, NJ: Princeton University Press.

Sakamoto, Tatsuya. 1995. [*David Hume's Civilized Society—Industry, Knowledge and Liberty*]. Tokyo: Sobunsha. Published in Japanese.

———. 2003. "Hume's Political Economy as a System of Manners." In *The Rise of Political Economy in the Scottish Enlightenment*, edited by Tatsuya Sakamoto and Hideo Tanaka, 86–102. London: Routledge.

———. 2008. "Hume's Economic Theory." In *A Companion to Hume*, edited by Elizabeth S. Radcliffe, 373–87. Oxford: Blackwell.

———. 2011. "Hume's Early Memoranda and the Making of His Political Economy." *Hume Studies* 37 (2): 131–64.

———. 2016. "Hume's Philosophical Economics." In Russell, *Oxford Handbook of Hume*, 569–87.

Salmon, Wesley. 1978. "Religion and Science: A New Look at Hume's *Dialogues*." *Philosophical Studies* 33 (2): 143–76.

Samuelson, Paul A. 1971. "An Exact Hume-Ricardo-Marshall Model of International Trade." *Journal of International Economics* 1 (1): 1–18.

———. 1980. "A Corrected Version of Hume's Equilibrating Mechanism for International Trade." In *Flexible Exchange Rates and the Balance of Payments: Essays in Memory of Egon Sohmen*, edited by John Chipman and Charles Kindleberger, 141–58. Amsterdam: North Holland.

Sargent, Thomas, and François R. Velde. 2002. *The Big Problem of Small Change*. Princeton, NJ: Princeton University Press.

Savary des Brûlons, Jacques. 1723–30. *Dictionnaire universel du commerce*. Paris.

Sayre-McCord, Geoffrey. 1995. "Hume and the Bauhaus Theory of Ethics." *Midwest Studies in Philosophy* 20:280–98.

Schabas, Margaret. 1994. "Market Contracts in the Age of Hume." In De Marchi and Morgan, *Higgling*, 117–34.

———. 1995. "Parmenides and the Cliometricians." In *The Reliability of Economic Models: Essays on the Epistemology of Economics*, edited by Daniel C. Little, 183–202. Dordrecht, Neth.: Kluwer.

———. 1998. "John Maynard Keynes." In *Encyclopedia of Philosophy*. London: Routledge.

———. 2001. "David Hume on Experimental Natural Philosophy, Money, and Fluids." *History of Political Economy* 33 (3): 411–35.

———. 2005. *The Natural Origins of Economics*. Chicago: University of Chicago Press.

———. 2007. "Groups versus Individuals in Hume's Political Economy." *Monist* 90 (2): 200–212.

———. 2008a. "Hume's Monetary Thought Experiments." *Studies in History and Philosophy of Science* 39 (3): 161–69.

———. 2008b. "Temporal Dimensions in Hume's Monetary Theory." In Wennerlind and Schabas, *David Hume's Political Economy*, 127–45.

———. 2009. "The Evolutionary Context of Hume's Political Economy." In *David Hume on Norms and Institutions*, edited by Wojciech Zaluski. Florence: European University Institute. http://hdl.handle.net/1814/12934.

———. 2014a. "'Let Your Science Be Human': David Hume and the Honourable Merchant." *European Journal of the History of Economic Thought* 21 (6): 977–90.

———. 2014b. "Philosophy of the Human Sciences." In *Routledge Companion to Eighteenth Century Philosophy*, edited by Aaron Garrett, 731–52. London: Routledge.

———. 2015a. "Bees and Silkworms: Mandeville, Hume and the Framing of Political Economy." *Journal of the History of Economic Thought* 37 (1): 1–15.

———. 2015b. "Hume on Economic Well-Being." In Bailey and O'Brien, *Bloomsbury Companion to Hume*, 332–48.

———. 2018a. "Hume." In *Knowledge in Modern Philosophy*, vol. 3, edited by Stephen Gaukroger, 129–46. London: Bloomsbury.

———. 2018b. "Thought Experiments in Economics." In *Routledge Companion to Thought Experiments*, edited by Michael T. Steuart, Yiftach Fehige, and James R. Brown, 171–82. Abingdon, UK, and New York: Routledge.

———. 2020. "David Hume as a Proto-Weberian: Commerce, Protestantism, and Secular Culture." *Social Philosophy and Policy* 37 (1).

Schabas, Margaret, and Neil De Marchi, eds. 2003. *Oeconomies in the Age of Newton*. Durham, NC: Duke University Press.

Schabas, Margaret, and Carl Wennerlind. 2011. "Retrospectives: Hume on Money, Commerce, and the Science of Economics." *Journal of Economic Perspectives* 25 (3): 217–30.

Schaffer, Simon. 1997. "The Earth's Fertility as a Social Fact in Early Modern Britain." In *Nature and Society in Historical Context*, edited by Mikuláš Teich, Roy Porter, and Bo Gustafsson, 124–47. Cambridge: Cambridge University Press.

Schama, Simon. 1987. *The Embarrassment of Riches: An Interpretation of Dutch Culture in the Golden Age*. New York: Vintage.

Schatz, Albert. 1902. *L'oeuvre économique de David Hume*. Paris: A. Rousseau.

Schiebinger, Londa. 2004. *Plants and Empire: Colonial Bioprospecting in the Atlantic World*. Cambridge, MA: Harvard University Press, 2004.

———. 2017. *Secret Cures of Slaves: People, Plants, and Medicine in the Eighteenth-Century Atlantic World*. Palo Alto, CA: Stanford University Press.

Schliesser, Eric. 2003. "The Obituary of a Vain Philosopher: Adam Smith's Reflections on Hume's Life." *Hume Studies* 29 (2): 327–62.

———. 2007. "Hume's Newtonianism and Anti-Newtonianism." In *The Stanford Encyclopedia of Philosophy*, edited by Edward N. Zalta. First published January 5, 2007. https://plato.stanford.edu/archives/win2008/entries/hume-newton/.

———. 2017. *Adam Smith: Systematic Philosopher and Public Thinker.* Oxford: Oxford University Press.

Schmidt, Claudia M. 2003. *David Hume: Reason in History.* University Park: Pennsylvania State University Press.

Searle, John R. 1995. *The Construction of Social Reality.* London: Free Press.

Sekine, Thomas. 1973. "The Discovery of International Monetary Equilibrium by Vanderlint, Cantillon, Gervaise, and Hume." *Economia Internazionale* 26 (2): 262–82.

Sekora, John. 1977. *Luxury: The Concept in Western Thought, Eden to Smollett.* Baltimore: Johns Hopkins University Press.

Semmel, Bernard. 1965. "The Hume-Tucker Debate and Pitt's Trade Proposals." *Economic Journal* 75 (300): 759–70.

Sen, Amartya. 1977. "Rational Fools: A Critique of the Behavioral Foundations of Economic Theory." *Philosophy and Public Affairs* 6 (4): 317–44.

———. 1987. *On Ethics and Economics.* Oxford: Blackwell.

———. 1993. "Capability and Well-Being." In *The Quality of Life*, edited by Martha Nussbaum and Amartya Sen, 30–53. Oxford: Clarendon Press.

———. 2009. *The Idea of Justice.* Cambridge, MA: Harvard University Press.

Shaftesbury, Third Earl of (Anthony Ashley Cooper). (1711) 1999. *Characteristics of Men, Manners, Opinions, Times.* Cambridge: Cambridge University Press.

Shapin, Steven. 1994. *A Social History of Truth: Civility and Science in Seventeenth-Century England.* Chicago: University of Chicago Press.

Sheehan, Jonathan, and Dror Wahrman. 2015. *Invisible Hands: Self-Organization and the Eighteenth Century.* Chicago: University of Chicago Press.

Shell, Marc. 1995. *Art and Money.* Chicago: University of Chicago Press.

Sherman, Sandra. 1996. *Finance and Fictionality in the Early Eighteenth Century: Accounting for Defoe.* New York: Cambridge University Press.

Shovlin, John. 2007. *The Political Economy of Virtue: Luxury, Patriotism, and the Origins of the French Revolution.* Ithaca, NY: Cornell University Press.

———. 2008. "Hume's *Political Discourses* and the French Luxury Debate." In Wennerlind and Schabas, *David Hume's Political Economy*, 203–22.

———. 2018. "Commerce, Not Conquest: Political Economic Thought in the French Indies Company, 1719–1769." In *New Perspectives on the History of Political Economy*, edited by Robert Fredona and Sophus Reinert, 171–202. New York: Palgrave.

Sidgwick, Henry. (1874) 1981. *The Methods of Ethics.* 7th ed. With foreword by John Rawls. Indianapolis: Hackett.

Sigot, Nathalie. 2001. *Bentham et l'économie: Une histoire d'utilité.* Paris: Economica.

Silver, Allan. 1990. "Friendship in Commercial Society: Eighteenth-Century Social Theory and Modern Sociology." *American Journal of Sociology* 95 (6): 1474–1504.

Skinner, Andrew S. 2003. "Economic Theory." In Broadie, *Cambridge Companion to the Scottish Enlightenment*, 178–204.

———. 2009. "Hume's Principles of Political Economy." In Norton and Taylor, *Cambridge Companion to Hume*, 381–413.

Skorupski, John. 1989. *John Stuart Mill.* London: Routledge.

———. 1998. "Introduction: The Fortunes of Liberal Naturalism." In *The Cambridge Companion to Mill*, edited by J. Skorupski, 1–34. Cambridge: Cambridge University Press.

Slack, Paul. 1995. *The English Poor Laws, 1531–1782*. Cambridge: Cambridge University Press.

———. 2015. *The Invention of Improvement: Information and Material Progress in Seventeenth-Century England*. Oxford: Oxford University Press.

Smith, Adam. (1795) 1980. "The Principles which Lead and Direct Philosophical Enquiries; Illustrated by the History of Astronomy." In *Adam Smith: Essays on Philosophical Subjects*, edited by W. P. D. Wightman and J. C. Bryce, 31–105. Oxford: Oxford University Press.

———. 1987. *The Correspondence of Adam Smith* [1740–90]. Rev. ed. Edited by Ernest Campbell Mossner and Ian Simpson Ross. Oxford: Oxford University Press.

Smith, Pamela H. 1994. *The Business of Alchemy: Science and Culture in the Holy Roman Empire*. Princeton, NJ: Princeton University Press.

Smith, Pamela H., and Paula Findlen, eds. 2002. *Merchants and Marvels: Commerce, Science, and Art in Early Modern Europe*. New York: Routledge.

Smith, Vernon L. 2007. *Rationality in Economics: Constructivist and Ecological Forms*. Cambridge: Cambridge University Press.

———. 2008. *Discovery: A Memoir*. Bloomington, IN: AuthorHouse.

Snyder, Laura J. 2011. *The Philosophical Breakfast Club: Four Remarkable Friends Who Transformed Science and Changed the World*. New York: Broadway Books.

Sonenscher, Michael. 2007. *Before the Deluge: Public Debt, Inequality and the Intellectual Origins of the French Revolution*. Princeton, NJ: Princeton University Press.

———. 2009. "Ideology, Social Science and General Facts in Late Eighteenth-Century French Political Thought." *History of European Ideas* 35 (1): 24–37.

Spencer, Mark G., ed. 2002. *Hume's Reception in Early America*. 2 vols. Bristol: Thoemmes Press.

———. 2005. *David Hume and Eighteenth-Century America*. Rochester, NY: University of Rochester Press.

Sperling, John. 1962. *The South Sea Company: An Historical Essay and Bibliographical Finding List*. Boston: Baker Library.

Spiegel, Henry. 1971. *The Growth of Economic Thought*. 3rd ed. Durham, NC: Duke University Press.

Stafford, J. Martin, ed. 1997. *Private Vices, Publick Benefits? The Contemporary Reception of Bernard Mandeville*. Solihull, UK: Ismeron.

Stern, Philip J., and Carl Wennerlind, eds. 2014. *Mercantilism Reimagined: Political Economy in Early Modern Britain and Its Empire*. Oxford: Oxford University Press.

Steuart, James. (1767) 1966. *An Inquiry into the Principles of Political Œconomy*. 2 vols. Edited and with an introduction by Andrew S. Skinner. Chicago: University of Chicago Press.

Stewart, M. A., ed. 1990. *Studies in the Philosophy of the Scottish Enlightenment*. Oxford: Oxford University Press.

———. 1994. "An Early Fragment on Evil." In Stewart and Wright, *Hume and Hume's Connexions*, 160–70.

———. 2000. "The Dating of Hume's Manuscripts." In Wood, *Scottish Enlightenment*, 267–314.

———. 2005. "Hume's Intellectual Development, 1711–1752." In *Impressions of Hume*, edited by M. Frasca-Spada and P. J. E. Kail, 11–58. Oxford: Oxford University Press.

Stewart, M. A., and J. P. Wright, eds. 1994. *Hume and Hume's Connexions*. University Park: Pennsylvania State University Press.

Stigler, Stephen M. 1986. *The History of Statistics: The Measure of Uncertainty before 1900*. Cambridge, MA: Harvard University Press.

Stockton, Constance. 1976. "Economics and the Mechanisms of Historical Progress in Hume's History." In *Hume: A Re-Evaluation*, edited by Donald Livingston and James King, 296–320. New York: Fordham University Press.

Strawson, Galen. 1989. *The Secret Connexion: Causation, Realism, and David Hume*. Oxford: Clarendon Press.

Stroud, Barry. 1977. *Hume*. London: Routledge and Kegan Paul.

Sturgeon, Nicholas L. 2015. "Hume on Reason and Passion." In Ainslie and Butler, *Cambridge Companion to Hume's Treatise*, 252–82.

Sturn, Richard. 2004. "The Sceptic as an Economist's Philosopher? Humean Utility as a Positive Principle." *European Journal of the History of Economic Thought* 11 (3): 345–75.

Sugden, Robert. 2005. "Why Rationality Is *Not* a Consequence of Hume's Theory of Choice." *European Journal of the History of Economic Thought* 12 (1): 113–18.

Susato, Ryu. 2006. "Hume's Nuanced Defense of Luxury." *Hume Studies* 32 (1): 167–86.

———. 2015. *Hume's Sceptical Enlightenment*. Edinburgh: Edinburgh University Press.

———. 2019. "How Rousseau Read Hume's *Political Discourses*: Hints of Unexpected Agreement in their Views of Money and Luxury." *European Journal of the History of Economic Thought* 26 (1): 23–50.

Swift, Jonathan. 1727–28. *Short View of the State of Ireland*. Dublin: S. Harding.

Sylla, Edith Dudley. 2003. "Business Ethics, Commercial Mathematics, and the Origins of Mathematical Probability." In Schabas and De Marchi, *Oeconomies in the Age of Newton*, 309–37.

Taylor, Jacqueline. 2015a. *Reflecting Subjects: Passion, Sympathy, and Society in Hume's Philosophy*. Oxford: Oxford University Press.

———. 2015b. "Sympathy, Self, and Others." In Ainslie and Butler, *Cambridge Companion to Hume's Treatise*, 188–205.

Temple, Sir William. (1673) 1814. *Account of the Netherlands and Observations upon the United Provinces of the Netherlands*. In *The Works of Sir William Temple*, 4 vols. London: F. C. and J. Rivington.

Terjanian, Anoush. 2013. *Commerce and its Discontents in Eighteenth-Century French Political Thought*. Cambridge: Cambridge University Press.

Terrall, Mary. 2014. *Catching Nature in the Act: Réaumur and the Practice of Natural History in the Eighteenth Century*. Chicago: University of Chicago Press.

Théré, Christine. 1998. "Economic Publishing and Authors, 1566–1789." In *Studies in the History of French Political Economy: From Bodin to Walras*, edited by Gilbert Faccarello, 1–56. London: Routledge.

Thomas, Keith. 1964. "Work and Leisure in Pre-Industrial Society." *Past and Present* 29: 50–62.

Thompson, E. P. 1971. "The Moral Economy of the English Crowd in the Eighteenth Century." *Past and Present* 50: 76–136.

———. 1993. *Customs in Common: Studies in Traditional Popular Culture*. New York: New Press.

Thornton, Mark. 2007. "Cantillon, Hume, and the Rise of Antimercantilism." *History of Political Economy* 39 (3): 453–80.

Tolonen, Mikko. 2008. "Politeness, Paris and the *Treatise.*" *Hume Studies* 34 (1): 21–42.

Traiger, Saul, ed. 2006. *The Blackwell Guide to Hume's Treatise*. Oxford: Blackwell.

Trentmann, Frank. 2016. *Empire of Things: How We Became a World of Consumers, from the Fifteenth Century to the Twenty-First*. New York: Harper.

Tribe, Keith. 1988. *Governing Economy: The Reformation of German Economic Discourse, 1750–1840*. Cambridge: Cambridge University Press.

Tucker, Josiah. 1755. *The Elements of Commerce and the Theory of Taxes*. n.p.

———. 1774. *Four Tracts on Political and Commercial Subjects*. 2d ed. Gloucester: Printed for R. Raikes.

Turgot, Anne-Robert-Jacques. (1750) 1973. *Discours sur le progrès successif de l'esprit humain (On Progress, Sociology, and Economics: A Philosophical Review of the Successive Advances of the Human Mind)*. Translated by Ronald L. Meek. Cambridge: Cambridge University Press.

———. (1759) 1913. "Éloge de Vincent de Gournay." In *Oeuvres de Turgot*, vol. 1, edited by G. Schelle, 595–622. Paris: Félix Alcan.

———. (1770) 1971. *Reflections on the Formation and Distribution of Riches*. Translated by William J. Ashley. New York: Augustus M. Kelly. Originally published 1766 in Paris as *Réflexions sur la formation et la distribution des richesses* in the journal *Les Ephémérides*.

Valls, Andrew. 2005. "'A Lousy Empirical Scientist': Reconsidering Hume's Racism." In *Race and Racism in Modern Philosophy*, edited by Andrew Valls, 127–49. Ithaca, NY: Cornell University Press.

Van de Haar, Edwin. 2008. "David Hume and International Political Theory: A Reappraisal." *Review of International Studies* 34 (2): 225–42.

Van den Berg, Richard. 2012a. "Richard Cantillon's Early Monetary Views." *Economic Thought* 1 (1): 48–79.

———. 2012b. "'Something Wonderful and Incomprehensible in Their Œconomy': The English Versions of Richard Cantillon's *Essay on the Nature of Trade in General.*" *European Journal of the History of Economic Thought* 19 (6): 868–907.

———. 2017. "'A Judicious and Industrious Compiler': Mapping Postlethwayt's *Dictionary of Commerce.*" *European Journal of the History of Economic Thought* 24 (6): 1167–1213.

Vanderlint, Jacob. 1734. *Money Answers All Things*. London: T. Cox.

Vanderschraaf, Peter. 1998. "The Informal Game Theory in Hume's Account of Convention." *Economics and Philosophy* 14 (2): 215–47.

Vaughan, Benjamin. 1788. *New and Old Principles of Trade Compared: or a Treatise on the Principles of Commerce between Nations*. London.

Velde, François R. 2012. "The Life and Times of Nicolas Dutot." *Journal of the History of Economic Thought* 34 (1): 67–107.

Velk, Tom, and A. R. Riggs. 1985. "David Hume's Practical Economics." *Hume Studies* 11 (2): 154–65.

Venning, Corey. 1976. "Hume on Property, Commerce, and Empire in the Good Society: The Role of Historical Necessity." *Journal of the History of Ideas* 37 (1): 79–92.

Vickers, Douglas. 1959. *Studies in the Theory of Money, 1690–1776*. London: Peter Owen.

Vickery, Amanda. 2009. *Behind Closed Doors: At Home in Georgian England*. New Haven, CT: Yale University Press.

Viner, Jacob. 1927. "Adam Smith and Laissez Faire." *Journal of Political Economy* 35 (2): 198–232.

———. 1937. *Studies in the Theory of International Trade*. New York: Harper.

Volckart, Oliver. 1997. "Early Beginnings of the Quantity Theory of Money and Their Context in Polish and Prussian Monetary Policies, c. 1520–1550." *Economic History Review* 50 (3): 430–49.

Voltaire, François Marie Arouet de. (1734) 1961. *Philosophical Letters*. Translated by Ernest Dilworth. Indianapolis: Bobbs-Merrill.

Wakefield, Andre. 2009. *The Disordered Police State: German Cameralism as Science and Practice*. Chicago: University of Chicago Press.

Waldmann, Felix, ed. 2014. *Further Letters of David Hume*. Edinburgh: Edinburgh Bibliographical Society.

Wallace, Robert. 1758. *Characteristics of the Present Political State of Great Britain*. 2d ed. London.

Wallech, Steven. 1984. The Elements of Social Status in Hume's *Treatise*." *Journal of the History of Ideas* 45 (2):207–18.

Waterman, Anthony. 1988. "Hume, Malthus and the Stability of Equilibrium." *History of Political Economy* 20 (1): 85–94.

Wei, Jia. 2014. "Maritime Trade as the Pivot of Foreign Policy in Hume's History of Great Britain." *Hume Studies* 40 (2): 169–203.

———. 2017. *Commerce and Politics in Hume's History of England*. Woodbridge, UK: Boydell and Brewer.

Weintraub, Roy E. 1974. *General Equilibrium Theory*. London: Macmillan.

Wennerlind, Carl. 2000. "The Humean Paternity to Adam Smith's Theory of Money." *History of Economic Ideas* 8 (1): 77–97.

———. 2001. "The Link between David Hume's *A Treatise of Human Nature* and His Fiduciary Theory of Money." *History of Political Economy* 33 (1): 139–60.

———. 2002. "David Hume's Political Philosophy: A Theory of Commercial Modernization." *Hume Studies* 28 (2): 247–70.

———. 2003. "Credit-Money as the Philosopher's Stone: Alchemy and the Coinage Problem in Seventeenth-Century England." In Schabas and De Marchi, *Oeconomies in the Age of Newton*, 235–62.

———. 2005. "David Hume's Monetary Theory Revisited: Was He Really a Quantity Theorist and an Inflationist?" *Journal of Political Economy* 113 (1): 223–37.

———. 2008. "An Artificial Virtue and the Oil of Commerce: A Synthetic View of Hume's Theory of Money." In Wennerlind and Schabas, *David Hume's Political Economy*, 105–26.

———. 2011a. *Casualties of Credit: The English Financial Revolution, 1620–1720*. Cambridge, MA: Harvard University Press.

———. 2011b. "The Role of Political Economy in Hume's Moral Philosophy." *Hume Studies* 37 (1): 43–64.

———. 2014. "Money: Hartlibian Political Economy and the New Culture of Credit." In Stern and Wennerlind, *Mercantilism Reimagined*, 74–93.

Wennerlind, Carl, and Margaret Schabas, eds. 2008. *David Hume's Political Economy*. New York: Routledge.

Westerfield, Ray B. (1915) 1968. *Middlemen in English Business: Particularly between 1660 and 1760*. New Haven, CT: Yale University Press.

Whelan, Frederick G. 1995. "Robertson, Hume, and the Balance of Power." *Hume Studies* 21 (2): 315–32.

———, ed. 2009. *Enlightenment Political Thought and Non-Western Societies: Sultans and Savages*. New York: Routledge.

Willis, Andre. 2016. "The Impact of David Hume's Thoughts about Race for His Stance on Slavery and His Concept of Religion." *Hume Studies* 42 (1–2): 213–39.

Wilson, Douglas L. 1989. "Jefferson vs. Hume." *William and Mary Quarterly* 46 (1): 49–70.

Winch, Donald. 1996. *Riches and Poverty: An Intellectual History of Political Economy in Britain, 1750–1834*. Cambridge: Cambridge University Press.

Wise, Norton M. ed. 1995. *The Values of Precision*. Princeton, NJ: Princeton University Press.

Wood, Paul, ed. 2000. *The Scottish Enlightenment: Essays in Reinterpretation*. Rochester, NY: University of Rochester Press.

Woodmansee, Martha, and Mark Osteen, eds. 1999. *The New Economic Criticism: Studies at the Intersection of Literature and Economics*. London: Routledge.

Wootton, David. 2009. "David Hume: 'The Historian.'" In Norton and Taylor, *Cambridge Companion to Hume*, 447–79.

Woozley, A. D. 1978. "Hume on Justice." *Philosophical Studies* 33 (1): 81–99.

Wrigley, E. A., and R. S. Schofield. 1981. *The Population History of England, 1541–1871: A Reconstruction*. London: Edward Arnold.

Wrightson, Keith. 2000. *Earthly Necessities: Economic Lives in Early Modern Britain*. New Haven, CT: Yale University Press.

Xenophon. 2013. *Oeconomicus*. In *Memorabilia, Oeconomicus, Symposium, Apology*. Translated by E. C. Marchant and O. J. Todd. Revised by Jeffrey Henderson. Cambridge, MA: Harvard University Press.

Young, Arthur. 1771. *The Farmer's Tour through the East of England*. Vol. 4. London: W. Strahan.

Young, Jeffrey. 1990. "David Hume and Adam Smith on Value Premises in Economics." *History of Political Economy* 22 (4): 643–57.

Zahedieh, Nuala. 2010. *The Capital and the Colonies: London and the Atlantic Economy, 1660–1700*. Cambridge: Cambridge University Press.

Zaretsky, Robert, and John T. Scott. 2009. *The Philosophers' Quarrel: Rousseau, Hume, and the Limits of Human Understanding*. New Haven, CT: Yale University Press.

Zubia, Aaron. 2019. "The Making of Liberal Mythology: David Hume, Epicureanism, and the New Political Science." PhD diss., Columbia University.

INDEX